Et Nunc Manet In Nos

A (MODERN) LOVE STORY, 1942-1945
(true to the letter)

An Epistolary Novel

The words of Aaron Kelman, as told through his son

Gary Kelman

Hardcover ISBN: 978-1-63263-700-0
Paperback ISBN: 978-1-63263-701-7

Published by BookLocker.com, Inc., St. Petersburg, Florida.

Printed on acid-free paper.

BookLocker.com, Inc.
2018

First Edition

Cover art by Jeff Urquhart

Dedication

To my Dad, of blessed memory, the most ethical, decent, and kindest man I ever met

TABLE OF CONTENTS

PREFACE AND PROCESS

In January 2016 my 93-year old mother died peacefully in her sleep. Having suffered from increasing dementia for the previous 5 years, and living (existing) in a near-vegetative state, her passing was not a surprise. But what *was* a surprise was the cache of treasure she left behind. While going through the obligatory, difficult, somewhat cathartic practice of cleaning out her apartment, I came across several old worn carry-on travel bags (advertising "Pan Am" and "Eastern" airlines), stashed away in the back of a closet, buried beneath a lifetime of forgotten items (clothes from a bygone era, outdated appliances, boxes of loose photographs that had never made it into an album, tarnished candlesticks and miscellaneous *tchotchkes*). Not wanting to risk discarding anything worth keeping, I quickly opened the zippers and suddenly, shockingly, found myself stepping through the looking glass into a bygone era. I did not exactly discover the Dead Sea Scrolls or a lost original of the Declaration of Independence, but assuredly something even more personal and valuable to me.

Neatly tied up with string were a series of bundles of letters dating to my own "prehistoric" time, when my parents were courting while living apart from 1942-1945. Though they had known each other from early adolescence, their romantic relationship was still in its infancy then, just beginning to root and sprout buds, and that time period embodied the growth and development of a love affair that lasted their entire lifetime, and of which I was one of the products (along with my older brother and younger sister). God only knows when those love letters had last been read, or whether my mother had known they even still existed. But exist they did, in nearly pristine condition, still in their original envelopes, with 3 cent postage stamps, bearing postmarks from Boston (where my father was living), emblazoned with the WW II slogans of "Support Our Boys, Buy US Savings Bonds." The paper was somewhat yellowed and fragile to be sure, but the writing remained clear and unmistakably my Dad's chickenscratch (he was penmanship-challenged to say the least). The letters were arranged neatly in chronological order, and (lovingly) tied with twine likely manufactured in factories and sold in stores bustling with the war effort then ongoing. They *were* the Dead Sea Scrolls to me, chronicling recorded history of years and occurrences that I knew little to nothing about, and detailing the experiences, hopes, dreams, plans, passions, etc of the man I would one day call "Dad". Suddenly I had a window with a direct view from street level into the development of a relationship/ soon-to-be-marriage in gestation.

Search in that apartment as I might, I failed to find the corresponding letters from my mother to my Dad, only those from him to her. Yet they were enough, and told the tale of love, trust, and commitment that never wavered, which, through the lens of hindsight, seems likely the winning combination for a successful and lasting union of man and woman.

Writing this book was a personal, perhaps somewhat self-indulgent, labor of love to learn about my past, my history, the DNA that is me. I subscribe to the philosophy that *everything* (not just looks and brains but personality, likes and dislikes, opinions and choices, etc) is genetic, and once sperm meets egg our entire future (personal) evolution is determined. I can often hear my own voice through my Dad's words, things that I still say, expressions I still use, reactions I still have. This book was borne of a love and admiration for my Dad as well as my own natural human interest and curiosity to know who I am and where I came from. Our present-day near obsession with uncovering our background and heritage (through ancestry.com, 23&me, etc) is a feeble attempt and pales in comparison with meeting our parents and ancestors *before* they were our parents, like Marty McFly in Back to the Future (how amazing would that be!).

The process of telling this story was quite simple: I allowed my Dad's words to wash over and envelop me as I transcribed them verbatim. I followed one rule and one rule only: be true to my Dad, even if confusing and incorrect in the rush and informality of letter-writing. Despite the spelling and grammatical errors inherent in the spontaneous flow of words on paper (as in letters, as opposed to more polished writings such as essays or books), I chose to memorialize my Dad's words exactly as he wrote them, feeling that his stream-of-consciousness was the truest most accurate reflection of his thoughts and feelings at the time (which is really what this book is all about). Rather than use spell-check or interpret the letters with my own spin, I wanted the book to be about my Dad and Mom, not about me, and his very words, available as they are, seemed to be the surest road to that end. A few letters were typewritten (with multiple errors of their own consistent with the manual typewriters of the day); but most were in long-hand, often difficult to "translate into modern English" because of the rushed and somewhat sloppy handwriting of a busy twenty-something writing with a fountain pen, often smudged and nearly hieroglyphic in their appearance. I assume that over time my mother "figured it out", as I did. Unfortunately, as time went by, the writing became even worse and nearly indecipherable (part of *his* process of becoming a doctor). But I did my very best, even if "my very best" meant guessing at my Dad's words and intentions. But mostly I think I really got it (mostly) right.

THE SETTING

My Dad's best friend growing up was Solly Berson, a local kid who lived in the neighborhood and was a classmate in elementary, high school, and college. The Jewish community of the day lived together and studied together, not exactly removed from their surroundings but definitely inbred. Being a frequent visitor at the Berson home, my Dad met Solly's sister, Gloria, and the rest is history. They started dating and fell in love.

After graduating from City College, and with an interest in Science, my Dad initially hoped to be a Biology teacher; but that career never really got off the ground. So he decided to shoot for the stars, go for the gold, and become a doctor. While awaiting acceptance to medical school, he worked in the research department of the American Museum of Natural History, while Gloria attended Hunter College with a degree in Social Work. Year after year no medical school offer was made, but he kept trying. Finally he was invited to attend Middlesex College of Medicine, in Waltham, Massachusetts, and, with no other place to go, and with Gloria still living at home with her parents in Brooklyn (the custom of the day for young unmarried women), he reluctantly accepted this assignment, and moved the 220 miles north in early 1942.

****

So much for the backstory. Now come, enter into my imagination, memory banks, and time machine; travel back 70+ years and see things as they really were for two young people in love during the sentinel period of their lives, during one of the most critical periods of humanity, when the world was at war and annihilation of the human race was a real consideration and possibility…and my future was in the balance…

1942

Wednesday
(undated)

Dear Gloria:

Your letter was very welcome. And thanks for writing so soon. It was a swell letter too. The feeling was very clear—the style mature. It's a whole lot better than I can do. But I didn't mean to get critical of your 'literature'. I just wanted to say something of what the letter meant.

It's a funny thing but homo sapiens just doesn't remain in a state of hopelessness indefinitely. I've known that for a long time. Yet it's brought home to me time and again. Objectively I've seen it among the people I studied. Some of them were, to my perspective, in so hopeless a state I didn't see what kept them going. Ill, physically handicapped, deserted mothers too old to think up a better future…Yet they kept on going. They adjusted to the present and did not collapse. We did our work with that peculiar power of adjustment "homo" has.

So with myself. I couldn't continue to stay as depressed as I was last Friday and Saturday and live. Either I perked up or committed hari kari. Being physically comfortable made me perk up, I guess. So your letter with its reechoing of the deep depression I was in last Saturday came as a bit of a shock. It was as tho I had been able to distill my feelings, put them in a bottle and then drank some of the stuff several days later. Your ability to reecho so faithfully is a remarkable example of your sympathy. I hope you'll always retain that capacity for me. It's like a second violin vibrating softly while a first is being played. In this case, the vibrations were reinforced.

Don't mistake me. You're quite right. There is nothing new in the situation. I still, intellectually, feel exactly as I did before. And as you so aptly put it—an ex-medical student is a rather hopeless business. But with a routine established and an awful lot of work to do, I've, to some extent, put all the 'hopelessness of it all' into the background and concentrate on the immediate now.

In the final analysis, I'm going to do just as you suggested. Complete the course, if I can in the time at my disposal; stall for time when payment is due, and try to get something as soon as possible. Altho what I'll be able to get is beyond me at this point. Agreeing that I made a mistake in coming here, I'll just have to make the best of it and try to get out.

On Monday I began to work—and in earnest. The crazy instructor expects me to do a year's Organic Chemistry. Maybe two years. In the time I've got, the job looks slightly impossible—but I've not discussed it too much with him yet. I want to see just how rapidly I can go. The set up is something like this: I was given a place in the laboratory, access to the laboratory supply room, bought a lab coat, textbook and laboratory manual—and told to go ahead. So I go ahead. God knows whether I'm going in the right direction—or rapidly enough. I get to the lab at 9—and leave at 4:30 or 5. By late afternoon I'm pretty groggy from concentration at doing the experiment correctly, understanding what I'm doing, fumes, and explaining to every student in the school what the devil I'm doing in the laboratory and why I'm doing what I'm doing. From 6:30 on I have to do the theoretical material from the text. And the stuff is brutal. The only recreation I get is writing these letters to you, thinking of what I'd like to write, what I'm going to write, and reading your answers. So write away.

I've come to one rather definite conclusion in the past few days. Everybody should go to an out of town school. A small one preferably—and live on the campus. Not for the rah-rah! stuff. But it's the only way to study. Everything else recedes far into the background in the normal case. There is little else the boys can do at night but study. And the enforced companionship, if congenial, should lead to intellectual stimulation. This is a far cry from what I find myself in, but objectively it's what I think it should be.

I was going to tell you something about the people I've met, the College itself, the feeling in regard to current events at the school, and my observation on small town life—but I've got to write home and then get back to work.

Yours,
Aaron

April 9 3:15 pm

Gloria—

Just realized I have tickets to the Belgium piano quartet at Washington Irving for this Saturday evening.

Would you phone me at Columbus 5-6239, ext. 26 at 9:15 Saturday morning if you're interested?

I may have an extra one for Miriam.

Regards
Aaron

Wednesday 12:15 PM
(undated)

Dear Gloria—

I've knocked off early this morning as I didn't know what to do next, and the professor won't be back until 1 o'clock. They've given me a key to the laboratory and stockroom, so that I feel something like a boarder. I get in first, and usually leave last.

Except for a few sticky days the weather out here has been magnificent—what I see of it. This time of the year nature is going wild in its splurge of love and reproduction. Just outside my window is a fairly wooded section. In the morning and evenings the birds try to warble their lungs out. No sparrows out here. Robins are hopping all over the place, thrushes perch high up in trees and sing away; yesterday I surprised a very brightly colored bird that I've never seen before.

In Waltham, at least the more expensive part, one finds few, if any, hedges. This is almost a shock—because if you look around in Brooklyn you'll see that every bit of green in front of the houses are enclosed in hedges. The effect of removing them is remarkable. One almost feels that the whole street is in a park with houses in it. Now don't get me wrong. I'm not romanticizing. It's just that it occurred to me one day that this was so much of a difference. The tree that stands out here is the grey birch—you know, the one I pointed out at the Palisades with papery white birch bark and catkins hanging down. I suppose Hiawatha used the bark to write letters. One sees very few of them in NY. The place is littered with them here. Since I've been here the Forsythia has bloomed, followed by the cherry tree, the Apple tree, Magnolia, dandelions cover whole fields; the tulips are coming up now. Things appear to be in bloom wherever one looks. A la Candide, every Walthamite seems to be busy tending his own garden.

Of course two days ago I walked thru what is probably the proletarian part of the town. Not quite as nice. There is much less garden and lawn space, the houses need painting. But they still have light and air—and the streets are clean.

People just don't rush much around here—and good for them! Stores all close at 6 pm. There is nothing anyone can do about it so everyone gets his shopping done early—or once for the entire week. There isn't much of anyplace to go—so why hurry.

So much for Waltham or "My Impressions of a Small New England Town."

It's interesting that Sol conceded about marrying Miriam right away. Of course I'm no prophet—but my guess is that he's not going to marry her at all. Of course he has a good deal of guilt feeling at the present time and it will probably be manifested by over-solicitude on his part. He'll "love" her more than ever for a while. After a while something ought to happen which will break it up. The specific incident is unimportant. Miriam might precipitate it even. But I am forecasting now—so I'll stop. Maybe I'm all wrong. I often wonder just how you'd act under the same circumstances. Wouldn't you succumb pretty readily to the family pressure? So don't condemn Solly whatever the outcome.

There really isn't anything I can write to Solly tho. Everything that I have I pour into these letters. (Don't be too disappointed tho—I just don't know how to write personal letters. Or else I don't have the personal security to be able to put down my feelings simply and clearly without a bunch of defense mechanisms).

You might tell Sol tho that even tho I'm on vacation this is one time that I'd write "Glad you're not here." I'm happy that he's at Bellevue. He knows a good deal about the College. I'll give him some more of the same thing when I get back. As a pre-medical student he probably knows more about it than I do.

It's almost one now, so back to my test tubes and retorts I go. Maybe I'll blow up the place.

Yours,
Aaron

Tuesday 7:00 PM
(undated)

(To be read as the very tired deep inside)

Dear Gloria:

I've just returned from a few hours of "Apartment hunting" for a furnished room. No luck so far. I want a room that's both habitable and inexpensive. Both seem difficult to find. I suppose my best bet will be to ask around among the veterinary students who leave in June for their summer vacation. I suppose that in the back of my mind I'm looking for an attic—a nice, bare attic; large; cool in the summer, warm in winter; access to a modern bath and showers. A garden onto which one of the thru windows looked would help. And since it's only an attic—I'd rent it for a song. So does literature, movies, and French opera poison the mind.

I don't know just what is the matter with me today. Let's blame it on Spring. Just as an illustration, in the lab, I completed a rather long series of operations on a chemical, and then had to separate it from some water. It's done with a separating funnel whose operation is obvious. (*graphic illustration depicted*) The two liquids, an oil and water, don't mix. I want the oil. By turning the stopcock the water drains out and I keep the oil, throwing the water out. So I kept the water, and threw my preparation, the oil, down the drain. So it goes. Never-the-less, either I've impressed the professor with my sincerity and good intentions—or he's too lazy to do anything else—I'm being allowed to quit Friday at 4 pm (at the end of 3 weeks, that is) and will not be given any examination. I can have a 90% for the asking. So the grind is over. Your comments on how hard I must be working make me feel like going under false pretense.

What I'll do will be to get to NY Saturday morning and go right to work. I won't be able to go home first you see. So that if you'd care to come into NY Sat at about 5 I can leave my grip checked and we can spend some time together before I go home. Let me know at any rate.

It's interesting that you feel the way you do about time. Many people, of course, have noticed it before. The only generalization I can make is that in thinking of the present and future, time literally doesn't exist when the interval is charged with emotion, positive or negative. In retrospect, however, this emotional period looks very long. And the converse appears true, too. When going along unemotionally, the time passed in retrospect seems to have condensed to nothing. For example, the first few days or weeks of being in a new situation appear very long in retrospect. The following ones shorter. The first few ones were filled with new experiences (each charged with some emotion) which later on became routine and emotionless. So the baby's first few days are immeasurably longer—in this new sense of relative time—than a good deal of the rest of his life. And consequently the enormous influence on his later adulthood. The first week here felt like a year; the second flew by.

When I returned home at 7 o'clock I found a note that a telegram was being held for me in town. I phoned in to get Sol's message asking me to meet Miriam's aunt in Boston at 6:55. Will you tell him that I'm sorry I can't control time to that extent. If they come over to the cottage tomorrow, I'll be glad to tell them what I know. But you know it all, already. Sol could have given them all the information I have in N.Y.C.

Writing letters takes me an awfully long time. Particularly the ones I write to you, and when I feel so deflated. Altho the danger of an examination and nonadmittance to the school is past, I still want to finish the work I had planned out of sheer conscientiousness.

You may have been able to gather from my letters, I do miss you.

Yours,
Aaron

Tuesday May 26
10:30 PM

Dear

I'll be over on Friday, tho without a bike, probably. Bicycle riding after dark would be a solo affair for us, I think, as most bike stores close with sundown. Maybe we can compromise on rowing—why not?

But more seriously. The only two topics I can think of are "Social Control of the Mentally Deficient" and something on "Juvenile Delinquency." I recently had to write papers on both. You'll find a book by DAVIES "Social Control of the Mentally Deficient" interesting, easy reading. That should give you all the information you want as he's up to date. If you'd rather write on Juvenile Delinquency, I've read a book by CARR—"Delinquency Control" (1941)—very easy reading—recent, interesting. I thought his concept of "deviant pressures" interesting. If you want it, I have a bibliography of about 10 books on the general topic of Juvenile Delinquency. But I think you'll find loads of stuff in the library. Much too much probably. I'm sorry that's all I can think of. Good luck!

Your letter was swell. Maybe one of these days I'll be able to say nice things in a letter, too. But I rather doubt it. You'll just have to take me on faith as far as letters go—at least for the time being.

Yours
Aaron

Wednesday July 1, 1942
3:10 PM

Darling—

I'm here and can think only of going home. Probably being away from the things that give me acceptance and security creates the feeling of deep black depression. In fact it must be contagious—Dave is now worse than I. Faced with the reality—one somehow feels small, hopelessly inadequate, and helpless. I'd give anything in the world to be employed at some fairly interesting, remunerative work (notice the cupidity even while wishing) and be together with you. There is so much that we could do together in such a situation.

More specifically—the trip up here was completely uneventful. About 8 ½ hours of discussing Middlesex's chances for recognition. Dave was trying to convince himself; I wasn't strong enough to help him do so. To make myself feel better I was very pessimistic about the whole thing, made Dave argue vehemently that it had to be recognized, and took what comfort I could from his arguments. Rather shoddy—the very common procedure. The trouble was that I was so convincingly pessimistic—Dave is just about ready to go home. At that point I tried to cheer him up a bit but he was too far gone. If he really does change his mind and does go home, I'll be sorry. It's nice to have some link with home up here. I can discuss my problems with him, talk to him about you, etc, etc.

We came into Boston late last night—so I stayed over at Dave's mother-in-law's place. It's a very nice frame house. All modern renovations. Wouldn't mind owning one like that at all. I stayed in Dave's room in the attic. It's something on the style of what I wrote to you that I was looking for. An attic with modern improvements. I think he's crazy for not going to NYU, though there is no official news about clinics or anything so far. The juniors still have the same program as before. Twenty three lectures a week—a few hours in that phony place they call Middlesex Hospital (!)

All we did this morning was get our books and equipment. It took until 3 o'clock. Tomorrow the Dean is to give us a pep talk: "I know what question is on every one of your minds. Rest assured that I will do all in my power…" You know.

Unfortunately, as I had suspected, we have classes all day Saturday. That just about knocks working part time into a cocked hat. Recognition wasn't really bothering me it seems. I'll probably only be able to delay induction until next Spring. I know how this will make you feel, and I'm sorry dear, but I want to give you the picture just as I see it. Not make up a false front which will be shattered. What I say, you know, comes (figuratively speaking, Anatomy professor) from the heart.

Write soon, and at great length. It'll help a lot

Yours
Aaron

My Address:
Aaron Kelman
82 ½ Bacon Street
Waltham, Mass
c/o Ellis

(Forgive the yellow paper-- I haven't had a chance to shop yet)

July 2, 1942
9:00 a.m.

Dear Gloria—

I've been up here 2 days; it feels like months. Wasn't it a long time ago that we trudged through Manhattan buying odds and ends for my stay at college? Interestingly enough, my conception of what I had to buy was a little silly. Waltham is quite adequately provided with Woolworth's, clothing stores…I really didn't need to bring soap, toothpaste…all the way from New York.

I'm living in the "dormitory".

A few minutes walk from the main building (Medical), which looks as though a moat, drawbridge, and 2 knights would be very apropos, is a row of 10 cottages. Euphemistically it's called University Park. This is the dorm. The other 85% of the students room in Waltham proper. The series of bungalows is very similar to the set up in a children's camp from the outside. Small, neat, white, grass and flowers all around, surrounded by fairly wild stand of trees. At night I feel that I'm in Camp Emanuel with the kids all asleep and the counselors ready to leave for town. My room is about 10 paces by

4. Contains bed, dresser, desk, chair, closet. The bungalow has 4 such rooms. Very clean, very modern. The bathroom is quite ultra (at least for a camp), heat is supplied by hot air and regulated by a thermostat. The noise of the city is completely gone; birds chirp in the birches all day long. The smells are typically country ones. Objectively this would be a swell place to spend a vacation—or honeymoon.

Fundamentally I'm lonely. The boys are all right, lots from Brooklyn, Jewish and Italian. But I'd give a lot to be home with my friends, and go bike riding with you. I suppose I might have been able to enjoy a month up here if it were simply a vacation, with no aftermath. But the depressing thought of the future keeps jarring me every time I feel a little better. Funny kind of business. After a few days here, I feel that your first impulse was right. I should have gone to Belmar. The idea of becoming a doctor, though, with all its emotional overtones, swayed my judgment considerably. I also thought of several years hence. As an unemployed physicist or social worker, I'd be in no position to marry anybody—as a doctor I would probably be able to do so. But the set up appears rather hopeless. Although there is a possibility that the school will be recognized by the AMA in a year or so, I won't be able to put myself through. There don't appear to be any scholarships or assistantships anywhere but in the bulletin. If I can get a job it would be only possible during the first year. Highly improbable during the second, and practically impossible for the last two. As the set up is now, the first 2 years are for clinic, lecture and lab courses. From what I see and hear, these are probably as good as anything given in 9/10 of the recognized medical schools. Then comes the rub. The school doesn't control a hospital. So instead of getting the instruction in Junior year at a hospital in conjunction with lectures and demonstrations the guys are given lecture courses in Boston to take the place of clinic experience. (So the fellow in the bungalow next door was trying to visualize how to take a baby from a book's descriptions.) For the last year they are farmed out to small Boston hospitals as Junior Interns. They pay tuition and act as interns in these hospitals. If the school is able to get control of a hospital all will be well and the picture could drastically change.

But all this is only of academic interest to me. I'll never be a member of the 3rd year class, probably not even of the 2nd. To the boys here who don't have to worry about that—the school's being recognized looms as the all important problem.

I've been pouring my heart out I notice. If you'd rather I didn't get you depressed with my pessimism just let me know. I'm sure I can fill paper with descriptions of people here—or something.

Some hitch came up about my course. The prof was in a hurry to get home Friday. So he's arranged to begin Monday morning—and said that I'll need a full month! That would be quite a mess. But I'll give you the details later when I get them.

As I better leave some time for study I'll quit here—I do miss you a good deal.

Aaron
Write soon and at great length
Regards to your family

My address: Aaron Kelman
Cottage #8
University Park
Waltham, Mass

Saturday July 4, '42
12:30 PM

Dearest

I just received your letters—both of them. They're warm and full of love. Write as often as you can, dear, it's the only contact that I have with you, and the only thing that I can do up here that is at all pleasant. From now on I'm going to spend a lot of time either reading your letters, thinking of what to write to you and then actually writing. This letter has no thought at all behind it. Maybe none of my letters will have any, but be just my expression of feeling after reading your letters and experiencing another day or two in the "wilds" of Waltham.

We've already had two days of lectures. The actual laboratory work will not begin until Monday, so we are really only marking time. The program is remarkably simple: Anatomy in the morning, Histology and Embryology (as one course) in the afternoon. This goes on every day, six days a week for the next 16 weeks. Even the method of teaching both courses is the same. We get an hour lecture first and then go to the laboratory for two hours. You remember the school was built by its present owner, Dr. Smith. It's really quite quaint. One of the towers has 4 lecture halls superimposed one on top of the other. The first year class uses the 4th floor, the third year class the third floor, etc for all their lectures. The idea being that as you progress in your study of medicine your dignity (or something) is enhanced and you need not climb so many stairs to the lecture hall. The whole school is quaint that way—though not very efficient from the point of view of teaching. The lecturer for example enters the hall from a separate door and stands on a podium. This is so constructed that he is unable to come over to the class as he is separated off by a railing. Do you remember that French movie we saw about a girl medical student in a French med school? Middlesex reminds me of that place. To add to the resemblance, a lot of the professors are German or French. Yesterday, my first lecture in Histology made me feel this strangeness by the method the lecturer had of being so terribly formal. Behind a strong German accent he lectured—never talked—to a class of about 115 students. His assistants scurried around giving out the papers…I hardly heard what he said (not important, just introduction) as I continually felt that I was in that French medical school. Do you remember the attitude of the students in that movie? Wishing to be doctors though rather dubious of ever using the degree. The similarity is obvious.

The dean didn't even bother to give us a pep talk. Just talked about "Medicine". Yesterday, however, Dr. Konikov, the chief professor (Anatomy) took some time out to tell us we needn't worry! The school has petitioned the AMA to grant them the use of a grade A hospital for 3 years. Probation is what it amounts to. No reply as yet. If they say "nix", as is likely, the school will immediately tie up with one of the smaller hospitals and sink $50,000 into it. They already have this money and more pledged by the alumni. Either move, said Konikov, means state recognition; AMA recognition is bound to follow. In any event the last two years will be bona fide clinical years under full time professors in whatever hospital they get. So there you are. It may be only a pep talk—or there may be something in it.

As for me, you know, the question is a little academic. So is the idea of taking a chemistry course and applying to Grade A schools. I won't have tuition for the April year.

But until then there is still hope, darling, especially with the kind of letters you write to me. This breathing spell will give me a chance to see you a few times anyway. It'll be easier to get to N.Y. from Waltham than Australia.

So much for the school. This letter is very long but the first few days in a new place are always full of strong impressions.

Have a good time at Oskowana—but don't pick up any poison ivy. You should know what it looks like by now. Incidentally why did Solly go as a waiter? Couldn't he have earned more (considering his car fare) by teaching in the Dental School even at the reduced figure? And what's new on the Miriam front? Is your mother campaigning yet for you to forget me? If she is she's going to be plenty disturbed by the quantity of my letters. There is so much to write about—and you're really the only one I want to write to.

Until Monday dear
Aaron

July 7, 1942
6:30 PM

Sweetheart

So a whole week is gone—can you imagine that it's only a week! It seems so long ago that I left you standing at Dave's car obviously holding down a lot of tears. But so it goes. Do write often. As time goes on I'll find it necessary to write to you even more frequently – as the novelty and "hecticness" of the new situation wear off; while you won't find it so necessary to write so frequently—as you make new friends. But write as often and as "full" as you can. I love you a great deal.

When I returned from school today I found your letters on my desk. On your insistence I'm sending out the application blank. We'll see what happens. Interestingly enough Dave received an exact copy of the letter Sollie got from Flower. And is proud. He feels that he <u>almost</u> got in. In fact he has already sent in the application blank + $. The bastards. I was going to show him the letter tomorrow but I'm not going to. If it makes him feel better to think he's going to get in next year—why not. And if he gets in, no harm done—if not, what difference would it have made his feeling badly.

On Sunday my housemate, Morris, and I went canoeing on the Charles River. No girls, darling, just Morris and I. It really was delightful, the nostalgia. It's got anything New York has to offer but a long way. The river is fairly wide, landscaped, and long. No currents or waves. The canoe glides along as you paddle gently. You can stop at a bank or small island and rest. What we could do with a beautiful day on the Charles! It'll probably be the last financial expenditure for anything that can be called "relaxation" for a long time. Of course the natives are no dummies. They know a good thing when they see it—so the whole river is lined at some parts with concessions renting boats. The bulk of the people congregate like schooling fish in a few parts of the river, leaving the rest of it wonderfully peaceful. But enough of "canoeing on the Charles." I wrote it up so nicely I don't believe it myself.

Yesterday we were introduced to our cadavers. Nothing happened. No one fainted, or anything. They made the very callous cracks about the condition, features…of the bodies, complained about being given the skinny ones or too fat ones, and started in cutting. No feeling that it's human at all. Me either. No different than working on a cat or frog.

The work is piling up. Not facts or interesting stuff; completely rote memory—and I'm having difficulty committing it to where it belongs. The class is quite bright from first impression. Sol is all wrong. No flunks or anything like that. 95% Jewish, they all had the same problem Sol was faced with the past 4 years, and they came to Middlesex hoping that it would be recognized. I'm going to have my hands full keeping up with them.

Morris is going down and is taking the letter to the letter box. More soon.

Yours
Aaron

Incidentally—how are my letters and handwriting?

Thursday July 9, 1942
8 PM

Darling—

You've spoiled me. Breakfast isn't complete unless I have one of your letters with my coffee. My landlady, a sentimental soul from whom I get my breakfast, places my mail (your letters) on the table every morning and is tickled at the way I go for it.

I really did make an effort to get a part time job. The details sound like one of the better stories my clients told me. Last week I went to the United States Employment Service in Boston—after spending about 2 hours finding the place I was directed to the one in Waltham which is 10 minutes from where I live. I didn't think this place had a branch office. At the U.S.E.S., when I finally got there, I was registered with all due formality. The employment interviewer spent ½ hour trying to find a "circle" for me, finally decided I was a "research worker-Biology" and filed me away. I protested that if I'm going to be filed, my ego would not be damaged if it was as a "salesman-supermarket" or something equally practical. But the dumb ninny just smiled at me and wouldn't cooperate at all. Just said they never got a call for part time work anyhow.

I tackled the managers of all the markets in town and about ½ dozen of the larger stores. No go. Maybe when the season starts in September. Also the high school kids are out and beat me to it. Also maybe I just don't give a good enough first impression to get the jobs. I may look too small, timid, and all sweated up.

Yesterday, following my landlady's advice I inserted an ad in the local newspaper. I haven't read it yet. But it's a typical "situation wanted" ad, which the clerk at the newspaper office said would be very unlikely to bring results. But 75 cents for six days isn't bad and it gave me the satisfaction of achieving a secondary goal.

Finally, I spoke to the President about NYA. There is none right now. Congress is still debating the issue. And probably by the time they finish debating I'll be 24—and so too old.

At any rate, you can see that I tried. This "secondary goal" stuff, tho, is very interesting. While shaving yesterday it occurred to me that most of us set ourselves secondary goals which are rather easy of achievement and to a large extent derive satisfaction from reaching this secondary goal completely forgetting the value this achievement has had toward furthering our original, primary, aim. For example, my idea in lathering my face and scraping a razor over it is to remove a lot of the hair from my face and thereby look very clean. But I can just go through the motions and be content not even noticing whether the result means anything or not. Again, my primary aim in going to the employment agencies, to the stores…was to get a job. Nothing else. I get a certain satisfaction in achieving even a "successful" search—successful in that I found the agency and got the interview—even tho there was no job as the result. Actually a thousand such successes would get me no further toward my real purpose—but such is the flight from reality. A final example. I am told to learn the spelling of a word. I decide to write it 10 times (secondary goal). I write it 10 times very mechanically and have done my homework with whatever satisfaction that may entail. I've completely forgotten that I was supposed to learn the word.

Does the idea get across? I'm not too clear on it myself. Maybe you can think of other examples. At any rate—it does seem one of our more subtle rationalizations which sugar coat reality.

I have written along this time, darling, haven't I.

I guess we're both of us looking for jobs. I hope you get one before I do. You'll be a long while if you don't. Do you have any other suggestions tho? When I'm thru, I send the story to the department of Welfare so they won't be so damned condescending to the clients. I swear that if I ever get back to that work I'll never again tell one of them that it would be easy for him to find work if he'd only look.

Do send me Howie's address, and the addresses of Bellevue and Long Island. If you still have time you might get me one of those applications for Student Instructor. I actually received a rating of 76% in that, and I think you have to be OK'd by the draft board, but maybe if they need me badly enough, another application won't hurt. As you see, I'm treating you like a wife already. Shipping you all over town on errands.

I'm enclosing a front page article from the local newspaper to show you the kind of thing that's big news here. I wonder what kind of a splash we'd have if someone got a job paying all of $1800.

Good night dear—
Aaron

Monday July 13, 1942
8 PM

Gloria dear—

Your letters aren't mush—they are the most beautiful things I've read. I've read your letters far more times than my assignments. I'm so proud of them that I almost am tempted to read them to my "roommate", Morris. But, of course, I won't, darling. The feeling you pour out goes just where it belongs; and I keep drinking it up with no feeling of satiety at all. I can't imagine anything less satisfactory than your mother's "technique" on your father in this courtship days. It's so immature to "keep him guessing", and so come out "winning." But if one "wins", so that the other "loses", don't both really lose? Isn't the relationship anything but the warm love that is so precious? Keep on writing, dear. You needn't worry about boring me with your feelings. I love you far too much to want to hear any less of them.

Things haven't become routinized yet. Until they do, each day is an event. On Saturday I went home with Dave to see Chlea off. She had been in all week and was returning to New York with her sister. We tramped around Boston while waiting for the bus and I was shown the Italian quarter where pushcarts line narrow, twisting, cobblestone streets, and where one can go into a Pasticeria and eat the most delicious cakes you can think of. I was shown the famous "Old Howard"—a barbecue house. (You see, anything in New England gets a swanky name and becomes a landmark or something. I'd never think of pointing out the "Garity" to a visitor to New York as one of the "sights".)

But Boston is full of hypocritical contrasts. The newspapers are full (front page) of the "girl problem". It seems that the good people are disturbed about the army and navy picking up girls. The pulpits are shouting that the country will go to Hell. The first solution they thought of was to impose a 10 o'clock curfew on Boston Common. Can you imagine the police clearing Central Park at 10 each night? "No more spooning", shriek the good citizens. Police cars roam the main streets, and woe betide a girl found walking with a soldier or sailor. Our boys! I don't suppose they mean officers, tho they might be "good people's" sons.

The "Young People's Baptist Society", or something, have formed "volunteer vigilantes" to patrol the Common from sundown to the curfew, to prevent "sin." And the Old Howard, in the heart of Boston, features the finest in strip teasing. Oh well!

Maybe I'm so hit up because we had such wonderful times in parks. And it was the nearest thing to God I know of.

Would you let me have the exact name and address of Sol's place of work (The Laurel Country Club or something) by return mail. I'm going to use it as a reference on Thursday night when I go out looking for a job in Boston. You've got to have references I find. Don't forget, darling.

Otherwise things continue to just roll on. I miss you terribly. I haven't realized yet that I may not see you for months. When the realization does really hit, I'll probably take the next bus home. Let me know what you do—even the little things. Have you cut your hair yet? Did you start business school. Have you been over to Columbia? And, oh, so many things that I'm vitally interested in.

Good night, dear,
Aaron

Thursday July 16, 1942

Gloria dear

I'm sorry your grandfather died. Just as yourself, I'm mostly sorry for the living who really miss him. But sorry too for the old man himself. Life is very precious to the old, and they wish to leave it as little as the young. There's a play by Euripides which deals with the subject in a very clever fashion. I think it's <u>Alcestis</u>.

I'm glad you like my letters. Usually people tell me that I don't know how to write letters at all. But maybe the inspiration is different. I find that I don't have to think about what I'm going to write at all. I just write.

At school, I'm overwhelmed with work. It's CCNY all over again. The standards are plenty high. As I may have written, the conception which outsiders have of the place is apparently all wrong. There are no students in the class that flunked out of other medical schools. One tried to enter the school without telling; the office found out right away, and now he's no longer with us. Because they are trying to become recognized the faculty set very high standards. They have to lean over backwards, you see, to show that it's not just a "diploma factory." I understand that there are about ½ dozen Phi Betta Kappas in the class, and a few other honorary societies. We have several Ph.Ds, a few men who taught biological subjects in other universities, and dentists and pharmacists. All evidently siphoned into medical school because of the war—and into Middlesex because they were Jewish. We had an Anatomy exam last Saturday. I received a 95% grade—the class average was 93%! My God! CCNY and Brooklyn College are well represented. And the boys know how to cram. The ugly fact of it all is that, just as in CCNY—the diploma means so little. And for the same reason.

Now that's off my chest. I suppose I'm always on the defensive about the school. But will just let it go as my impressions of the school after 2 weeks. They may change enormously in a few more weeks.

I'm very tired now. I've been at it since 7:30 this evening. Trying to memorize about 30 unrelated names of structures located under the armpit. The names of some of these muscles, nerves and arteries are much longer than the structures. It's when I'm tired and small that I need you particularly. I'd give a lot to have you here for a little while right now. I suppose you can understand the flow of energy that can pass from one person to another under the circumstances. You could even be next door.

I'm going to continue "reading" for a short while before going to sleep, darling, so good night until Monday.

Yours,
Aaron

Monday July 20, 1942
11 pm

Dearest

I'm very tired and I want to see you. Those are the major aspects of my consciousness right now. Do you know, it's getting worse. I want to kiss you more as time goes on. And when I feel tired, I really need you here. The civil service commission of NYC sent me a notice to take an oral part of the test for health inspector on July 15. I wrote that I was in Waltham and requested either postponement or a change of date to a Saturday. They answered on July 11 that both were impossible; and my mother just sent the reply to me. So my fond hopes of seeing you for a few hours during the weekend when I would come in for the exam came to nothing. Damn it!

Do you remember that article you sent to me about instructors wanted in the air corps? I received an offer (certification) today as student instructor. With it comes a questionnaire to the draft board evidently trying to ascertain whether or not I am deferred at the present time and how likely that this deferment might be changed. I'm writing to the War Department requesting that my name be suspended until I notify them that I can take the job. From the looks of the questionnaire, I'm afraid to send it to the draft board. The same reasons as is the case of the signal corps. This was mailed up to me very late also. I was supposed to have answered in 5 days, but it's about 10 days past already. I'm going to write home and ball them out. I don't know whether it's an oversight—or that my mother wants to make sure that I stay in Medical School.

I also received a mimeographed letter from the War Department about my application for meteorologist (you remember?). They say that I'm being considered for the class starting December. Maybe I'll get the offer. And if I do, and can see no hope of staying in school—well you'll be able to talk of your smart, young lieutenant. If I'm sent to NYU we'll be together for 6-9 months anyway. Of course the aftermath isn't pleasant. Australia or such. But c'est la vie.

Both Allan and Abe have written requesting a correspondence course in medicine. I haven't answered their letters yet—nor do I think I'll write to anyone else very much. I pour out first about everything I have to say to you. And then there is nothing left. I just sent postcards home saying that I'm well. You ought to drop in at my home some day. You can give my mother an awful lot of information about me that I just can't repeat in other letters home. What I write to you is spontaneous. I can't possibly repeat it. Mother knows, of course, that I'm a little "dizzy" about you, that we were out together every minute I had before I left, and I'm sure she'd like to talk to you. She misses me quite a bit, her letters indicate. You needn't be bashful either. My mother hasn't any preconceived antagonisms about my girl at all. She'd probably be very fond of you. Altho, as she's a very emotionally insecure person, she'd not be able to show it for a long time. As you know, my whole family are emotionally reserved. But enough autobiography.

What I'd like to do is write to you every day. That would almost be a telephone conversation. But I found that I didn't have the time, so that I save it up and try to write it all in my two or three letters a week. But I can't ever write all that I want to. There is so much that goes on. Little things. But the kind that I want to write about. And about school. The queer ducks who go there and who comprise the faculty. How the courses are run. I always tell myself that I'll spend a whole letter on how they run their courses here, or something; but I just let my pen write away and never get anywhere.

Solly is a good man. I have more and more respect for him every day. I expect to be at his wedding, and hopefully it'll be soon. When you work as a waiter when you can go to Maine for a vacation—that's love, I guess. I wish we could do the same thing, but wishing doesn't help…

It's almost twelve, darling. I'm going to sleep. Writing to you, and getting your letters are the most pleasant things that I do up here. I love you.

Aaron

Thursday, July 23
1942

Gloria dear—

Altho I don't generally reply to any one letter of yours but just write what I have to say to you at the moment, yesterday's letter in which you mentioned not getting along with your mother requires some elaboration. Not so much that you might have had a temporary spat, that isn't too hard with your mother—but the letter just oozed with the overtones of a psychological low. What's the matter, dear? Do you really quarrel? And why to such an extent that you feel so badly about it? Is there any new angle to your mother, brother, and girl triangle? And what is she saying about us lately? In any case I'm really concerned about your feeling under par and would try to help if I knew the details.

Of course today, your letter was on its regular emotional plane, so maybe that was only a temporary mood. But let me know.

You asked for some idea of what my studies are like. Well you asked for it:

If you were to stick a pin into the skin under the armpit for about two inches you would be in a small space called the axilla. It is bordered laterally by the humerus bone, the short head of the biceps muscle, and the Costocoracoid muscle; medially by the Serratus Anterior muscle, first 5 ribs, and adjoining Intercostal muscles; anteriorly by the Pectoralis Major muscle, the Costocoracoid membrane, the Pectoralis minor muscle, and the Subclavius muscle;

posteriorly by the Subscapularis muscle, the Latissimus dorsi muscle and the Teres major muscle; the apex lies between the Clavicle, anteriorly, the first rib, medially, and the superior border of the Scapula, posteriorly. Within this region lies about 6 lymph nodes, the axillary artery and its branches, the axillary vein and its branches, and a good part of the Brachial plexus. The Brachial plexus, after arising from the 5,6,7,8 Cervical nerves and the first (and possibly 2nd) Thoracic nerve, gives up the following branches: from the medial cord we have – Ulnar, (2) medial, antebrachial cutaneous, (3) medial brachial cutaneous, (4) medial anterior thoracic; from the lateral cord we have: (1) musculocutaneous, lateral anterior thoracic, (3) subscapular (4) dorsal scapular (5) subclavian; from the posterior cord: (1) axillary (2) inferior subscapular (3) thoracodorsal (4) superior subscapular. From the plexus we also have the Long Thoracic and the Intercostal Brachialis…And so on, and so on. And this would be the first 20 minutes of one lecture. I'm not kidding, either. We get one of these every morning, another in Histology in the afternoon. There is nothing to think about. The chances are that those damn nerves do come off where Gray's Anatomy says they do. It is of course very important to know the stuff pretty well. The professor does, at least, try to tie up the anatomy with medical applications. So much for that. If you show the least amount of curiosity I'll give you all the muscles that these nerves go to. But I'd much rather write about other things.

If you have the occasion to be in the city you might drop over at the Academy of Medicine and inquire about Middlesex. We don't know what's going on up here. Rumors are manufactured every day. The more intelligent pay no attention. So far nothing concrete has actually happened but I've an idea the AMA in New York could tell us more. So if you do go over let me know what you find out and I'll start another rumor.

Now that you've mentioned it, I think I do smell some faint fragrance from your letters. But it isn't necessary, darling. Nor the very beautiful paper. Altho I'm really proud to receive letters which are on such expensive stationery, I'd be as anxious to receive, and as happy to read your letters if written on scrap paper. In fact, if the expensive paper is even subconsciously cutting down on the 10 page letters you could send, go to the nearest Woolworth's and buy the cheapest paper you can find.

There is a lot more to write—about job hunting, the war, the students, and the way I want you here. But it grows late and I've a lot of work to do. While you're thinking of defense courses, I'd suggest CCNY, where they have a central information bureau. They can give you a list of all the courses and you can then select.

Good night darling
Aaron

Wednesday, July 29
1942

Dearest—

I've just received your letter from Camp. For the past week I've been dying to yell "Bravo" at you, or something. But I couldn't write as I didn't know whether my letter would have reached you at home. Now that you're actually in camp, I can start writing again.

Good for you! I honestly was laying bets with myself about your not going. I was sure that your family would object. I can't for the life of me understand what got into your folks to make them give in without a struggle. But maybe Sollie has softened them up. They may be easier to handle from now on.

But no matter what the reasons, the summer at Camp will be swell. I know. I spent one of my nicest summers in a camp. And it wasn't anything as nice as Red Wing. Your letter made me so nostalgic for lakes, mountains and canoes that it almost hurts. And to be there together would really be superb. But at any rate I know that you are where I would like you to be. Nothing like it for the summer. Even more than that it'll be your first real break from home. You'll find that it's really remarkable how other breaks are more easy. Trips to other cities, for instance, like Boston. I remember that we had a great to do at home about my first camping trip, but later on I went bicycling over New England, walking in Pennsylvania, and now look at me.

This business about taking a trip into Boston being impossible is ridiculous. You've got to arrange it. I was practically all set to go into New York some weekend. Now that you've moved—we'll have to dope out something else. Don't rush the idea that you want concessions at camp right away. But gradually drop the hint and take the opportunity when it presents itself. You come to Boston, not Waltham; see what the train schedules are, and how much it'll cost. Then we'll plan the trip together. I will, of course, go to Boston. Or maybe to some point on the way. Some stuff, isn't it? Making a date with a girl to meet her in New Haven, Connecticut for lunch! Well, well. But it'll be worth it. You can guess how much I miss you.

Back here I worked for the past two week-ends in a place like Nedick's in New York. You know, coffee, coke, hamburger, hamburger, and more hamburger. It's really more like White Tower. I look really ducky in an apron and little cap. But the job is quite unsatisfactory. I don't believe I'll continue. From the employer's point of view, I really won't do as he needs me for the "wee" hours of the morning on weekends. The last train in from Boston to Waltham is 2:20 am on Friday and Sunday nights—12:30 am Saturday nights. That won't do at all. Furthermore, you've probably heard of the meat shortage in New England. Well, no meat=no hamburgers=no employees. From my point of view the job is too much for me. Friday, Saturday, and Sunday nights! That gives me exactly 3 nights to get all my work done. I'm no good on Saturday or Sunday afternoons, and fall right asleep Monday. All of which is very complicated, but you get the idea. I'll let you know what develops—and probably at great length.

I've had so little time to study during the past 2 weeks that I'm taking tomorrow off to study for our quarterly examination in Anatomy. I better pass. Anatomy, as you now realize from my crummy sample, is pure rote memory. The boys, many from CCNY and B'klyn (no Hunter College) sit up all night, every night and study. Everybody got 99% on the quizzes so the instructor is raising his standards. There ought to be a union.

Incidentally, I forgot to say that my job was doing counter work (a la White Tower) and when in the mood I'd handle the grill and make hamburgers, Hamburgers, and HAMBURGERS (a la Kelman). But the people eat anything. It's remarkable. You better never fry any hamburgers for me. I'll consider that as valid grounds for divorce. Altho, if I don't go back this weekend I may forget all about hamburgers and even get to like them again.

Just one more thing, darling. You're the only person to whom I really can speak to about those secondary goals and emotional satisfaction from this achievement. That trick really is very subtle and is at work all the time. We, for example, take a lot of lecture notes and then commit to memory. The boys take pleasure in all sorts of interesting arrangements of their notes. Card indices, pictures, retyping...completely losing sight that the only criterion for any of these devices is whether they will facilitate memory. Nevertheless, distinct pleasure is derived from putting all the muscles down on cards, per se, without any connection with the original purpose.

I do the same thing.

Good night, darling.
Aaron

Tuesday Aug 4
4:30 pm
1942

Sweetheart—

You ought to read your last few letters. They're a study in contrasts. Very normal, of course, they reflect your changing moods beautifully. Camp and what you expected it to be, reaction to the actual work involved and its terrible insecurities, and the very rapid adjustment. It's swell that you adjust so easily. Solly would have come home. Stay on, and have as good a time as you can.

Of course I visualized camp life as a councillor. It's the only way I ever knew it. And I remember the set-up so very clearly. Your letters bring it back very vividly. From what I remember the waiters just didn't exist. The other councillors were personalities—the waiters part of the environment. And it wasn't their fault. One chap I remember was an entymologist—and I completely ignored him, I suppose, even tho as nature councillor I knew almost nothing about insects.

The sharp cleavage between councillor and waiter is an excellent example of that intangible, tho very, very real thing—class distinctions and caste. It's all so unconscious for most people, yet so consciously fostered by the people who do the directing of things. The Army affords another wonderful example of the same thing.

Where is the reason that the waiter, who, for the most part, is as educated, cultured, even as wealthy as the councillor, is given no status at the camp; the same individual getting the job of councillor is given a great deal of status. And in hundreds of little ways. As I recall, the cleavage was very sharp. We were introduced to visitors; we had gatherings in the recreation hall with the administration; etc, etc. As a co-ed camp, the men took out only councillors and the girls went out only with councillors. The social stratification was complete.

The administration gives this "status" to councillors, as, "willy-nilly", they must have the respect of the kids. They must lead them and have some discipline. So they are invested with "status". However, the primary cause has long since been forgotten, particularly by those who enjoy the slightest taste of status so much, and the "status" is carried over even when it no longer is functional.

In the Army you see the same thing more clearly defined. The theory is that one salutes the uniform, not the man. But how soon is that forgotten. What officer doesn't consider himself immeasurably different from the enlisted man? How obvious the stratification, and how complete.

And this stratification is eagerly lapped up and entered into by all of us. We all want STATUS. Men die for it.

In the Department of Welfare the investigators to a large extent "stratified" themselves off from the clerical staff. By and large the clerks were as educated, and intelligent, and far less neurotic. But the administration subtly fostered the cleavage into "clerical staffs" and "social service staffs." And the investigators fought for their distinction tooth and nail. They wanted the "status." Fundamentally, the administration wanted to instill a sense of responsibility to the client and to the department. And they did it (as well as they could) by giving the "social service" staff "status" over the clerical staff. I suppose "status" is a relative thing; someone must be on bottom.

What gets me, tho, is the way the damned stuff is lapped up, and so eagerly. We're all so starved for a little ego swelling. How few people, who are given this so-called status with an ulterior motive by those who are able to give it out, ever really see that they are just little cogs who are no better than the little cogs they boss around. That the status of true worth may have little to do with the position.

I don't know whether I'm able to develop this any further. It may all boil down to economic class distinction with those who have having all the status and giving a little of it out to a few of the others (the "have nots") for their own ends.

That was some tirade, wasn't it? I'm exhausted. I don't know whether it makes much sense, but it's good to try to do some critical thinking. There is none at all up here. Just rote memory. No critical thought allowed—on any subject.

Nor are the students stimulating. I somehow have a soft spot in my heart for the radical. We generally see eye to eye—even if we don't agree in details. But this bunch of middle class boys is terrific. I don't feel lack of them at all. By and large they're the most dull bunch you've ever met. I haven't heard mention of a book, painting or composer. The Boston Symphony gives free concerts on the Esplanade in Boston—I'm dying to go and just can't. I haven't heard of anyone hearing even one! The fundamental topic of conversation besides the current subjects of Anatomy and Histology is how to have sexual intercourse soon.

But the weather is lovely just now, and I'm very comfortable. So I'll not complain.

I could go on practically indefinitely. But I've got to do some studying. I miss you terribly.

Love
Aaron

Thursday August 6, 1942
6:00 pm

Darling—

You've broken me into bad habits. When I don't have your letter waiting for me when I return from school, the day is ruined. Silly as Hell, isn't it? But that's the way it is.

We're still pounding away at the same material. Gross anatomy in the morning; microscopic anatomy in the afternoon. It'll get to the point where I'll be able to identify any region on the body I touch (pardon me, palpate!) It's remarkable how well people get along without knowing the names of the muscles which comprise the lower extremity. They just know they've got feet, and somehow are able to manage.

In medical school, one builds up a tremendous vocabulary, and a bad handwriting, so that one's learned discourses may be extremely unintelligible to the layman.

Every lunch hour for the past few weeks, we (Dave, I and a few of the others) have been sitting on the grass, propped up against a few trees and discussed the eternal question—Recognition. No one has any additional information so it's just a matter of rehashing the same stuff. Practically every morning we get a "shot in the arm" from Dr. Konikov, the anatomy prof. The story to date is (union formed) that the AMA has given the school permission to tie up with a grade "A" hospital—with the hospital not losing it's A rating thereby. This permission to last for three years "to show what you can do." If true it would be tantamount to probation. But this is so far unconfirmed. The big day is now supposedly Sept. 1, when clinics will be made available to the Juniors and Seniors (Hospital, if any, not announced). But, as I said, all this is rumor. If you had been in New York, you might have inquired at the Academy of Medicine. They ought to know.

Life has become more or less routinized now, and time (except while I'm actually working in the lunch place) passes rapidly. August is rushing by under me. I miss you more as time goes on. Instead of getting used to the fact that I can't be with you, I want to be with you more all the time. I don't know whether I've said that before, but it's true now, too.

There is very little variety to what I do. That is why it passes so quickly in retrospect. And I'm so busy, that it passes very quickly during the actual living of it. The only "luxury" I am allowing myself are these letters to you. As you can see, they take up a lot of time. Not all, of course. But some, not necessarily the longest, are certainly time consuming. As there is too much work for me to do adequately in the time I have, I'm always catching up. So that tonite I'll try (but obviously not succeed) to catch up on 2 weeks worth of Histology and about 3 days of Anatomy. About two days after an Anatomy lecture, I begin to realize what the fellow was talking about—my questions are, then, dated. He must think I'm awfully slow. The boys here, to a large extent, are quite good, as students.

The day, at present, starts at 7:30, breakfast is served by my landlady, Morris (my housemate) and I walk to school (1/2 hour), I am driven home by Dave at 4 pm. Wash, eat, and then I desperately try to catch up on all the anatomy I should have learnt 3 days ago, ultimately get very sleepy, and so to bed. This for the 4 "school days." Friday, Saturday and Sunday are just a blur to me. I rush to Boston Friday at 4, and then I'm at school Monday morning.

Until next week, darling
Aaron

Tuesday Aug 12, 1942
11:30 pm

Gloria

I received your letters today. Both of them. Now I feel considerably better. To say the least they're interesting. When you wrote about sunning yourself with a refugee who was telling you all about sex, I was curious no end. But you didn't elaborate. What on earth did she tell you that you don't know already? Come now, don't be bashful. After all, I'm going to be your husband, and possibly a doctor. As you can imagine, the boys up at school are devilishly sex starved. What with 2 girls in the class (very respectable) and over

100 men, I'm affected probably even worse, as I'm not only sexually deprived, but also deprived of the entire gamut of emotions in our love relationship. I can't, as some of the boys do, think of sex per se, and see what they can find. I can't think, in this construct, of any other form but loving you. It's all a mess, I know, but maybe you can understand the feeling if not the explanation.

You seem to be having a lot of fun at the camp. I'm "enormously" glad you went. You ought to be a little more grown up for the experience. The hard work won't harm, and tumbling out of rowboats sounds wonderful. The most important thing about camp life, of any kind, for me, was the wonderful sense of security it gave me. I was cut off by the confines of the camp from the hosts of little insecurities that followed me around at home. There was always something bothering me about "something has to be done." I should be preparing for an exam, or getting a new girlfriend, or seeing 3 people like Allan, Abe and Willie, or doing something about getting a job, or a better job, or something. As I was rarely able to do what I thought I ought to, to my satisfaction, those feelings of inadequacy and with them horrible insecurities came along. In camp, on trips, those problems were taken out of my hands for the time and so I escaped for the week or month.

But of course this may not be affecting you at all, darling. I'm just reminiscing. I know that I love camp life, hiking, etc, whatever the reason may be.

You ought to be getting "terribly" healthy. What with all the fresh air, a raidable icebox, and plenty of exercise, you'll be healthy enough for the rest of the year. Next summer, you can go to camp as a councillor, and get healthy all over again.

Don't work too hard, tho. I don't want you ill or something. There are so many parts to your body, that I am more amazed every day that they are all there and keep on functioning.

It's a funny thing. The students behave so strangely, that altho I seem to recall that it was somewhat similar at CCNY, I can't understand it or get used to it. Competition is rampant. Every student looks upon you as a rival (for what, I can't imagine). They go out of their way to knock one another. Altho a lot of it is in jest, the substratum is in earnest. Everyone denies that he ever looks at a book or studies, and accuses all those around him of grinding. The weaklings get a terrible riding. Factionalism over class offices…, which mean absolutely nothing, is terrific. It's really amazing, and so vastly different from what I've been used to for the past 4 years. I'd had the experience, at least since college, of a mature acceptance; I did my job; the others did theirs; we each accepted the other as a person who was on our own level, and got along quite well. Someday I'll try to figure it out. Maybe you can.

Personally I'm not victimized by the set-up very much. I don't have any time to bother about the boys' attitudes. Nor would it be easy for the students to ride me. I'm largely curious about it, and annoyed. Annoyed to see pettiness, conceit, selfishness, ego, stupidity, and immaturity so much around me. Where are the sensitive souls who ought to be healers? Very few, if any of the men, are interested in medicine. I wonder how many doctors are?

Oh well, I notice that I'm rambling. I'm desperately tired and sleepy. I'd give anything I own to have you here with me right now. I could bury you within my arms and sleep very contentedly.

Good night darling
Aaron

Thursday Aug 14, 1942
10:45 pm

Dearest—

Well, I've decided to try to give up the idea of catching up on about a week's worth of Anatomy and go to bed. It's been raining steadily all day. To add to the weather, I've a cold. I'll be darned if I know where I got the thing. It just happened. I sniffled more and more until now I feel real rheumy. A little sunshine would clear it up I think. My landlady brought up some aspirins and hot lemonade (which is quite cold by now), brought out some blankets, and suggested I climb into bed. I'll try that as soon as I finish this letter.

Your last letter was swell. Long and warm. Do you notice how we both constantly feel the same way. I, of course, write to you before receiving your latest letter, and yet the letter I do get echoes mine in an uncanny fashion. As tho you had read what I was going to say.

You're really experiencing quite a lot in these few weeks, aren't you. Do you find it at all difficult to live so close to the others. There is nothing like continuous, forced, company to turn an acquaintanceship, or mild friendship into strong enmity. That's why, I suppose, you either love your wife—or actively hate her. At best in dreams.

During the past week I had a group of human bones at home. My landlady, coming upstairs and seeing me surrounded by bones like something out of Dance Macabre, timidly, and hopefully asked whether they weren't cowbones. I reassured her that they belonged to some animal—HOMO SAPIENS. Now she feels better.

Abe wrote recently from Radar. His letter still indicates that he is having a pretty nice time. He relates that they have invented a wonderfully new way for detecting submarines. (Incidentally, I just ran out of paper; my housemate gave me this. As he lives in Panama, he uses this paper to write home, air mail.) To get back to the deeply guarded military secret. The idea is to spread green paint on the ocean. The submarine captain is decoyed to where the battleships are by fake SOS signals. He rests a little to get a good look. The paint covers the periscope; he thinks he is still underwater, so rises out of the water and is at the mercy of the American cruiser...So goes research at the signal corps Radar labs. He is still going to school.

The boys today sitting near me confided that they wished they had some nice girl to love. And they meant it. It would be a really good reason to go home. Someone to go home for. They're certainly right. Even tho you're 250 miles away, a something or other carries across in the mind which makes for all the difference in the world. It gives purpose to activity. There is something to look forward to, plan for, hope for. Anything else becomes sterile after a while. Even success and honors become routine and a matter of course. In fact, a lot of success simply means that one doesn't look forward with pleasure to succeeding, but with dread to possibly not succeeding. As one professor said—some students study because they're afraid of failing; others are afraid of not getting "A's" in the course. The point is obvious. The only thing that really can continue to mean more and more is a personal relationship, if built up over a long period of time. It can flower into greater and greater satisfactions.

All of which boils down to that I love you very much, that it's become so much a part of me that I'm taking it for granted, that I want to see you very soon.

Good night darling
Aaron

Friday 10:00 pm
August 21, 1942

Gloria dear

I've the uncomfortable feeling that all is not well at the other end of the line. You're angry with me or something. Yesterday your letter said "This is a quick letter because you're a big bum, but I love you anyhow." Do you feel that my letters aren't frequent enough in response to yours; that I don't show enough enthusiasm? Whatever it is, honey, out with it. Doctor can't prescribe unless you open up, nor would he need to prescribe if you do.

Of course by the time this gets to you, your mood may be totally different. This kind of letter may strike the wrong note entirely. But that's the difficulty of having to wait a day and a half to get an idea across, and another day and a half for an answer. It makes for the most peculiar kind of conversation. Nevertheless, at this minute I feel that there's something amiss. Write soon and let me straighten it out.

Now back to myself, dear. I'm practically writing an autobiography in these letters to you. I hope you're interested; they may sound too egotistical—I, I, I etc. But the new experiences that I hit would be the things I would tell you if I were to come home evenings to you. So I substitute the letter as the same idea.

Last week-end I quit my job, and worked instead in a supermarket in Waltham. My job was to assist the cook who prepared the delicatessen for the meat department. The hours were much better than my previous job: 4-9:30 on Friday; 9:30 am to 10:30 pm on Saturday. That gave me Friday evening, all day Sunday and Monday evening to myself. Even Saturday evening after 10:30. But the work was fierce. You know how I sweat, even at ordinary temperatures; especially when ill at ease. Well put me in a steaming kitchen, at manual labor, and very much ill at ease as I didn't know how to do such elementary things as peel potatoes, cut celery…I poured.. My glasses became wet, I kept on wiping them, becoming more flustered as this slowed me up even more, so I poured even more if possible. I used up my 2 handkerchiefs, my apron, every dry, clean rag in sight. The avalanche was not even temporarily dammed. But like all things Saturday ended; I went home; undressed, washed and spent the rest of the evening reading Julius Caesar. I had never read this one of Shakespeare's plays before. It's a swell play. And I enjoyed it immensely. It was the first "leisure" I had really "done" since I came here. And I needed it.

It was a good thing that I had quit the other job at this point. I had fallen so far behind that I would have done miserably on last Saturday's anatomy quiz. Although I know it's not too important, long habit insists that I rank in the upper brackets so I try. As I was able to do some work last Friday night I was still up among the top 30-35% of the class. Sunday was swell, too. I didn't study much, but had a good time lounging around, talking, listening to the radio.

With my new found leisure I'll probably not study more, but relax more. It's funny how enormously relative everything is. How much pleasure I (or you) can now get from spending a morning in bed reading. How little it would have meant to us a short while ago.

Tuesday evening I visited Lou and Dave, as I've written to you. Just an example of the use I make of the time I gained by sweating buckets for a day. But such is homo-sapiens.

Tonight I worked at the counter. Quite an improvement. Altho I'll probably be fired soon. When I got the job I said that I was going to stop having Saturday classes by September. I think I said I "expected" that to happen. One can expect anything. I'm sure nothing of the sort will happen. But I'll worry then.

From my letters one might conceive of my stay up here as primarily concerned with anything but medicine. Medical school just being a slight incidental. That isn't so of course. Practically all my waking hours is permeated with Medicine. The amount of work is terrific, or I'm a dumbbell. It's just brutal memory; I never was great shakes for remembering things. I can't remember names, faces, addresses. At school I was most proficient in the analytical courses; math, physics…this term is all rote memory. The orbit of the eye consists of seven bones, they are…ad infinitum. After spending the morning learning the names of the bones, muscles, ducts, glands, nerves…that compose the eye, we spend the afternoon learning the names of all the parts one can make out under the microscope of bone, muscle, glands…Anatomy and anatomy. Gross and microscopic. And I forgot. We learn where the structures came from every Friday afternoon. More anatomy—developmental anatomy.

I think I could rave on like this forever. But I have to do some studying for tomorrow's exam, and I'm getting very drowsy. I think I'll go to sleep. Exam be damned. Aaron is becoming a new man. I never would have said that at CCNY.

Do try to make it out here next week. I can't put into words how much I'm counting on it. I tried not to, but I'm largely swayed by emotion, irrespective of mind.

I really need you here all the time. But a short while is infinitely preferable to none.

Good night darling
Aaron

Tuesday, Aug 25
1942

Dearest

I'm sleepy, warm, and just in the mood for you. God willing, I'll see you Saturday night. I'll probably be much sleepier; tired, and needing you even more then.

It's hard for me to know whether you've been getting my last few letters or not. Something is wacky in your postal set-up.

Yesterday, I received your letter which you dated "Saturday 2:30 pm" in which you gave a host of arguments for my abandoning the medical profession as a bad job; today I got your letter dated "Thursday 9:00 pm" in which you want to know where my letters are. You've got me. I do write at least twice a week. But maybe we can get it straightened out this weekend.

The meteorologist problem more or less solved itself. They sent me the forms to fill out and an appointment to report for a mental and physical exam. In it was a little nigger in the woodpile. To wit, I have to agree that if in the opinion of the examiners I wasn't fit for Aviation Cadet training, I stay in the Army as an enlisted man in the Air Corps. The visual requirements for officer training are considerably more than I can muster, but I thought I might be able to squeeze it out by squinting and stuff. I thought that I'd have nothing to lose if rejected. As it stands I'd be planted right into the Air Corps as an enlisted man. The lasts Corps I'd wanted to enter. So I wrote saying—no thanks. Maybe in about 8 months.

It made me feel very warm inside to read at the back of your arguments your strong desire to have me in New York. Let me tell you, it was one of the best reasons I had for joining. But there was really no guarantee I'd be sent to school in NYC. There are excellent courses given up here in MIT and Harvard—also in California Institute of Technology. I think it's mostly chance as to where they send you. So for a while, at least, I continue to study Medicine. It's a wonder I can get anything done; I never know how useful it's going to be.

Today we had our first medical demonstration. Some old gardener has a hydrocoele-- accumulation of fluid in the scrotum. We had studied this area previously in Anatomy. This morning this chap was sat down in front of the lecture hall, and the Anatomy prof who was formerly a urino-genital specialist put in a needle and withdrew 500 cc of the liquid. He lectured, of course, while working. Symptoms, diagnosis…I felt almost like a real med student. (From that last sentence I realize that if something doesn't happen soon, I'll develop a feeling of inferiority that will be something to put in psychiatry books.)

As for the weekend. When you arrive at South Station walk across the street to the Essex Hotel and take a room. Dave (the Junior) recommends it. His girlfriend stays there when she comes up to Boston. It's greatest asset is its convenience to the station. I've never seen the place. I'll be thru work at 10:30 pm; will wash, change my clothes, and dash madly for Boston. Expect me about 12:30. If for any reason you don't stay at the Essex leave word at the desk so I'll know where to find you. I'll only believe it when I've got you in my arms. Maybe not even then, for a little while. I do love you so much; and miss you terribly. In fact it's the knowledge that you're there, somewhere; that I'll be with you eventually, that makes it possible for me to continue just "living." It's something to strive for. If that were gone, I think I'd give up the struggle and take a path of lesser resistance.

Incidentally, if your plans change, telegram. Otherwise I'll be at the Hotel Essex Saturday night.

With all my love
Aaron

Wednesday 4:30 pm

Gloria dearest

I really won't believe it's true until I've got you in my arms. You know that I'm an unaccountable pessimist. But I really don't want to let myself go too much on the idea that you'll be in Boston in a few days. I'd go right home if it didn't work out. Yesterday, for example, I had a terrible few hours. I think you wrote in one of your letters that you'd have to come to Boston via Buffalo. I went into Boston yesterday and inquired at the station. It's 12 hours for the trip from Buffalo to Boston! I felt horrible. But I feel better now. Later in the evening, I went over to the place of 2 Juniors, Dave and Lou, whom I met while up at the cottages. Both were familiar with Schroon Lake and assured me it was about 4-5 hours from Albany. Thank goodness.

I hope they're right. Let me know at once if not. At any rate, I'm enclosing a timetable that I obtained. You can get a train at

Albany at 3:35 pm and arrive in Boston at 9, or at 11:40 am and arrive in Boston at 4:40. The fare is $4.45. It's $5.05 from Boston to N.Y. by train; less by bus. Trains leave from Boston to N.Y. every hour. So much for timetables and such. I send all this to you as I don't know whether you have facilities for getting the information at Camp. Tentatively all you have to do is make reservations on a bus so that you can get to Albany by 11:40 am, write for reservations on the Albany-Boston train, arrive in Boston's South Station Saturday afternoon or evening, take a room in a hotel and wait for me to arrive. I'll get to Boston Saturday evening and stay over. We'll have Sunday, all day, and possibly Sunday evening, too. You've got nothing to do you see.

If it looks as tho all this can work out I'll send more information about hotels, where to meet, etc, etc, etc. I still don't believe it.

You know dear, it's absolutely uncanny. I've got your letter in front of me where you bring up the meteorology commission. The same day I received a notification that I was accepted. I'm going slightly bats. To accept; or not to accept. One of these days I'll pull a Hamlet and do something drastic.

This is the way I've thought it out. I'm going to write it out as well as I can. Read this stuff, think about it, and let me know what you think right away. I have to answer the War Department at once.

1. The situation at school is none too hopeful as far as recognition goes. There is nothing new, but the general tone is low. Maybe because no news is bad news. The status quo is very bad; we must have change. So far nothing official has come out. We were told by the Anatomy professor that AMA has agreed to allow us to tie up with a Grade A hospital, without endangering the hospital's status. Rumor has it that the 3rd and 4th year men are to get clinical facilities at Boston City Hospital. Three other medical schools are in there already. I suppose they have room for one more. That's all unconfirmed. My hunch is that State recognition is pretty probable; National AMA recognition dubious and a long time proposition.

2. If I am able to meet my living expenses as I'm doing now, I can stay for two school years (18 mos)—just barely. The federal

assistance to medical students was finally passed. It is available right now only to those who can finish in 2 more years. So for a while I'm not eligible to participate. It is not clear whether Middlesex, as an unrecognized school, will come under it; how much the student can really get of the theoretical $500 per year maximum; or what the machinery will be. With $1000, tho, and meeting expenses by working, and some luck, I may be able to make it.

3. Accepting the Commission means that my job in Welfare (I'm on leave until December) will be held for me; I'd be drawing a decent salary; living at home for about 9 months while going to school as an aviation cadet; learning a pretty good "profession"—meteorology; be in a fairly good spot in the army and would be in danger of being bombed to hell.

4. Boston College of Physicians and Surgeons—another unrecognized school—has also taken in a Freshman class. Probably going to try to get State Recognition again, too. Their graduates, like Middlesex's, are the poor white trash of the Medical profession. They have been running since 1882 and have the clinical facilities of Boston City Hospital, which they obtained way back. The AMA is unable to take them away. I understand tuition is very low, and they make all sorts of arrangements. I'm writing for information. As a last resort, if they are still up, and have State Recognition, I might go there for my last two years. Their graduates know some medicine, and all are doing well somewhere's in Mass. This is also largely unconfirmed.

I don't know. You can probably think of a great many other angles. I'd love to wait until I could see you, to talk it over with you, but I ought to write at once. Let me know, as soon as you can, what you'd do.

I've ten more pages to write, darling, but I have to do some work. I love you very much; I just throw my problems into your lap.

Aaron

September 2, 1942
5:45 pm

Darling,

Your letter that got to me Friday afternoon completely floored me. I must have read it a dozen times since. I'll probably read it a dozen times more—and then not fully understand what went on in your pretty little head at the time.

At first I was going to write to you, in the best Cyrano de Bergerac style.

"My dear young lady, you will have to change your brand of Love Story Magazine. It gives me a very deceptive picture of "LIFE". Did it ever occur to you that:

1. Hotels generally have more than one room to let at a given time.
2. 12:30 am on a Saturday night isn't a disreputable hour to be out—even in Boston.
3. That nevertheless, I couldn't very well have asked you to meet me on the corner of Boylston and Washington streets at that hour.
4. That the best place that we could have met would have been at the hotel (a la Astor) you were staying.
5. That I worked until 10:30 pm on Saturday, and preferred to go home, nearly exhausted, change my clothes and take a 2 hour trip to Boston so that I could see you as soon as possible, instead of waiting till Sunday morning.
6. That we then would have had all day Sunday to walk along the Esplanade, visit Harvard, row on the Charles, eat Italian pastry in Boston's North End, and time permitting, take the bus into Waltham to show you the College and introduce you to some of the boys.
7. What the Hell do you mean by "sordid" anyway?

But even tho all that is true, that obviously isn't the problem. Those points are fairly obvious. You certainly couldn't have believed that there would be even the remotest possibility of my forcing intimacies on you if you didn't want them.

The situation would have had "possibilities"—and you were afraid of them, evidently. And the conflict over the situation resulted in a welter of emotions. Your letter fairly spilled over with deep emotional strivings.

But you needn't feel badly, dear. That kind of conflict would be inevitable in you. Remember your limited experience and background. The conflict will have to be worked out. You'll do it. And I won't be able, nor will anyone else be able, to solve it for you. Emotional blocks are only solved by Clara Blake's. It's a growth process which will take some time. Maturity isn't achieved vicariously. What I do want to do tho, is to be around to help and give support where you need it. Explain when I can. Reiterate what you already know—that my feeling for you is deep and strong. It doesn't change with change in circumstances, or situation. That I'll be myself either in B'klyn or Boston, whether you're a librarian or typist…

Today's letter was another variation on the same theme. You're going to have quite a year ahead of you. A little late, perhaps, you're starting to establish a personality of your own. But you haven't done so yet. Hopefully you'll do so soon—and become Gloria, not Sol's sister, or Mrs. Berson's daughter. And I do want you that way. Not "Aaron's wife". It's quite a conflict, this establishment of an independent personality. It involves a great deal of unhappiness. But to the degree that this is accomplished can future happiness be achieved. Very few people achieve full maturity; some none at all.

Lots of stuff has been written on what constitutes maturity. Mostly incomprehensible as is all psychiatric stuff, unless backed by a great deal of experience. Nor do I have the experience. In a word tho, my criterion of maturity would be the degree to which the emotional response to a stimulus approximates the magnitude of the stimulus. The same thing has been said in different ways by philosophers and psychologists since Aristotle. I never understood them until I figured it out for myself in that way and realized that they had said the same thing in other words.

Write what you feel, dear, your relationship to your family, friends. What do you want to do, what are you afraid of doing, what makes you miserable at any particular time. I'll try to understand. Even that'll help.

I was, of course, disappointed not to see you Sunday. Maybe another opportunity will present itself. Write frequently dear.

Love
Aaron

Sunday, Sep 6, 1942
11:00 am

Gloria dear—

Your last letter sounded kind of anxious. As tho since you hadn't heard from me since your letter cancelling your trip in, you were wondering how I was taking it. And if I weren't punishing you by not writing. By now you've received my letter and know better. I didn't write sooner as I wanted to make sure you were home before writing. I answered the first letter I received from you, postmarked "Brooklyn." After all!

I'm a little sleepy now. The day has been beautiful. I stretched out in a rocking chair on the lawn, put my feet up on another rocking chair, fortified myself with a box of matches, my pipe, tobacco, and—a histology book, and was at peace with most of the world.

I'd never appreciate it if I didn't have so little of that kind of leisure. And even that is snatched. Of course, I didn't read any Histology. It was far too nice out in the sun. My body fairly soaked in the Vitamin D. A few back numbers of Harper's, I found in the house, substituted. Either I'm terribly out of date, or the kind of stuff they wrote about hasn't changed much, as I didn't know I was reading 1941 issues until I was thru.

Most of the afternoon, tho, I mused on the comparative advantages of the big city as against the small town. I still have no answer. Living is more pleasant away from subways, crowds, streams of automobiles pouring fumes into the air, noise, tall buildings, endless pavement, humidity, dust, anonymity. The mere living, the slow rhythmic pulsation that is life going on thru time, is more keenly felt in the small town. One is simply more aware of the natural things that go on. A premium is placed on talking, thinking, walking, eating. Not on other activities to which these are necessary evils.

I think better people come out of the country. People who aren't so aggressive, who can sit and not feel a tremendous need to forge ahead, usually at the expense of others.

Dr. Thurrot, the psychiatrist of whom I told you so much, once said that the few healthy people he knows came from farmers. That we ought to go to the country, to the farmer and his family, for mental hygiene.

Of course, intellectual sophistication and development go on much faster in the big city. The farmer's son doesn't think of these problems. Free education is pretty much unheard of on the college level. Washington Irving Concerts, Schools of Social Work, large well-equipped hospital and Research labs…

Without trying to solve the problem for mankind, I know that I should like to live in a pretty small town. A car would get me to a nearby Big City inside of an hour. There isn't any better way.

I watched a neighbor's little boy of about 2, running around the garden, trying to mow the lawn, chasing the cat, and getting the kind of play, both physically and mentally, that neither of my kid brothers ever had. He'll be a healthier kid, in every way. Much more than the "mere" good the exercise gives him, or sun, or decent air—the feeling of security that he feels in his own garden, with quiet all around, with familiar faces the only ones he is likely to see, with "mummy" within call—is something that will become part of his very soul. I know something deep inside of me went out to the picture, and I wanted all kids to have that kind of situation in which to grow up.

You might as well resign yourself, honey—no penthouse apartment.

Would you send my best wishes, etc to Milton and Eva. The lucky dog. How about Solly? Incidentally I'll write to him before I write to anyone else except to you or my mother. He's not being slighted. I haven't had the energy to sit down and repeat in a letter what is spontaneous when I write to you. You might read Sol the unimportant facts of my letters to you. That'll keep him informed of my progress anyway.

I received an invitation to the wedding of Aaron Braverman and Esther Gavritz which was held this afternoon. Aaron's one of my oldest friends—I've known him for about 16 years. So it goes. Damn the war!

I'm practically asleep now…and quite chilly. Guess what I'm thinking of.

Good night dear
Aaron

Sunday, 9/13/42
12:15 am

Gloria dearest—

I suppose this might conventionally be called Saturday night. But it's past midnight, and very late for this part of the country. All good citizens are asleep by now. About an hour and a half ago, I returned home from work, pretty tired, got into pajamas and sandals, munched fruit and cake, read tomorrow's comics and then lit my pipe before starting to write. The atmosphere is perfect for writing letters—completely quiet except for some persistent crickets, no lights anywhere in the house or within my window view—except for my desk lamp.

And your last few letters certainly open a lot of room for answers. I meant to answer them as I received them but just couldn't get the time to do so. My eyes have become pretty badly strained so that I'm already tired when I get home from school.

But to get a little organized. You asked about my opinion on Delinquency. What to do with the criminal. I don't know. Nor do I think anybody as yet does either. A great deal of thought and research has been done on the subject (Like in almost every other field, I know something about it—but not much.) To understand what to do with the criminal one must know the individual criminal; his complete social history, physical makeup, IQ, and emotional setup. The complete job is pretty much beyond present methods. Only in the sophisticated, willing adult can the psychiatrist get anywheres in doping out what makes him behave as he does.

Then there is the problem of the person who would commit crimes despite the best present day treatment—too far gone emotionally, too low IQ.

Finally there is the problem of "protecting society"—and private property. A lot of people have impulses to crime. Many a worker would like to take his boss's money away. Many a wife would like to kill her husband. Pretty strong taboos must be put up to prevent chaos.

There is also the large field of prevention. I read a swell chapter someplace (Juvenile Delinquency—Carr) which "proved" by a very elaborate mess of data that it seems probable that most delinquency is correlated with poverty. Very surprising.

The social approach which would eliminate the crime for want, ease family tensions by making separation easier, abortion legal...might help a lot. The remaining group would have to be segregated and treated psychiatrically. With our present knowledge even, a lot can be done to return the simple minded prostitute to social life, healthy, and usefully employed—under close supervision.

Those are just a few ideas at random. If you become at all interested, there is a wealth of literature on the subject. A lot of it very good.

About whether to read ancient or modern philosophers? Whatever you enjoy. Don't, whatever you do, read the stuff to become cultured. Pick up an introductory book to find out who the philosophers are. Read the ones you enjoy and understand. My reading in philosophy is shamefully meager. I really would like to read Plato, Spinoza, maybe even Kant. Even more, the contemporary philosophers. They talk my idiom. I just don't get the chance.

I'm getting really sleepy now honey, but I'm going to answer those letters from you that are on my desk.

Oh yes—I don't mind, of course, whether you go out. You sound a little as tho you thought I might. But I was disappointed in your approach. It so lacks sincerity—not to me, dear, to this other chap you went out with. You feel that you can't tell him you're in love with me but are going to let circumstances, the Army, solve the problem for you.

What is wrong with that? I'm not sure I'll be able to tell you, especially in writing. My own ideas on the subject aren't too clear, I discover. But I'll try.

The personality is that something inside the person which we can't possibly see. We judge of it (subconsciously for us, consciously for the analyst) by the personality reacting to what it meets. To some extent, each of these reactions in turn affects the personality so that it changes a little. After childhood these reactions have but little effect in changing the personality. The emotional component isn't great enough.

What I love in people, I think, more than anything else is sincerity. It's a very big term. It means everything we usually think of by the words and a lot more. It is the synonym of "simple" when one spoke of the simplicity of Milton, whose verse was extremely complex.

A child is usually a sincere personality—maybe that is why I'm so fond of children. At least the sincere ones.

The reactions are clear, simple, and not too hard to understand.

In this case you are not being sincere, and that if left as is in the path of least resistance, will set a pattern. I'd like you to be able to do things simply. Above all sincerely.

I could probably ramble on for 10 more pages, making myself no clearer. If you can get some concept of what I'm trying to get across—swell. Let me know. I have a deep conviction that what I say is true—but don't have the ideas too clearly formulated in my own mind.

We'll be able to discuss this soon, tho, if you want to—I'll be home next Sunday and Monday. But I've all week to write about that.

It's 1:15 now. Wow. Good night dear.

Aaron

Tuesday, 9/15/42
6:30 pm

Gloria dear—

From the letter I received today (you wrote it Sunday night) I think that my last letter wasn't the best medicine in the world for you. You seem so very much like the "babe crying in the wilderness"—the everlasting picture of man.

You ought to feel lost. I remember pretty clearly that awful feeling of "not belonging" I had after I commenced. It was quite horrible. My ego was about the size of a peanut when I was in school; (I did my best to compensate with high grades) and after a few weeks of "not belonging" you couldn't find that ego of mine with an electron microscope. But circumstances helped. Recognition as a person from the day I entered the Museum to the present has helped unfold the ego, if you will, so it's not a shriveled up little nut desperately needing warmth and sunshine to keep it from hardening into a microscopic particle. And they've fancy names for the end stages too if they go far enough—like Dementia Praecox.

Like everything else it's a matter of degree. By no means do the "little egos" become Dementia Praecox cases. But, God knows, very few of us are completely sane, and emotionally balanced. You remember my eloquent discourse on "status"? Most of us are somewhere on the line and need the ego sweller badly.

Very often I feel lonely and small. Very small. At other times I feel normal again. To the extent that the fluctuations aren't too violent, I'm nearer to the golden mean of emotional balance.

I don't think I'll ever forget my first few days at the Museum. I drank it in like one dying of thirst. I was accepted by those around me as an equal; the situation commanded respect; I belonged.

And that is what I meant by the development of an individual personality. It's one that has worth in its own eyes, that is fairly capable, that can accept people on an adult level insisting upon its right to individual fulfillment; yet without emotional upheavals in its relations.

You're hitting the same kind of low evidently. Neither of us will ever be very strong people, in all probability. But a lot can be alleviated. Taking a beating only aggravates the situation. Fortunately the situation in regard to jobs is far different now than in 1938. A modicum of aggressiveness and you ought to hit something. You'll have to get that first push. You'll become more aggressive after you are pleasantly surprised to learn that people will trust you as an adult, that you can take care of yourself, that you have learnt to be pretty much self-sufficient, and that you will have enough warmth inside to shower it around you.

Why don't you try the Radar labs at Belmar? Don't wait for the Civil Service Commission. Go down in person—and don't take your mother along. Tell them that although you don't have much Math, you do have the fundamentals and would make a good trainee. Live with some of the girls. You'll feel marvelous.

Take Philadelphia if that doesn't work.

In any event get work on a <u>professional level</u>. Work that will make you feel good, not ashamed of what you're doing.

Boy oh boy. Haven't I been the old pedant handing out free advice! But it's written, it's sincere, maybe it'll hit a responding chord. Let me know.

As for me, I'll give you all the details personally.

Abe was shipped to Ohio and points west; Joe Feldman is going to study Meteorology in Chicago (not N.Y.). Nothing is certain anymore.

I know how you feel darling. The worse I feel the more do I feel I need you.

Until later,
Love
Aaron

Thursday
(undated)

Darling—

I'll arrive on the SilverDart Bus at the Trailway Bus Depot 241 W 42 St (I think it's the Dixie Hotel) at 7:35 am on Sunday according to the time table. I'd love to have you there. The buses are usually prompt nowadays.

I'm scribbling this just before rushing off to school.

Until later,
Love
Aaron

Tuesday
9:30 pm, 1942

Dearest

As you can see it's comparatively early in the evening. I haven't even tried to study, but I'm going to sleep as soon as I finish my letter. The trip in was very uneventful. The whole flying visit to New York feels like some kind of dream. A restless one at that. I was always using a huge amount of energy while in New York to simply keep awake. It'll take two or three days more before I'm normal again. Those first thirty six hours of no sleep with all the excitement piled on top making further sleep impossible, just about put me in a daze.

It was all worth it tho and I'd do it again the first chance I get—just to see you. Besides trying to keep awake I spent whatever mental energy I had left in trying to be with you as much as possible. I seemed to be trying to shoo people away from us all the time. New York has too many people.

The night right now is really lovely. The moon is full, the streets are deserted except for some persistent crickets. It's warm out. The stars are pale because of the moon's brilliance. We would be very happy here tonight. It's just pleasant in a mild sort of way, alone.

I can't write very much more tonight, darling. My eyes are drooping more and more. You know the bus pulled into Waltham at

7:45; we went to my room, washed, ate, and then went to school. I don't know how I've stayed awake so long.

I wish you were here with almost a physical longing.

Good night dear

Aaron

Incidentally, Clelis informs me that I received 100% on the In-Service Training Exam given to all the staff of the Department of Welfare several months ago. Cute?

Thursday 9/42

11:30 pm

Darling,

I've just reread your letter—it makes me feel swell. I think from your description that you're almost as fond of me as I am of you. But let's not argue the point.

After a few days of my normal quota of 10 hours sleep I feel much more normal again. I just feel sore that I had to leave New York before I could really absorb some of the enjoyment of being with you. After all, that was my main reason for going. My next trip in had better be far longer than 2 days. I need that long to get over the bus trip.

You're right, of course. We have something that will be with us always, I think. Words won't put any of the feeling across unless one is a poet. Fortunately you know what I mean.

School continues rolling on as tho nothing had happened. As tho I hadn't gone to New York and seen you at all. It seems funny.

Today the regular College session began. That meant that first year Veterinary students, liberal arts students, etc descended on the College en masse. In fact I have one inflicted on me, too. When I got home this evening I found my former housemate's room occupied by a boy from New York (NYU) who is entering the Vet school to avoid the draft. Don't know much more about him tho except that his name is Addie and that he's partly bald. Also he's very worried about what the Draft Board will say.

Now that you're studying typing you have some idea of what Anatomy is like. Only Anatomy is much worse. When you learn to type groups of words you don't forget individual letters. Or better still, in your shorthand, the word combinations learned help in retaining the simpler forms. In Anatomy, a perfect knowledge of one muscle has nothing to do with learning the rest. So that when you learn the tenth, you've forgotten the first two.

But have a good time. I tried to learn to type at home since 1936 or so. I still type at a snail's pace with about 2 errors to a word. No manual brains at all. Eons ago, I had the bright idea of learning shorthand. I got the Gregg book and started to learn word forms like mad. But I lost my enthusiasm, or the book, somewhere in the middle. At any event you can relate your troubles in a professional manner and I'll be able to understand you. I think I must have tried everything but playing Polo.

I'm sleepy now. And my eyes are tired. Maybe it's the light on my desk which isn't adequate. My eyes tire very rapidly so that I have to quit studying after a pretty short session.

But it is especially during this time of the day (night) that I miss you terribly. I can't possibly explain what my tired feeling and wanting to sleep and relax has to do with you, but there it is. Not that I wouldn't be much happier with you in my most energetic moments. But at this hour, and hours like these, it's pretty bad.

It would have done my heart lots of good to have justified that worried expectancy of your family last Monday night. One of these days we won't disappoint them.

Good night darling
Aaron

Tuesday 5 PM
9/29/42

Gloria darling

I come home from school every day to your letters. They're my "shot in the arm" that all of us must get pretty regularly. Only the sternest can go on living just for future goals.

I can imagine how you would miss me an awful lot on Saturday night at 10:30. What the Hell, you would normally be out somewhere. I can think of a lot of places where we could go together. But that'll have to be one of those distant goals that I'm living for.

You asked a book on marriage for Thelma. I really don't know of any. I suppose if I ever become a doctor I'll have to learn a few for the naïve little girls who come into their family physician's office asking for advice. I'll probably be embarrassed as the devil.

But seriously, the only book I did read on the subject was required reading in one of my courses: Long—"Sane Sex Life and Sex Living"—or something. It wouldn't help Thelma at all as it was written for the newlywed some 25 years ago. His main thesis is that the love play associated with courtship should not cease at marriage, but should, on the contrary, assume its correct place in our physiology—pre coital stimulation. He never even heard of contraception.

I don't believe any book would deal with the right and wrong of pre-marital sex relations—and favor it. Society has as its mores that a woman is supposed to remain virginal until marriage. (the origin of the idea is very interesting and may date back to the days when primogeniture was the rule. Then everybody wanted to make sure that his wife's first child was his, as his property was going to descend to him. After the first one I suppose the husband wouldn't care particularly.)

Be it as it may, such is the convention, and I don't think any book would buck it. On the other hand, society (as in the case of abortion and contraception) is completely hypocritical about this. Studies have been made which show that a very small number of women are still virgins upon marriage.

The question Thelma would have to answer is "what does she want to know?" Is it what society will think; is it danger of conception; her status in the eyes of her boyfriend? These can probably be answered. But these questions, which are the ones which bother most girls when confronted with the situation, have nothing to do with ethics, or a sense of values.

If what is bothering her lies in this area (and I mean really, not the fear of conception being sophisticatedly denied and "values" put in its place) I'd have to talk to the girl to find out what her "values" are, in what they are based, and whether they are realistic. Finally, going even deeper, are those "values" covers for other emotional attachments or blockings.

The question, on the level of "values", is not too simple. It used to be for me. It is very easy to say with the fake sophistication of 17 that since reproduction was a natural function, like eating or excretion, why limit it? When we're hungry, we eat, etc, etc. Yet what do I think of the girl who is promiscuous? Can I love her? Do I feel that she really can love me? To what extent is sex a physical expression of an inner feeling? How much can you divorce the two and then expect to unite them again in "the real thing"?

But if you want more about my "ethics" on the subject let me know. For Thelma, the question is "Exactly what bothers you?"

Good Lord! I've certainly ranted on. I hope it's interesting even if not very helpful. In any event, I'm not an authority. There are probably plenty of better sources for material.

I feel very warm about your shopping around for my birthday present. You would be the nicest one I could think of. After that it's not very important. I'm interested in your love. Its expression in any form is swell.

Until later dear
Aaron

P.S. I told Howie Schneider that Sol would like him to write. I don't think he will. I'd look up Eddie's brother if you give me his full name and connections. "Who is a friend of who"

Thursday, 10/42
11:45 pm

Gloria darling-

My new housemate (Ed) says I'm a sissy. Just when he's about to really get started on his work, I'm quitting and going to sleep. But I can't help it. Comes 10-11 pm and I'm thinking of how nice it would be just snoozing peacefully. What's more I'm sick of sitting and learning after 4-5 solid hours. To be sure I'm falling more and more behind, but when I'm sleepy—I'm sleepy.

You certainly are very sensitive to how I feel. My eyes were constantly tired and under a severe strain for the past month or so. I hated like the devil the idea of sitting down to read. Imagine! My housemate took one look at my antiquated lamp with its feeble light, and let out a yell. I bought one of those daylight bulbs the next day and things are much better now. As soon as I can I'll get one of those scientific no glare affairs and then all will be O.K. As is, the daylight bulb is swell. The remarkable thing is my going along—very uncomfortable, without enough brains to do anything about it. Even an amoeba has more sense.

In about two weeks finals hit us. My God! It looks like an impossible job preparing for them. The stuff just piled up. And unlike any other subject I ever took, what one learns today just makes it easier to forget what I learned yesterday.

Interestingly enough they are already planning on dates for the makeup examination for those who fail. We're quite certain that the makeup will be easy enough to pass anybody. Rumor hath it that the questions might run

1. Name a muscle. For the "A" minus, name another
2. The radial nerve is (a) a muscle, (b) a nerve, (c) an artery, (d) don't bother (eg square root of -3)
3. Make this one up, and for the "A" minus, answer it.
4. Etc, etc

Tonight I studied the stuff that Solly lectured at me the day I was in New York. I mean I studied the stuff from the text. He undoubtedly knows his stuff very well, and I'd be in a better position to understand him now. I still don't know the stuff 1/3 as well as he does but an examination tomorrow which will cover substantially what he lectured about (while I concentrated on holding your hand very tightly) will tell the story.

I don't know anything yet about our schedule during exam week etc. I'll know in a few days. We may get time off between semesters or not. Our class president goes in to see the Dean every day about it. All the boys want to go home for awhile. The status of the school is very discouraging and morale is low. Our first enthusiasm based on hope generated by daily "shots in the arm" has gone and everybody feels rotten. The status quo remains unchanged. God (and maybe the AMA) knows whether anything is going to happen. There isn't anything I can do about it, but make the best of it I suppose, but it would be much easier if I knew that at the end of the grind, a decent reward would await me.

The weather is generally quite beautiful out here, tho getting colder now. It's very quiet now. About five minutes walk from this house, we would come to a section that is typically "country." Houses separated by large tracts of ground, beautiful trees, autumn flowers. Not a soul around. The good citizens safely at home minding their own, or a neighbor's, business. The only light is from the moon, stars, and the occasional house. We'd like it along the road. You'd feel, for the moment, completely cut off from reality and its problems. But only for the moment. Reality has a nasty habit of intruding. We'll have to make reality conform to what we want so we can walk along those old roads on quiet nights and enjoy them together.

Good night dear
Aaron

Tuesday October 6, 1942
11:00 pm

Darling—

I can almost stretch out as I start to write on decent size paper again. Somehow, I simply felt cramped writing on those small sheets. But my money ran out one week, so I compromised. I'll get some man-sized envelopes tomorrow; and then all will be well again.

Your letters are swell. I've a bunch of them on my desk now. Particularly the one where you threaten to propose to me in 1944. Dear me! You don't really have to. Somehow, if you think of it, I never did propose to you formally. It wasn't necessary at all. I honestly can't recall how a transition was made from the friendly interest to a pretty perfect love and understanding. When we're together words seem unnecessary. Our mutual impulses always coincide. Here, too. As soon as the situation looks possible, we'll take advantage of it. Don't hesitate (leap year or no leap year) to let me know what you think. But we'll probably both be able to stay apart for only so long.

I still don't know what the school's plans are for intersemester. Finals are the 17th and 19th of the month. We haven't been given the dates for the beginning of the new term. According to some reports we may start next term on the 20th! Some fun.

What does Thelma think about the sex problem now? I'm really curious to know how she reacts to the situation, and how she justifies her actions. I'm glad that she's in love with someone out of town. It gives you two something in common. Altho she is probably able to see her boyfriend pretty regularly.

In any event, I know now that as an amateur psychologist I'd make a good butterfly catcher. Do you remember my brilliant analysis of the Sollie and Miriam relationship? How I was certain it would break if Sollie got into Med school? So they're going to be married. The moral of the story is, not to believe any of my theories—even when they sound interesting. I'll undoubtedly continue to make up theories, but don't take them seriously.

One of the boys in the class is a rather queer duck. One of many. In his late twenties, married, a father as of this morning, he has become the most ridiculed and disliked person in the class. His difficulty must be of long standing, as men who knew him from college days speak disparagingly of him. But disparagingly! As I might have told you, the normal sympathies one finds (sometimes) in our everyday world seem to be lost in the school. Emotion is quite primitive, and very aggressive. He has been taking one of the worst beatings I've ever seen.

Somehow I couldn't help simply accepting him as a person—not a heel. I suppose my social work training made me unconsciously accept everyone. The result was startling. The chap is oozing gratitude from every pore. He'd go way out of his way for me. Of course that doesn't last. I'm in no position to administer therapy even when rapport is established. So whatever makes him so disliked will undoubtedly crop up. But I became interested in knowing just what it is that can bring out all that latent hostility of the pack. I hope I don't bring some of that onto myself by association.

As usual, I write to you just before I go to sleep. It seems the best time. I'm not particularly hurried, and go to bed thinking of you. It's too bad that I don't dream—then I could dream about you too.

Good night darling
Aaron

Friday 9:00 a.m. 10/9/42

Darling—

I certainly do need someone to take care of me. Right now I'm being very sorry for myself as I sneeze, wheeze, and sniffle. I've caught another cold, and have resigned myself to staying out from school today to doctor it. Like every layman I've taken aspirin, drunk hot tea, gargled, and then went to sleep at 9 o'clock last night. This morning I decided to write to you as soon as I got up. So, Hello dear.

My stay up here, away from the supervision of a very solicitous mother will either kill me, or make a man out of me. I'll just have to learn to take care of myself. And it's quite a trick after not doing anything of the sort for the first 24 years of one's life.

Your letters are swell. I'm glad you miss me as much as you do. I miss you even more. You'd find it difficult to adjust away from home too, I suppose. It would be really a swell thing for you to get a job in another city. Completely overlooking the idea that you, or I, would then be able to make flying trips to see each other; it would be a marvelous growth experience for you. Think of all the fun you could have.

I received a letter from Lester a few days ago. He's the chap who stayed on at the museum. I had written to him for a letter to N.Y.U.—he just returned from vacation and wanted to know whether I still want the letter. But the point is that I was swept with a terrific feeling of nostalgia. But terrific. His letter brought back skiing at

Lake Placid, climbing Mount Shissing, frogging in the Adirondack's—all pretty much with a lightness of heart that I haven't felt since war was declared.

The others have just about stopped writing to me after I didn't answer their letters. I just couldn't keep up a large correspondence. The only letters I enjoy writing are these, to you.

Abe wrote to me recently. He, and his "classmates", are going to the school run by the Philco Co. After learning what to do when a radio breaks down they will be shipped all over the country to fix, and install radios wherever needed. In a way it isn't half bad. He gets $6 a day, in addition to his salary for "traveling expenses."

The weather, right now, looks gorgeous from the inside looking out. It probably is swell at that. The past few days have been pretty perfect hiking weather. Gosh! Imagine romping over the trails in the Ramapos with the leaves every color from green to deep red. There's nothing like it. The weather keeps one's body warm; the cold air feels marvelous coming in. The leaves crackle underfoot. Occasionally a small toad hops across the path. And it's all real too, not just some author's pipedream.

The semester is rushing towards its close. I've an impossible amount of material to learn and review. Finals start a week from Saturday. We're still hoping that we can get the bums to change their minds but it looks as tho we start the second semester the day after the final examinations. I did count on coming in to New York. But I'm not being given much choice in the matter.

Until later darling,
(I love you very much)

Yours
Aaron

Monday 10:30 pm
10/13/42

Gloria dear

I came home this afternoon to find your miniature art gallery waiting for me. It's really magnificent. Of course, getting an art book from you for my birthday was no shock—your letters for the past two weeks have been permeated with your browsings in the book stores. And that's just the way I always want it to be. No surprises. I'm too much in love with you to want any surprises.

I can't think of a nicer way to spend the week before your birthday than to go shopping for a gift for you—together. That would be far more enjoyable than anything else I could possibly do.

I've unwrapped the book, browsed thru it, and will renew my acquaintance with a lot of old masters during the coming cold nights. I'll have no other chance to look at beauty while up here.

Your taste is very similar to mine. We'll add similar volumes to "our library" as time passes.

My parents shipped out a big box of food. Cookies, dried fruits, etc, etc, too.

What an afternoon. Can you picture me during the rest of this week sitting propped up in an old chair, munching away and looking at magnificent reproductions?

My last letter was written in between sneezes. I really felt crummy. But being a medical student, I did just what any layman would have done—aspirin, tea, Rem ("Remarkable Remedy for Coughs") and got better. I'm much better now, but still insist that I'm not fit to take care of myself. My early training was pretty bad.

This week we practically have no classes. Just reviewing for finals. As the semester ended, the material began to come into a clearer focus. It makes considerably more sense than while studying it.

The entire term was spent in having your body (don't be offended—anybody's body) described. Altho the material was divided into three courses for practical purposes, it really is one course. There is a tremendous amount of overlapping. But that is just what you'd expect. Imagine yourself making up a curriculum for doctors-to-be. The first thing is to become familiar with the human body. Just what does the damn thing contain anyway? What do the lungs, heart, liver, kidneys, intestines, ovaries, etc, etc look like? How large are they normally? Exactly where in the body do they lie? In what relation to the other organs? And while we're at it, what is the skeleton like, what muscles are draped over the skeleton? Theoretically the answers are derived from actual observation of the cadaver. The body cavity is opened and you look at the liver; see its shape, where it lies, what it covers, are duly impressed with its great size. But the description can't end there. There are a lot of things inside the liver one can't see with the naked eye. Slides are made. The liver is described in greater detail, and they call it "Histology". Just where one begins and the other ends is of course very hazy. Theoretically the things you can see without the microscope is Anatomy—otherwise Histology. Everything you look at, of course, is put under the microscope for more details; bone, muscle, kidneys, liver. So the liver shows a rather complex structure of blood vessels and bile ducts. Their ramifications have been worked out. Now the student knows what goes on inside the big, brown liver. And hopefully he knows what's in front, behind, and to the sides of that same liver.

Finally, the question arises—How come? Why (or rather "How") are the structures as they are? And the Embryology course simply describes the development of the liver from a couple of cells in the embryo.

So there you are. If one knows the material, he has a limited knowledge of what the body looks like beneath the skin. No attempt is made to answer the question of the workings of the organs—or the reasons for that little group of cells becoming a liver, and not a nose.

Again I've gone off the deep end raving away. Good night darling.

Love
Aaron

Thursday
11:30 pm

Gloria darling—

Against the loud remonstration of my housemate (Edward) I've decided to quit studying, write to you and go to sleep. So far I don't know whether this chap ever sleeps at all. I've never seen him go to bed, or get up. Maybe he just doesn't need any sleep at all. Mmm…

Seriously, darling, I'd much rather write to you than study Anatomy—with all due respect to Anatomy professors. The past few days have been Indian Summer up here, too. Leaves all over the ground swishing as you walk through. Very quiet and peaceful. In marked contrast to the newspaper headlines…

You'd like it up here in the Spring and Autumn. Trees all over. Something like living in Prospect Park.

I'm told it'll get real cold here soon, tho, and I'll be yearning for my nice warm apartment in New York.

Despite my better judgment, I've been browsing through my new art book. My better judgment tells me (shouts at me) to study for finals—but to come back to the art. Rockwell Kent and I argue frequently about some of the pictures. Tho sometimes he blasts with a phrase that I enjoy very much. His brief statement about Grant Wood, for example, that whether we like him or not, he's American, and "God Bless America" didn't echo my sentiments at all. I think Wood's stuff is as good as Rockwell Kent's. But you better let me know whether you had a chance to go thru the volume before you sent it to me. In any event I'm really looking forward to our going thru the book together. Many times. It's well worth it. To supplement it, we'd need art books on individual paintings. Ones we're particularly fond of. Hold on there, I'm not asleep yet!

Clelis came in this week. Dave's younger brother died of a bad heart; he's all broken up, so she came up to Boston to help him get over it. Dave is 29-30. Clelis thinks of him as her baby. Is very clever in handling him. She's planning to send him to Waltham as he'll be able to see more people and forget his brother…I don't know, of course, exactly what will happen. When I saw Dave last he just wouldn't let anyone get near him. Wouldn't talk to anyone; brooded by himself. After a few days of that, the boys just left him alone. Strange and sad.

So far things continue about the same. You remember my picture of man surrounded by a constant circle of worries, some more immediate, others more distant. Constantly changing relative positions with circumstance? I'm a swell example of that. I can always think of something to be concerned about, if I choose. Most immediate are exams; next is the possibility of Saturday classes next semester and its effect on my working; then my inability so far to borrow next term's books; then my inability to get time off to go to New York now; then recognition; then the war; then my soul, God, the universe...Catch on? When I had a cold, that was first. Most of all I'd like to have you with me. I don't even care if you and I were so busy I couldn't pay any attention to you. Just to have you in the same room. Oh well!

Good night dear,
Aaron

Thursday 11:30 pm

Gloria darling—

The new term's begun. No "acclimatization" or anything. Accelerated program means "accelerated". I'm on strike, tho, this week, and refuse to work. I think they're just a bunch of "meanies". I went to a movie Tuesday, spent last night looking at pictures, and tonight reading Shaw's "Doctor's Dilemma" and the New Republic. At this rate I'll be snowed under in no time—but as I said, I'm on strike for better hours for med students.

But much more important. That stuff about your Aunt Charlotte having a place up here is very exciting. Come now. Put on the pressure and spend a week or two in the historical city. Very educational and all that. After all, your mother can't object to your staying at your aunt's house—much. And pressure can probably wear her down. I really need you pretty badly. Try, honey, at any rate.

Eleanor is quite a girl, isn't she? Sounds very sophisticated and arty. Different species of animal from me entirely. All I want is simplicity. Comfortable surroundings; and you—(sounds like a modern version of The Rubiyat). As I don't drink wine; will have to get milk; but the book of verses and trees are O.K. At any rate she must be having a hell of a time. Does she have any sincerely deep feelings in her? Can she switch it from Billy to Victor to a stablehand? Like hot and cold water. Damned convenient.

I'm thru with last term's courses. This trimester (or semester under the old system) I'm taking Physiology, Biochemistry, Clinical Diagnosis, and Neuro-Anatomy. Incidentally, in view of the fine lecture I received from Sol on the Sympathetic and Parasympathetic Nervous Systems, I was able to hit 100% on the exam covering the subject. You might tell Sollie. It'll make him feel good. Don't tell him that I didn't hear a word he said as I was far too busy thinking of other things, nor that the class average was about 95%. I'm enclosing some examples of the Anatomy quizzes we got. Sollie may be interested. Class average ran about 85-90%.

Dave is moving to Waltham this week. At first it wasn't clear. Now, it is becoming apparent that he's not getting on with his in-laws. He's so anxious to move, that he is coming in to live at a hotel for a week, when a furnished room will become available. He certainly must hate them. I've come very much to the conclusion that familiarity really does breed contempt. I've noticed it over and over again. How do married couples avoid it? Is that the one great issue? Is it that familiarity brings to maturity the seed that was always there? That if you (for whatever unconscious reason) hate someone (in the broad sense) familiarity will bring it out, and if the seed of love is there, familiarity will bring it to full blossom?

A sweater is a wonderful idea. Make it heavy, as I'm told it really gets cold up in these parts.

It's awfully late for me now. Good night, dear.

Love
Aaron

P.S. Are you moving? When? Address?

Tuesday 11:50 pm
October 19

Gloria dear—

Well it's over! Wow. I've never "ground" so hard in my life. I can understand now what they mean by a "grind" at College. All of us are grinds at Medical school; I never had to at College.

It's funny the way Medicine is taught. It's so unlike practically anything I've ever studied before. I've taken courses at Brooklyn College Evening, New School for Social Research and N.Y. School for Social Work, but I've never quite met anything like this before. My experience has always been that there were a limited number of facts in a course, rather readily memorized, all tied up in some logical fashion. We all were able to memorize the actual material in the Embryology course...the trick was to understand the logic behind it and fill in, on the questions asked. This stuff, as I've probably written before, is sheer, brutal memorizing of millions of facts. I've just put away my Anatomy lecture notes—187 pages on both sides! If one knew every word in those notes he would be assured 100% in the final. To the extent that you don't, the grade is lower. It's very simple. The professor lectures on topic after topic, in each case describing something. The ear, heart, lung, an artery...The examination question simply asks for a regurgitation of some one lecture. "Describe the Radial Artery." So that if you can give back, word for word, what he gave us, all's well.

Of course seeing things in actual dissection helped, but fundamentally, the Anatomy course was a set of lecture notes. I understand that the same is true for all clinical medical courses.

Our entire educational system is ridiculously inadequate. As soon as I'm Commissar of Education we'll revise things considerably. You can be Vice-Commissar. After throwing out most of the teachers, the curriculum would have to be changed to cut out its huge emphasis on memorizing. After all, if you think back to your Academic Courses, that is fundamentally all you did. And a pretty nice waste of time it was. Actual experiment (not me as an example) shows that we retain practically none of the facts we memorized at school. Only as they become functional, later on, do some of those facts take on significance and stay with us. The concepts which we do retain (if we do) can be taught as concepts. I can learn the concept of evolution without having to memorize the bones of the skull of 10 different animals. If anything, the latter method actually confused me. I can't see yet how one proves that one animal evolved from another on the basis that both have mandibular bones when we name those bones both "mandibular" because we say that they both did evolve from a common ancestor. Or am I way off on a deep end?

But to get back to Medical school, willy nilly, the stuff is very necessary. It's got to be committed to memory, and over and over again until one knows it. My only plea would be for more time. Cut down the pre-professional course to 2 years—all "cultural". Give six years of medical school—all "medical". The courses I took in "Comparative Anatomy, Physiology…" help a little, but would have been much better done without, if I could have had twice the time to learn Human Anatomy, Medical Physiology…

Well! I certainly did go off, didn't I! It's just the reaction, as I'm pretty sure I passed my exams. I'm really thru with Anatomy. So passes the first semester.

I'm on my third page, and I haven't told you that I loved you once. I'm ashamed of myself. Don't let that tension you're under build up and burst. I want you in one piece. My prescription would read "Rx Aaron Kelman applied in large doses, at least 8 hours a day. A Kelman".

But I don't know just where you can get it filled right now. Hold onto it. We'll find a druggist yet. At any rate, you've the most faithful absentia fiancé in the world. I haven't even looked at another girl since coming up here. The class ran a dance several weeks ago. I didn't have the slightest urge to go. Stayed home and read Harpers.

Sincerely, darling, I do miss you a lot. I'm sublimating by working quite hard. Considering all that I've got to sublimate I ought to be a genius.

It's way past my bed time, dear. Good night, darling.

Love
Aaron

Tuesday, Oct 27, 1942
12:15 am

Gloria dear

I'm a sissy. It's only a little after 12, Ed (my housemate) has settled himself for a good night's studying, and I'm simply too sleepy to go on. Furthermore, I'd much rather write to you. By all the laws of Medical School practices, and by the state of the am't of work I have to do, I ought to forego sleep altogether. But—

It's cold out now; the windows are covered with mist. I was out a little while ago for some food—typically wintry weather. Bright stars, no people, a few lights in the houses along the street.

But it's pretty lonely. I don't think I'd mind living up here if you were here. We might be self-sufficient to the point where we'd enjoy the solitude.

Today, we did blood counts. I didn't take my own; maybe I'd find out I'm anemic or something, considering our technique on the first few trials. It wasn't bad tho. We pricked each other's fingers and counted all sorts of things under the microscope. It's a good idea to do these things. No matter how often I was taught the general method and significance of blood cell counting, it really never meant much until I did it. I can't explain the psychological process very well, but it's there.

I came across an interesting concept you may want to think about some time. Altho, I heard about it before, as with everything else, it takes on added meaning with detail.

In general, the idea is that the human (or other animal) parts that are really alive [the cells as distinguished from the bones, teeth, nails, surface layer of skin...] are very limited in the kind of environment they can live in. The range for life to go on is quite definite as to temperature, acidity, food, oxygen, water content...Almost the slightest deviation from the optimum leads to death. Death of the cells, of course, would result in death of the individual.

Now the actual environment of our <u>living</u> parts is not the environment one generally thinks of—the Habitat. But the conditions, whatever they are, <u>inside</u> the body. And this "internal environment" (Claude Bernard's phrase, years ago) is the important one, and the one that is kept remarkably constant. As you know, your bodily temperature is 98 degrees approximately, despite wide fluctuations in the temperature outside. Similarly for all the other factors. A host of mechanisms are constantly at work, to affect the changes in our external environment and keep the internal one constant.

So the body is a little house, steam heated, air conditioned, ventilated,…for the living cells (brain, muscle, glands…) to live in.

It struck me as a very neat concept so that I had to pass it on to you. If you were here, I would have sat you down and poured out, willy-nilly. So forgive me, if it doesn't strike you as anything at all. It's not new, or original.

I'm desperately sleepy dear. All I can really think of right now, is all the things I could feel if you were with me.

Good night darling,
Aaron

I'll expect you to be a ballerina very soon. Command performances etc.

Friday, 1:30 am
10/30/42

Gloria dear

I'm up late tonight. My sins are evidently catching up on me. The subject matter is somewhat different this term—and lends itself to long hours of study. That is, it's not as tiring as simply banging in Anatomy. Last term, I simply had to quit after a few hours of the most difficult kind of study I can imagine, almost rote memorization. Now, it's more a matter of understanding. The Physiology book can be read (unlike the Anatomy), while Biochemistry requires plenty of "figuring out." And while Aaron figures, tempus fugit (or something). Grades will probably be considerably lower this term than last. The Physiology prof, Kaplan, must have some secret hate for all medical students. He flunks more men in his course than all the others put together, and thinks that 75% is perfect. Last year's class still remembers that he flunked the whole class on his first exam.

And darling, I'm not a genius. Maybe it'd be good if I were, but you ought to know by now how very ordinary my mental functions are. Even if love is blind—don't be under false illusions. You've just to resign yourself to a run of the mill kind of fellow—who happens to be very much in love with you.

It's very quiet in the house now. Winter adds even more to the desolation of the neighborhood. Everyone in the house is asleep—even Edward. My desk lamp is the only light that I can see. My window must be the only one lit up for a large area. It's a funny kind of feeling. Sort of all alone in a lot of darkness.

This week we used our blood equipment for the first time. I'm still full of punctures where I drew blood for a dozen different tests. As my technique is not reliable I'm not jumping to any conclusions. But if I had any faith at all in my readings, I'd see a doctor. (Don't worry honey, it's the technique, not my blood) Incidentally, I typed my blood today. It's group A. Like in AARON. What's yours? I'll let you know whether I can safely give you a transfusion.

School seems to have put routine into your life again, and made it more bearable. That's a good thing. But are you content to simply get a job as a steno as the ultimate? Are you doing anything which might place you in something more professional? Or are you too tired of useless thinking to try anything else?

As I've said many times before, I will care for you just as much no matter what you do, but I don't think you'd be happy for very long as a steno. You'll love it for the first few months—pay days, novelty of working, new associates…but I'm almost sure you'll grow to hate a typewriter eventually. I knew a lot of stenos in the Dept. of Welfare. The time they put in working was just a meaningless hole in their existence.

But don't let my pessimism get you down. You're young enough to switch professions several times. And then maybe my viewpoint right now is colored by the hour. I'm practically half asleep.

Good night dear,
Aaron

Tuesday, 12 Midnight
11/4/42

Darling

I ought to write to you every day. Not as a duty—not at all. It's my only contact with you now, and I need those contacts.

Interestingly enough, I spent some time Sunday with 2 Juniors, Dave Ausabel and Lou Gitlin, in Boston. Dave is, in relation to his girl Pearl, in much the same boat as we are. She's been waiting back home for about 3 years now. Dave is a pretty decent chap; probably worth waiting for. Pearl writes very regularly; Dave answers faithfully; and being a better letter writer than I am, he writes at great length, essays and discussions. Pearl must, by now, know practically every word that I ever said in Dave's presence. I hope she's not disappointed in my non-Aristotelian utterances. I understand that she has boxes stuffed with Dave's letters. C'est la vie.

On Sunday we discussed topic after topic, just as an exercise (mostly) of the intellect. "So help me," I'm getting rusty in doing any original thinking. Imagine the powwow one can have on such topics as "Psychogenic vs. organic basis for mental disorders"; "The Ethics of Sexual Intercourse without love", etc, etc. I didn't feel that the day was wasted from the academic angle, as I borrowed a Physiology notebook which (hopefully) ought to save lots of time. Some rationalizing!

It's raining out now, and the wind is really howling outside my window. Could I enjoy your company right now! It seems almost like eons since I saw you last. Sometimes I wonder whether it wasn't all a dream; whether I hadn't always been trying to keep up to a maddening pace in some medical subject or another. Your letters bring me back, and I realize that reality for me lies in New York, that existence now is an interregnum—marking time.

From your letters, Thelma seems to be wonderfully happy. I'm glad. I know practically nothing about her personally, but got the impression from what you say that she's a swell girl who deserves all she's getting. You can pass along my best wishes.

How is Solly's proposed marriage coming along? December isn't very far away. I'm really more interested in his love life and happy marriage than anyone else's—except yours! You can tell him I'm having the Devil of a time learning Biochemistry. My 3 week Organic course is no substitute for a good year's course. I memorized lots of stuff at the time, but for lack of repetition the stuff never became part of me, so that I'm really learning a lot of the organic I should have known, now.

Today we worked on the heartbeat of frogs, a standard physiological experiment. It required us to mash up the frog's brain with a needle, open up his chest, and stick pins, drugs…into his beating heart to get various effects. I didn't like it. You know I must have operated, and killed, thousands of frogs at the Museum, but it was all under anaesthesia. And I never did like killing them. Particularly for didactic purposes, it seems somewhat unnecessary to kill large numbers of animals. The students know no more after today's experiments than they did before. There are good answers to that chain of reasoning, but right now I still don't like it.

Good night dear
Aaron

Thursday 10:30
11/6/42

<u>Sweetheart</u>

I feel very important receiving mail marked "air mail". Dave and Sid came home with me after school today and found your letter on my desk. They said you must love me—just by seeing the envelope. So there.

Work is piling up but heavily. I'm swamped again. Today we received results of our first Physiology quiz. I hit a clean 70%. Three or four in the class managed to pull off 75%. They are either genius or have some drag with the instructor. Physiology is a swell subject. So are all medical subjects for that matter. If only they were taught correctly. So much has been discovered—there is so much to learn. Any attempt to really learn what goes on in Anatomy, Histology,

Physiology, Biochemistry seems impossible in the time allotted. All I'm getting is, to me, a very superficial picture of these subjects. Maybe that is all that one needs for medicine. After all, I suppose one cannot become an Anatomist, Biochemist…Medicine uses these subjects as a basis and then goes on to describe actual treatment of disease. But, nevertheless, I feel very unsatisfied. I only have vague ideas, not clear conceptions. With sufficient cramming, I'll pass exams, but I don't feel that I can step back and really scan the subject and feel that I know it. Dave says that I'm too damned curious. It isn't enough for me to memorize that in muscles Glycogen is converted to a monophosphate glucose and ultimately to Lactic Acid and phosphoric acid. I want to really see how this happens—10 very complicated formulas to date. Maybe so. But if I don't get an understanding of the underlying mechanism, I simply won't remember what happens. So I'm swamped, but good.

So far we haven't any Saturday classes (keep your fingers crossed). They started a First Aid course on Friday late afternoons. I'm trying hard to duck it as I'm supposed to be at work during this time. I don't know what'll happen there. When one is treading on very thin ice, so many small things become problems.

You're absolutely right. We're in the perfect example of an ivy-tower here. I didn't know that there was an election, what the issues were, and was only mildly surprised or concerned about my new Governor. I don't read more than one paper a week on the average, and a Boston paper at that. Do you remember how concerned I was over politics and economy? Abe and I used to tear the paper apart every day trying to get behind the headlines. Now, I'm lucky to know who the present Governor of New York is. You'll have to keep me informed about the real world. I'm lost in the world of Chemistry and disease. "Mine" is the more liveable one. The other, the one which will affect us most and about which I must be informed in order to survive.

The war is a long way off. I have a 2A card, no date, and can do nothing about getting a commission. I can just mark time and hope the draft board doesn't get new orders, or change its mind, and request my getting a commission—or else. For in that case, it would have to be—or else.

Do you think the thin ice I'm on will crack?

Here I'm about to the end of my letter. I've been so concerned with myself I haven't even mentioned you. You know how I feel, of course. Your daydreams echo my sentiments. I would have the same daydreams if I had time. As is, I simply continue on with a deep longing which is never gone.

Good night dear
Aaron

Tuesday Nov 10, 1942
11:30 pm

Darling—

Don't worry, dear, about being a horrible baby all your life. You're not much of a baby right now—and you've a pretty good life expectancy yet.

Both of us are the soft, sensitive kind. We shall never inherit the earth. That remains for the strong and tough—the doers.

I remember, tho you probably don't, my deep feelings of immaturity when I left College at the ripe old age of 19. I'm much older now. Mostly because of the jobs I had the chance I received to meet people almost on a self-sufficient basis. Going to school, seems to me, to be one of the "infantilizing" processes in our society. One is completely dependent on others (parents, family) and thus is treated like a child by a bunch of other adults, the teachers. When you can calmly walk over to a teacher and say that if she doesn't stop chewing gum you'll go to another school for your instruction—one has achieved an adult relationship. So long as teacher is "god"—one is still in a childish relationship. Incidentally, we are now faced with that kind of relationship up here. It tends to break down some of the mature confidence and put in its place the inadequacy of childhood.

After you've gotten over school and started to work you'll probably find that you'll subconsciously be acting somewhat more independently. You'll discover one day that you're an adult. That you'll buy the clothes you want when you want them; go to the theater to see the movie you want with whom you want...You'll do these things without apologizing.

The sophistication that comes with "living" isn't too hard to acquire. With time one makes trips to Mexico, to Lake Placid, sees many plays, reads many books, has love affairs (or affair!) and is able to speak of, and look at his world, more broadly.

Much more important is a calm feeling of inner strength. Without that, no matter how many scalps one can show, the personality is in danger. The ability to tell someone else, politely, to go to the Devil is important. No emotion should accompany it. The ability to have opinions, any kind, and not constantly be apologizing for them, and deferring to others (as an adult) is indicative.

Don't misunderstand me, dear, I don't mean that one must be contrary or stubborn. Not at all. The more intelligent rarely get excited about other people's opinions, or wishes, clashing with theirs.

But to have the feeling that one is perfectly able to come to conclusions for oneself; that you are amiable to other views, but will in all probability not adopt them; that 9 times out of 10 the other person has an axe to grind and is trying to sell you something; that, by and large, other people may know more about a small subject than you do, but in general we all know damned little.

I don't know what I've written all boils down to. I've poured it out as I feel it. It's real to me, every word of it. Maybe it's not too coherent. Let me know what you think.

There isn't anything much you can do about your feeling. As I expected, a good night's sleep and breakfast helped to put Thelma and her "nasty" ideas far away. I wouldn't worry about it at all. You're one of the "swellest" persons I've ever met; you're intelligent, sensitive, and full of warmth. You'll get sophistication—willy nilly.

Good night darling. I've been writing for about an hour now. At this rate I'll never pass Physiology.

Love
Aaron

Thursday 11:30 pm
11/12/42

Gloria darling,

I miss you even more than usual tonight. Hormones maybe—or just that I'm more aware of a pretty constant longing. I'm so horribly rushed that it really feels good to forget all about proteins, circulation time, rickets and heart failure, and bathe in the feeling that you love me any how. And I love you.

I'm really working hard now. I didn't bother to take such helpful courses as Organic and Biochemistry, Physiology, Bacteriology in College. Now I'm trying to learn what to most of the boys is review, and then do the new work, too. Wow! Every once-in-a-while I come up for air. Never-the-less the stuff is far more interesting than Anatomy. It's not such routine memory. To some extent (not too much, tho) it makes some sense.

Examinations in medical school are unlike anything I've ever been up against before. No matter what course I took, the questions asked were always rather specific—particularly on information exams. When not of the short answer variety, they were still rather specific. Compare one thing with another; give 3 insects and a way of combating each…up here it's totally different. No matter what the course, you're always asked to reproduce some part of the lecture. And God help you if you deviate!

It's always, "Give all the mechanisms you know that affect blood pressure" or "Describe the eye". It's always "Tell all you know about—". Sort of silly. What is really wanted is that bunch of words the lecturer spouted at you a few days ago. Just reproduce it and all will be well. It's hard to explain, but the difficulty is still there. Just memorize, memorize and reproduce. No attempt at understanding or discussion to bring out understanding.

How are you coming along now? I'm constantly writing about myself; and reading about myself, magnified by affection, in your letters. I'm very interested, as you can imagine, in what you're doing. Are you really learning typing and shorthand? Do you have much opportunity to get around? What's cooking on Broadway?

What do you read,…? I'd know all that if I were in New York. My only way to get that now is via the U.S. mail.

And don't cut your hair! I'll stand for all the difficulties I may get into as I get tangled in it. In fact, I'm quite sure that I'd like nothing better right now than to be good and tangled in your hair. Permanently. I better not go on in this vein, or I'll be hopping a bus to New York. That wouldn't do at all. But I just can't discipline myself tonight. Matter has taken prevalence over mind…I want you pretty badly—and it's staying right up in the conscious part of my brain all the time.

Good night darling
Aaron

[I've just run out of stationary, so I'm using this rather than wait until Monday to get more].

Thursday 6:30 pm
11/20/42

Gloria darling—

I haven't written to you for several days now. You can just imagine the amount of work I'm up against. When I went to sleep during the early part of this week, I was too tired to think.

Your letters kept coming. They're grand things to receive. It's almost unbelievable what an integral part of me you've become. And except for a very short period—we've been in contact by letter only. I suppose the saving feature was our knowing each other so well before we "fell" in love. We didn't have to get acquainted as well.

Tonight I'm going into Boston to attend a meeting of the AIMS (American Association of Interns and Medical Students). The chapter to which I belong (Middlesex) is in the midst of debating whether or not to put up an independent fight for recognition. Independent from the Administration. I hope we'll have some fireworks tonight.

The whole situation is very confused. We, as students, don't know very much about what's going on. It is felt pretty generally that the Administration doesn't give a damn. The school is owned by a Dr. Smith. His one idea, apparently, is to make money. If he can make more on a "B" school than an "A" school, why, he'll keep up a "B" school. Good medical schools lose money.

The idea then appears to be (from the agenda of tonight's meeting) to have the entire student body apply for Commissions in the Medical Reserve together with a petition to the Surgeon General to grant us Commissions on the basis of our desire to serve and the present need of doctors. [At present, Middlesex men who pass a state board and have a year of internship get their commissions]. We expect to be turned down. Then to get publicity on this basis on the peculiar situation where doctors are desperately needed, a Medical School exists which has no clinics and can't really help in the war. The publicity, if effective, should bring things to a head. Maybe nothing at all will happen. The whole thing may be squelched at tonight's meeting. I'll let you know very soon. All in all, we do many things up here, besides discuss medicine.

Boy, do I wish I had you up here for a while, so I could talk to you. There is so much to be said all around the topic. I need encouragement which only you could give in person.

Right now Dave is lying on my bed and Eddie is leaning on the dresser discussing our respective schools. The eternal topic of conversation. It practically drowns out sex from our conversation. Dave is raising Hell, to get me to get going. I better do so and mail this now. I hope the dean shows up as planned, and says something definite.

Oh well, the tribulations of little people.

So until tomorrow darling,

With all my love,
Aaron

I'll write to Sol very soon. Don't worry, dear, I'll make the letter nice. Let me know exactly when Sol is getting married.

Aaron

Monday 12:30 am

Gloria darling—

I wanted to write directly I returned from Boston, but the meeting lasted so long I'm just getting over losing almost a night's sleep. Now I'm O.K. again, and in the early part of "tomorrow" am just in the mood to write to you.

The meeting was very hectic. Like many meetings we've both seen before, a lot of heat, little light. Cross arguing, useless debate, parliamentary difficulties…I suppose people never do grow up enough to conduct a really sensible one. All in all it was a lot of fun. The Dean was there, said practically nothing as an introduction, continued saying nothing in the body of his speech, and then ended by saying he was going to leave the gathering so discussion could be free. I think he wanted to get home to his wife. As I don't blame him, I'll forgive the fellow this time. But the boys are up in arms. They (we) want action. A second front, or something. All out for recognition. No more stalling. Think of our allies. Now is the time to strike a blow for victory. Gosh, maybe the slogans got all mixed up. But the sentiment is good, I think. We voted to empower the chapter to do everything it could to achieve recognition—including open pressure on the administration. Hopefully there'll be some Hell breaking loose.

A petition was drawn up to go to Washington, requesting our being granted Commissions as second lieutenants while in school. It'll be denied, of course. Then the idea is to publicize the contradiction, of a medical school operating which is not being used to its possible capacity, when doctors are needed so badly.

A parents' group is being formed; the first meeting is in New York's Hotel Astor next week. We're going to give them a clear picture of the situation; maybe they can bring some pressure to bear. Etc, etc, etc…

But I can tell you so much better in person. How I'd like to go in for Thanksgiving! Honestly, I'd give almost anything to have you with me. The fellows around here think I'm queer or something; girls don't even make a dent; I don't seem to realize that they're women. Somehow I've locked all my love in some closed compartment of my brain and mailed the key to New York. You're the only one who can open it, I'm afraid.

You'd better not put your stamps on upside down to tell me you still love me. Suppose you were to forget? I'd spend a week trying to figure out what unconscious motivation made you put that stamp on right side up. I'd start reading Freud, Adler, Karen Horney et al, disregard my assignments, lose weight, get rings around my eyes…on account of a postage stamp! Nix, you better put them on right with an explanatory note underneath.

I'm a little woozy tonight. Three of us spent a good deal of yesterday writing up Physiology notebooks. We raised much more commotion than erudition. What can you expect? At any rate, the room we were in had a radio so I heard Beethoven's 7th and the Emperor Concerto. The music raised a terrific nostalgia in which you figured prominently.

I've obtained a large map of the world and tacked it up on my wall. Now I think I'll be more certain of the continent the fighting is on. It's tough to be an ignoramus.

Do write frequently darling. I look forward to your letters as the warm part of an otherwise bleak day. I think my letters are becoming less intelligible with time, and probably more sentimental. I feel less intelligible and more in need of telling you that I love you. I'll try to be more erudite if you really want me to.

Good night dear,
Aaron

Thursday Nov. 26, '42
12:00 midnight

Gloria darling

So Thanksgiving is over. There are some things to be thankful for, I suppose, but I do hope we can spend the next one together. As it was, I had my Thanksgiving dinner alone in a small restaurant, wishing to be several hundred miles away.

A holiday to the medical student (at any rate, the medical freshman) is just another opportunity to try to catch up on past work.

The subject matter is very interesting. I'd bore you to death, if we were together, explaining how brain lesions affect behavior; how clever God was to make our blood pressure stay so constant, and so on. I'm not going to do anything of the sort in my letters, dear, so don't worry. I don't have very many opportunities to tell you how much I do miss you, that I can waste them on Physiology. That'll wait until I know the stuff better and can tell you in person over a long period of time.

Fatalism, you say? Yes, I think I'm a fatalist. But not in the same sense that your mother is. I don't think that the actual details or minutiae of our lives are "written". But I do believe that our actions, and so our "free choices" are governed by our personalities. And our personality was laid down in our very early childhood, with comparatively little room for change. So, I don't think it was destiny which led Sol to Miriam (or vice-versa), but the things Sol wants from a wife, his relationship with his wife, the problems he will have,…will all be determined by the kind of a chap he is. It sounds awfully obvious, yet has loads of complications (and implications). Worry some of them out and pass them along.

Our vacation starts on Christmas Day. I'll probably be able to come in by the 26th. But let's not even discuss it or make any plans. I'm getting superstitious. I was almost certain that I'd see you in Boston—and made elaborate plans; I was pretty sure I'd be home between semesters—and made elaborate plans. So altho I'm pretty sure I'll be home for the week between Christmas and New Year's, just try to forget all about it. I'm going to let you know exactly when I'll get in. We'll have nothing planned—and everything will be grand. All I know is that I'd like to see Sol for a few minutes, my family for a few more, and then spend the rest of the time with you. I'll try to be actually rude to anyone we meet, so they'll let us alone.

Incidentally, I've asked everyone I know—and some fellows that I don't know—who are about my size, about a tux. To my relief, nobody has one. I'll hire one if you've set your heart on going, honey, but I'd much rather spend the time anywheres we'll be alone and comfortable. Once we get used to being together all the time that we wish, we won't treasure a few hours so greedily. It would be kind of nice, wouldn't it, to know that we'd have tomorrow, and tomorrow, and tomorrow…

I didn't mean that Sol was to go thru all my letters to you with his critical eye! Rather, that he can get all the information he'd like about what I'm doing from well chosen excerpts. I'm not in the least ashamed of my love for you, and even the elementary way of my expressing it. But, darling, I think my feeling for anything as being sacred would be that love. And its intimacy.

All in all, today wasn't so bad except that the mailman doesn't come on Holidays.

Good night dear
Aaron

Tuesday 1:00 am
Dec. 1, 1942

Gloria dearest—

I got both your letters today. A bonanza! I can't still think of anything I'd rather do than first, get letters from you, and second, write them to you.

One of your letters had quite an anticlimax in it. I wondered whether you noticed. You said that just thinking of my not coming in for Christmas gives you the most horrible sensations, you're not sure what you might not do in such a case. Why—you might even cry, and your mother wouldn't like it!

Don't worry, darling, I'll be in. I'm really very anxious to see you. Much more so than I can put across on paper. I never could write decent letters.

But the fire up here was really something. It hit home to this region far more sharply than does the war. Frantic parents were calling the school all day yesterday to make sure their sons had come in. One of the seniors was burned to death; another medical student (Sophomore) lost his girlfriend. The stories of the ghastly few hours really are something. It's murder all right. But not the 16 year old busboy's! I think I was more angry than sorry Sunday and yesterday.

And now that the first awful shock is being gotten over by the natives, they too are beginning to get angry.

There is absolutely no excuse, in Heaven or earth, for a catastrophe like that in these times. What with fire-proofing materials, automatic sprinklers, fire escapes, scientifically determined exits for capacity crowds, laws to enforce these being used, inspection to see that the law is carried out! No such thing should ever occur. And when it does, the whole damn bunch, from the Mayor down to the owner of the nightclub ought to be hung as an example to future grafters and politicians.

Some of the facts are cute!—No fire escapes, no sprinklers, one door (revolving) for 800 people, windows barred, the decorations very inflammable, the paint used was made with a cellophane base—the same kind that burned so well in the Normandie, the owner is one of the big politicians in Boston—and right now is running another place just like the "Coconut Grove."

So don't blame the 16 year old kid. I'm sorry that he's getting into any difficulties at all. But just so long as the few are allowed to do as they please at the expense of the many in this anarchic society of ours, we shall continue to have human flesh burned, maimed, and starved.

Golly! I went off didn't I? I feel quite strongly about it. Remind me one of these days to let you know what happens. Are new laws passed? Is the fire commissioner kicked out? (the place was inspected and <u>passed</u> a few days ago). Etc, etc.

How I'd rather tell you all this! I could tell you what I think so much better. And could end it all, so nicely, with a kiss. Putting ideas down on paper doesn't nearly satisfy my hunger. But I send them for your approval in the same spirit that I told you so many of them.

Good night dear
Aaron

Thursday 12/3/42
10:20

Sweetheart—

I'm knocking off early tonight you can see. Tomorrow is our supposedly "easy day" and I'm too lazy to try to learn any more Neuroanatomy tonight. I feel kind of mellow right now—despite the freezing weather up here—and couldn't resist closing my books to write to you instead. It's a damn good thing I don't give in to my inclinations and do this every night. Usually the pressure of the following day's work makes me (more or less) toe the mark.

I've picked up a cough. One of those pesky, lingering things. Not exactly uncomfortable, but very annoying. I probably roamed around on a rainy day without my rubbers—or something. I'm seriously considering wearing a hat. It's my pride against my cough. If the cough gets stubborn, I think it'll win.

I'm glad you went out, dear. I really think we know each other well enough to trust each other completely. You can go out with anyone—I'd continue to be perfectly certain of your love for me. For heaven's sake, tho, don't sit and mope at your escort! Have a good time, darling. Just so long as the guy doesn't try to make love to you, it's O.K. with me.

It just so happens that I'm not interested in seeing any other girl at present. I'm too busy to waste my time trying to be nice to someone. The only girl I have any urge to see is pretty obviously more than a short ride from Beacon Street.

Gosh, but I'd like to see you! Nothing has really been accomplished by the students so far. I'll keep you posted on what happens. Blow by Blow. So far, a meeting has been scheduled between the representatives of the student body and the trustees. We want to know, officially, where we stand; what they are doing towards getting clinics, etc, etc. In the meantime the parents are holding their meeting in New York Dec. 6. We'll get some information from that. I don't think the plan is to make it a public issue as yet, PM…The idea in "Medical Circles" is to appear very conservative. Arousing antagonism is just the wrong thing to do. If possible, one gets in there as quiet a way as is possible. You can imagine the epithet "radical" getting into the heads of the powers that be. I suppose, tho, that if everything else fails, no harm can come of writing to the papers and asking for support.

It would be a lot easier to forget about recognition—or better still, not to have to worry about it!

Now that it's getting cold you can start learning to ice skate. It's a grand sport, tho rather painful at first. But, like typing, it's amazing how one progresses with shear plugging. If you're not falling quite regularly at the beginning it's because you're not learning. You've got to let yourself go to learn—and falling goes with it. It's worth it. I'm becoming awfully soft. No exercise at all. It's a rotten way to live. Maybe I'll do exercise every morning, and regain that sparkle, so you'll be proud of me when you see me. I'll be proud of you in any event.

I'm writing a lot of disjointed stuff lately. My head is getting crammed with medical information. If I could have you with me I'd pour it all out and then have lots of time to tell you that I love you.

Aaron

Friday 11:30 pm
12/4/42

Gloria dear—

I've succumbed again, you can see. I just can't help writing to you again tonight. Your letter that came this afternoon was either particularly sweet, or I'm in a particularly receptive mood. I love you far more than I can put into written words.

It's very lovely out now; cold, still, and dark. Stars are very bright. Walking to my house was almost like walking thru the park at night, it's so quiet and dark. I'd prefer to be with you here, where we'd be so much more alone and together than in the city, where there are so many separating influences; people, noise,…

So bake your cookies and send them up. I'll appreciate their taste, and because they're yours. In any event, I'll have to get used to your cooking. To prove my faith, I'll eat them without trying one on

Edwin or the cat. Enough faith can digest any kind of cookies; even if it can't move mountains.

Incidentally, thinking about cookies reminds me of my mother. She sent me some that she baked some time ago. If you get the chance you might drop in at my home and just say hello. Mother knows that I love you and would enjoy seeing you. You can say that you were walking by when "lo and behold" there was my house—so you dropped in. Or anything else equally silly. My mother isn't like yours at all. She would accept any girl whom I loved-- that was Jewish and fairly respectable. Even if outside that wide limit, she would disapprove but wouldn't dream of doing anything actively about it. My choice is ultimately mine—with my parents' advice, possibly influencing, never deciding it.

Of course, the whole train of thought is quite academic now. It was of some interest before. You'll fit in quite well with mother's picture of an "approved" spouse for me. I love you. That's both mine, and mother's, criterion.

I'm not very tired now, so that I really could be excellent company if you were with me. I'd tell you at great length about my professors, the kind of men they are, the new things that I'm learning every day, my questions about them; the eternal question of recognition...and how much I care for you. If I got too tired of talking about such mundane things as professors and students, we could look at the book of prints you sent up. Some of the paintings are wonderful and bear a lot of looking. I'll tell you why I like Tintorello and Elgrew, and can't stand a host of English painters.

A fine thing for a medical student to be doing! Spending his time writing letters! They do take a lot of time, dear,-- an hour on the average I guess. So you can imagine at what time I finish them and get to bed.

Yet I can't help it. Wishing is almost a tangible link, and affords some emotional release. If you've reread all my letters—am I getting worse? Is there anything you'd like me to change? Fire away darling, I'll be very amenable to criticism. God knows I mean well. But that doesn't necessarily make for good letters.

Good night sweetheart

Aaron

Tuesday 11:45 am
12/8/42

Gloria dear—

Chemistry lab was called off today, so I have two hours to myself now. For the first time in "ages" I can write to you during the daytime when I'm not 2/3 asleep and only can rely on my feelings to express themselves in their own sure way.

Don't be angry, darling, at my picking you up on a phrase in one of your letters. I really didn't mean anything by it—and just thought you might be interested. I know what your feelings are basically, and I don't look to your phraseology for proof of your love. Don't ever look to my letters for proof of anything. Simply assume that I do care for you very much, and then go on interpreting from that point on.

You know, I've been writing to you so consistently, that it never occurred to me that I didn't give you a pretty good description of what I'm doing, the curriculum…Maybe I can bring something more of my school life into my letters—if I can find room enough when I finish telling you in one way or another how very much I miss you.

The courses we're taking—and have taken—are remarkably well organized. The medical curriculum is something which grew up over several centuries, and has had plenty of time to get organized. The big job is to transfer a huge mass of information to the student. What he will do with this information after he gets out is between the doctor, the patient, and God. Generally, the doctor and God come out all right.

Last term everything we did was based around an "understanding" of the body's structure. That's pretty fundamental, isn't it? And the body of knowledge which is transmitted is pretty much static. The doctors of a century ago studied pretty much the same Anatomy.

This term it's the normal functioning of the body we're trying to understand. Now one comes to an entirely different approach (not in the way it's taught—just philosophically speaking). The question is not what does the muscle look like? But how does it work? And look at the consequences of that kind of question. The muscle, we say, contracts and so moves a bone. But how does it contract? The muscle fibers are studied, the properties of muscle fiber contraction worked on, the effect of chemicals, electric shock, fatigue on the strength of muscle contraction are studied. A million facts are collected thru very ingenious experiments—telling us something about the properties of muscular contraction. Laws are formulated and we say that when a muscle fibre contracts it gives all it can, heat is given off…the question still remains, "How does that fibre contract?" "What's the mechanism?" So they go deeper and measure the energy given off, notice the kind of fuel used to get the energy from, and the chemical equations which describe the processes whereby food is converted to muscular energy. The nerve impulse is studied and laws are formulated for the amount of stimulus a nerve must give to a muscle fibre so that the fibre will contract. Still the question remains, "What is this influence the nerve exerts, and how come the muscle contracts?"

As you see the original question is far from answered where I left it. It is far from answered at all in our present knowledge. But a lot is known, not about the ultimate nature of muscle contraction, but about observations which can be made of the process.

This is Physiology.

There are lots of other examples of course. The question of sugar in the urine, eg, comes up. "How come?" So they go back and describe how a certain hemorrhage in the brain gives sugar in the urine. (Why?) So they find out that this hemorrhage causes a lesion in the brain which in turn sends a stimulus to the adrenal gland, which in turn liberates a hormone, which makes the liver mfg more sugar, so the blood sugar is raised, so sugar passes into the urine. How each one actually leads to the next is quite a problem.

Maybe this will give you some idea of what Physiology is like. We've all taken it before to some extent; one of the authors I'm reading compares knowledge to a flight of circular stairs. At each level we survey the same field but with different perspective.

I've got to rush back to school now, darling, so

Love
Aaron

Thursday, 6:20 pm

Darling

I'm writing in bed—so my quite illegible handwriting is probably impossible now. Nevertheless, I want to get this out to get to you before the week-end.

It's that cough. Starting out very innocently, it had me barking away pretty constantly. That provided me with a perfect excuse for a vacation. My first since the Lord knows when. Imagine: I've convinced myself that I'm too ill to go to school today and tomorrow, and really shouldn't bother studying either, to rest better. Pretty good? With enough knowledge, one can convince himself of almost anything. So here I am, propped up in bed, reading an old Harper's, dozing intermittently and letting my imagination picture us together in countless situations. Hopefully I'll be O.K. tomorrow.

This week we did another of our so called "mammalian experiments" in Physiology. We do one of these a week; using a dog, cat, or rabbit for the experimental animal. Six of us work together and the experiment bears all the earmarks of a bona fide operation. It's meant to give us practice in cutting into living things.

The surgical team is divided into surgeon, assistant surgeon, nurse, technician, recorder, and anaesthetist. We rotate positions each week.

On Tuesday we did a rather long experiment. (I wasn't surgeon yet. Don't know how skillful I'll be when I am.) The layout is something like this. The animal is on a board which is heated electrically so kept warm. The anaesthetist puts the animal under, keeps him there, and checks pulse, temperature, respiration, reflexes…to see how the "patient" is doing every 5 minutes. Depending on findings he varies the anaesthesia, or may call for artificial respiration. The surgeon and assistant do the cutting, the technician rigs up the apparatus and runs it for the actual experimentation. (to be con't, darling, my ability to write now isn't so good)

Love
Aaron

Thursday, 12/15
11:15 pm

Sweetheart

I was becoming depressed at receiving only two letters from you last week; but "perked" up immediately at the sight of the sweater. It is gorgeous. And doubly welcome. Winter—and a real New England winter—is here to stay. Beautiful to look at; cold to live in. I'll be wearing your sweater just about all day, every day, and appreciating it very much. I've already showed it off to Edwin and Mrs. Ellis; very proud indeed, I am, of having someone think enough of me to do a job like that. During Christmas week, I'm going to kiss you once for every stitch on the sweater. Won't that be fun, tho! (If I have time, I'll drop a stitch and start all over again)

I hope you've made up your mind about what you want for Christmas, as we're going to go shopping for it together. Somehow I get a real kick out of contemplating having you along when I go to buy something. Sounds silly I suppose, but I get pleasure out of things like that.

Come to think of it, I can't promise to think of you more often "as I wear your love close to my heart." I think of you just about all the time as is. I've even begun talking about you. I think Eddie is getting sick of hearing me make reference to you no matter what the subject of conversation starts with. And for me, that's a bad sign, Honey. I'm in a really bad way.

Did I mention Nature Friends for New Year's in any of my letters? I've been wracking my brain out trying to remember. You see, I've been thinking about it a lot, hoping that we could go there for a few days. It's beautiful and refreshing. And we could really be together 24 hours a day. Maybe Manny would go along and chaperone us. Try to think of something, darling. Things move terribly quickly now. We ought to grab what we can. My whole outlook on things is changing to the "Carpe Diem" idea. It's become the tempo of most of American life. The old concepts of planning, of denying oneself today for a greater reward tomorrow is going by the board. "For who knows what tomorrow will bring." Or will there be a tomorrow?

Good lord! I certainly went off on a tangent, didn't I? Yet, I suppose that feeling is strong in me at present, and so had to come out for your approval.

Which reminds me, I'm not an idealist at 24 who used to be a cynic at 23. Things don't change as simply as all that. Nor are points of view very firmly and sincerely held if they change so fast. I still don't know what love is. I'm in love. I can tell you what I feel about you. But I can't explain it too well. Just as I know that a liver will make more sugar if certain hormones are present—but don't know how. I don't know—specifically why I happen to love you so much, and other girls not at all…

But what's the difference? I'm perfectly content not knowing. The only psychiatry I want to practice is on other people. Not us. We're not going to have any "marriage of convenience." So we ought to have the fortunate start of really loving each other for our sole purpose in deciding to live and share together.

If we can spend as many happy weeks together as there are stitches in my sweater—we'll be an old, old contented couple.

I've gotten my bus ticket for the Bus (Greyhound) that pulls out of Waltham on Sunday, Dec. 27, 9:00 am. It's the earliest one I could get more than a week ago.

Good night dear
Aaron

Thursday 12/17
12:30 am

Gloria dear

Unlike a lot of other weeks that I can remember, time is crawling right now. I suppose, however, that I'll soon see the passing of a few more days and find myself on a bus to New York. "What's New York got that Waltham hasn't?" they shout. I'd never be able to really tell them. Either they've been in love and know, or they don't.

Our professors this term are of a more Americanized variety than last semester, and more of them. Fundamentally, as I write to you, we're studying a big fat Physiology book (some 2000 pages just bursting with information). If one knows what's in that book—understands, not just memorizes—he has this term's work under his belt very thoroughly.

The major Physiology course is based on covering most of Best and Taylor. The Biochemistry course gives one the chemistry necessary to understand the Physiology. The Neuroanatomy gives the Anatomy needed to understand the "physiology of the nervous system"; and the course in "Clinical Physiology" is a very silly name for the endocrinology part of this massive text. All in all we really cover the book. During the day we spend our time in the laboratory doing experiments so that the principals are more readily understood and remembered. You know about "learning by doing."

But to get back to the profs. Dr. Singer, lecturer in "Clinical Physiology" (endocrinology), is the most interesting. He only gives us a two hour lecture each week, but also teaches each of the other years. From my impression of him, and what I've heard tell, he is really an interesting man. A refugee, who has been here only two years, he speaks English very well, is connected with several of the large Boston hospitals. His lectures are swell. They're the best thing I've heard up here. He knows a lot, has confidence in his knowledge, and can put it across. With that, he's terribly conceited, and has a tendency to play to the gallery, telling the worshipful freshman that most doctors are dumb bunnies…I forgive him his faults for his merits. Two weeks ago, I took him at his word, and submitted some questions based on his previous lectures. I really couldn't find the answers anywhere in the text. Well, he came in that Friday, and simply roasted the stupid student (my name wasn't on the paper) who submitted such idiotic questions, for about ½ an hour. I was sweating bullets. A lot of the fellows became pretty angry at the attitude he took. It seems either I was going to the movies every night and not studying (a knave) or a fool. I still don't know the answers. So there you are. One must listen, learn what the professor says, and regurgitate on exams. Nevertheless, Singer is really good. I would rather listen to him, with his faults, than to anyone else I've had.

So you see, the old rule about this school I laid down last term still holds true. The foreigners are very good men. They're teaching in this school because they're foreign. They are much superior to the Americans connected with the school. More of what you expect a professor to be. Sharp, keen minded, facts at his fingertips, possibly eccentric, scientists.

It's really late now. It just occurred to me that Sol can't find a camp. Silly! Let him try Chester Zunborgs. Details are in the Standard which Miriam gets. I've never been there but hear it's wonderful. We'll not spend our honeymoon in a New York hotel if we can help it.

Good night darling
Aaron

Monday 12/27/1942
12:00 midnight

Gloria dear—

I'm getting this letter out to you air mail, dear, or else, considering the mail service here, you'd get it—literally—next year.

Things have gotten a little complicated. I've just gotten a letter from home saying that my brother Arthur is ill, and suggesting that I not come in to New York. Since I can't stay away, I'm coming in as I planned, but may have to find somewheres to stay. The tables are turned. Will you ask Sol if he knows of a fairly good hotel or rooming house, preferably in Brooklyn—tho Manhattan will do—where I can stay. Not the Astor or Hotel Pennsylvania. It'll make things a little more inconvenient, but not impossible. When I get to New York Sunday evening, I'll call up home and find out whether it's all right for me to go there. If not I'll have to find a place to stay right then. Let me know what Sol suggests so I'll have quite a variety to choose from, hopefully.

Don't things always get complicated.

Today we had our Physiology mid-term; and I went to a movie this evening to clear a lot of cobwebs out of my brain. As I've said many times before, Physiology and any other course in Medical school, are all taught on the same basis. They tell you an awful lot about a subject, then during the examination booklets and questions are handed out, the proctor says, "Ready, set, go!" and you start to write like mad. At the end of 2-3 hours he says "Stop." And papers are handed in. God alone knows what you put down during the actual writing period. If lucky, with the material at the fingertips, you don't make too many mistakes. Unlike Anatomy, Physiology is quite comprehensible to the layman. It deals with things we are all familiar.

"In drinking a lot of water at one time exactly what happens?" (one of the questions on which one can write four pages). You know that if someone suffers a severe hemorrhage, various symptoms appear. Anyone can see them. Faintness, rapid pulse, increased breathing, pale skin, cold skin, blue color under nails and lips. The trick is to explain how the loss of blood can account for each of the symptoms. And you can—in about 20-30 minutes of writing.

So it goes. Things we see about us every day. In muscular exercise we notice an increased blood pressure, rapid breathing, rapid pulse, sweating, rise in temperature. How come?...

Such things as exercise, drinking water, changing posture, eating…are called physiological states. We study those first, and learn the mechanisms whereby what we do affects changes in our "internal environment."

But then comes an even more interesting part. Pathology. What goes on when something goes wrong. Next year is spent wholly around Pathology; this year we only touch on it. It's very interesting.

The development of the subject here is not quite perfect. It has to be practical. What has happened was that diseases were described (eg, swelling of the legs, deep breathing which becomes gasping on exertion, rapid pulse, possibly blue coloring of lips, cough). The cause is found to be heart "failure"; and then an explanation is given for the way in which inefficient pumping by the heart can cause all these symptoms. The next step is: what caused the heart to go bad. When you've given all the possible reasons, eg, high blood pressure, the question may be "What caused the high blood pressure?" Reasons are given. One reason is kidney disease. So "what caused degenerative changes in the kidney blood supply?" etc, etc. So you see, as I've probably said lots of times before, that we keep going back, back, until—we don't know. Then they call it "primary something." Like "Primary High Blood Pressure" is one in which they don't know the cause.

It looks as tho I spout the stuff whenever I get the chance, doesn't it darling. I find it interesting, and would ordinarily tell you about it. I write instead.

I'm taking the Greyhound Bus that leaves Waltham at 10 AM on 12/27. You can find out when it arrives at the Capitol Terminal by calling up. Let me know whether you'll meet me.

Love [a great deal]
Aaron

1943

Tuesday 1/5/43
11:10 pm

Sweetheart—

Tho I can just about still feel the pressure of your lips, I'm back again to the routine that appears not to have changed. To make the illusion of two worlds still more complete, it snowed all night as I came up; Waltham looks like a picture postcard of a New England Hamlet. It'll take some time tho before I get over the feeling that I have to take the next bus back to New York. Particularly now, the feeling is strong, and getting stronger.

I suppose you'll be reading this in bed, all stuffed up with a cold. It's a damned shame that anything as annoying as a sore throat can result out of something as beautiful as walking around in a daze. There's no justice. So write soon, tho; my imagination will build up your sniffles to something quite serious.

And despite it all, a "Happy Birthday" dear. Your coming out of your teens in pretty troublous times; I hope we spend your twenties in more auspicious ones. Your locket ought to arrive with this letter. I tried hard to get one that you'd like. If for any reason, you want a different one, just ship it back. Most lockets come in the shape of hearts, apparently. You don't need to have my heart mailed to you now; I never took it to Mass. with me.

Yesterday I was pretty dizzy. No sleep, I guess. The bus ride in is quite vague. I arrived in Waltham about 5:30 am; got to my room; undressed and slept until 7:30. Then we went to school. I was just able to get thru classes. One instructor sprung a quiz on us. I couldn't tell you what the questions were.

Today I stayed home all day to try to catch up. I need a week. Staying at home isn't very efficient, as I miss lectures which have to be copied…But I tried. If I had the stuff in me, I'd stay up until 3-4 am for a few nights and do it. Instead I'm going to go to sleep. Probably, I'll dream.

I'm out of stationery, but will make up for it later in the week.

Good night dear,
Aaron

January 1943
Waltham, Mass.

To Gloria, coming out of her "teens". With all my love
Aaron

Darling—

I hope you like it. When we get the chance we can put pictures into this locket and look at changes time makes…

Thursday 1/7/43
12:50 am

Darling—

I've just gotten in from a "Bull Session" with Dave and Joe, and a few of the other boys at the Cabins. We're still discussing the school—instead of women.

And right now discussion is rather hot and heavy—and very depressing. We were notified yesterday that our school was turned down by the manpower commission for inclusion in their plan to militarize medical schools. That is, apparently, that. It's what I had expected, you know, but the hope that springs eternal was still making itself felt. I dreamed—and thought of how wonderfully we could live together during my years at school. Yesterday sort of hit me pretty hard—and made me wake up to hard, brutal reality.

Exactly what will happen to us now, we don't know. You can probably guess, tho.

Damn it!

I love you very much and feel even worse at the idea of knowing what I'm missing in being separated from you. I'm sorry dear. You probably never had a worry in your pretty head until you fell in love with me. There must have been lots of them there since.

The tension in me is remarkably up. I'm torn by several major worries, all claiming precedence. Do you remember my theory of worry? That man is surrounded by sort of concentric circles of worry, each one being a little further away as it's less immediate. As the nearest one get's less important, the next one takes its place…I wonder if it isn't a good thing, that generally one can only feel bad about the innermost one, the most immediate and pressing one. The toothache, sick baby. And temporarily forgets the war, rent, health…At present I think that I'm in the peculiar position of having two immediate problems thrusting their way into first place. They're even fighting in my mind for dominance. Both are highly charged with emotion. They are 1) I have to continuously keep studying to try to do more than I can do. A terrific emotional drain; 2) the problem of the school. A terrific worry.

And lurking just behind them are the threat of others you know about. The two major ones are fighting each other and increase the emotional tension.

I have really gone off the deep end tonight, haven't I? Maybe it's the hour. This letter, it seems, would go well to the slow movement of Beethoven's Third Symphony.

Perhaps I could have used the time to tell you more effectively how much I miss you. I do want to keep my heart completely exposed to you, tho. So that you can see just what goes on in it: hopes, fears, longings,…that way you'll know me completely, understand what I do, and our love can rest on a secure foundation. I know that you do the same.

Get better soon darling. I hate to feel that our being together—even in the rain—made you sick.

Good night dear
Aaron

Thursday, 1/13/43
12:00 am

Sweetheart:

As you can obviously guess, I'm writing this in bed. "If you get sick—how can I stay well" would be the appropriate quote from somewhere if I could find it. I've been feeling under the weather since I came back to school, spent an impossible night on Tuesday and saw Dr. Blumenthal yesterday. He was very nice. Professional courtesy and stuff. Told me I had Intestinal grippe, and sent me to bed. So here I am loafing again. I'm to eat nothing but fruit juices or Pepsi Cola for a day or two. I've got the stuff all around me. In fact, I even bought a thermometer so I'll know when I'm well enough to go down.

Strange isn't it? We're very much alike. I hope I don't ever break a leg. You'd probably limp for weeks.

This Dr. Blumenthal is one of our graduates. Out since 1935 or so, he has a tremendous house in Waltham and a great practice. He's a good doctor, as well as a likeable chap. The medical students all go to him, rather than to a lot of other doctors who are connected with the school. His method is apparently very rapid diagnosis followed by a check-up. And his diagnosis, from what the other boys tell me, is very often right. Since he didn't have to use the bedside manner on me, my examination lasted about 5 minutes. All the rest of a physician's examination, unless complications are apparent is evidently to impress the patient. He told me what was wrong with me from the symptoms as I gave them to him; then checked my temperature, heart, lungs, and throat to make sure. He said that he was certain we'd be allowed to practice. One man's opinion. He (and the other doctors of our school, I guess) don't charge the students. Professional courtesy. He hopes that I'll do the same when I'm practicing. I sure will!

I received your very accurate echo of my feelings about the school yesterday, dear. You're right of course. There isn't very much we can do, tho. Yet in these times of rapid change my best bet is to hang on for the next year, too. We sent a delegation down to Washington to get information. They found out very little. The army and navy said simply that under no conditions would sub-standard schools be used in their plan. They will select all students to enter medical school for the December (?) 1943 class. This would leave no entering classes for the unapproved schools which would be forced to close down. The Selective Service Board said that they took orders from the War Manpower Commission. The War Manpower Commission hasn't made up its mind yet.

So there we are.

Altho there is little comfort in the idea, the only way you can get along without feeling very depressed about the situation is by not comparing it with what "might have been." Bellevue paid for going to school, living together in New York, 3 sure years of security, a first rate doctor when thru, a military status later which is so useful in civil service jobs...compared to that I ought to shoot myself. But on the other side of the picture, the great majority of men,-- in fact everybody but the handful in dental and medical schools—had to give up their jobs and lead the uncomfortable and "precarious" life of the army. Some will come back; a lot won't. Their jobs—all but city employees—will not be waiting for them. The maelstrom of existence will keep whirling them after, as it did before.

So compared to them, I'm in no worse predicament. My letters get to you in time—And I can get yours regularly. We love each other enough to have gotten married, or decided to get married even if I entered the army I think. Only my ability to go home to see you might not have been quite as much.

Of course you know what I feel about smug people. "Things could have been much worse" philosophies never push one forward. But sometimes one has to look at the total situation to get a perspective.

Incidentally, if you visit my parents don't say a word about my illness. They'd only worry unnecessarily. You see you're my only confidante. It would be awful if I had nobody to tell my troubles to.

Until later darling,

Love
Aaron

Monday 1/18/43

6:30 pm

Sweetheart:

You want to come up to Waltham anyway. Get married—"if I'd have you." What do I think?

That's a big order, Honey. As usual I don't know all the answers. But I'm going to try to give you some of them. The rest, when you get them figured out, pass on to me.

First, tho, stop being a little goose! If I'd have you! As soon as you get here, or arrange for me to do so in New York. We'll be married. You know that.

From the purely selfish point of view, I ought to urge you to come very earnestly. I'd have everything to gain: Gloria waiting for me when I get home, meals that aren't 80% poison, an apartment of my own, and, of course, the deep satisfaction of spending all my nonworking hours with you…I can't lose.

But love isn't like that, I guess. There are two of us. And it's you I'm concerned with.

Just what is the situation up here anyway?

1) We don't know what's going to become of us ultimately. For the near future probably nothing will happen. Our delegation to Washington was told that, although we definitely will not be included in the present Army Navy plan, we should continue our studies; existing facilities will not be discarded. Probably then, we will be allowed to continue then with our 2A classification. State recognition will eventually be achieved (tho to complicate the situation, there will be no entering class in October 1943, as all pre-med students will be in the Army and sent to "A" schools. That would mean that the school would just die a natural death. It would be interesting to be around then to see just what they do about it.)
2) If I even had the next three years up in New England, I think it would be a pretty good idea for us to be together rather than separated. But I only have enough money to pay my next year's tuition. I, apparently, gambled and lost. Money was lent to Med students. With the new

program, it probably won't be. There isn't any way for me to meet $1000. Possibly (and the draft board mayn't like it) I'll go to Boston P.& S. for my third year. I'd only have to get $150/year then. It would be nothing but an army evading move at that point. Most probably I'll be drafted at that point.

3) In the interim—It depends, as I'm trying to make clear, upon what you are capable of handling.

As the situation is, I, if not a liability, would certainly not be an asset to you. I can't be the strong, protective husband you may need. The situation is too big for me.

Altho money won't get me into a recognized school, it again would be the principle problem we'd be up against (I'm beginning to hate the filthy stuff). As you know, if the Dept. of Welfare comes thru with my vacation money, or I can work during vacation—and if I don't get sick too often, or lose my job--...I'll just make books and tuition. I won't be able to take care of you, support you,...the way you should be. I couldn't do anything at all! It's the most helpless feeling you can imagine. Cold attics notwithstanding, we'd have to live comfortable, to live. You probably are thinking about that attic I looked for when I first came up here—with shower, bath, electricity, running hot and cold water, steam, and a good view.

4) Finally: If you were somewhat older, been out of school for several years, and had been taking care of yourself...it wouldn't really make much difference whether you did so in Waltham, Washington or New York. Except for the fact that we'd be looking rather anxiously toward October we'd have a lot of fun together. Several of the boys have wives up here.

So the question ultimately boils down to your own capability and your own strength. Do you think you could go to a small town on the outskirts of Boston and take care of yourself? If you could, since

I'm more or less taking care of myself, we could spend our time together as husband and wife.

The question I pose, in answer to yours, is not easy. You probably don't know the answer. You've been so beautifully sheltered. Maybe you'll know better after you finish business school and have a chance to work and look for jobs.

Looking it over, I really have remarkably little to offer you:

1) No future. The Dep't of Welfare even accepted my resignation.
2) Drafted within 6-7 months. Realistically that may kill or incapacitate me.
3) I can't even help support you 'till then.

These are the facts. I'd give anything to be able to be the kind of husband I should be. To offer the security compatible with married happiness. My intentions are good, God knows, but Hell is still paved with good intentions.

Think it all over darling. I don't know whether it's clear. If you want more of my opinions on any point just shout. You have all the facts which bear on the situation that I have.

This letter is quite a brief! At any rate, you won't be able to tell our grandchildren that I married you under false pretenses.

The Neuroanatomy outline arrived today. Thanks. I'll try to make good use of it.

Good night dear,
Aaron

Thursday 1/21/43
11:15 pm

Gloria dear—

I'm not exhausted now. But I'm just going to quit anyway. I'd rather write to you than study anything.

It's snowing out tonight. But snowing. If it keeps up, I probably won't be able to get to school tomorrow. I've never seen anything quite like it. They say that tremendous snowdrifts are common out here. Already it's way beyond anything I've seen in New York.

To sort of balance the cartoons (they're good) you sent up, I'm putting some pictures of the school and a clipping, in tonight. Both need a word.

The pictures are wonderful examples of what a good photographer can do. The school would make quite a lovely finishing school for girls. But a medical school should be more business like, and smell of iodoform—not lilac.

About the article. It's a brief note on the tremendous amount of intrigue and unrest going on underneath the surface of the school. I don't want to pour out rumors. They're awfully disappointing. But the story, pretty reliably, is that a battle has been going on between the Dean and the owner, Smith. The Dean represents all that's Holy in American medicine; Smith is a blackguard who has been making money by selling "MD"s, and many other kinds of underhanded skullduggery (!) in the past. Under his control, the AMA wouldn't look at the school.

This article announces the resignation of Mr. Ruggles Smith (the old man's son) as president of the University. And of several prior Smith trustees to make room for new men. Particularly significant is Frank Kingdon, a really good man.

It may mean absolutely nothing. The boys felt very happy at the news. It is felt that the greatest handicap to the school since it started was its administration. The administration is, hopefully, changing. I think they saw the handwriting on the wall; and decided to try to keep their salaries as minor officials (Ruggles is now registrar) in an approved school, than own a school which will be closed down.

Maybe.

Maybe not. It may just be surface changes, like the manipulations of the French Cabinet when things got hot. Never-the-less, this is the first concrete information I could give you, so I pass it along.

So you know, dear, a school year has just about passed. I can't realize it. Time more than flew; it disappeared. It was pleasant after a fashion. Yet a little heartbreaking. Mostly I missed you. And the constant feeling of helplessness at the probable futility of it all. "Would I be able to finish? And if I did, would it be any use?" Fortunately tho, I'm very much interested in the material I'm studying. Time just zooms along.

Edwin has gone to sleep early tonight. It's almost midnight now. The only sounds are the ticking of my clock and the scratching of my pen…I'm not sleepy strangely enough…I'll probably be awake for awhile thinking of how warm you'd be.

For someone who never was able to think of what to say in a letter, I'm showing a remarkable facility in covering page after page. I have enough to write every day. I just don't have the time.

Good night darling
Aaron

Tuesday, Jan 26. 1943
12:35 am

Darling:

I'm back at the old habit of writing these midnight letters, it seems. Anyway, it's the best time for them. I'm thru working, and feel comfortably set to take as long as I like to write to you.

I'm very behind. And on Sunday, Dave and Joe inveigled me into going to see "Now Voyager." Really, I don't have the time for movies now, but they convinced me. See it—if you haven't done so already. It's very good. You know, I see you almost everywhere. I saw you in Bette Davis, during the few moments on the screen, when she was portrayed as a sweet girl of 20. There are differences of course. But we can go over them after you have seen how a movie psychiatrist works. It's about the destruction of a girl's personality by the domination of her mother. They don't go into the subject very deeply; it's a Hollywood production. Underneath the dominance must have been some real (tho probably, unconscious) hatred and rejection of the daughter (Bette) from the day she was an infant. Even tho the mother proclaimed constantly that she was doing everything "for her daughter's sake."

Your letter today, with its dry tone of dejection because of a quarrel with your mother made me think of the movie again. Get your mother to see it. There are some speeches in it, put very well, that I would have liked to have said to her myself.

The only difficulty with the movie, is that the patient is cured in about 3 weeks. I don't think a lifetime of therapy could have done that job at her stage.

Interestingly enough, the romantic angle, tho somewhat "hammed" at times, had a message. The message that Dr. Thorot used to pound out—"Love as a healing force." This poor, sick girl had an ego that was very shrunken, was terrified and lonely. Her symptoms of fear, and unhappiness sprang from it. In the warmth of a love and affection from a chap who had a lot of it to give; who wasn't 'sick' himself so that he desperately needed his ego bolstered; who could accept the girl, simply, without flinching in the face of her difficult behavior; she grew stronger and healthier.

It sounds good anyway. Maybe you'll think that this is all crazy and I ought to stick to my Best and Taylor.

Yesterday, I had supper at Sidney Kafka's, a classmate. He's married, just had a baby, and recently brought his wife up to Waltham. Give the man credit. He can devote himself to a wife, daughter, and Physiology too. Compared to that I'm just a big loafer.

I love you very much. We'll be married in October if that's the time you want. Unless of course I'm drafted. I don't think I'd want to go to war leaving you tied to something as uncertain as that. But if I can stay out, I'll get the finest birthday present any man ever received. You have a lot of courage darling. When I reread my four page theme on the subject, I felt that the situation as presented might look too black for you. I sent it anyway, as I wanted to be completely honest in this—as everything else.

Good night dear
Aaron

Incidentally—Arthur wrote asking for Arrowsmith

Tuesday
12:00 midnight

Sweetheart—

Gosh, I'm sleepy! I was going to stay up until 2 or so tonight, but I'm going to go to sleep. I guess I'm a sissy. Finals are crowding up over the horizon, but lectures are continuing right along. I've got all I can do to keep up with current work, let alone do anything but feel very apprehensive about the exams. The pace in Medical school really is terrific. Or maybe I'm getting old and feeble. Or maybe it's the way things are taught at Middlesex. Or maybe it's not expected that the student do anything but study week-ends. I don't know.

That sounded just like my Physiology test. For every question, practically, about 10 answers are given with no real indication as to whether any of them are right. Everything is all very vague.

Compared to Physics, Engineering, or even Chemistry, Medicine is still in the dark ages. They don't have fundamental concepts yet from which to reason. You know, that in math or physics a lot of experimental work is done, but a great deal of what is known can be arrived at by reasoning from fundamental concepts. It is these concepts, eg gravity, relativity, energy, entropy…which form the backbone of the science. You know that you have a little truth when from your basic concepts a host of observable phenomena can be predicted and explained.

Medicine is very largely descriptive. The body was dissected and described. It required no great synthesizing mind to write the first Anatomy book. A good, careful worker did it. They have been copying it ever since. So, for everything else. Description after description. Diseases are described, bacteria are described, symptoms are described, treatment is described. A huge amount, as you can imagine has been described during the past 1000 years. But fundamental knowledge is entirely lacking. There just don't seem to have been any Einstein's, no Newton's, or Marx's in Medicine. Someone to take the huge volume of description and make something of it.

Someday I hope somebody will crack the problem. What they have been able to ascertain shows a great deal of cleverness and ingenuity. But the genius isn't there. I'm learning about nerves now for example. I learned, at length, many new words for old ideas. I was told that in order to excite a nerve, a certain minimal stimulus must be given; that different nerves, under different conditions react to different degree of stimulation…ad infinitum…But fundamentally what is this thing called nerve impulse? How come all these things described are so? What is the fundamental concept, so that these results can be arrived at by reasoning, instead of mere memorization…nothing doing. In discussing disease, the same thing happens. "If the cornea of the eye starts to degenerate we call it a cataract…"; from then on lots of description about what happens in such cases. Just how does it happen that the cornea starts to degenerate?

So you know, darling, I'd be pouring all this out to you if you were here. I'm not too clear in my ideas, at all, but I'd love to get them off my chest and tell you just what ideas get into my head.

Your letters are regular and grand. Coming home from school is a pleasure. I miss you terribly.

Good night darling,
Aaron

Thursday, Feb. 4, 1943
12:15 am

Gloria dear—

Comes midnight or thereabouts, and my thoughts leave the tracts of the spinal cord to focus on New York. You must be quite used to these midnight and early morning letters. Are they any different from the ones I sent in more "sensible' hours?

I'm not particularly tired now. When I got home this evening I was full of eye strain, so that I took a nap. So for all practical purposes it's only 10:30. I really ought to go right back to those cranial nerves! Nope. I'm going to write to you, and "sip" the writing slowly. <u>Then to bed</u>.

Altho finals don't begin until next Saturday, I took Chemistry practical today. It was quite interesting. You know, I guess that the chemistry we study deals with the stuff inside of us. One of the most important things the chemist can analyze, when it comes to people, is blood. The other is urine. It looks funny at first that such an enormous amount of research has been done on the composition of blood and urine. After all the urine is a waste product—at least so the layman believes. But to the physiological chemist, urine is a gift from Heaven. He just grabs it and will analyze it all day. You never know what you might find. Like a jig saw puzzle I guess.

Seriously, tho, the reason they make such a fuss about highly complex methods of urinalysis is the ease with which one gets a sample from a patient. He's glad to give it to you. And all you want. It's really much easier on him if you can diagnose his liver trouble by playing with his urine than by looking at his liver during an operation. So that a careful correlation of urine constituents and disease is an indispensable diagnostic tool. Even more valuable is the blood. In fact they'll use anything they can get out of the patient to analyze. His expired air, his vomitus (taken with a stomach tube),…[not a very savory topic, I'm beginning to realize, but I really was curious about it]. Of course, besides being a convenient method of diagnosis, these bodily secretions do give us information that can't be gotten any other way. If a certain waste product is supposed to come out and doesn't—it tells you something about the organ manufacturing the waste product, or the kidney,

Before long, you'll be able to take the state boards in medicine. Do you mind these digressions? Sometimes I can't say anything else in letters but that I miss you terribly; that I want you to hurry up, and come up here. At other times, I want to talk to you about what's in my heart at the moment, just as I would if we were together, and it comes out in my letters.

I'm not repeating my lectures, darling. The stuff that gets into the letters are what I think of the material I learn. I have to memorize, you see, a lot of things that are present in urine, average constituents, and pathological variations. No one told me why.

Today, as I started out to say, I was given a sample of blood, and was asked to find out how much sugar and salt there was in it. There are some cute methods for doing it. I'll tell you about them, if you're interested. I handed in answers, but I don't know yet how close I came to the true value.

You certainly are getting a lot of interesting stuff from your friends. I'm sorry for Solly. But things seem to go like that. They are rarely simple. God knows what makes people feel and do the things they do. Maybe even he wonders sometimes. I can't quite understand what the logic behind the chap's behavior is. We'd have to hear his story first.

I haven't been here for a month

Tuesday 12:00 am
2/9/43

Sweetheart

I'm a little groggy right now. I've been writing a Physiology notebook all evening. Very tedious. Completely useless. I always did object to reports, and notebooks. Particularly notebooks. Sometimes I even went so far as to lose credit by handing in obviously quick jobs. But I always felt they were wasting my time. And particularly this one! Exams start on Saturday; I'm not prepared, and I've got to sit up writing a Physiology notebook! Damn it. I don't know how I'm ever going to pass those finals. We may be a Grade X school, but the exams are always Grade A.

Oh well, darling. I've gotten some of it out of my system. How are you dear? Boy, could I use a little of your warmth to relax in now. I feel as tho I hadn't seen or kissed you for years. I'd like to have nothing to do for a couple of months but just be with you. I wouldn't make love to you all the time. Just to hold on to some part of you, talk about whatever came into my mind, let the outside just go by in a grey cloud.

The year is rushing to a close. Lectures end on Thursday. Exams right thru the following week. My perspective is undoubtedly way off, but right now those exams loom ominously important to me.

Before I forget what they were like, let me tell you something of the instructors, who played such a big part of my life up here in this tight little world of ours.

I told you about Dr. Singer, I think. The very sarcastic, very competent, fascinating lecturer in Endocrinology & Vitamins. His lectures got better, his sarcasm is still there. The saving feature of the Anatomy department is Dr. Bergmann. Young (38 or so), slight, nice looking, delightful Viennese accident, he is a younger Singer. He is extremely capable—one can't know much more Anatomy--; he is completely sincere in his effort to teach. His lectures, tho not as polished, or incisive as Singer's, are wonders of patient explanation of a rather complex subject, Neuroanatomy. He prepares every lecture very thoroughly; knows we are students; and goes to great lengths, from cutting paper models to drawing up onto the ceiling, to make himself clear. He is right up to date, attends the Anatomical Conferences, and is one swell egg. He's warm; Singer is competent and cold. Bergmann doesn't want to practice. He likes to teach. Every year the professor of Anatomy has been letting him take over more and more. This year he gave the Neuro Course. If I don't know much it's not his fault. No teacher could do more.

The other two are only negative. The Biochemistry prof, Dr. Davidson, is a queer little duck, who may or may not know any chemistry, who is a good Republican; has outlined the text, and laboriously parrots it out. He saves me the trouble of doing it. Rumor hath it that he is a Eunuch or a cryptorchid (undescended testes); no hair on face; queer solitary life; strangely alien to the social world about him. In general, a harmless, little fellow who at least doesn't hinder your studying. He'd help, if he could.

But Harold Kaplan, the Physiology prof…It's not the notebook, darling. I've really detested the guy all along. He apparently has ability and once knew his stuff. Ph.D. from Harvard under Cannon. But he hates his job. And with it the students who are part of it. He wants to be in a good school where he can go places. So his attitude just hovers over and smothers the second semester at Middlesex. Physiology this semester is the most important course. He hasn't prepared a lecture apparently for years. Has a book of notes; rattles off into the air for an hour; marks the place; and picks up next session. He doesn't give a damn about our understanding what he says; or about saying anything correctly. Mistakes are legion. Since he's not prepared he can make simple things more complex than anyone else I know. He keeps the grades down to as close a failure as possible; and then flunks more than the others put together. He knows that writing 200-300 page notebooks is a tedious farce, but insists on it. Some dark night one of the boys will meet him in a dark alley and…

So there you are, darling. The insignificant which becomes so important up here. Silly stuff to write about. I love you so much, I want to write that instead. But I get off on a tangent, and cover lots of you and time.

It's really late now. By the time you see me again I'll look like the devil if I don't keep more reasonable hours. And then what would you say?

Gosh I miss you…

Good night dear
Aaron

(undated)

Darling—

The Physiology notebook is finished. *Tis a thing of beauty and a joy forever—and I hope Herr Kaplan chokes on it.* Probably he'll pass it with all the obvious faults of composition. Now I have to try to get enough information into my head to pass the exams. Well, well.

I'd love to be home with you dear. My going in, as compared with staying up here and working someplace isn't something that I'm debating about on the basis of preference. I don't think even an idiot (let alone a moron) wouldn't prefer to be home, lounging around with a girl he loves, listening to good music, eating good food…than to stay in a small town, with all the other students gone home, working 6 days a week in some smelly factory at a laborious and tedious job. Come now, there's really little to choose from. But I'm stubborn. If I can get a job for the month (and I probably won't) to make it worth while staying, I'll stay. If I can't, I'll go home.

I want to shut it out. I can't tell very well what will happen to the school. But I've cast the die. My only real hope now lies with the school. If I can earn enough between now and October to see me thru my third year—probably the school will see me thru the fourth—Everything else being equal. And "everything" else is a lot.

But don't worry yet, sweetheart. I haven't even tried to get a job yet. If I don't find a plant that can use an experienced chap for one month, I'll rush home very quickly.

Your new stationery is very pretty. I'll have to get some new kinds also. This is the paper on which I've been writing to you ever since I started—long distance. It gives me lots of room to pour out my feelings. And your letters are swell, darling. I feel as tho I've been in New York all along sometimes. I can tell Solly, Manny and sometimes even Milly more-or-less what they've been up to these past months. I'm glad all the newlyweds are maintaining their honeymoon into married life. And I envy them collectively. Never-the-less, my conviction still holds that it is a rare couple indeed who are completely satisfied and secure in each other. And it is even a rarer one who admits to it—even to himself. Nonetheless, send my love to Sol and Miriam. Considering the battle they put up to get married, they deserve many years of marital bliss as reward. Everybody is married I suppose. Aaron, Sol, Milly…it's becoming contagious.

You don't have to convince me that marriage is a nice institution. I'm all ready to be an "inmate."

Since last letter I've been doing nothing but sit home and work. As of today, lectures are thru for the end of the first year. I cut yesterday and today, hoping the profs wouldn't say anything interesting. They rarely do.

How is your shorthand and typing coming? Has it lost its novelty yet? Are you any good? What's school feel like now?

Just about a year ago we went to the Metropolitan. You wore a red dress, and were dressed so carefully. It could have been a grand year if I didn't spend most of it several hundred miles away.

Good night dear
Aaron

Tuesday, 11:00 pm

Gloria darling,

Your valentines were charming—both yours and Silly Millie's. I had hardly realized Valentine's Day was here—nor would I have thought anything of it if I had. But you're very sweet. I love you a great deal. It's really a good thing that I'm so swamped that I have little time to be introspective. I don't think I could stay away for very long if I did. The pressure tho is one form of sublimation. I rush about, then study until fatigue sets in—and then go to sleep.

Sometimes I dream. Often it's about you. Oh my!

Right now I'm in the midst of finals. Two gone—two to go. On Thursday afternoon I'll be thru, for better or worse. I have little idea how I've done so far. The questions were pretty broad. I even wonder whether they'll grade the Physiology exam I took yesterday. Herr Kaplan is much too unconcerned to bother reading about 800 books.

Tomorrow Biochem

Thursday Clinical Physiology

It really froze up here this week. Temperatures dropped like mad, and people tried to keep warm. There has been lots of frostbite around. I'll probably catch cold if this keeps up, just to be consistent.

Waltham looks like Snow Village. It's really quite pretty. Some parts remind me of those "typical scenes" seen in postcards or calendars. You'd like it. But I wouldn't want you freezing. It's never like this in New York. The snow, tho, is very pretty after it falls. They don't clean it off in this town, so it just lies there, very white and beautiful, transforming an ordinary street into a pretty scene.

I'm glad you're developing. Not for my sake, darling. For yours. It's probably remarkable how little that phase of your anatomy, by size, means to me. I'm very much in love with you, dear,-- all of you. I hardly notice what any part of you is like. Or what you say or do at any one time. It's the fundamental you that I respond to; what comes out of it will be right as long as the basis is right. Your "prettiness", softness, warmth, understanding...; that isn't reflected by any one thing.

But if the more matronly bodice will make you happy—I'll be very happy, too. Just you wait until I see you!

Have you gone over to my home for dinner yet? My mother would really like to have you, I think. Not only because of our connection; and the fact that she might as well get used to you—but for herself. She's a lonesome woman. Very few social contacts, and misses them very much. Not very stable, she is pretty much unable to really "go out" to people; so she is left very much alone, and respected by all her acquaintances.

I give you this so you can handle the situation as constructively as you can. There's no question here of any antagonism, rather the opposite.

Enough of the psychology.

I'm going to bed now.

I miss you very much.

Good night dear,
Aaron

(undated)

Sweetheart:

I've just stopped a rather long discussion with Edwin. We talked about women and "life." You know. I talked mostly about you. He must be getting tired of hearing you brought into all our discussions, but I really can't help it. I talk about what's on my mind.

I feel a little mixed up. We finished our first year yesterday. I started to work in a defense plant this morning. I want to go home to you.

I want you darling. There is a full moon out tonight, the night is full of the hint of spring coming. I'm not too tired to feel, and know what I feel. I want to talk to you, hold your hands, and love. I don't want to stay several hundred miles away.

I'll call you long distance this coming Thursday at eight o'clock in the evening. I want to talk to you, even if it's for a few minutes over the phone.

I don't know dear; we're hitting an awful lot of difficulties in getting to see each other. It's small consolation to know that they are less difficult than from Africa.

You'd better write some long, warm, and very loving letters. I need them. They won't substitute for your long, warm, and very loving kisses; but they can at least get to me.

I'll give you the details of my job in my next letter. Right now I want to write about you. It makes me feel good to just let out like this. When I start taking you for granted—like all husbands are supposed to do; and you don't like it,-- as all wives are supposed to do; show me this letter and I'll reform. Right now, I can't think of anything I'd rather have than you with me.

It's funny. I think I'd go home, but for you. Quite a paradox. I feel that married love might possibly flourish under insecurity; but has a far better chance under happier circumstances. I want you to be happy, and always proud of me. As the wife of a physician, you'll have an easier job of being both.

Briefly I work in a plant that turns out grinding wheels. I was put on a lathe doing a simple operation 7:30 to 5:30, 6 days a week; 35. The plant is about a half block from where I live. More later.

Darling, do you think you could come up here for a while to visit me? All the boy's girl-friends do it. You could have my room, while I stayed at a hotel. Or you could stay at a hotel. I'd meet all your expenses; it would, in fact be quite a saving for me. I'm not sure that I could keep away from you for the month. Even a four day trip—Friday to Monday—would be grand.

It's quiet now. I'm going to sleep, a little saddened. But I'm very glad that I love you.

Good night dear,
Aaron

Tuesday, 2/23
11:00 pm

Sweetheart—

I really could write to you at more sensible hours, but it seems that I've just gotten into the habit of ending a couple of days each week with an hour or so "devoted to you." I don't have anything else to do, and can just let my feelings, and my pen, wander leisurely. (that sounds a little mushy, darling; I mean it tho; slap me down if I ever tend towards sentimentalism)

As you know by now, I've been working since Thursday night. I'm a little tired when I get home, but it's not too bad. I've read Erskine's Private Life of Helen of Troy and Alas Pasado—42 Parallel. I'm in the middle of 1919 now. It's a grand book. He writes very well. I'd love to read some of the stuff to you. In fact, I'm going to.

What do I do? Well, you know what grinding stones are. When the stone wheels are first cut from the material they make them from, they are only approximately the right size. My "department" trues the wheel. They make sure that the dimensions are exactly right. So, my machine is one form of lathe. That is a wheel spinning. The motor spins a series of wheels up near the ceiling. Each machine is attached to one of these wheels by a belt, so the machine spins. The grinding stone is attached to the machine, so it spins. (it's a wonder I'm not spinning, too.) Finally I push (using controls) the cutting tool, over to the stone and the stone is rubbed away. When it has just the right thickness, and is perfectly flat (true) my operation is over and I start on the next one. Very entertaining. The dust raised, as the grinding stone is ground away, is terrific. We breathe sand diluted with air. But it won't hurt for a month. Other fellows are doing it, too. Other defense plants want to know why you're deferred; and then won't take you for a month. The first day, I cogitated over the relationship between angular and linear velocity. I once knew a formula; I now saw a practical relationship. I've thought a lot about the word "LABOR." Everybody talks about it. I'd make the very pot-bellied, soft-voiced, dainty-fingered little intellectual who is always thinking about what would be good for "LABOR", as tho the men were cattle or pigs, work in a tough factory for a while. They'd knock some of the condescending tone out of him.

When I'm thru with studying to be a doctor, I will have learnt quite a lot that's not in medical books. I wouldn't voluntarily learn this way, but if I must—it won't do any harm. I've heard a lot of junk, and said a lot of junk. Each year I wonder how I could have been so immature the year before. I guess I'll never really grow up.

Except for the few days just after I left for school, I've never missed you as I do now. My evenings are free. Free to feel lonely and frustrated. Both of us, I guess.

You mention in your letter that you'd like to come up for a weekend. Curiously enough (or is it, obviously) you'll find the same idea in my last letter. How about really doing it? I hate to toy with ideas. Your mother ought to let you come. It's quite a common occurrence up here. And after all, one of these days you'll have to ask her to let you take a trip to Waltham so you can get married.

I love you very much darling,

Good night dear
Aaron

Friday 9:00 pm

Darling—

I'm writing in bed again. That hoarseness you heard last night developed into a full fledged sore throat. So here I am. I don't know whether I'll be well enough to go to work tomorrow. This cold has been coming on for a few weeks now. I kept on hoping that it would hold off during exam week. And it did. But it's here now.

It was very nice talking to you last night. Three minutes went remarkably fast. And there really was nothing to say that wouldn't take hours. But for a few minutes I knew just where you were, what you were doing, and thinking. Not several days later.

From your account of your attendance record at school, I'm beginning to think your father wasted his poor hard earned money.

More power to you darling. I've always wanted to cut classes—and didn't very often.

Winter's here again. I wish they'd make up their minds about the weather. I daresay you're having a milder version of what they proudly call up here "New England Weather!" I think they'd be proud of the Devil if they thought he came from New England.

I'm going to cut this short dear. I'm going to read for a little while and then go to sleep. It's strange that the most beautiful letter I'd ever received had a paragraph telling me that my letters were great and yours mediocre.

Good night darling,
Aaron

Sunday, 5:00 pm

Darling:

I've spent a very lazy Sunday, loafing around the house and finishing USA. My cold has developed into a swell case of laryngitis so I can't talk very well. I rumble. I don't think I'll go in to work tomorrow. My plans for the immediate future are rather vague just now.

I'm glad that you got me so curious about the book. It's very well done.

Dos Passos describes a great many people; different kinds of people. But one thing seems to stand out. The people continue to be the same, as they get older and get into new situations. The old idea of mine, that personality is fixed at an early age, and that you'd have to have experiences of monumental emotional importance to make any alterations, stands.

Charley Anderson was a small, little-ego, uneducated chap, whose world ran between his lathe, a poker game, getting laid, and getting drunk. When, by luck, he became very rich, the same character persists—although more exaggerated now, and doing more harm as his power is greater. His life continues to the end to be gambling, an attempt to find a woman he can thrill, an attempt to convince himself that he was a big shot. Desperately trying to inflate that ego.

J. Ward Moorehouse, the cold, blue-eyed, bluff as a youngster—is still the same person as the big public relations man. I don't think he's so vicious, as stupid.

And so down the line.

So you noticed that nowhere's did you find peace, contentment; or love in the sense that I use it? All the people are a frustrated lot; trying desperately hard to satisfy their little urges. Rich or poor, everyone is working to get something.

Very rarely did we find parents giving children love and security. Generally the parents were much too unhappy themselves to make anyone else happy.

A lot of babies were born unwanted. Many were accidents. Abortions prevented others.

It's difficult to know what to do with a picture like that. The picture of people and their meaningless lives. My cynicism tends to agree, that that is just what life is like. You'll never believe it, really, I think—until possibly you experience it. Just so long as we long so desperately for status, and need constant props for our egos we'll always be pushing and groveling for more.

Fundamentally, although I think the book is extremely well written, I can't help feeling that it's being cowardly to write in that fashion. I much prefer, and admire the author who says what he thinks about anything at all in a simple declarative style with whatever proof he wants to give.

Don't misunderstand me. There is room for poetry, novels and the drama. But I think their function—as all art—is to deal with the emotions. Make me feel.

An exposition on the social conditions of the time, the major drives of adolescent girls…is most honestly put down in essay form. I know that I would be tempted to put down my ideas in story form. People can interpret as they like, and can't argue with you—if you write well. But it's not as brave as the other.

So there you are. Now you can tell me that I'm way off the deep end. But go ahead. I like people with convictions—if they are sincere and intelligent.

In one sense the book was no good for me. I'm sex starved enough as it is. And his graphic, and realistic, descriptions of American sex life isn't the stuff to tone me down.

But don't worry darling. You know my ethics in the matter. I don't believe in a double standard, and will hold out for you in exactly the same way that I'd expect you to wait for me.

All my love—
Aaron

Wednesday 9:30 pm

Darling—

It's a crazy town this. Just a few days ago spring was here; now it's snowing like mad out. And so are my plans. I think I'm doomed to live the very well planned, "planless" life.

On Monday, as I said, I quit my job grinding big stones down to little stones (the phrase sounds familiar, somehow). That was Monday morning. Tuesday morning I started to work in a defense plant which makes the casings for incendiary bombs. Very interesting. And pretty dangerous. At any rate I'll get about $45 for a 54 hour week, working nights, as of Sunday.

My letters are beginning to sound like a diary more and more. Something is always happening. When I feel particularly lonely I just pour out my love and longing. Sometimes I write those things that I want to tell you: about what I'm doing, and thinking…

Just what am I doing now? Well…you know that there are fundamentally two methods for making the part of any machine, or motor. "Machining" and "Casting." Casting in a mold usually comes first; and goes for the larger parts of the engine. That is, a mold is constructed of sand, or wood or metal; the metal to be used is melted, and then poured into the mold. When it cools, the metal is removed and you have the part. The process is then repeated. Right now I'm mixed up with something like that. The incendiary bomb casing is a hollow cylinder made of magnesium. So, we work in a large stone room. Bars of magnesium are put into the small pots (large enough for a cannonball) and melted down to a silvery, mercury-like liquid at about 1200 degrees F. They then transfer it to the large pot in the middle. This is heated too, so that the metal is kept liquid. Now there are men stationed at each mold who prepare it to receive the metal. After it is poured in from a ladle (by a chap who makes the circle, refills and starts again), we remove the cast, and prepare to receive the metal again. This goes on all day. In fact, since they have 3 shifts the furnaces are always going, melting metal.

As you can imagine it's pretty hot. The roar of the furnaces, the smell of burning sulphur (used as a flux), the clink of metal as we manipulate the molds, the terrific glare of magnesium when some of it starts to burn all make for an interesting picture. Usually we don't bother to look at the "picture." We think of the heat, how to get breathers; and look at the hot, pouring metal and hope that it won't spatter and burn us.

I bought a cap that you've seen pictures of "factory men" wearing, and wear heavy gloves. Edwin says that I look like Socrates in overalls.

Incidentally, the other aspect of machine and engine manufacture is pretty well shown in the grinding job. The <u>cast</u> part is never exact. A machinist puts it on a lathe and cuts it down to specifications.

By the way, dear, if you see my mother don't mention anything about the danger involved. She'd worry.

My plans are still, as usual, indefinite. If I catch another cold or something, I'll quit of course. Nor do I relish night work.

But the situation is a rather definite one that I'm facing. I'll try to explain it, dear, so that we both see it the same way. At least you'll understand my point of departure for taking jobs, leaving them, staying in Waltham when I could be with you in New York.

I can go home at the end of the week; come back when school starts, and, barring accidents, continue to work in the meat-market and put myself thru my sophomore year. In October I'm thru.

In order to stay sane, I must tackle only those problems that I can do something about. The others lead to neuroses. Recognition for the school is out of my hands. If we're not recognized—at least I tried where I could.

My problem, darling, is to pass my courses, support myself in decent health, and pay tuition. Just how to adjust my time and energy so that I do all is the problem. By October, if I'm to stay at school I will need to have earned about $400 over and above my maintenance during that time. That figure looms to me.

So you see, dear, that it's not a matter of wanting a few extra dollars during vacation, but every day that I can put in, will go toward meeting that sum. It'll be far too late in September to start getting desperate. Of course, if the Federal Gov't comes thru, I'll be glad to "go back" to a comfortable, leisurely routine.

So there you are darling. You have my Modus Operandi. Lord knows, I want to be with you—but there'll be no "together" for us, orange blossoms, and night-long kisses unless I can stay in school. My program is just theoretical. I see no way of really carrying it out. So far the horizon looks pretty dark. As soon as any signs of dawn appear, I'll rush to you with the news.

Good night darling
Aaron

Sunday, 5:00 pm

Dearest—

I'm lazying away this "day of rest." Altho it's five now, I haven't really gotten dressed yet. We are absolutely wasting days like this. All day and nothing to do. I've been lying and daydreaming; we could do a lot.

I received my grades. They are:

<u>First Semester</u>
ANATOMY (Dr. Konikov) 84
HISTOLOGY/EMBRYOLOGY (Dr. Weisenberg) 98

<u>Second Semester</u>

PHYSIOLOGY (Dr. Kaplan) 79
BIOCHEMISTRY (Dr. Davidson) 92
CLINICAL PHYSIOLOGY (Dr. Singer) 94
NEURO-ANATOMY (Dr. Bergmann) 96

The overall average is 90+%. Subjects are not weighted up here, as far as I can tell.

So you see, I'm not a genius. Now you have to love me for my other (?) admirable qualities. Strangely enough, (or is it, "obviously") my grades vary directly with what I think of the professor. If you recall my comments you'll notice that I detested Kaplan, felt Konikov was a bluff and a windbag; thought very highly of the foreigners: Singer, Weisenberg, and Bergmann.

I'd give a great deal to get a transcript of 75% average from Flower than 90% from Middlesex. But, what can I do.

You've probably learnt by now, that my logic varies with how I feel. Don't let my "convincing" arguments ever shake your belief in anything you really think.

So although I'm sure I very ably presented the case for my staying up here right thru—I'm going to come in next weekend. School probably starts on the 17th or 18th so I'll have several days with you.

I just don't have the guts I guess to stay away from you. We're doomed.

I understand you've a wedding Saturday the 13th, so I'll probably come in Sunday night. There's no point getting off the bus without the expectation of your lips, and hands around my neck.

Yesterday I was pretty tired. One really should get used to hard labor as a child. Tonight I start on the night shift for a week. Barring accident, I'll work thru Friday night, rest up Saturday, and take the bus in on Sunday morning.

How does that sound, darling?

Now you know how much I love you. I plan a career; chart a course of action; decide upon the correct course with my best intellectual ability—and chuck it all to see you.

More later dear,

Aaron

Thursday, 10:50 pm

Darling—

I've been so busy recounting my adventures these past weeks, I haven't answered your letters at all. Just shows you how egotistical and self-centered we are; I did mean to answer any questions you brought up as I read your letters, but by the time I wrote one, I was full of information and would have burst at the seams if I didn't impart it.

As to your nutty Aunt. I think it's really very convenient. First, she'll furnish us with a topic of conversation. Secondly, if our children act kind of balmy, we'll be able to pin it on heredity, rather than the more embarrassing environment furnished by its parents. But seriously, dear, you know that all my training holds for the concept that mental disease and mental health depend upon the environment to which the child is subject. So your aunt will have as much effect upon the stability of your offspring as the weather in North Dakota.

I'm glad you visited Mother and Dad. I told you they'd be pretty nice. Your description of what went on made me quite homesick. But I'll arrive on Greyhound, at Capitol Terminal at 7 pm this Sunday night. So we'll have several days together at any rate. Probably I'm a traitor to my principles. But who wants to be an iron man anyway. I hope you can get to the station.

This past week I've been dabbling in my reading. One really needs leisure (if you're as soft as I am), leisure divorced from the tiredness of labor to read meaty material. When I'm really tired, and have just another tough day to look forward to, I want to read mystery stories or something.

I started Veblen's Theory of the Leisure Class; Wolfe's Web and the Rock; Beard's America in Mid Passage. The library out here is wonderful. Nobody apparently takes the books out. They even get

In Fact, and hide it between some less disturbing literature. But it's there for the initiated.

So barring accident, I'll see you in a few days.

Good night darling
Aaron

Thursday, 10:00 pm

Darling

From Sunday to this evening was like a blur. I really have difficulty distinguishing between the days that passed, what we did, and when. All I can readily bring to mind is that I arrived Sunday evening after a long bus trip; kissed you; and then found myself in Waltham again after a long bus trip. Maybe it was the same bus ride.

Because of the conditions under which we've been seeing each other, I still can't visualize you as part of a normal, day to day existence. Where kisses are simple and gay, not touched with the heightened emotion lent by sadness.

I made the bus—but only by practically grabbing its tail light as it pulled out. You see, my watch loses about 5 minutes a day. Usually I watch for it and correct it. These three days vanished for me; but not for my watch (the unemotional thing) so that I really had some tall hustling to do to catch the bus. The driver made some uncomplimentary remarks about wanting to drive a train that left on time—but he was a good driver and got me into town for my first class.

More and more I'm getting to believe in the theory of compensations. "Lucky in love…" When I arrived here it was very beautiful out. Spring was just around the corner. We could have done wonders with a day like this. Do you think that we'd have a much more easy courtship if we didn't love each other so much? Or do we want each other so intensely because we have so many difficulties? What's the difference?

I sat thru my lectures today but don't have much idea about what went on. I'll tell you about my program next week when I have a better idea of what it's like. So far I don't think I have Saturday classes.

I gave the letter from my draft board to the ex-President, Mr. Smith, who said that he hoped it was just routine. I hope so too. He'll write the usual form letter to them. I guess that is all I can do. Early in April I'll know what action they've taken.

I'm desperately sleepy now. I hope the letter makes sense. If it tells you that I love you, am suddenly very lonely, and feel small and inadequate at being unable to keep us together—it's right.

Good night dear
Aaron

Tuesday 4:30 pm

Sweetheart—

Slowly we're getting into the swing of things again. Lectures and laboratory go on; we take notes, discuss the "state of the union"; and watch time go by. Things aren't pressing yet as no quizzes are in sight, so I'm able to write at this sensible hour.

Your letter was waiting for me today. Despite my taking your love for me very much for granted, and feeling comfortable in it to the point of smugness, I still get quite a lift to see your letters on my desk when I get home. I read them even before I get undressed. Then read the letter more leisurely later.

I agree with you completely about religion. I've never yet seen anyone who could defend organized religion on rational grounds. But then religion isn't rational. Fundamentally it's "faith." In any event, Thelma, as an intelligent person, ought to think it thru for herself and try to see the rationalizations she's making. A happy, true relationship can only exist, I think, if she is sincere about the convictions, and is loved for them. Becoming temporarily religious for Elly's sake isn't so good in the long run.

Sunday, I spent the afternoon at Lou Gitlin's. He's Dave Airsubel's roommate. Dave did finally enter B'klyn Jewish. He asks that we don't spread it, as it was evidently done thru contacts.

As I told you, they have a beautiful apartment. I appreciated it even more now, as I tried to visualize our occupying it. If you can make the trip to Boston in the near future, I promise to show it to you. It was so comfortable just sitting in soft chairs, listening to the radio, and talking to Lou, that I slept over, and came into Waltham just in time for my first class. Was I sleepy yesterday!

I borrowed three of the five books I'll need this term. Dave lent them. Would you buy one for me? The only two places I know of are Barnes & Noble and a book shop located right near Bellevue, that sell second hand medical books:

TEXTBOOK OF BACTERIOLOGY
Zinsser and Bayne Jones
8 Edition—1939

There are a lot of older printings of the same edition. I'll take the oldest; it's much cheaper. The book lists at $8.00; I can get a 10% discount up here. But I hope there may be an old, weather-beaten volume, of 1935 or so, that'll be cheaper. Ship it up and let me know what it costs—if you don't have the money with you, leave a deposit and let me know.

See, I'm ordering you around already.

My Anatomy grade was an error of transcription. It was 94%; not 84%. My opinion of Konikov is unchanged. But it makes my grade average better; and tickles my vanity. (tsk, tsk). To add to my swelled head I was top man in Histology, despite being one of the few who hadn't taken the course in College. So there. I'd still swap for a 76% at Bellevue tho.

The two big courses this term are Pathology, given by Dr. Mathias, a refugee; and Bacteriology (Immunology, Parasitology…) given by Dr. Schweinberg (another refugee). Both men are excellent men in their field. Minor courses fill in the week: Obstetrics, Pharmacology (Materia Medica part); Minor Surgery, Public Health, Pharmacy (prescription writing). Some of these courses continue for a year, or two. This term the subject matter is becoming more medicine.

As the Pharmacology prof put it (Dr. Mountner; a refugee; noted Viennese pediatrician; also teaches Pediatrics): The first year in medical school is very similar to Pre-Medical College work. It simply takes the same subjects applied to man. We dissect a cadaver instead of a cat.

This year, as in the future, the stuff is strictly medical school property. The subjects are essentially the Anatomy of <u>diseased</u> organs (Pathology) and the Physiology of diseased organs (Pharmacology, Internal Medicine…). The story now is to learn general principles about disease, and then specific diseases: TB, Cancer…

Later on we'll learn how to recognize the disease by its symptoms (Diagnosis)—and then what to do about it (treatment). Then you're a doctor—provided you can take and pass the State Boards.

Do you notice, my letters keep getting longer and longer. What do I write about so much anyhow? I suppose I'm just loquacious.

I love you very much darling.
Aaron

Friday 6:00 pm

Darling—

I hate to admit it—but I'm out for the day again. Grippe or something. Don't get angry honey—I really don't like it. It makes it pretty tough catching up on missed lectures, laboratory, readings,…Last night I went over to see the doctor with my tail of woe. I've been catching or losing colds all the time I've been here.

He gave me some green pills to take the fever down, some red medicine for my cough, and told me to go to bed. Then he prescribed vitamins! So when this cold's all over, I too, will become a vitamin eater.

That's if there's enough sale of meat to hold my job. The little vitamin pills (considering the pretty brochures that doctors get advertising them) are expensive.

As for the Bacteriology book, you'd better get the best buy you can (up to $7) and ship it up. I'm over a week behind already. Solly won't have an old copy.

In a few of your letters I found a little thread of an idea that maybe I was going to jilt you to vindicate my theory. Don't be silly! I ask for nothing more than the opportunity to marry you, and live with you for a very long time. I have completely accepted that, and take my love for you as much for granted as the seasons.

My opinions about personality problems are completely academic. As far as we're concerned I don't know that I could love you any more, no matter what attributes you possessed. As it is, I think I'm "loving to capacity."

Neither of us is a perfect specimen of "American Youth." Nor is it necessary that we be so. My whole conception of love describes it as being strong between us, just as we are.

I'll have to close right now, dearest. Edwin is taking this out to be mailed—and is getting impatient.

I don't know how long I'll be laid up this time—but it's in times like these that I feel very lonely for you "extra strong."

All my love, dear
Aaron

Saturday March 27
9 pm

Sweetheart

I'm lonely now. So although I wrote yesterday, I can't think of anything I'd rather do now than write to you. I do wish I could talk to you for a while.

I stayed in bed yesterday, and in my room all day today. The doctor scared me a little by talking about the prevalence of Virus Pneumonia in town, so I stayed home from work, read a little, and spent the day missing you.

They tell me it's been lovely out tho I don't appreciate it. I would like a few beautiful days out in the country to get well. Relaxed. You know, I've written several times that when I see you

I'd read to you from U.S.A., Hamlet, Shakespeare's Sonnets…but I almost never get around to it. I would really like to lay out in the field, head in your lap, feel the warm sun on my face, your fingers comfortably in mine, and read relaxedly to both of us. We'd have to have lots of time with no thought for "musts." No parting in the offing.

I'd like to walk with you down the street my house is on now. Out into the outskirts of the town. I'd probably say very little now, but look at the big stars, feel the cool air, breathe very deeply, and hold you very tight. It's very quiet out here in the country; and we'd be very much alone.

Yesterday, some of the boys were up to see me, and offer condolences. Looking thru our Rockwell Kent they noticed your dedication to "our library." They were old enough to wish very much that someone were planning for a life with them, and thought I was very fortunate. I am. I don't allow myself much abandonment to my feelings; work presses. But behind all the efficiency I can muster lies the solid, the quiet, assurance of your warm love. It's not so conscious in my hectic days when I'm trying to keep my head above a multitude of problems; it's extremely conscious when I'm tired and lonely. It is then I feel that it's not as bad a situation after all. I am building toward something definite and beautiful.

Shakespeare said the same thing in a sonnet much more adequately.

Tomorrow, Lou Gitlin (Dave's roommate) is coming over to see me. If I feel well enough we'll probably stroll around town, absorb a lot of fresh air, and talk about trivialities. He'll undoubtedly get very bored of my talking about you. Somehow the conversation inevitably gets to women…

I'm going to read a little longer, take my medicine, and go to bed early.

Good night darling
Aaron

Tuesday March 30

12:00 Midnight

Darling—

This is more like it again, isn't it? Writing letters to you at midnight.

I'm pretty much recovered, tho I still keep up a pretty neat cough. On Monday, I returned to school to find out that they were doing without me very well.

Right now I find myself swamped with work again. I'll be trying to catch up now, for the next 8 months.

Pathology is the big course this year. I'm still in somewhat of a daze as to exactly what it means or what they're driving at. Probably as I work with the subject I'll get the idea. Another name for the subject is "Morbid Anatomy"—and it certainly is morbid. In brief, it is a classification of the things which are found on autopsy. From time immemorial (or there-abouts) physicians who were also scientists made post-mortem examinations of as many cadavers as they could get their hands on. They described what was eventually to become the "normal cadaver"—or what the body actually looks like in a healthy adult. Probably best seen is someone who died by accident—if the wound is discounted.

Then they realized that almost every cadaver had some changes from the so called normal. The head was larger, or the lungs were more distended, or the large arteries had yellow patches, or the liver was yellow instead of brown...With time the changes found were grouped, classified, given names. Then the organs were studied microscopically so as to see these changes better. Finally the changes found in the body at death were linked up with the disease the person had before he died.

So yellow patches on the arteries, and arteriosclerosis go together. (a bad example) A certain color of the liver, and a certain histological picture go with jaundice...

Now the big trick remains. To explain the disease on the basis of anatomical changes. Heart disease is explained on a definite damage done to heart valves. This damage can be seen in the heart at autopsy.

I hope this is more clear to you than it is to me. Right now it's the best that I can do. I was studying a book of Medicine this evening. Every disease ("millions of them") has to be learnt in regards to its: etiology, incidence, pathology, pathological physiology, symptoms, signs, Differential Diagnosis, prognosis & treatment. If you can make the diagnosis; you can look up the treatment. So the whole medical training is largely devoted, evidently, to preparing the student to make a decent diagnosis.

There. I've wasted a whole letter on an essay "On Medical Schools" or something. Say the word darling and I'll write on some other topic. I never plan the letter. It just happens.

Congratulate Manny for me. I hope he becomes a very successful dentist.

And I hope you become a very successful wife in the near future.

Love,
Aaron

Friday, 11:00 pm

Gloria darling—

I'm very sleepy now. But I feel nice in a way. I came "home" to find your book here, a letter from Abe telling me all about California (I think I'll enclose it; you'll like it, and I've long since decided that you can read, see, or hear anything that I do), and a card from Lori, asking about my cold.

Thanks for getting the book for me, dear. I'll send you a money order for it on Monday or Tuesday. As soon as I can get to the post office.

Yesterday I started to work at the market on Thursday afternoons too. It'll give me several more dollars a week. You see, I'm concerned about really having the money for books, registration and first installment on my Junior year. According to the way our program is set up, we're thru at 2 pm on Thursday. I'll continue to work at this pace as long as:

1. My health holds up. (I'm still coughing, tho somewhat less. I think it's bronchitis, and I will get over it, if the weather gets nice and I don't overwork and keep healthy otherwise)
2. I can keep up with the class. (There is a huge amount of very interesting work this term. It requires a lot of home study, and correlated reading. Attendance at the Clinics—Pathological Conferences held every other week, on Tuesday evenings, by our school in Boston would help. Also attendance at autopsies. Right now I'm frightfully behind in my lecture work)
3. The market continues to want me (the point system has gone into effect. Good lord! Am I dizzy! Tho there is plenty of meat, there aren't very many people who can buy it. Sales are way down)
4. They don't schedule classes "unofficially" on Thursday afternoon. (Yesterday the Bacteriology professor pulled a fast one and gave a lecture from 2-3 pm. I cut, as I said I'd report to work at 2. But I can't do that often.)
5. The army doesn't draft me (I haven't heard yet)
6. They don't close the school down (No news yet. The fatal hour approaches.)

Otherwise I'll continue with my current program this semester. Oh yes. Barring earthquakes, tidal waves, etc, etc.

Now, how are you darling. I miss you very much. Hurry up and finish school so you can achieve enough independence to visit me occasionally. In fact, I'd like you to commute. Dave Rosenberg and a few other boys of my class went in to New York this afternoon after school. I really envied the lucky devils.

Now that I know you're on your way with a cold, you'd better let me know how you feel right away. Altho I can't prescribe I'll feel better knowing just how you feel.

You know practically how I spend every hour of my time. In fact, I think you could look at your watch and know just where I am and what I'm doing.

I don't really know what your days are like tho. Now, don't send me a detailed "daily schedule" in your next letter. But fill them all up with the little details about yourself, in which I'm so interested.

Good night darling,

Aaron

PS. Your new stationery is lovely (But I don't really care)

Tuesday 11:30 pm
April 6, 1943

Gloria darling:

I'm remarkably sleepy now. All I can think of is yawning, going to sleep, and what I'm missing in not having you up here at the moment.

Last night the boys convinced me to go see "Gone With the Wind." All of it. It seems that there are two kinds of people. Those who have seen "Gone With the Wind"—and a few numbskulls who hadn't. So I went. Did you ever sit thru it, dear? I can't possibly imagine what prompted the critics to award so many prizes to the movie. The producer tried hard, the director tried, but the book is pretty hopeless, and some of the acting terribly wooden.

Probably, from the historical aspect, it might be good stuff. The Civil War from the point of view of the south—and all that sort of thing. But as a novel—as portraying real people—just nonsense. I never saw a stage filled with so many morons in any dramatization that pretended to be Grade A.

To which we can add the complete lack of understanding evidenced by the author of the causes of the Civil War, the anti-Negro character of the picture, pro Ku Klux Klan aspect, and its total lack of social consciousness.

Oh yes, the Technicolor was pretty.

Now you see what you're up against, darling. "Always belittling."

In any event I'll have to get a grip on myself and start to do some tall studying. I just can't seem to get to work. This is the second movie I've been to this semester. Write a scathing letter or something, so that I can promise to be good, and get to work.

I received two letters from you yesterday. It didn't matter which I read first. Both (or all) your letters are impressions of emotion at the moment. They make me feel better—in any order. But your reminiscing about last spring made me very nostalgic. Unless you keep a diary, your memory for details is wonderful. The days you describe came back with a rush as I read your letter. Came back with a lot of the emotion with which those instances were clothed. I agree with you. The days I liked best were those we had together for the whole day. No place to go by noon, or by 5 o'clock, or by evening. Just let the day flow by as we moved along slowly. We both want the same things.

You know, I never really write "love letters" to you. I was surprised at the first time you mentioned that some of my letters were love-letters, others discursive. But I never sit down to write a love letter to you. I just write. I love you very much. Right along. When I write, and when I'm doing something else. Sometimes they just come out more longing, sometimes more intellectual. In either event, my scrawl is always saying that I'm very much in need of you, and miss you.

Good night dear
Aaron

Incidentally, thanks for the book, darling.

Friday 10:30 pm

Darling:

I got home from work about a half hour ago. I'm tired, sleepy...I want to write to you now, and then go to sleep. Incidentally, when you see my mother, you can tell her that I still love them all, even if I don't write home nearly as much as I write to you.

The situation at school is quite tense. Nobody knows what will happen. I don't think you'll have much of a problem deciding whether we'll get married this October. We'll know very definitely before then. As the poets have it, the times are ominously portentous. Things are very quiet. Classes go on routinely. The instruction is very good this year. I have Americans for only 2 very minor courses. The whole week is practically devoted to lectures in several Viennese or Berlin dialects. The men are good. I don't believe any medical school in the country can produce better. But, as you know, the AMA is but little interested in what kind of teachers we have.

Rumors, good and bad, fly about like a plague of locusts. They infest every spare hour. By and large they cancel each other. I'll pass on bona fide information as I get it. As you said. If I become a doctor, it'll really be quite a miracle.

If you were here, I'd be telling you rumors galore probably. It makes up a good part of our conversation here. You'd soon get used to them and pay little attention. In fact, temperature, pulse and respiration are by this time hardly affected by rumors, good or bad.

Recognition, or no recognition, the situation looms so enormously. These next few weeks, or so, are deciding our whole lives. Like many things, life here is an all or nothing affair, isn't it? With recognition, I'd be assured of staying alive and healthy for the next two years at least, assurance of being allowed to complete medical school, a recognized doctor when thru, a life from then on a professional plane which would make living very worthwhile, we'd be married as soon as convenient with the blessings of our friends and families and a hopeful future with which to plan…

Without recognition --- I don't know. You can visualize the picture for yourself, dear. It'd be pretty horrible.

So we wait…

There you see, I started out by saying that I wouldn't discuss the question of recognition, and then proceeded to do so. I really can't help it. You're the one I turn to to pour out what rests most heavily on my mind and "heart." You'd get much more of it, if I could talk to you regularly. Maybe in a sense you're lucky that I'm restricted to the letter.

So you're finding school tedious at times? I don't blame you. There is nothing very stimulating in shorthand and typing. Once you are proficient it will just be a matter of putting in the necessary hours and being paid.

I don't think it'll do you any harm, tho, darling. I'm tired of looking forward to seeing you blossom forth, as you have to meet critical disapproval from lots of people who won't have any interest in your welfare.

Good night darling
Aaron

Wednesday April 14
6 pm

Gloria darling—

Your letter today on the very expensive letter-paper was of course a reminder of our first letters. I dare say you still have some of the swanky stationery. Now that you know that I welcome your letters as much on any kind of paper, you need not use the expensive linen. You ought to buy stationery, tho, with lots of room. I love to read your letters—and the more room you have…

The reason that I haven't written much about my courses so far is that I don't yet know enough about them to write about "Bacteriology" or "Pathology." I would have to write about some specific bacterium or pathological disorder—very dry reading, I'm afraid.

But I can tell you something of the clinicopathological conferences—even if I've never attended one, not having the time. These conferences are held in every good medical school, presumably, and in large hospitals. Some of the conferences held at Massachusetts General Hospital are published weekly in the New England Journal of Medicine; the origin of the AMA in New England (Dean Rushmore is one of the Editorial Board, by the way). I've read quite a few.

The patient who enters a hospital has a disease—whatever that means. The disease manifests itself by symptoms (prostration, fever, rapid breathing, pain, rash…) and signs (what the doctor can ascertain by feeling the body, and listening thru the stethoscope—

breath sounds, heart sounds, masses in the abdomen,…). Information is also available from laboratory tests—Red Blood Count, Whiteblood Count, urinalysis, X Ray plates, hemoglobin %, clotting time, BMR,…

Now the trick is: What's the matter? (And you'd be amazed how little the average doctor knows about what's the matter. Very often he guesses all wrong. A good diagnosis is something to be proud of. The reason that people don't die more frequently of their illnesses is that the disease per se is not fatal if the patient is kept warm in bed, given fluids, moderate diet, and symptoms treated as they arise: one drug for headache, another for fever, morphine for pain…This is called "symptomatic treatment." It is used when the doctor doesn't know what's the matter. Or when medicine doesn't know what to do about it. So for Erysipelas, for example, even when you know what it is, you "treat symptomatically." There isn't anything else to do.)

It is important to know what the trouble really is if you're really going to give the patient all the assistance in fighting the disease that medicine has to offer. He might get better on his own defense mechanisms anyway, but he might not. Pneumonia serum, surgery, drainage…will increase the patient's chances a whole lot.

So to get back to the Conference.

An actual case history is prepared, mimeographed and presented to the audience. There are the symptoms and signs the hospital was faced with. The doctor presenting the case (his case usually) gives the diagnosis made at the time and why.

Then the wolves fall to. The various specialists "comment." The hematologist, pharmacologist, pediatrician, neurologist, cardiologist…agree with the diagnosis, possibly for other reasons, and possibly have different diagnoses.

The visiting doctors and students ask questions, make comments. They don't see how you jump from a pulse rate, breathing rate, blood pressure…to tumor of the brain.

Then the denouement.

You see, each case chosen for discussion is one that did not survive—or at least needed operation. Usually the former. Not that the diagnosis was necessarily wrong, and the patient treated for pneumonia when it was heart failure. But very often there isn't anything you can do. Even knowing it's a tumor of the brain, or cancer of the liver doesn't often save the patient.

The Pathologist gives the autopsy report. Then you know whether the diagnosis was right. Was it heart failure, or kidney disease…He gives the actual findings and explains their significance. And one is very much impressed by the erudition and ability of their specialization hitting the bulls eye so often.

As one chap told me about the clinic-pathologic conference held at our school yesterday (something like little Vienna, all the participants great men in European medicine): he felt he was looking in on a meeting of the Gods.

I'd like to tell you more about the faculty. These Europeans are magnificent. Maybe soon.

There you are dear, I've filled a whole letter with the stuff you probably know about.

Incidentally, when do I get that picture? What with Spring coming and Remembrance of Things Past cropping up, I'd like to do my reminiscing looking at you.

Until later dear,
Aaron

Saturday 11:40 pm

Gloria dear—

I've been home from work for about an hour. I'm tired and will go to sleep after I finish writing to you. It's remarkably quiet now; everyone asleep, Edwin in New York for the Passover holidays.

Sunday 10 am

Darling—

I guess the situation was too much for me…

It's lovely out now. As you've probably gathered, weather in Waltham and New York are very similar, only, I think, it's a lot more exaggerated here.

My letters were tardy last week. I know. But I'll get into stride again pretty soon and have them go out to you more often. Nobody can really believe it, but sometimes there isn't the time to write a little letter. "The spirit is willing…"

Don't be too excited about the AMA visit, darling. I know what it means to us, but realities must be faced. Rumors, of course, abound, but they just about cancel each other out. I haven't been able to get anything very solid.

Actually there are no reasons why the AMA should recognize the school now. (I mean probation, of course—that must precede recognition.) They were here many times before, and must be pretty tired of looking at our castle. Nothing is here now that wasn't here two years ago, when they turned down the school last.

My feeling is that the decision of the AMA is not based on the simple merits of a school; the faculty, buildings, equipment, student body…Rather, on much broader principles of 1) the number of doctors in the country (a good union always is out to keep the members of the trade to as low a figure as possible); 2) the location of the school (a school is opening in New Jersey I understand with the AMA's blessing; that is all right; every state is entitled to one school; it's a completely closed shop with no applications being given out; 3) the politics involved.

So that although the boys were up here for several days cross-examining the professors and looking over the labs, I believe they came to find reasons for whatever action they had already decided on.

The trend (certainly in normal times) would be for an emphatic "No." Based upon the agreement of the AMA that there are too many doctors anyhow, and far too many schools in Boston.

Times, tho, aren't normal. I hope—very desperately—that some kind of compromise is worked out by virtue of governmental pressure. If not…

Keep sending your letters, darling. You probably know how much I look forward to them. Make sure your longest, warmest, most loving letters get here on Friday and Saturday. That's when I almost feel like chucking it all. Your new stationery is very pretty, rough edges and all. My opinion of the worthwhileness of letter paper you buy depends to a large extent on the size of the paper.

I heard from my draft board. They classified me in IIA until October 10, 1943; my 25th birthday. Quite a coincidence, isn't it? I expected my deferment to continue. It depends on the school on whether I'll hold this status unchanged till the date set.

Now I'm going to try to study. A Bacteriology exam is looming for Wednesday.

All my love dear
Aaron

Thursday 9:05 am

Darling—

I don't have a 9 o'clock class on Thursday. Probably this letter will sound sort of hazy and not quite awake, but it'll prove that I love you even when I just get up in the morning. Isn't that supposed to be the acid test?

Everything up here is at a standstill. Everybody is waiting—either to whoop with joy, or pack up and leave. All the ambitious plans of the school: to repairs of the buildings, fixing up laboratories…are apparently suspended, waiting.

A nice, restful atmosphere. Like being in a London bombing.

You're going to be finished with school soon and going out to get a job. I'm very much interested in exactly what happens. Here's hoping you land a very soft, interesting, well paid job at your first try. Far more important to me than your actually working or earning money, is whether you are able to assume more maturity and independence because of your work. It doesn't necessarily follow. But it may. I want you to feel secure enough in yourself to listen to others if they are insistent, but to be able, with very little emotion, to tell anybody to go to the Devil. At the point when you don't care whether everyone likes you, and you're not distressed by the fact that someone actually dislikes you, you are starting to be a complete individual.

All this is nonsense to you probably. Without specific experience to back it, it means very little. I just want to give you some idea of criteria you can use to measure self adequacy. One of the things I always notice about little children is their great need to be liked. Everybody must like them. The idea of someone actually disliking them was very disorganizing. Eventually, the relation of the child to other people becomes far less emotional and more intellectual.

Very important too, is the "Emancipation from home." Frank Williams' book on Adolescence makes a tremendous point of it. Not that the adolescent must leave home, but his relation to the members of his family must assume a new-emotional one. His activities, the little everyday things, are done, based fundamentally on his own whims and fancies. Criticism from parents or siblings are accepted unemotionally and not resented. Simply comfortably discarded.

All this very patriarchal lecture on maturity, darling, isn't meant for you to take to heart & reform yourself. Ridiculous. As you see, I place a tremendous emphasis upon the emotional set-up which I don't think is a matter of changing at will.

But the thing that I hope you find soon is—"Gloria!" Find out that you are a complete individual, with your own ideas, convictions, desires. That your happiness is fundamentally your problem. That with maturity and the finding of yourself, your environment will have to take notice of you, not that you must bend to please everyone in the environment. Your personality must become complete in itself—and able to give support to others. Such is the "integrated personality."

Wow!

I have to run now, darling.

All my love—
Aaron

Tuesday April 27
11:10 pm

Dearest

I've been so engrossed in my problems up here, that I kept on telling you about them; almost taking for granted that we both knew that I loved you very much. It hit me particularly hard when I got your letter; saying that it wanted to make me feel better if anything bad were happening. You're very sweet, darling. There is very little else you could possibly have said that would have made me feel better.

And I'm very thankful for you…I'm so sure we could be very happy if we only had half the chance. There is so much that I want to do, and in all of it you figure so prominently. There is hardly anything I think of which doesn't someplace in it, have the element of doing it with you—or at least telling you all about it.

As you know "Spring is here." Birds are warbling, grass is greening. And I feel it all going to waste. What with this being the season for a young man's fancy turning to love—my fancy is really getting very intense desire of being with you. I would have given a great deal to have been with you this Sunday. It was lovely most of the day. Easter Sunday—with the local populace all dressed in their new spring finery walking along the streets…It's very hard to tell you by letter how beautifully we could have spent the day. There is no place to go. Just feel good to live and be healthy and be together.

Now that you're going to start working I want you to start planning on a trip to Waltham in the very near future. One of my classmates had his fiancée come up last week-end. It was all very proper. There is a small hotel in the town, about 5 blocks from where I live, where the girl stayed. The place is not only very comfortable and clean, but very proper and respectable. I couldn't even go past the door if you were staying there; and I'd probably have to get you in by 11:00 pm. But I'd even submit to that if you could be here so I could see you for a little while. Bring your mother if she insists. (But don't let her insist.) You can come up if you really determine to do so, darling. I don't know when I'll be able to get into New York.

Theoretically, no vacations at all are scheduled until October 24th! If nothing drastic happens in the meantime.

Incidentally, give Manny my best wishes. I hope he never gets his pretty uniform very dirty. He'll make a good dentist, husband and father some day.

All of us have to have some immediate incentive in order to keep even fairly content. The "raison d'etre". With the world in such turmoil around me, my work and future career being tossed around as tho by a gale, I rely on you for my incentive. Your love, the letters, and the expectation of having you up here for visits soon are important. Undoubtedly it will rain during any week-end you should happen to be in Waltham. But we'll simply have to chance it. What's a little rain?

There you are. I've frantically transported you several hundred miles with a scribble of the pen.

Good night darling
Aaron

Friday 4/30
10:40

Gloria darling,

Your letter today with the letterhead of the Social Security Society of Hunter College did surprise me at first. But as soon as I saw the salutation, "My darling", I knew that the letter was from you, and that you had picked up some stationery somewhere. Nobody else writes to me like that dear. Tell Thelma that I'm proud of her.

But she's quite wrong about the cause for lack of fertility. As far as I know, conception will take place if a viable egg meets a healthy sperm somewhere in the female body; pretty much irrespective of the psychological state of the donors of the respective germ cells.

Your observation was very apt. Many an egg was fertilized to the chagrin of both parties, and often with very definite anti-fertilizing feelings involved. Girls have become mothers who were raped; artificial insemination is pretty much absolute proof that you don't even need the sex act to have babies.

If the couple find that they can't conceive after several months of hard work, I would suggest a good doctor. Preferably a specialist, urologist and gynecologist. The problem would then be to see whether the male is sterile, completely or partly. Examination would be made to determine whether there were sperm in his semen, adequate in number and healthy.

If the male is all right, his wife would be examined to ascertain, if possible, whether an egg, capable of being fertilized, passes down from the ovaries to the uterus each month. Easily said; not easily done. Many things can be wrong. The oviduct may be plugged; the eggs may simply not be healthy and formed right; spontaneous abortion may occur.

If the cause of the sterility in either partner is determined; treatment might be possible. But no amount of wishing or talking is going to open up a plugged-up tube.

I haven't studied the problem of sterility yet, so I'm not giving you official stuff. There is probably a lot that I've left out.

It's remarkable how many couples are sterile. Most people spend their time & money trying to prevent conception. But an awfully lot are equally energetic trying to have children.

I think the psychiatrist enters the picture in response to what the situation does to the people involved emotionally. You can imagine what a girl who fundamentally never did like the chap thinks of him as she convinces herself that her husband is to blame. Or the feeling of incompetence in the husband if he is convinced, too.

You asked for it, darling. You know very well that I'm not a "fountain of all knowledge"—but when you pose such interesting questions I'm bound to let go with what I do believe.

This week we practiced Schick tests on each other. I'm negative. So far, that is the second one. Theoretically I can't get Diphtheria or Smallpox or Scarlet Fever. Well, well. We're going to go thru the whole list and I'll send you my batting average as I react.

Medicine is a wonderful science; geniuses have lived, millions of dollars were spent, many animals and some people died…to produce the artificial immunities we now have. But they don't have any immunity against bullets and shrapnel which will take in a year what they've saved in 5 decades.

Love
Aaron

Tuesday May 4
12:30 am

Darling—

It's pretty late now. But time just disappears when I get down to study. The material is pretty fascinating—hours go by without my being aware of it.

How are you darling?

Did you start to work yet? Remember, I want a blow-by-blow description of just what you do, now that you're finally thru with school—and how you like what you're doing. I don't think you'll have any difficulty getting a job at present. Only don't take one you won't want to keep for the duration—as the War Manpower Commission may not let you change later on. Job freezing…How do you feel being thru with school—probably for good?

The situation at the school is not so hopeful. Apparently the prognosis is very negative. Nothing definite has been said, but the consensus of all rumors are quite uniformly bad. I'm sorry dear. It looks as tho I gambled and lost. Altho I don't know whether any other "card" available would have been better. Smitty was drafted last month; Abe is in IA as of last month. There isn't anything for me to do but wait for action. We're not clear as to what's going to be. But it won't be anything very wonderful…

At any rate, the stuff I'm studying is very interesting. (Damn it! I could have been quite content not being a doctor 2 years ago; now, I don't think I'll ever be happy in anything else I do.)

If I could see you, I'd probably talk on endlessly about infectious disease, immunity, inflammation, repair of tissue…until you actively took measures to shut me up. The layman knows so little about Medicine. Boy, has the AMA kept its information a trade secret! Of course there are far more questions unanswered than answered. But there is so much information that is available—whether practically applicable or not.

You know, ever since I can remember, I wanted to know. It didn't matter much what I was learning—but I always felt good when I was learning new relationships, concepts…Botany, trees, stars, frogs, geology…And in Medicine one finds a tremendous amount to learn, and then learn again at a higher level of understanding.

In Social Work or Education, I felt that there were really few facts and few real concepts in the field. Mostly it was a lot of inflation of a few sound ideas. The psychiatrist had much more to offer. But first there is medicine in general with its huge mass of information; facts and theories open to the willing (and able) student.

Well, I'll keep on studying while I'm up here. Rather ironic, of course. Someday, I do hope to be able to start something—and finish it. But I'm rapidly becoming a fatalist, if I haven't been one right along. Something will have to come along and insist that I complete what I had started—so that I'll see it thru.

A little muddled dear? It's probably the hour. But then you probably can understand me by now—even muddled.

Good night darling
Aaron

Thursday, May 11
10:40 am

Darling—

Our pathology lecturer is sick this morning, so we were told that classes are off until one o'clock today. Maybe he's out looking for a job…

So you're working finally. How do you like it? Things are far different now than when I graduated. A job—any kind—was a rarity. My very intelligent friends worked for $10-12 a week, as shipping clerks, canvassers, salesmen. Ultimately some were lucky—and got clerical jobs in Civil Service at $1080 a year. They went to Albany &

to Washington to take these insignificant jobs. A lot of people who graduated with me had to work for WPA in various pseudoprofessional capacities. Those who could afford it took advanced degrees—Columbia, NYU, Harvard…A few even went to professional school.

All this was based on the simple fact that despite ability and a lot of willingness—there were no jobs. Staying in school seemed the only comfortable thing to do.

Why must we have a war, and the slaughter of millions of young men to provide the situation as we have it today? Our "prosperity"—really no more than what should be "normalcy"—is literally being bought with quarts of blood.

Of course when the war is over, we'll go back to that other war—those of us that are left—to the war of daily living & fighting. It's a rotten set-up, darling.

I miss you an awful lot lately. It's Spring, and made for love. I was out Sunday evening, walking toward Livington. A few minutes walk and I could hear the tree frogs whistling in the valley. Trees, stars, the moon…One really lives out in the country here. I think I could enjoy it, if underlying it all there wasn't always that feeling of loss. It's something like the feeling I had when we were together last Spring. It was beautiful, yet sad—as the end loomed so near. This kind of emotional state is not too healthy, I think. Everything must end, and one should enjoy the moment as deeply as possible. After all, if all pleasures are to be saddened by the thought of their ending—even life itself would be a very sad thing.

But as I've no doubt said many times before, we rarely feel what is best or healthiest. Unfortunately, our emotions are not open to intellectual decree.

Do you know, it's really a strange thing that of your $30 salary, you decided to give your family half. That's exactly what I did. My folks and I didn't quarrel over what I would do with my money. I was always a very quiet, conservative chap, so that the issue never came up. What's more, I grew up more-or-less imperceptibly.

Have a good time, darling. Buy all the pretty hats you can get into your room. Go horseback riding, and play tennis…

I sent my mother a fairly pretty card on Mother's Day. She ought to get it sometimes this week. Actually I think the whole business is Communistized tummy rot—but my mother would be very hurt if I didn't do something about it. Last year I was up here at this time, too, I remember; and sent mother a card.

Time passes and I'm going out to eat and then back up to school to get a Bacteriology lecture.

Until later darling,
Aaron

Friday 11:30 pm

Darling—

Spring finally came to New England today. The sun shine, robins hopped around, and the air felt good. Tonight is warm and fresh. The stars are larger, like you see them in the country. The streets are quiet and dark; I'd love to have you here with me now. We could spend some really beautiful hours together.

Sometimes I think that I'm going to be sorry leaving Waltham. Whether for the Army very shortly, or to go to Boston in October. Life is so quiet, the air is clean and free of New York odors, the things I'm studying are very interesting…Fundamentally of course, I'm lonely for my friends, family—and very lonely for you. But the year I spent here won't have been an altogether bad one—if it must be ended aimlessly.

But why in so pessimistic mood? No real reason. Just Friday night I guess. Your letter was waiting for me tonight. You're very sweet. Your letters on my desk when I get home are like getting your kiss as I come in. Not nearly as good, but they serve the same purpose. They're there waiting for me; are the first thing I see when I come in; and set the tone for the rest of the evening.

Don't worry about avoiding the "pitfalls of married life." I don't think they can be avoided. I think that particularly in this relationship, people do what they must do. Are what they are. No amount of resolutions and advice to the lovelorn can be of much good.

I've always believed that marriage changed nothing. That the people are "nice" people after if they were so before. Basically to the extent that the people involved are mature; strong in themselves so that they can understand and accept others; capable people, able to manage without too much effort the problems which living in today's complex society presents; physically compatible; interests in common—to that extent will marriage be a continuous building of an ever deeper and stronger union. In other words, good people are good in every sphere.

So the details of living, the getting away for an afternoon, and the schools for junior, are solved as they arise evident friction or emotion—rather in an easy, smooth understanding.

I do believe that for a really ideal marriage, one needs two very mature, secure people. Insofar as there are so few such people—marriages are usually far from the ideal.

Being allowed 6 minutes to visit a friend, or needing an excuse to go to a ballgame—these are symptomatic of an infantile relationship. This relationship would continue, no matter how often they resolve not to do this or that specific thing.

Of course a lot of people who don't approach my ideal are married and apparently "get along." Of course, there is every gradation from the horrible mistake to the ideal situation. And most people are somewhere in between, being happier married than single, and adapting to the situation, more or less successfully.

Well, well, well! How does this little dissertation on marriage sound? Like I had been married at least 5 times, doesn't it? Pay no attention to the tone of assurance, dear. It's the way I write. You can believe my point of view, or write back telling me that I ought to read Doris Blake. But at the moment that is what came out of my head in response to your letter!

It's very late now and I have to get up at 6:30 tomorrow. Maybe I won't be sorry to leave Waltham at that.

Good night darling,
Aaron

I don't know when I'll be able to get into New York. I do want to see you badly tho.

All my love
Aaron

Friday 5/7
10:30

Dearest

You're probably working by now, and getting used to your first job. It ought to be interesting—the new experiences, new people, filling up your day. As the work becomes more routine you will have to find some "extracurricular" activity to keep things interesting and be your "raison-d'etre." We all need something in which to bury ourselves in. Medicine, or the Benevolent Order of Young Hebrew Women of Boro Park. But something. I think, the level of the person can usually be gauged by his main interest. Look around you and see whether or not I'm right. Doesn't everyone have some major interest from which he gets a lot of satisfaction?

Spring, or summer, or something has hit us. We go around sweating, and getting drenched by the rain. All in all it's quite uncomfortable. They should have put the school up in some sensible place like California.

Up here, life-and-classes, go on. We don't know the why or wherefore, but the machine keeps rolling along its well-worn track and we keep moving with it. At least it's healthy up here; comparatively speaking.

On Wednesday and Thursday we have a Guest Lecturer in Bacteriology, Dr. Singer. He lectured to us last year, and will give us another course next semester; but he gave this lecture on blood grouping now. It was really magnificent. He is the finest lecturer I've ever heard. His lectures are very well prepared; he knows his material; he is a very keen intelligent chap; and speaks very well, despite his Viennese accent. Maybe the accent even helps.

With it all, he's terrifically egotistical. The saying has it that he believes that only he and God know the correct diagnosis—and he wouldn't trust God. In spite of that, I'd rather listen to him every day, instead of to some well-meaning, nincompoop.

You can imagine the quality of the lecture, when he kept a restless class absolutely absorbed for a 2 ½ hour lecture! It's almost a record I think! And when he finished, the boys applauded.

I knew quite a bit about the blood groups, their importance in transfusions and in paternity problems. In the lecture, tho, he summed up everything I knew rather neatly, tied it all together, and then went into the details of the facts I knew nothing about, bringing it up to the latest papers on the subject.

Not only do they have the original Landsteiner Blood Groups A, B, O, and AB; but they now also divide people according to their blood having factors M, N, MN, P, and Rh.

As Singer always puts it: at first we knew nothing about a subject; then a substance was discovered which seemed to explain it all; then we find out that there are many substances, very complicated relations, and we don't really know very much about the mechanism after all.

His constant theme is "What is the mechanism?" How do you account for the facts? By what means do you get from liver disease, obstructed bile duct, and infancy—to prolonged bleeding-time in each case? What is the underlying mechanism?

A far cry from my Pathology prof—who says that a lot of things are simply known by experience, and it is better to learn "the facts" than to try to cook up explanations. He is quite content to know that in Vitamin B deficiency (Beriberi) you find, at autopsy, nerve disease, dilatation of the right ventricle, and stomach disorders. The connection? What's the difference?

Lots of luck darling

Good night
Aaron

Friday, May 14
11 pm

Darling,

The AMA sent us a brief letter telling us that they couldn't recognize us because of "deficiencies."

Yesterday the Dean made the announcement. I don't know what the deficiencies are specifically—or whether the AMA listed them. So the comedy goes on…

I have been trying to send you the facts as they are brought out without much coloring; you can decide for yourself what they mean.

At any event the school still keeps moving along; lectures go on; laboratories keep running; I keep on studying…

It's become pretty nice out; that helps a little. I don't know whether I wrote to you, but I stopped working on Thursday afternoons. The prof. was using them pretty regularly for lectures and extra labs, so that it became too difficult. It does give me an "extra" evening to study.

I received your communication darling and tore it up with due regard for its grave significance. But you do type well dear. Somehow I couldn't imagine you as an efficient stenographer. But I must have guessed wrong. At any rate, seeing is believing. After six months of your job, you'll probably be an expert. I hope that even much sooner than that you can get thru the working day without being exhausted at its end. Then you can go home with enough energy to do the things that would give you a lot of pleasure.

You know, you needn't be so humble about your political opinions, darling. Or any others. They're not stupid. On a great many problems there is no scientific method at arriving at conclusions. It is rather a matter of values, ideals…Here there really is no "expert opinion." And particularly is this true of the social sciences. They are sciences in that a huge amount of factual material has been amassed. But in the final analysis, as to whether we are to inflict capital punishment, tax the poor even more, permit birth control legislation, or kill off all the German youth—will ultimately come down to personal values. Of course a lot of facts which are pertinent to any question are available and many very clever men have usually wrestled with these problems before.

It, therefore, becomes advantageous, I think, to get as much on the subject as possible, so that opinion will be based on more substantial grounds. When you feel that there is something you need to know about the situation, try to get some of the facts; then make up your mind on the basis of the kind of a person you are and your sense of values, of ethics, of right & wrong.

And your point of view certainly will not be any less intelligent than your friends or mine. I'll certainly be glad to give you everything that I know on a subject, but I'm afraid I'm not half the authority you think me.

So pass on what you think, dear. I don't think that your ideas are in any way inferior to mine. If they differ, I'll love you just as much anyway.

I really will have to try to get in to New York in between terms. I've got to kiss you soon.

I'm real sleepy now, so I'll get to sleep fairly early tonight.

Good night, dear
Aaron

Wednesday 5/19
11:00 pm

Gloria darling—

You're right, of course. I don't know just what will happen to me or the school; or how soon. And I suppose I'll continue to plod along until something happens to me. I can't think of anything else to do; can you, dear?

I do want to see you pretty badly. Spring is in Waltham. Birds are chirping, flowers are blooming; some nights are balmy. My imagination just runs riot. But only my imagination. You had better start accumulating sick leave or something so you can drop in on me and let me kiss you a few times. Or do Civil Service Employees have any such luxuries during war time?

May is the loveliest part of the year, I think; but it's all going to waste now.

How is Solly deporting himself these days; like an old married man? I really can't imagine taking you for granted, although I know that that's the way all couples get. How does Solly do? After all, considering his stormy courtship he ought to doubly enjoy being married.

Sunday evening, I spent a couple of hours with Lou Gitlin in Boston. We strolled around the city; talked about Medicine; Middlesex; women; and sailing. Particularly sailing. In Boston, evidently, there is a club for those who enjoy sailing. For $15, one can join, be taught to operate the small sailboats the club owns, and then sail around on the Charles to one's heart's content. The Seniors who are not yet in hospitals are spending more time on the river than in school. I'm going along as soon as Lou passes his test, and I'll give you a blow-by-blow description. We'll probably capsize.

School routine is quite established by now. We get in at 9 and are chased around until about 4. The time disappears. It's twelve midnight before I know what's happened.

Very much like last year, the subjects are very well integrated. They make sense. The medical curriculum was established thru long experience, I guess, and shows it.

As I've written, this year we are interested primarily in the pathological changes which can happen to organs. Fundamentally, that is what disease is based on. A weak heart means that the valves don't close just right, or the actual heart muscle is diseased and thinned out. Glandular disease (diabetes, eg) mean that some gland is either overworking (tumor?) or not working enough…So that the basis for understanding of what really goes on inside somebody who is diseased, is to be found in the autopsy room; where the person who died of the disease is opened up, and we can see just what went wrong.

Frequently the organs have to be examined under the microscope to see any changes from the normal.

Practically anything can happen to organs, and just about everything does, in some case. The fundamental approach is to the cells as the unit. What has happened to the cells of the organ?

As the injuries ("lesions" in pathological language) were studied, they found that cells can be killed, injured slightly or stimulated to grow. Depending upon what happened, which cells, which organs, and how much, the particular disease manifests itself. If the Islands of Langerhans of the pancreas degenerate, we find diabetes; if a group of cells started growing wildly, we have a cancer.

The next question, of course, is why? Why the destruction of cells in a heart valve, or of the liver,…(In medicine this "why" is the "etiology"). You can probably imagine that innumerable agents can kill cells: burns, poisons, wounds…Most important, tho, are the Bacterial poisons (toxins). And that is why the "Infectious Diseases"—due to bacteria—play such a large role. These poisons kill off cells, cause lesions, are the various diseases that are so familiar.

That is also why we are spending most of this semester studying Bacteriology; to acquaint ourselves with the parasites that are the "etiology" for so much of the Pathology we study.

Of course, the other big "lesions" are the tumors & cancers. But we know little of their cause, & can do little about them; so we concentrate on learning about those diseases one can help.

In the pathology laboratory we study organs sent from the autopsy room of City Hospital, Boston, and slides of pathological specimens to get microscopic detail.

In the bacteriology laboratory we make slides of the various living bacteria, Diphtheria, Tuberculosis…and study their appearance, growth…

Good lord, I've really raved on this time! Does it make sense?

Good night darling

Aaron

Friday 5/21

11:00 pm

Darling—

I've run out of paper and can't get any until Monday, so I'd rather write on this than wait.

Your letters have been swell. Your job seems to get along with you all right. Now use what time you have, and your money to have a good time.

You needn't send me any presents dear. There really isn't any occasion for it. Tho I would like a nice big picture of you.

In my last letter, I wrote something about Pathology. The study of the basis of disease as seen in organic lesions. Maybe you'd like some ideas about why we study Bacteriology.

You see, the disease can be looked at from several points of view.

Considering that large group of diseases to which I was referring as having a "lesion" behind them, the doctor must be concerned with what to do now that this distribution of some tissue is present—no matter what the source. The patient who has a lesion of the pancreas and has, therefore, diabetes, must be given insulin; the heart case whose valves are damaged must be kept quiet; the chap with a weakened heart muscle is given digitalis…No matter what the injury, we must know its effect on the whole body, the body's response to it, and what to do to help.

There is another point of view.

Among all the agents which cause lesions, there are, as I said, the Bacteria, and other parasites (fungi; protozoa, worms…). Most of our serious diseases are caused by their activity, you know. Well, one can approach the study of diseases, as a study of these organisms. Their chemistry, life story, things they need for food, methods of reproduction…they injure man, not because of viciousness, but they just are living and trying to get along the best they can. We kill and eat other plants and animals, too.

The more we know of the invading organism, the better we can fight him. So each parasite must be studied in very great detail, and weapons developed for preventing an invasion, and to kill the organism once it is in the human body. This problem is actually exactly the same, whether the organism is a bacterium, or a fungus or some small animal.

We have learned a great deal. But compared to what they don't know it's a drop in the bucket. As you can realize, we once more are face to face with fundamentals. We want to know what makes a bacterium, a single cell, tick. And fundamentally, of course, that is the problem of what is this stuff called "life"—and we don't know.

Yet so much is known about these particular parasites that for convenience, the field "Bacteriology" is set up.

We do have a lot of weapons now, learned from studying the bacteria. Vaccination, antitoxins, sulphanilamide…are based on knowing something about the life of bacteria. The whole field of immunity comes in here.

In class, our job is to take each of these organisms separately and learn what is known so far about it. How to recognize it, its chemistry, what it does by just trying to "earn a living" in our body, weapons found against it.

There I go again, darling. Two such letters in succession are probably too much. Do I make sense?

Good night sweetheart
Aaron

Monday

Darling

You've become so much a part of me, Mrs. Ellis picked these from her garden for you.

Until later
Aaron

Thursday 5/27

Dearest:

I was elected to Osler. It's the "Phi Beta Kappa" of Middlesex. There are usually about a dozen Osler men attending Middlesex Medical School at any one time. So there. You can be proud of me darling. I'll get a certificate (which I'll send home) and a key (which is yours as soon as you come up).

Yet, I've been terribly depressed all the past week. Yesterday, I think I hit a new low. Just a little lower, and I'd pack up, and go home. You'd find me sitting on your doorstep in an infantry uniform.

I don't know what it is dear. The futility of it all, I guess. Feeling constantly that it's all a game. Having to drive myself, practically without let up, without ever getting the necessary satisfaction of small goals achieved. We can't feel, after a difficult examination, or completion of a course, "Well, that's over. 8 more like that and I'm a doctor." It's "That's over. What next?"

I don't know. Maybe it's the state of my hormones. I have an overwhelming desire to make love to you. That kind of frustration just adds fuel to the fire. It's largely an emotional need—as well as sexual. I want to pour out a great deal of the emotion that's building up inside of me. And I have no other outlet but you. Probably I oughtn't to write letters as depressing as this, but there isn't anyone else to whom I can talk to without restraint. As you know, we've always tended to support my mother emotionally, rather than receive support from her. So channels for expression are very limited.

You know, if you were here, you'd be getting this kind of thing nearly every day; only more concentrated. Lord, what an effect that would have!

I'm getting terribly tired dear. Tired of the "What's the use?" feeling. Maybe I ought to be psychoanalyzed and get it out of my system. But it's been with me for so long. I don't know why the feeling should be so strong in me. Do you know anyone else that feels that way? That it's all rather hopeless, that nothing will probably come of what you're doing?

At CCNY the feeling was there. Courses went on: History, Biology, English...While graduating class after graduating class became soda jerks, salesmen, and WPA workers. At the laboratory, it was an intangible getting "of results"; funds from foundations; the lab was the museum's stepchild and threatened with closing every week. We all felt that it was very temporary. The Dep't of Welfare—Nomar can tell you the general feeling there. It is considered by the public as the least desirable of Departments as it spends a great deal of money on the "worthless." Payrolls are to be cut whenever possible; caseloads determine number on staff. But for the war, and the resignation of 1000 of us, there would have been the mass dismissals that we all foresaw. Nor are the employees proud of their jobs. I've never seen an investigator say that he was a Social Investigator without using some defense mechanism.

And now Middlesex…

There, darling. I've poured out a lot. I hope it doesn't get you down too badly.

I'm glad you enjoy working so much. I felt that you would. It gives us a sense of "belonging", and of doing something useful. But don't expand either in width or breadth. I consider that grounds for divorce.

Until later dear
Aaron

Tuesday 6/1
5:00 pm

Hello darling—

My last letter apparently was a lulu. It was undoubtedly a combination of the situation, the rotten weather, and "biliary stasis." Or maybe lack of Vitamin B1. What I should have done was to tear it up after I wrote—particularly knowing the effect it would undoubtedly have. With my letters, tho, you get just what I feel as I write them. By this point you have a written record of my moods over a period of a year. I think we might be able to do a little research and see whether I don't correlate with the phases of the moon, sunspots or something. Some research workers believe that men have a sexual cycle which corresponds with the oestrous cycle in women. Who knows?

You may also catalogue that I (the research animal under consideration) smoke periodically. I smoke until I catch cold, get a sore throat, blame it on the pipe, and put it away for good. Or until I get better. I am now in the smoking stage.

So far my health, and mucous membranes, have been holding up under the strain since my last cold at the beginning of the semester. I've even put on some weight. I attribute all this to a judicious use of cod liver oil for the past 2-3 months. Or maybe it's the warm weather.

There you are, dear. You have me down on black and white. No one can ever say that you married blindly.

The weather picked up a bit—and my morale lifted. But it'll go right down again pretty soon I guess. I'm not tough minded enough to cope with the situation.

You'll get the key as soon as I receive it. I won't be a meany. In a way, tho, I'm almost sorry. First of all, I'm reserved enough and don't mingle too well with the boys. (It's difficult for anyone to get by my unconcerned politeness); Osler is another barrier. Secondly, it forces a certain expected standard of performance. And third, it'll hurt that much more to have it all come to naught. It's remarkable, tho, the respect that one is accorded by fellow classmates. No one at school knew I had a Phi Betta Kappa key or such. I steadfastly denied it for the reasons I gave. But I was shown up.

Edwin is home on vacation. The Vet school has a month off. So it's pretty lonely up here with the house to myself. I'm using his room as a study and mine as a bedroom. Some class, for $3 a week! That is until Mrs. Ellis decides to lock his room up.

I miss you a great deal. If I could be with you without the feeling that I better get in all the kisses I can before leaving, I'd talk to you for hours and hours. After which I'd have nothing to say, and you could get in a word or two.

If you get the chance drop in on my mother and tell her that I still love them despite my infrequent letters, that I'm terribly busy, and that I'll try to come in as soon as the term is over.

Until later, darling
Aaron

The student nurse article for your amusement; The clinicopath case history to impress you.

Friday 6/4
10:30 pm

Gloria dear—

I had planned on taking a long walk tonight—into the night. But as usual, "The spirit was willing,..." Instead, I'm in pyjamas, sandals, smoking, and writing to you.

But it's beautiful out now. There's this to be said for New England Weather: It's very much like "the little girl who had a little curl right in the middle of her forehead..." (You know the rest, I suppose.)

Tonight was simply made to order for boy and girl. You know the kind. Just like in movies and cheap novels. It almost hurts to watch it go by. I'm like a starving man shown lots of wonderful food that he mustn't touch because of his health.

I don't feel terribly passionate now. Probably there is no stimulus. But I want so very much to have you near me—together with the feeling that you're going to stay there. That I can talk to you and make love to you today, and tomorrow, and tomorrows...

Mrs. Ellis told me a few days ago that her husband feels something of the sort. He usually gets home from the store, sits before the stove, and reads. She sits nearby and knits, or does nothing but watch him (a lazy cat completes the picture). She once said that she was going to bed early as she wasn't doing her husband any good just sitting there. He told her that, even that was a great deal just knowing that she was there...They've been married for about 35 years...

There is a certain kind of intimacy that's built up between two persons—from which strength can be drawn. To feel completely accepted, in caresses, desires, beliefs, aspirations...It's a difficult thing to achieve, But once obtained is always something to turn to.

So tonight, I want to take that very long walk with you. Into the night that is scented with lilac, that is lighted by the brilliant stars, that is even more silent because of the mating calls of the crickets and the frogs, and that cries out "Carpe diem."

God, I'm getting poetic!

It's been so long since I was in, that you're becoming hazy—like a dream...Waltham, my courses, profs, exams...appear to be the reality. And in my day by day routine, there is no connection between the two worlds, except our letters. No places we've been to together, or friends we know in common…

I'll finally be in, in-between terms—but not because of any vacation. My mother must misunderstand my letters regularly. Possibly because they want to collect as much tuition as possible, our program calls for 32 weeks of school (1 year) with a month's vacation in-between years. I'm planning to simply take the few days off after Mid-Year exams to come in to see you. If you don't come up here several times before then, they're going to have trouble getting me back to school.

You are the reality, the part that I expect to become interwoven with the material of my future life. Waltham, Middlesex…will probably be an abortive detour.

Incidentally, when you see my mother again you might straighten her out. I can't get it across by letter to her. Also about the loan. She was apparently prematurely optimistic; but nearly right. The details are complicated. The school was granted about $18,000 when the appropriation was made last July or so. This was distributed. In April of this year, Mr. Smith, seeing the boys working in local factories, getting ill, and losing out at school (and possibly worrying about his tuition) wrote to Washington requesting more money. He got several thousand more. Now at the same time, I just reached the point of being within 2 years of graduation (theoretically we get out March 1945). So naturally I applied. That's what I wrote home. I could only apply for tuition + $25 a month for April, May and June. As the appropriation made by Congress expires on July 1, 1943. That means $225. Tuition was due this week—and I was one of the boys to get the loan.

It'll help. But I actually need one or two full $500 loans. As no more money is being appropriated by Congress (the schools are in the Army), I'm still left in a very precarious position. Yet, I can finance myself thru about half my junior year now. The deadline was pushed back.

Of course the big problem still remains about whether I'll have a Junior year.

Why do they lend me money? God knows. I don't think one bureau of the gov't knows what the other is doing. When they find out & get together, they'll draft us & close the school, probably.

Do you think I ought to enlist and try to get into a Med. School from within?

Good night darling
I love you very much
Aaron

Tuesday 6/7
12 Midnight

Gloria darling

Well, we're off again. "Writing to my love at midnight." Romantic as the devil, isn't it?

Oh well, if I can't write brilliantly at this hour, blame it on the Parasitology course we just started. It's just a riot. They're trying to pump an MA in Parasitology into our already overstuffed brains in 3 weeks. They say that it's an accelerated program! I read in a recent Readers Digest of a Princeton man, who went out to get a smoke; and found out when he returned that he'd missed his whole sophomore year. That's how I feel now. I've never gotten nowhere so rapidly before. Every day I marvel at the capability of the human mind to keep on adding to its store of information. But any day now, I expect the top of my head to pop off with a "Hsssss…"

Now you have some idea of the state of my mind, darling. Brush your hand over my feverish brow in make-believe. Maybe I'll feel better anyhow.

Your letters (I received two today) are swell. Either I'm more in need of them, or they get better continuously. As you can tell from my letters, we're both more than a little in need of each other's company. Gosh, darling, I miss you terribly…

Incidentally, your typing is remarkably good. You know, I still don't really envision you as a very efficient little stenographer. But I really am glad that you are. Warmth and tenderness you have; capability will only add to your personality.

In due time you ought to be quite able to handle any kind of "Mr. Anthony" problem. What with all the problems your girlfriends are faced with. If you have any idea on solutions for the problems you throw out, let me know, darling. I feel more and more, that I know less and less. I've been out of touch with reality for so long, that it's nice to be reminded that people are concerned about other things than their livers and gall bladders.

Your taste in records is quite all right, dear. So is your taste in art, ballet, and the theater. In fact, when I'm a great man and very busy, I'll leave all those things to you. I'll just tag along and enjoy the stuff…

You might add Sibelius to your list—if you don't have him already. His Violin Concerto is magnificent, and his first two symphonies are something to listen to, also. But you know that as well as I do.

How is your relationship with your mother coming along? Is it any different, now that you're the only one home, and employed?

Altho it's probably far more lovely up here now, I'd give a lot to be in New York…I look at your picture occasionally. I'm glad you sent it up. It brings up quite a wealth of emotion.

I love you very much darling. Good night, dear,

Aaron

Friday 6/11
10:30 pm

Dear

The night is beautiful—and I miss you. As you know by this time, sometimes I want you more than at other times—but lately it's pretty constant. Do you think we'd love each other as much if we could see each other whenever we wished? Or does the fact that so much emotion must be crammed into so short a time heighten the level of feeling, making it a more intense one?

Frankly I wish we had the chance to try a little of this "see each other whenever we wished" stuff. Right now, it seems to me that if I could see you for 10 years all day long, I'd spend all that time making love to you.

One must eat, I suppose, but I just can't seem to fit it into my plans for us. As you can see, I'm pretty starved for you.

By all means come up to Waltham with or without your mother, father, partner, his wife, and even his children. I don't promise to be polite to any of them, but if they just leave us alone, I'll try not to get nasty.

But it would be so much more satisfactory if you could get on a train and come up for a weekend yourself. No end.

1) We'd have a long evening and a whole day together. Imagine!
2) No relatives.
3) It would show, that you can do it. And that is "terribly" important darling. At some point you'll have to be able to tell your mother you're going to another city; buy your tickets; make your reservations; kiss her good night; make the trip without getting into a jam or running out of funds; and return on time, unruffled. The first time would have some emotion tied into it. Later, it should be almost routine.

You see, darling, we're going to get married pretty soon, in any event. But I feel that it's very important for you to achieve an emancipation from home—before you're married. Now is about the time you should be maturing rapidly, and the situation, I think, will help.

It's extremely important that one make decisions in all things primarily for oneself. Of course, consideration is frequently given to the wishes of those we love—we want them to be happy. But our actions must not be dictated by the habit of filial duty—either to parent or husband or wife.

So come up—however you can manage it. My exams will probably be held the week before July 4.

How do you like the Tribune articles? This one is very good I think. The writer is a sensitive chap, and between the lines I think you'll find a lot of truth and some pathos. Do you think we fit into any of his categories?

It's getting very late now, darling. These letters may not show it, but they take me lots of time to compose. Even with an inspiration. I couldn't do anything without one.

Good night dear
I love you
Aaron

Tuesday 6/15
11:45 pm

Gloria darling—

On the basis of your last week's letters, I think that you'd better write them to me in longhand, and at home. First, your handwriting brings you much closer than a typewriter (tho you type beautifully), and secondly, you're much freer in what you say when you're not afraid someone will peek over your shoulder. I'm glad you love me…There is really very little else that I look forward to…

Tonight I went to see <u>The Commandos Strike at Dawn</u>. It wasn't bad, tho rather overdone. I think Irwin Shaw and Paul Muni are capable of greater art. In any event, it made me hate the Germans a little more; and love the Norwegians, British and Americans still better. So my morale is more in line with the rest of my neighbors. Muni is a great actor. He was a little miscast here, tho.

I needed the release. The Parasitology course has been driving us crazy. Since it's a three week course it was 2/3 over today; we had an exam; and I went to a movie.

You've been leaving me up in the air in your recent letters, darling. You say that you're having a grand time "doing the things you've always wanted to do." But just what are they? I'm very curious. You'd better let me in on your escapades.

I'm enclosing the letter from the Board of Estimate. I could probably find out just how to go about getting my money, identification,…by mail, but it took about 4 months for them to answer my first letter. See what you can do by telephone. I hope you don't mind my treating you as tho we've been married for ages, and having you buy books for me, and handle my finances. My father could handle it. But I get a distinct pleasure in your doing it. You explain it.

It's gotten very late; I'm going to sleep...I love you very much, dear. I'm looking forward to seeing you enormously, but I can't give you any details on my coming in to New York until I know them.

Good night darling
Aaron

Thursday 6/17
11:15 pm

Dear

It's teeming out. Somehow I like the sound of a terrific rain pattering on the windows—when I'm inside and warm and dry. There is undoubtedly a Freudian explanation. Maybe you can figure it out.

Incidentally, you wrote something about Haverlock Ellis—his living a very happy life with a very talented wife. [Wow—the thunder then was practically in my room. I take it all back about liking the rain]. But to get back to Ellis. I have a faint recollection of hearing that his wife was frigid or a lesbian or something—and that their sex life was anything but satisfactory. Check on me, dear, I'm not too sure. But at any rate, it might account for the two room arrangement. Also for his becoming an expert on sexual relations.

Right now, my head is getting more and more cluttered up with Parasitological data. Ask me a question-- you know, the whole approach up here is so different from what it was at College. Then, even in Science Courses, the emphasis was entirely on "getting the idea." The actual facts were not important at all. We learned, for example, that there were lots of parasites among lower forms (protozoa, worms...) and that they frequently attacked man. Also bacteria were likely to do the same thing. Finally, we were told, that in some cases a parasite could be carried by an insect (eg Mosquito and Malarial parasite); these insects are called vectors.

But in med school all this is just gravy. Anybody can see that. We memorize diligently that "The disease kala azar is carried by the mastigophoran Leishmania Donovan; which in its life cycle goes thru a crithidial stage in the fly phlebotomus." Then multiply that by 350 or so, and you have a rough idea. For many we also learn the life cycle of the parasite; the things it does in the body when it invades; the symptoms of the disease; how to diagnose the disease if you suspect a patient has it from the symptoms; treatment; prevention;--and anything else they can think of.

Nobody is interested in your getting the idea here. No "culture" is being taught. The idea is always "Specifically, what happens?"

And that's been true in every subject, and will continue to be. No place for discussion. There are no opinions. "The following 10 Tabanid flies are of medical importance: Tabanis sp; Chrysops discalis; Chrysops silacea…" ad infinitum.

Retention is very low—25% I guess. The only saving feature is that the stuff is repeated fairly frequently in different courses, under different emphasis; so that a lot of what is important finally sticks.

Of course, real medicine doesn't actually begin, until you're in a hospital.

Final exams are scheduled for July 1,2,3. In response to our urgent pleas, we were given the following week off.

(The rain has eased considerably by now.)

Good night darling
Aaron

Tuesday 6/22
11:30 pm

Dear—

Altho it's quite lovely out, it's frightfully hot in the house. I must have sweated a gallon of water today—we had our Parasitology finals. Wow! Somehow, dear, I'm not what I used to be—or maybe I never was much. I just don't have the push now to put much real effort into getting a grade. I dare say I'll pass that little Parasitology course, but not with too much to spare.

The accelerated program of study has hit me as a student particularly. I think I finally doped out why. My proficiency in school was not due to a phenomenal memory. Really, that is what makes the little school geniuses, I think. My memory is, and always has been, average at best. If anything, I think it's poor. And still, the greatest asset in school work, (which is largely committing to memory a body of facts to be repeated during examinations) is a good memory. How did I get the grades I did? Fundamentally it was on an emotional level. I was so put together, that I was the more conscientious student. Combined with a good I.Q., this makes for top-notch grades. The memorization was done by sheer hard work. The concepts were gotten by a good ability to see relationships. But the primary quality of being able to read a chapter, hear a lecture, or see a specimen, and, retain it was never there.

It was considerably easier in the more thoughtful courses: English, Math, Philosophy, Education. I always had a heck of a time in Biology courses. (Imagine).

Now, the accelerated program hits just the point where I really used to bolster my rotten memory. At present there is no chance for review and repetition. Just a ceaseless pouring in of new facts to be learnt practically verbatim.

Don't worry, darling, I can get thru Medical school. It's just that I finally figured out what seemed at first a paradox, and thought I'd let you know.

You'll have to love me, even if I'm not really a genius, dear.

The excerpt from Moon and Sixpence was swell reading. Send all you like; I don't have the nerve to go to the library myself.

What do I think about love and things?

Did I ever tell you of the time, probably 5 years ago, when a girl I had known for a long time once asked me whether she ought to marry an acquaintance of mine. Very platonic, of course.

So I spoke thusly:

There are 3 essentials for a successful marriage. First you ought to be fond of the chap. Like him (or her) for those qualities you treasure in people: Introversion, extroversion, humour, sincerity…Some people like Bach, others Benny Goodman…

Secondly there must be a strong sexual compatibility. You must want to be made love to by the person, and good healthy passion develops. Having only the first, there is the basis for a nice friendship; only the second, a brief, usually unsatisfactory affair; both together, we have Romance.

Finally, if you can feasibly live together for a long stretch—get married. This brings in similar interests, background, racial & family problems, financial problems…This, of course, is the part that parents always stress.

Depending on the relative strength, or lack of each of the three factors, the marriage will be successful or not.

In concluding I pointed out that since she was rather soft, & the chap very hard—it wasn't a good idea. They were married shortly thereafter & probably lived happily ever after.

Good night darling,
Aaron

Friday 10:40 pm

Gloria darling,

To say the least, the idea of getting married now tempts me. It's surprising how many people have nearly the same problem. Within the past two days I've discovered 2 other chaps at the school who want to get married to their respective sweethearts; who feel very unhappy separated; and who are afraid to attempt it. I don't know the answer now. We'll talk it over as soon as I come in, and decide. We can say more in a half hour's conversation than in volumes of letters. That is if I can talk coherently and intelligently as soon as I get home.

But, did you hear the oft repeated adage about the most dangerous man is the one who has a plan—any plan. And that probably goes for women, too.

It would be nice having you here right now. Incidentally, I don't really dislike planning what I'm going to do next. I find that the nicest "spontaneous" things that happen are very carefully planned in advance. It's just that I don't like to make a fuss about what I'm planning & hoping to do, discuss every angle pro and con, live every minute of it in expectation…Because of two reasons:

First, the terrific build-up is bound to lead to disillusionment. Secondly, if the idea fails then there is an awful letdown. Finally, there is ingrained in me the knowledge that there is no status quo. One either moves forward to greater, or down to less. That is a platitude I know. But its significance grows with each new experience.

Therefore, I like to take the good things that happen in stride, feel good of course, but discount them at once and see what further obstacles are looming. There always are some.

There you have some awfully homely philosophy, darling. I wouldn't dare to write it to anyone else but you.

My folks, by the way weren't against our getting married at any time. I think they'd even prefer it.

But we can go over all the angles in about a week.

The weather conditions are driving me crazy. I can't study. Yet finals start on Thursday. I'll flunk out this term if it doesn't cool down soon.

About School of Social Work & Thelma's plans. I thought I'd leave that for the time that I could tell her or you what I knew about it. I didn't want to waste a letter on the subject. So I'll tell you all I know and you can pass it on…

The "Intern" comes out only once a month. But I've been getting these articles for you out of every issue I come across. They're pretty cute.

Good night darling
Aaron

Wednesday 6/30
10:00 pm

Darling:

I'm very much in a funk now, as you can imagine; cramming in all sorts of stuff that I'm going to forget as rapidly as possible after Saturday.

I arrive in New York, Greyhound's Capitol Terminal, Sunday evening at 6:50 pm—as usual. They had me a bit nervous on Sunday. As I blithely asked for a ticket, the agent said that they were all filled up until after the 5th! After I recovered from the shock, I called up Boston hoping that the Silver Tart Bus Lines might have room. They no longer exist! It then occurred to me that maybe Boston-New York buses may still have room (Greyhound), but not the one that stops in Waltham. I was right.

So I pick up the Bus in Boston, and get to New York at the same time.

Barring accident I'll meet you as usual.

This week is exam week with a vengeance. In Bacteriology we were given an "unknown" to work out. That is a specimen taken from a sick person, and we are to ascertain what was the matter. Specimens vary: throat smears, urine, spinal fluid, sputum…I have a throat smear. I take it the patient must have had a sore throat and not Gonorrhea. On that basis I'm growing the little bacteria on different petri dishes and test tubes, making the prettiest stains possible…but I'll be damned whether I'm at all certain as to whether my patient had a septic sore throat (streptococcus) or diphtheria. Probably it was Tuberculosis. But so it goes. Maybe I'll know by Friday.

While we're working on this "unknown" they give us "little unknowns" to work out. Yesterday sputum was handed out with the question—"does he or doesn't he?" Having only time for a few preliminary stains, I got the nicest red bacteria in a very light, sky-blue background, and decided that the patient probably was getting close to dying of Tuberculosis.

Today we were given a culture of rod-like bacteria which might be Typhoid, and a serum which would clump them if they were. My specimen under the microscope showed these little rods scampering around like mad—serum or no serum. I reported "no typhoid." Probably I'll find out that the patient died of Typhoid. Oh well.

Tomorrow we get a final in Pharmacy. A minor course on "How to write a prescription" (if you ever have occasion to do so.) Latin or English; name your brand.

Rx: Acid Acetylsalicilic .3
Sig: 1 in aqua h.s.

That calls for aspirin at bedtime! Which is what I could use right now.

Until Sunday, darling
Aaron

Tuesday 4:00 pm

Hello darling—

I wanted to write to you yesterday but gave way to the elements. I got into Waltham with a heat wave. If you find any drops on the paper, it's the sweat pouring from me. You might try to imagine how I'd like to be back home with you. Just try. You really couldn't do it.

I'm going to enclose some sheets of the bulletin for our Medical School which just came out. You'll find the faculty listed, and their previous schools. The particularly interesting thing is the appointment of all the refugees, who are the backbone of the faculty since 1939. Most of them are even more recent. And our students are not granted state recognition subsequent to 1940. So apparently, we have the ridiculous situation where the far better prepared student is not considered as good as the one who was taught his medicine by the trash at the school before. We could well call ourselves "Little Vienna." And after all, isn't that where all the doctors went to become specialists? At least in the movies…

My program for this semester is quite complex.:

MON: Epidemiology/Surgery/Pharmacology
TUES: Pathology/Pharmacology

WED: Pathology/Laboratory Diagnosis
THURS: Physical Diagnosis/Public Health/ Pharm
FRI: Pathology/Laboratory Diagnosis
SAT: Obstetrics/Pediatrics

Professors:
Epidemiology (Lecture)--Schweinberg
Surgery (Lecture)--MacDonald
Pharmacology (Lab. Course)--Mauntnor
Pathology (Lab. Course)--Mathias
Lab. Diagnosis (Lab. Course)--Singer
Public Health (Lecture)--Pearlstein
Obstetrics (Lecture)--Kuhn
Pediatrics (Lecture)--Mauntner

The three important courses this term are, of course, Pathology (about which you are very well informed); Pharmacology (which Solly has just completed), and Laboratory diagnosis. You'll hear more about the courses as I take them.

I don't know what I'll do for a job. Saul says that due to the meat shortage there was nothing doing last week. Probably we'd have been laid off anyway. My next letters may be about my experiences at job hunting.

All my love, dear
Aaron

Sunday, 12:40 am

Darling,

I went to see "Talk of the Town" tonight, and came home to find an enchanted night. I stayed in the garden for awhile to look at the night and muse. Now I'm a little full, and let myself bubble over to you.

The garden was a little unreal, all lit up and silvered by a big, clear moon; the stars are very faint, but clear; the "Big Dipper" sparkles across the sky—each star winking…the shrubbery, and trees, and crickets, all seemed so unreal. Like something Hollywood would put out. I expected it all to fade any minute.

But the movie started a long chain of thought. It was amusing, but also packed a morale. And I asked myself once more that eternal question—What would I do if I were able to set up this Society of ours to suit myself? What is my plan of salvation?

You know, when I took my first Shop course in Public school, I remember being a bit surprised at the teacher spending a lot of time during our first lesson, and giving a great deal of emphasis to the Rule of the Shop: where to put our tools when thru; which to use; where to get them; cleaning our bench when thru; stopping work and listening for instructions when the whistle blows… I thought that he should stop wasting time and tell us how to saw wood…But the teacher knew that we'd all learn the many details of the course—as long as the shop ran smoothly. The most important thing was to set down the principles of conduct.

So for our more complicated society. What are our fundamental rules anyhow? What do men live by? I guess—not to kill; not to commit incest; and not to indulge in extramarital relations; of our most fundamental principles there are a few not too clear ethics; about not stealing, lying, or taking advantage of the helpless. Can you think of any more?

These principles it seems to me, need great revision, clarification, and exposition; they are outmoded, and date back to a civilization vastly different from our own today.

The rules of conduct that I can think of for us can be summed up as:

1. Nobody shall be in need of food, shelter, clothing, or adequate medical care;
2. A fair trial shall be given to all who transgress the laws of the land (to be determined democratically)—with no capital punishment. [We don't know what life is, nor can we create it. Let us not destroy it.]
3. No one is to aggrandize himself at the expense of another.

4. In all things let every individual do completely as he wishes, except in so far as he violates one of the above, or is incompetent to take care of himself.

Actually that is all that I can think of. They are far different from what is currently accepted:

1) We now generally believe that it is every man's destiny to get his needs for himself-- preferably honestly. Or else he's no good, a pauper, a chiseler…
2) Our law is that of retribution; eye for eye, tooth for tooth
3) No one practically would deny to anybody the fruits of his wit and intellect. If he can make a fortune by outwitting his employer, the consumer, his competitors…In fact he's a "smart fellow." But I don't think so. There is no room in my principles for that kind of smartness. There would be no room for the profit motive, or the stool pigeon…
4) And finally, the "live and let live" idea. It's the most important of all Christian ethics. If "Big Brother" would only let the little brother alone, and mothers not try to run their children's lives, and Hays Commission not worry about our movies, and League for Decency about our morals…We'd live in a far healthier, cleaner society, where fresh air would blow.

We have a Constitution. And a Bill of Rights. Something of my "ethics" are there. But what are they to most people? Curious facts we learned about at school, and hear of occasionally on Quiz programs or political speeches.

No. My "Ethics" must be engraved, not in piecemeal, but in the souls of all the people. They can be said simply and briefly. But understood, not as slogans, but rather as a way of life. Almost every day, a child will be faced by one of "these principles": in his relationship to his family, his friends, his school. How frequently do we all, constantly, try to convince others they ought to do what we'd like to do—go to bed early, or late, or go to College, or go to work, the kind of job, hair comb, kind of clothes, amount of clothes...We're always doing it.

I am pleading for the concern that is willing to hold one's advice, keep a watchful eye open, and step in, in answer to an appeal for help—verbalized or mute.

So that finally, if these "Rules of Conduct" were completely accepted, the things we want would go along smoothly. Like the Shop course, the details would work themselves out quite nicely. Science would go on, colleges would be built, architecture would improve.

Gosh, darling. Look what you've got this time. I really don't believe it myself. You'd better come up and let me get the stuff out of my system or there'll be a profound paper shortage.

It's very late now

Good night dear
Aaron

Friday 7/16
11:00 pm

Gloria—

It's a very lovely night. The kind that we ought definitely to spend together. It's lovely out, with a moon big & round, and lots of stars out. It's cool enough to be comfortable; not too cold, or muggy. I need you tonight, dear.

You know, I almost went in to New York this afternoon. One of the boys was driving in; he asked me to go along. But I decided against it. Tonight, I and Saul, the romantic lad I told you about, broke the news to the manager of the market, that we had classes on Saturday. He agreed to our taking the time off! We won't even be docked for it!

It was either my glib presentation of the case, full of tact and diplomacy; or the fact that the manager was ½ drunk. Probably tomorrow morning, as we start for school, we'll get fired. But life is like that. One never knows. Maybe it would be very dull otherwise. At any rate, I'm becoming more and more fatalistic. Ultimately I'll sit still all day, and contemplate my navel or something, and let things happen to me. There is nothing I can do about it anyway.

So these little problems are always with us. You know, I've had so many little problems to be solved in just staying in school, that I can't really worry about the important thing—the school. Yet that may be a very good thing. There is nothing I can do about this primary problem; worrying about something you can do nothing about leads to neuroses. Meeting problems that you do solve—more-or-less adequately, is far healthier. (Wow, I never thought that I could rationalize to that extent!)

Thelma & Elliot are lucky, aren't they? I suppose they'll get married now; both working; Elliot is a lucky devil. In any event give Thelma my best wishes. Also Elliot, if you see him.

School rolls on…As you can see by my program we continue in the mornings with Pathology laboratory, with demonstrations of lungs, livers, hearts…more-or-less as I told you. We continue to look at slides and make pretty pictures. Yesterday we finished the very big section on so-called "Constitution" with a lot of time spent on "Hereditary Diseases." Good Lord! Everything seems to have hereditary significance, from mental disease to deaf-mutism to Tendency toward Tuberculosis. More-or-less (taken with a big grain of salt) you pass on everything you've got to your unfortunate offspring. Of course, this isn't stressed much in Medicine, as there is nothing you can do about your patients' genes.

More about my other courses as I learn some more.

Good night sweetheart,
Aaron

Thursday 5:15 pm

Hello darling—

I'm glad you liked my treatise on "Society." I don't know whether my 4 ethics are so impossible tho. The Soviet Union based a great deal of its philosophy on them—and except for some variation has nearly carried out the program. Think about it. The way I feel;

only by mass education of youth in the Ethics I propose, so that the person finds exploitation or starvation as abhorrent as incest or murder, will the Society I envision be reached.

But enough politics, for now.

There isn't much that is new up here right now. There is a general feeling of depression and hopelessness permeating throughout the school. I don't know.

There is a book you can try to pick up for me. An obstetrics book which has lots of pictures and should be good reading:

A,C, Beck—"Obstetrical Practice", Second Edition, 1939, Williams & Wilkins Co.

There may be a later edition, but this will do very nicely. If you can get it for less than 10% discount (second hand…) pick it up and ship it to me. I can get it at that discount in Boston.

The lecturer is quite unintelligible so that I'll have to do some tall reading.

Yesterday I watched a routine pharmacology experiment done as it should be. It was to test the effect of certain drugs on a dog's heart.

The vein going to the heart was tied off with a hemostat and a cannula inserted. A cannula is a glass tube going into the vein so that blood can be allowed to flow out or things put in.

Similarly a connection was made from the trachea (windpipe) to a drum. As the dog breathes the drum moves up and down, the writing lever moves up and down, and leaves a tracing on the kymograph paper (which is revolving) of the respirations. Then a connection was made between the carotid artery and a "U" tube of mercury. The blood pressure is pushing against the mercury and lifts the column of the "U" tube. On the mercury is a cork, stuck into it is a pin, and to the pin a writing lever. As the blood pressure varies, the mercury sinks (or rises), the cork shifts, and the lever makes its tracing.

All the while the dog slept very soundly. The big job was to get this set up. Then a drug was injected into the venous cannula, it went right to the heart, weakened it, and the pressure dropped.

Digitalis was then introduced and the heart strengthened, and the lever (showing blood pressure) rose.

Do you enjoy this stuff, dear, or would you rather read this stuff in the library?

Love, darling
Aaron

Friday, 8/6
11:45 pm

Darling—

All's quiet finally; Eddie went out for coffee; little Davida's asleep; and I can write away.

Coming home tonight I was stopped by the beautiful night. The stars were out crying for attention, with a crescent moon. As I went by the river, the scene was a perfect setting for a romantic movie; balmy breeze, a canoe or two, and moonlight reflected in the water.

Speaking of light, Rembrandt is magnificent in his handling of light. More than anything else, I was deeply moved by this character in his work.

There is one etching in particular. It's a dimly lit church, in which the only source of light is a window in one corner. You can make out faintly a flight of curving stairs going up into the shadow, a crucifix, and an old man, representing a saint, reading from a big book in front of the window, and by its light. But the important part of the picture is not the church—or even the saint. They all just seem to accentuate the light coming in from the window. It's bright, and clear, makes dimly visible some of the things it touches. It's very difficult to realize that it's not a real light, of bright sun shining through the page, but only a drawing in black and white. For me, the true central theme of the picture was—light.

I must have heard something about this before, or else it may be that it's very dramatic and thereby appeals to my unsophisticated artistic taste. If I find more "discoveries" in Rembrandt, I'll pass them on. Altho I ought to be looking at drawings of pathological specimens instead of etchings…

The New York City Hospitals (Dep't of Hospitals, NYC) have removed their ban on Middlesex students for internships. Our senior class now has already made connections, and are entering these hospitals in November. Greenpoint, Gouverneurs…You remember that the Commissioner of Hospitals officially invoked a ruling against accepting us. The few who did get in by the back door were promptly ejected. Now it's officially O.K. It's a good break for the boys; excellent training, and living in New York near friends and family. These are facts. I've seen a letter from Gouverneur Hospital to Dave.

This doesn't affect us, of course. We can't take State Boards yet, or anything. But it's nice for the seniors. It's not that they like us better, but they like being very short-handed worse.

Let me know, right away, the details of your trip up here. The train you're taking, when and where you arrive, what plans you make (if any) for staying now…But soon. I have to make my plans to visit. Come soon…

Good night dear,
Aaron

Tuesday 7/27
12:45 am

Gloria dear

I'm back to my old habits of writing to you at midnight or thereabouts. Very romantic. This is just the time when I'd like to close my books and devote my full attention to you. So here goes:

There has been no let up. In fact the amount of work to be done this semester is about double. Yet it's by far the best term so far. The material is very good. Strange how each term got better…

You know, it's very fortunate that the staff is so good. I don't think I could stand it otherwise. The situation looks more hopeless every day. All the rumors are bad. The question is apparently not "Whether the school closes," but "When." No clinics; no building going on; no nothing. The wheels revolve, lectures and laboratories go on as they did in the past. Those who are interested even study. The most flourishing thing at school right now is the "Camera Club" (where the pictures are Jacks, Kings and Queens)—and you can get some idea of the morale, in that speculation is going around about the school taking over the bank! Maybe they'll even put in roulette wheels in the smoking room.

Medicine is a magnificent subject. And the books I'm reading are the theoretical basis for it. The "science part." In the clinic you get the "art" of medicine—the essential skills. But just as an academic topic it's awfully good stuff. So much work—and a lot of it brilliant—has been done! So much is known. Yet so much more is still not known.

I can't possibly do all the reading & studying actually required now. The pathology text and pharmacology are splendid; Dr. Singer gives top notch lectures; there's a big pediatrics book waiting to be read; and a lot of Obstetrics to be done.

And with it all there is the constant review (if done right). To be sure I studied the histology (microscopic structure) of the kidney in my first year—yet I don't really remember it—and have to go back and go over it again, before I can go into the various pathological changes one finds…the whole thing is very closely tied together. It's, after all, the study of one organism—man.

Sometimes I really wonder that throughout the years knowledge was continuously accumulated and added to the ever growing mass. It seems so orderly. Deceptively so.

Do write as often and as long as you wish. I look forward to your letters every time I come back from school.

I love you a great deal, dear

Aaron

Friday 7/30
11:00 pm

Hello Darling—

I'm pretty tired right now. Last night, for no particular reason, I stayed up till about 1:30 reading. Result: a very sleepy chap all day today. Tomorrow I get up at 6:00! Oh well…

It's funny, but my entire emotional set toward school in general is changing (& has already changed considerably) up here. When I was in High School or College, "Grades" meant a great deal to me, emotionally. The fear of not getting a "90%" or an "A" was a very potent stimulus which drove me towards doing a great deal of work. Completely irrespective of whether I was particularly interested. Result: good grades in <u>all</u> subjects. No marked proficiency in any one field.

But more and more, I just can't seem to get excited. Somehow I don't care about exams, grades…I won't go out of my way—to get that extra 2% on the final grade. More and more I read what I find interesting, learn what I enjoy, and only begrudgingly give of my time and energy towards memorizing details I'm not interested in; or reread my lecture notes which I don't find as interesting as the excellent texts.

It's probably a very bad approach from the Medical student's point of view. But I'm getting older I guess and rebel against learning masses of facts which I may not understand or be interested in. Also I'm getting lazy. It's good I made Osler last year; I wouldn't have now.

To get away from me. Your new stationery is very pretty, dear. The scent, tho, is lost by the time it gets here. I hope the post office employees enjoy it. After all, morale is morale. In any event, I'm very glad you've returned to writing letters again. On any kind of stationery, I'd prefer your more intimate & freer communication this way. Maybe, subconsciously, I like the idea of your sitting alone at night, in the perfect setting for love, writing to me.

So far I haven't been able to get Saul to write a letter for me. I suppose he's getting bashful. I did want to find out what other chaps write, and what their girls think is "just divine!" You'll have to go along accepting my more reserved letters, which usually reflect my mood pretty accurately. They should be telling you that I'm very much in love with you, by "tone of voice", in every line.

I haven't written home for over a week. I'll write tonite and go to sleep.

Good night dear,
Aaron

Tuesday 12:30 am
8/2

Gloria darling,

I've never been so rushed. 9 courses are just 5 too many. By and large I'm keeping one jump ahead of being thrown for a loss. I'm glad you're busy, too. It'll make this period, while we're marking time, go so much faster.

That very emotional letter I promised you, from my romantic colleague, Saul, won't be forthcoming—they broke up on Saturday.

You know—that made me very pensive all day.

But maybe I'm right after all, in my instinctive aversion and distrust of anything which is loud, obvious, exaggerated, superficial…call it what you will. That is why I like to see things start slowly with no words, or Hozannahs. And to let the deeds and facts speak for themselves. It's why I don't wear a Phi Betta Kappa key, or like women who are overdressed and oversophisticated. If anything is really good, you don't have to shout about it.

So I always felt uncomfortable about Saul's carrying a picture of his Eunice in each pocket; of her attested perfection; of her great solicitude for his welfare…

Similarly I always have distrusted those married couples who could never stop "darling" each other in public…

As some very wise one put it someplace, "He lives quietly with his love"…

There is a sincere, normal way of life. Particularly in such a relation must it be maintained—or there is no relation, I think. In all sincerity one can realize that no one is perfect or divine, that we have definite shortcomings, and discount them—and love withal.

Gosh, I've wandered far afield, haven't I?

Thanks for the book darling. It's as beautiful as the thought of sending it up to me. I'll take very good care of it, until we have the time to go over Rembrandt's etchings together.

Now that I have the Etchings; I need the girl to look at them. Do try to come up. The students have been having their respective soulmates up all summer, for week-ends. Two or three left for New York today.

So come up to the fair city of Waltham, and I'll thank you with the long deep kiss that can tell you more than my letters or monologues.

Did you see the article in the World Telegram on Friday, about Middlesex? It reviewed our plight in a rather favorable way. And even the Times mentioned us on Sunday. Boy oh Boy! We'll become national figures yet. But it really means nothing you know. The Mass. Medical Society hates us very thoroly—and that's what counts.

I'm practically asleep now, darling. I hope the letter is intelligible. At these hours I really don't input much.

Good night dear
Aaron

Wednesday 8/11
11:45 pm

Gloria dear—

It gets harder and harder for me to get any conception of time. Einstein was right. Somehow weeks just seem to disappear. It's like being on a merry-go-round watching the world spin by. And is it spinning! Summer is practically gone; and with it my second year of Middlesex. It was so far away only a very short while ago; when we discussed whether I'd stay for one or two terms…

Actually things move so rapidly that I don't even know whether I've learnt very much. I don't have time to really learn anything well; or to get a real good perspective. I become "familiar" with a lot of things, find that they are rather hazily present back somewhere in my mind, when those things are brought up again; but one thing can be said for medical training. It certainly is repetitious! You get the same material thrown at you by lecturer after lecturer, test after test, in course after course. Sometimes, from a somewhat different slant. But to a large extent repetition. Retention is very low. Because after having heard, read, and seen something for the 15th time I'd still be a little shaky if asked about it.

Don't worry about your job, dear. They won't lay you off. I've seen far more serious "crises" in Civil Service where at the end no one was dismissed. Positions are abolished, transfers are made, titles are changed, and everyone is happy. Nobody gets fired. I think I'd like to be in some nice little Civil Service job right now, with an apartment in Greenwich Village, books, record player, some paintings, weekends off for tennis, or country, an opera or symphony during the season…Oh yes, you can share it with me.

I guess I'm getting soft…

There is a course being given at our undergraduate school, "Introduction to Freud", or something. It's during our lunch hour so a few of us are sitting in. The prof, as usual, is a talented, very well educated, and well traveled Viennese. It's nice to hear the psychological concepts thrown around again. It brings back a lot of stuff that I once knew—and have largely forgotten. I can see now how easy it was to take 5 or 6 College courses and loaf by. These lectures require no real work; nice you understand, that's all there is to it. In the biological sciences, and particularly medicine, understanding is a luxury. First you must know. After the facts are crammed in, if ever, you can try to understand—"why". But foremost come facts.

Come up to Waltham whenever you can, dear. I dare say, someday you'll be able to make the trip without even a chaperone.

Good night dear,
Aaron

Friday 8/13
10:15 pm

Darling—

Well, I'm glad for your peace of mind that you weathered the "firing" storm. In fact, I was quite surprised that anybody was laid off; particularly at this time, with "Help Wanted" being such an overwhelming cry. Of course, at the war's end, all the departments will be liquidated that were set up to meet war needs. Many a man still remembers the stoppage of production in his plant, the hour the armistice was signed…

Up here there is nothing. Minor repairs are made on the buildings—enough to evoke passing interest. Lecturers berate us for not showing more interest, and give exams in which they consider the most important courses in Medical school—their course…the mills keep on grinding…

Last Sunday I saw a pretty bad movie. I was tense and wanted a quick & inexpensive way to relax. "Coast Guard" I think.

What struck me, was not the ridiculous & very heroic rescues attributed to the dauntless heroes of our Coast Guard; but rather the theme of the flimsy story around which the impossible rescues were based. Because it wasn't the essential part of the story, it had to be what the audience would take for granted—or else they would think about the plot and not marvel at the Coast Guard.

I don't know whether you've been unlucky enough to see it. But in brief, it makes the point that the good, nice, sober, well-meaning, honest, likeable chap never gets to first base with the girl. He has all the noble virtues. But the dashing, selfish, egotistical, talented, smooth, hard, extrovert can't keep her out of his hair. The more he beats the little thing, apparently, the more she appreciates him.

It seems to me (not from this one silly movie), that most women are masochists at heart. They like to be beaten tho not necessarily, of course, physically. I'd like to read a really good psychoanalytical study of the problem. If true, it implies a great deal and removes a lot of the truth from our platitudes about "equality of the sexes", and with Herr Hitler puts the fair sex into the kitchen and bedroom where they can enjoy being dominated by their lords and masters. [And just as some men are more effeminate, all the way to the pervert; so some women would be more aggressive, incisive and dominant, displaying "masculine characteristics."] Schopenhauer and Nietzsche would be right!

Oh well. You're a woman. Tell me that I'm all wrong. My line of reasoning certainly got me to a very unsatisfactory conclusion—didn't it?

Saturday mornings, I'm the original early bird. So,

Good night dear
Aaron

Tuesday 8/17
12:00 midnight

Darling—

Good. I'm glad you've finally arranged for a trip to the wilds of New England. I've reserved 2 rooms in a respectable inn in Waltham, and paid for them, so you'd better come even if Sol has to go A.W.O.L. I'll send more details later.

It's gotten almost cold lately. Right now, I've closed my window and am seriously thinking of putting on a sweater; maybe winter has arrived without worrying too much about Fall.

An Obstetrics book would still be useful. I'm told by the prof that the Second Edition is an old one, tho still very good, and should sell for about $5. So act accordingly…

Now that's over with.

So you remember the time when I was taking Biochemistry and was so amazed at the terrific amount of analysis that went into Blood and Urine. Well, if I was amazed then, I ought to be thunderstruck now. I'm taking what amounts to a major course in Clinical Pathology—which resolves itself to "what you can learn from a patient's urine or blood." It's given by the magnificent Dr. Singer—and is probably the best course this year.

The whole point is really very simple. Both the urine and blood are products of the activity of the whole body. The urine, this which is formed by the kidney, is primarily an indicator of how the kidney is doing. Normally the kidney should be passing out all the dirt in the blood. If it doesn't, it's diseased. Normally it shouldn't be passing out albumin—if it does, it's diseased. But also, the urinary picture has been tied up with some other diseases, too. Sugar in the urine, eg, often means diabetes.

But the blood! Singer can look at a drop of your blood, I understand, and diagnose flat-feet. Seriously, it is reasonable, and has been found to be true, that pathology of almost any important organ will lead to some change in the blood picture: Hemoglobin %; number of red cells, shape of red cells, size of red cells; white cells; coagulability; sedimentation rate; sugar, Calcium, phosphorus, sodium, bicarbonate, bile pigment, urea, creatinine, cholesterol…levels. A drop of blood is very easy to get. Opening up the patient to look at his liver, gall bladder, or kidney is very dangerous. Therefore, the great avidity with which the Medical Profession has pursued this lead of finding out as much as possible from these easy sources. And then there is, of course, a lot you can learn from blood that you couldn't tell by even opening up and looking. The liver may not be working and will still look normal. But bile will accumulate in the blood and give it away.

Finally, using blood, a tremendous amount of diagnoses can be performed in the field of Infectious Diseases. The bacterium is fought by the body producing specific antibodies against the bug. They are in the blood. If the doctor finds these antibodies he knows what disease you have. Wasserman for example.

Do I rave!

Good night darling
Aaron

Thursday 8/18/13
5:15 pm

Gloria dear—

This will just be a brief note. As I don't know whether you're going to be here this week-end or not, I'll have to simply assume you're coming and send these directions out tonight, so you get them by Saturday morning.

Your rooms are reserved at the BUTLER HOUSE, Main St. Waltham (just where Bacon St. intersects Main). There are two rooms; for yourself and Sol.

I think it would be best to have you come to Waltham and meet me here. It'll give me a chance to go home, wash, dress and try to look presentable.

So, from your station ask directions for getting to Watertown. (It'll vary depending on whether you arrive at North or South Station). At Watertown Square (where the trolley will leave you) you take a bus to Waltham; 10 minute ride. Get off at Baron St. and walk to my house. It's a block and a half from Main. You'll have to go into a driveway to get into the house, it's off the main street. I'll be waiting there for you.

There, aren't these directions specific?

Actually I don't really believe you'll be here. Somehow I can't imagine Solly being too anxious to give up the week-end when he's so pressed, just to be a chaperone for his little sister. I know, I wouldn't do it.

I'm rushing this off dear,

Love Aaron

Wednesday 8/25/43
5:30 pm

Darling,

I wanted to write last night; but, at 2 am I just fell asleep. No accounting for bad habits. At any rate, it's lovely out now, crickets are chirping away like mad; and I'm very much in love with you…

I don't know whether I bothered to tell you that I loved you while you were up here. Probably I did without saying so. But I understand that women all like to be told. So now you know.

As I expected, the week-end just disappeared; didn't it? Where on earth does time go to when we're together?

It's a small town all right. Three or four of the boys wanted to know who you were; the proprietor of the little restaurant where I eat asked me about you; Mrs. Ellis confided her little machinations for staying out with her fiancé after 10 p.m., when her mother expected her to be at home.

So far I haven't had to apologize for Sol and Miriam.

Incidentally you might as well forget about the obstetrics book. I'll buy it up here one of these days.

Classes are rolling on as tho nothing had happened. You could just as well not have come for all the difference it made! Can you imagine!

Monday morning I went in for the Epidemiology exam. It wasn't difficult.

Morale is pretty low. Nobody seems to give a damn about anything. Today the Dean came back from vacation. His first step was to forbid all card playing on College grounds. Very important.

Yet some of the upper classmen are doing quite nicely. Three of our Juniors, you know, are at Brockton City Hospital. Dr. Singer told us today that one of the boys diagnosed a case from a blood smear a week ago, against the diagnosis of the Technicians and Doctors of the hospital. The patient died. At autopsy, it was found that the student was right. They are calling the boys the "Three Viennese Consultants" now. Probably sarcastically, but the incident couldn't help impressing. Singer was proud. He taught them their Hematology.

Now Singer is probably doubly determined to make us learn to interpret blood pictures. I hope he can teach me the art. After all, that is what makes the doctor. Making a slide and being able to read it. Not just knowing what the tests tell you, in a theoretical fashion, about it.

Medicine is after all a skill and an art. The science is the foundation for the doctor. But in his actual use of his tools which science has forged, he must above all be a highly trained and skillful technician.

Love,
Aaron

Friday 8/27
10:00 p.m.

Gloria dear—

Friday somehow is my day of lowest morale. It's when I feel that everything is for naught, that we're not going to be allowed to take state boards or practice, that I'll be financially unable to push it thru…Last Friday was an exception, of course. I was too busy thinking of more pleasant things to bother with the obviously unpleasant ones. Now, if you were to come up to see me every week, think of what that would do for my morale. It's practically your patriotic duty, you see.

By this time, I have some degree of perspective about Medicine, as seen from the vantage point of a second year medical student. As you know, the biggest course this year was Pathology—so my concept of medicine is probably swayed by the emphasis placed by the curriculum:

Etiology (bacteria, viruses, parasites, malnutrition, aging, heredity, unknown) leads to Pathological Lesions leads to Laboratory Symptoms, Clinical Symptoms, all of which are treated with Pharmacology, Surgery.

There's the story of how Medicine is approached. Nearly all my courses thru the first 2 years are included.

The story is somewhat like this:

The cause, <u>Etiology</u>, of disease can be of many types; very frequently the cause is a living organism. We therefore studied in some detail these organisms to understand how they make their living on people, and what damage they do. You remember about my intensive courses in Bacteriology and Pathology. The idea there was, what is known about the organism, what does it do in the body, and what means are currently available for fighting them (sulfanilamide, antitoxins, immunization…)

No matter what the etiology, (and often we don't know what it is), <u>Pathological Lesions</u> are produced in the body:-- weakening of the wall of the aorta, destruction of a part of the spinal cord, inflammation of the appendix, blocking up of the oviducts, defects in the heart valves, narrowing of arteries, ulcers of the stomach, tumors of all kinds…

These lesions, by interfering with the normal physiology of the body, produce the symptoms which make us aware of the disease. They may be symptoms which you can get by examining the patient:-- pain due to an ulcer, murmur of the heart due to a bum valve, shortness of breath and swelling of the legs due to heart failure, a hard lump due to cancer of the breast…Or they may produce changes which are only detected by the use of laboratory methods:-- sugar in the urine due to an atrophied or non-functioning pancreas, bile in the urine due to a plugged up bile duct, bacilli in the sputum due to lung tuberculosis…So we take Physical Diagnosis and Laboratory Diagnosis.

From the data, one makes a correct (?) diagnosis, and then proceeds to treat. Now, treatment is preferably against the causative factor:-- salvarsan in syphilis kills the spirochete; sulfanilamide in pneumonia, vitamin pills in deficiency cases, extirpation of the tumor which is pressing on a nerve…

Or the pathology may have to be treated:-- Digitalis to improve the force of the heart after some bacterium or virus has already damaged it; extirpation of the inflamed appendix,…

Finally, if nothing better can be done, the symptoms at least must be treated: Aspirin for fever, morphine for pain, Phenobarbital for insomnia, castor oil for indigestion,…

So the two tools are given in two courses, Pharmacology for the drugs, and Surgery.

There you are darling. If one realizes that a good working knowledge of normal Anatomy, Histology, and Physiology (with Biochemistry thrown in) is needed to start to understand the Pathology, you get the raison d'etre of the first year. And if you then add 2 good years of really applying this stuff in a hospital, you get the rest of the medical school courses.

So now, you have a complete survey of Medical School. Bored?

I've rambled on considerably, haven't I? If you ever find anything bothering you, about some of this technical material I write, just pass it on.

Good night, dear

Aaron

Wednesday 1:10 am

Gloria darling,

I've been trying, all night, to do a blood smear. By this hour, I'm convinced that I'm really meant for Psychiatry. And if I don't get one done right pretty soon, I'll be certain that I'll need a psychiatrist. Apparently I have the manual dexterity of an artichoke. Singer said that he taught an intern to do a good smear in 1 minute...Well, I've been at it considerably longer.

Oh well, now that that's off my chest, I can relax and write to you about very much nothing. My mind is pretty close to a total blank at this hour,-- as you know so well,-- so I can't write of anything that requires any thought at all. I'll think about what you said about getting married this November and try to give you my ideas on the subject. All I can think of right now is that it's a very good idea...

In any case, when are you coming up again? Now that you've been up to see me once, and nothing dreadful happened, you ought to be able to come up again. Preferably unchaperoned...

I'm practically asleep now—so I'll include some material from the <u>Intern</u> to take my place in regard to the Medicine I generally include.

Good night darling

Aaron

Sunday 9/5/43
12:30 pm

Hello dear:

I know that I've neglected you terribly this past week; somehow, I was just too sleepy to write, even unintelligibly, during the early morning hours when I finally decided to try to do so. You know that I'm really kind of fond of you, tho, and I'll probably make it up…

This morning I got up late, and apparently am doomed to one of those very sleepy days; one really can't sleep any more, but feels too tired to do anything very constructive either. There are innumerable things that I ought to do today, and tomorrow (we did get Labor Day off!)—but I'll probably loaf all day, feeling very guilty about it.

I had read the PM article. In fact, a great many of the students received the editorial, (neatly clipped out of the paper) from anxious friends and relatives. Nevertheless, it makes one feel very good to get them from you. It's a warm and comfortable feeling, to know that you are always thinking of what would interest me…As you said, the article was very favorably written, but unfortunately, will reach the wrong people. The Boston papers won't touch it with a 10 foot pole.

Your blood donation was very exciting, wasn't it? So far I haven't donated any, feeling that I'm just managing to hold my own. You don't need to dose yourself on liver, darling. It won't have any effect at all. Of course, if you like liver, that's different. Just eat your normal diet, and forget about your loss of blood. You lose quite a bit naturally, during menstruation, without taking any added precautions. Meat in general is valuable, to supply the Iron that you normally need for the manufacture of Hemoglobin.

We ought to seriously discuss getting married, even. Altho you could, I guess, hop a train some Monday morning and arrive in Mass.; it might be more convenient if we made some concrete plans a little in advance. It's just my very lethargic soul that hates to run around like mad at the last minute. But it will be much easier to talk about than write if we can get down to earth when we're together—and really talk sense. I know it's difficult. So try to come up for a three day weekend or something soon. Maybe, I can come in for one of the Jewish Holidays.

In any event think the thing thru, dear. The practical aspect. We can neglect the angle which bothers so many other people—the desirability of getting married to each other. But we do have to see our way clearly, of making a working arrangement of it in these times. It's a difficult and mature question; and one which will mostly fall on you. I'm trapped between exams, the draft board, necessity for paying my way, and the AMA.

All my love dear

Aaron

Wednesday 11:45 pm

Gloria darling:

Your pictures are very sweet; the one taken two years ago does look more sophisticated. It's just probably the angle or something. Anyway, did you take that fancy haircut you spoke about—or did you give in to pressure? I want to see the result—good or bad. And don't let your friends and relatives hold you down. If you want a – whatever you call it—go right to it!

So Italy is out of the war…Funny that there was very little stir up here about it. The only people who seemed at all excited were the radio commentators. The fact that Italy would soon capitulate seemed almost a foregone conclusion. My big question is, what will the United Nations do with Italy? Keep the King in power and supplant Badoglio with another Fascist? Or will they make a clean sweep of all those who have held any office during the past 25 years; forbid anyone having any affiliation with the Fascist party to run for office, , and then hold elections in a nice democratic fashion? I hope they do it my way, but I seriously doubt it. People are becoming less stupid; they might set up a Socialist state. And our State Dep't is not waging a war to put Socialism into Europe…

Whatever is done, in Italy and Germany, must do more than change those who at present head the gov't—if it's to be effective. All the little officials: local mayors, police commissioners, civil service…must be completely swept out, and kept out, if the country is to take on a new complexion.

I hope my prediction of the "shape of things to come" is just plain pessimism.

Of course, things are looking considerably brighter now in Europe and on the Russian front. Who knows?

Yesterday and tonight, I interspersed my Pathology with Sinclair Lewis's Elmer Gantry. I know that I shouldn't waste my time like this, but I couldn't resist. It's a second reading for me, as I went thru most of Sinclair Lewis's good stuff years ago. Be sure to read it, if you haven't already. Besides being a very entertaining work, there's a lot of powerful philosophy about people and institutions packed into it. That boy certainly had a real solid punch, once...Tonight, I put the book in Eddie's room, and he's not to return it for a while. My eternal weakness of not being able to stop doing anything I like until exhausted is still there. I'd read the book all night, and then continue tomorrow, until I finished. You'll have to keep an eye on me, to curb that natural impulse. Moderation being the acme of sensible living, it'll be up to you. With me, it's usually all or nothing. I just can't seem to quit and do something else.

Your stationery is very pretty, dear. I prefer it to the blue one. You can write more, and it's easier to read. I have no imagination; so I'll continue to use this paper.

Good night darling
Aaron

Monday 9/13
9:30 pm

Gloria darling—

I guess that I'm going to the devil, darling. Today I played hookey—all day. Not that I was going to study for an exam or anything. It's just that I succumbed to that failing—to keep going on something I like. From 9 to 11 I read, and partly understood, "Heart Failure" by a chap at Mount Sinai, Fishberg. Eddie said that I was crazy, I completely agreed, but I wanted to see whether I couldn't straighten out some of my very unclear ideas on the subject. I still don't know anything about it, but they can't say I didn't try. If I had a week, I'd read all of it. As is I'll spend tomorrow night copying the pictures I missed. Well, you'll just have to resign yourself to a second rate student. I suppose it was in me all along, but I never gave in to the impulse much.

Now you ought to remove my pictures from your desk, for my peace of mind. After all, it makes me very self conscious. Imagine being in a paper-weight!

Friday, during lunch hour I strolled along the Campus (which is very beautiful now) and tried to define what I meant by <u>a disease</u>. At that time I was all ready to write to you a thesis on the subject, but probably you're lucky that I was too sleepy to write Friday night. Actually I still don't know what a disease is, although we constantly throw around such terms as shock, cardiac failure, Emphysema, Pneumonia, Typhoid, Hepatitis…If I really ever discover what a disease is, I'll be sure to let you know.

Among the diseases affecting man at the present time (not including wars, poverty, and general insecurity) Heart Disease and Kidney Disease (Nephritis) cause more discomfort than most of the others put together. Because of that I'd really like to get a decent understanding of those two conditions. Interestingly enough, the same chap, Arthur Fishberg, wrote standard works on the heart (<u>Heart Failure</u>) and on the kidney (<u>Hypertension</u> & <u>Nephritis</u>). I suppose that, since these conditions are what the clinician meets so frequently, and <u>treats</u> for a long period of time in each case that a lot of information has been accumulated. After all, when you find a Cancer or tumor, it's a job for the surgeon. In these cases it's up to the internal medicine man. He has to keep the patient alive and comfortable for as long as possible, using whatever drugs and prescriptions he has, while the underlying disease gets progressively worse until the patient finally succumbs. A tremendous amount of information is therefore available about clinical results, post mortem studies…

Someday I hope to be able to get thru both of these books, and to get some understanding. Tho I'll need to do a lot more than just read two volumes, I'm afraid.

And I thought that I wasn't going to write about medicine tonight.

Good night dear,
Aaron

Wednesday 9/15
12:30 am

Gloria darling:

You're apparently having a lot of trouble keeping track of your friend's difficulties, aren't you? But don't let it get you down. Somehow they'll all continue. After all, no problems would make things awfully dull, wouldn't it.

Last night there was a meeting held of the student body. We all, or a lot of us, went down to our Boston building, and were addressed by all the important elements of the administration. It was a pretty good show. They should have charged admission.

First the Dean spoke. We were supposed to have submitted questions to him during last week, and he was going to answer. Well, he told us nothing we didn't pretty well know already. In brief, the school, as you know, has until July 1944 to stay around. Until that date, the State can't "disapprove" the school, unless they ask them for approval on that date. The graduates who are not O.K come up for State Boards, and if nothing has happened by then, the State must make a decision as to the approval of the school, whether the school asks for it or not. If the school is turned down, and the graduates not allowed to take the Boards, they (or the school) can bring the case to court for a review of the decision. If it sticks, the school presumably closes…

Requirements for approval were listed. They were pretty stiff:

1. A good dean; (this was before Rushmore came here. Apparently it was his idea that the school needed a good Dean).
2. A library—the ridiculously inadequate library was closed last semester; about $1500 worth of books bought; 40 periodicals are now coming in; and the library is housed

in a large, pretty nice room of the administration wing. A real librarian was hired at that time who is good. (A refugee who has a Ph.D. in History of Medicine and was a Medical Librarian in Vienna or thereabouts.) But, the library is still very inadequate. Plans call for converting a barn on the Campus to the new library, and buying books.

3. More and better staff. Men have been hired, to wit our present refugee faculty. Still inadequate.
4. An endowment. They don't have a permanent endowment. The school is at present completely in the hands of the Board of Trustees (Rushmore, the former owner, Dr. Smith, is completely out of the picture. It is now a non-profit institution; which is running by meeting all bills out of tuition income. There are two small mortgages held by banks, which are in a good state of financing. The only kind of an endowment that they can hope to get in time, is a "living endowment." That is, donations, contributions from the students, alumni; trustees…to get the school approved. Once it's rolling, permanent endowment will probably come in.
5. Adequate Clinical Facilities in the Upper Two Years. There has been no clinical instruction in Middlesex so far. Boys went out on "clerkships" and picked up what they could. That situation is, in the eyes of the approving authority, completely impossible. Right now we have some working arrangement with two small Grade A hospitals in the vicinity for Clinical Instruction: Brockton City Hospital and Chelsea Memorial Hospital. There are a half dozen juniors there now, on a trial period. As of next year we "expect" that the doctors at these hospitals will be added to our faculty and be put on the payroll. Even so, those two small hospitals are inadequate for even the Coming seniors, let alone us, as Juniors. We "expect" further clinical facilities by that time, so that the whole senior class will get adequate instruction. That means adding 25-40 clinical profs to the faculty. Apparently

> nothing, tho, for our class—even being "expected." Negotiations are going on, but after all…

Rushmore didn't say all that. Rather, he was followed by Dr. Miller, the treasurer of the school, and active trustees. A really good speaker. Should have gone in for the clergy. He gave most of the information. He also spent a lot of time convincing us that since last year, when Smith was kicked out, we've had a new dean, everybody's pulling together, nobody (including Mr. Miller) is making anything out of us, and it was "unthinkable" that our efforts shouldn't be concerned with success (AMEN!). He pointed to the transformation (now going on) of the old library, to a lunch-and-locker room; the remodeling of another small building (now going on) into research laboratories for three of our good refugee profs, and the remodeling of the plumbing system of our whole school (now going on) costing $20,000.

Then other men reiterated. The representative of a law firm, that the school Parents Organization just retained ($5,000/40); the head of our alumni association, who is also superintendent of Chelsea Memorial Hospital, and who told us that he has $50,000 raised by the alumni, earmarked for clinical salaries; the Chairman of our Parents Association…

They're requesting $100 per student, at the minimum, to carry on this program…

To sum up, I think they're trying, but as you can see behind the brave words, they're not getting anyplace. We'll probably be there in July if the Army doesn't get us sooner. What do you think I ought to try next?

I miss you very much darling. How about coming up? Exams are October 23-30. Vacation Nov 1-Dec 1

Good night dear.

Love
Aaron

Wednesday 9/22
10:30 pm

Gloria dear—

I thought that I might write to you early tonight. If I wait until much later, you'll be out another letter; the spirit is willing…

There is so much to learn. If I were a genius, and could do without eating or sleeping, I think I could really learn a lot. As is, I'm just scratching the surface. They certainly have accumulated a lot of information since the first medicine man mixed his first witch's brew. The only saving feature is that it all ties in. Really nothing that you learn in one course, is not applicable to, and depends upon, the stuff they teach in another.

You're having quite a time now, aren't you? Moving to another apartment, living in a hotel…I'm not quite sure just what the arrangement is going to be. What hotel are you staying at? I was kind of thinking of coming in to New York for one of the Jewish Holidays (no promises). There won't be any fun having to see you in a hotel lobby! You know that I'm a kind of bashful chap. Also my mother would be a little upset if I spent the saved days riding around on subways. Not so good. Not so good. At any rate, I'll let you know my plans later. Actually, all the arguments (the good ones) point to my staying up here. I shouldn't miss 2 days of good lectures; I should study, particularly with finals so close; I should work in the market and make money; and I shouldn't spend my tuition savings on bus fares. However I'd like to see my family. And incidentally, I'd like to see you, too. If I can't spend 18 out of the 24 hours with you when I come in; I don't think I'll bother…

While studying the devious intricacies of blood cells in obvious diseases, I'm also trying to plan my approach to next semester. Problems galore. I need to find a place to live in Boston. Not only are places hard to find, I hear, but very expensive. My requirements are a neat little room, very quiet, warm, well-lit, cooking facilities, private bath if possible, charming landlady, across the street from school—for nothing a week. You see my tastes are getting more aristocratic.

Also I have to find another job. Since we'll have Saturday classes, this one day affair is over; and I hate like-the-devil to put in 3-4 days a week working late at night, for the same salary.

Finally I have to earn money during vacation month, too. Lots of it. To do that I ought to find a job. Since I want to be in New York at the same time, and the job I can find is in Waltham…

Did you ever hear of the white rat that was driven nuts by being forced into a position of choosing between difficult alternatives?

Besides all this I'm supposed to cram in 8 courses, pass the finals, one-a-day for 8 days or so; and worry about recognition. Maybe I'll start drinking or something equally naughty.

Now, I'll drag Eddie out for some coffee and try to make a night of it.

Until later dear

Love
Aaron

Friday 9/24
11:35

Darling:

Another week-end has arrived. I'd give a lot to make the weeks a little longer and the weekends shorter. Tho I've said this time and again; it has become inconceivable to me that time is really rushing by me so quickly. I have so much to do—and really so little time to do it in. I remember reading that phrase many times; I never thought that I'd be writing it, and really meaning it. If I had you with me, and could talk to you instead of writing letters, think of all the time I could save! There's an excellent reason for our getting married, I think…

So you know, I'm getting fat! For the first time in my life I'm beginning to think in terms of losing weight instead of gaining the precious avoirdupois. It's either Mass. air; Medical School; or my getting older, and with age, adiposity. It certainly isn't the food. My Lord! If Waltham air is putting girth on me, what will it do to you? We'll be just two little roly-polies. But at that I draw the line. As soon as I'm out of this terrific struggle to learn in 3 years of 5 nights a week, what is difficult enough in 4 years of 7 nights a week, I'll start Tennis, handball, hiking, swimming…And regain my erstwhile leanness. Anyhow, I'm a male.

But as for you, I demand a sylph like figure. After all, that's one of the disadvantages of having two X chromosomes—starvation, and also menstruation.

A few days ago I went to see Coney Island. I was all ready to pick out my house. But the picture was as complete a farce as was ever perpetrated on the great American public. Coney Island my eye. There's a song in it someplace about "Coney Island, Beautiful Coney Island, Nestling among the waves"—or something. And you know what I think about Coney. I was tempted to let the audience know what the "Showplace of the Nation" really is like. You know—the hinterland of this country, must now have a very queer idea, about my place of domicile. Oh well, they have plenty of queer ideas about lots of things.

I've arranged to come in to see you for the Rosh Hashana holidays—we'll get to New York sometimes Wednesday night, as I'm going in by car with one of the students. As I don't know exactly when we'll arrive, I'll call you at your home when we pull in, and meet you right afterwards. School was unofficially called off for the 4 day week-end.

This is against all my better judgment. Actually, as you know I should stay here, but…

I'm not giving up, darling. I still insist that you will have to achieve the personal security which will allow you to make a trip to see me dependent solely upon your desires…

Until I see you dear

Love
Aaron

Sunday 8:00 pm

Darling:

These are the last flowers of the year. Mrs. Ellis brought them up for me, thinking that you'd like to live in Waltham where flowers still grow.

All my love
Aaron

Friday, 10/9
10:30 pm

Gloria darling:

It's a little difficult to realize that a whole week has practically gone by. I'm back in Wells' "Time Machine" seeing the days go blurring by.

Your letters have been very sweet and warm. Maybe I'm getting more prejudiced, but I think they're even getting better. Maybe you'll write that great play we've talked about. That would be very nice.

Waltham has been having weather. Good weather and bad weather with a pretty low average. Everybody who is anybody has a cold, and I feel one coming on. Well, it's about time. It's quite nice out now, tho, so I've been thinking how nice it would be to have you around. We could go walking off into the darkness of Waltham and not embarrass anyone by our frequent pauses for refreshment.

Today's news was good on all fronts, one of the boys pointed out: the Russians crossed the Juniper; the Allies gained in Italy; and the Yankees beat the Cardinals. "God's in His Heaven…" All we needed was to be recognized and all would have been just fine.

Come to think of it, my trip to New York cost you a lot of money. Your Saturday afternoon's "absence without leave"…Yet, I suppose it was still considerably cheaper than your trip to Waltham. I guess we can't have everything…No matter what you do, it costs money. Silly stuff…

I'm sorry that Eleanor couldn't catch us Saturday—but I'm also certain that I'd have found some excuse for not being able to make a "double-date" of it. Try to explain to her that I don't travel 250 miles to see her and respective boyfriend, despite their very fine personalities. Why can't people be smart and realize that we want to be alone? Oh well, as soon as we get the drive of needing to be together all the time out of our system, we'll need entertainment, and will feel very annoyed with the people we know who want to be left alone.

I'm working at the market this week-end, and eating very normally. It's the first time that I've not observed these holidays in some degree. Nor do I feel very much about it. There is very little up here to bring back any of the feelings that would normally go with Yom Kippur and Kol Nidre. A great deal of our religious feeling apparently depends upon conditioned reflexes; the proper stimulus bringing about a certain emotional set up as its response. The stimulus is not here; the response is practically nil. I am sorry tho that I'm not able to stay home tomorrow and study. Finals approach ominously.

Good night darling,
Aaron

Wednesday
4:00 pm

Gloria dear—

No, darling; nothing happened during my 25th birthday—or on Columbus Day. I've been fighting a cold and trying to study at the same time. So far I'm not so sure what's winning; certainly my studies lose out in any event. The beautiful weather we've had during the past 2 days, has helped, tho.

That distressing incident you wrote about last week was very interesting. Do you remember? Some female star-lodger angrily demanding that you leave the bathroom! Significant was that you were very hurt by the experience; so much so that you even cried…

Now, that is something that you're going to face more-and-more, probably. And like myself, you're not going to enjoy it. In brief, most people are not interested in us; don't like us; don't want to like us; and want to be as comfortable as possible in spite of us. That is a very hard thing to believe emotionally. Easily enough, said. We just instinctively want people to smile when they talk to us, and feel terrible when they sincerely frown. Practically nobody can stand being insulted without getting excited.

What does it all boil down to? We're like kids who are very insecure in their own self sufficiency to take care of themselves, and in this constant fear (anxiety) continue by every possible means to get others, stronger ones, to "like them" and take responsibility for them. By being kind, sweet, and most of all helpless, the little child can get the tolerant smile of the adults he meets.

You and I, and most of our friends are still trying to keep people liking us, very much; and when they obviously don't—beyond all possibility of rationalization—we're hurt.

We'd be in a better position, probably, if we didn't really care. If we;-- "knew ourselves"; knew which people we liked; knew our goals; our rights; and lived by them without being unduly concerned about what others thought or felt—except insofar as our actions interfered with our ethical code of "Do unto others…"

This kind of person would not be emotionally moved by someone else's annoyance. Would do what is most appropriate at the time, and if necessary arouse even more annoyance.

In your instance (petty as the example is in this philosophical treatise)—you could decide rapidly who was right; whether serving your convenience (if you were right) wouldn't possibly make it more inconvenient later, because of the enmity aroused—and then to either tell the lady to "Go to Hell", or dash out apologetically. In either case, with no emotion involved on your part. [this is way beyond my capacity tho]

I wrote once, I think, that when you can tell somebody to "Go to Hell" and really mean it; and not feel much emotion—you've achieved something. You don't, at that point, have that need for people to like you…

My Lord, look what I got into this time.

I love you very much darling. But have to get back to work.

Aaron

Friday 10/15

9:45 pm

Hello darling—

Last night I didn't get to bed until past 2, so right now I feel kind of sleepy. Just a little you understand. I think I could almost fall asleep standing. Are we sissies!

Finals start next Friday, Oct. 20. They run Friday thru the following Saturday. Gosh. I'm pretty sure I won't flunk any courses this year, but I won't pass any too high; there is so much to know and I didn't have time to learn it…Anyhow, you'll love me anyhow, won't you?

The typical end-term rumors are floating around again. Won't we ever learn to stop giving ourselves injections of hope, only to get a terrific reaction at the let-down. There are all kinds. Everything that anybody says is passed around, magnified, and distorted. Every possible angle which looks favorable is worked over as the students gather in knots during lab and lunch hour, after school…Nothing different. The same thing has been occurring for years. And always, as during the past two years we know so well, nothing at all really has formed. There is talk going around now about our not going to Boston next year, but staying on in Waltham. Speculation runs mad. Other rumors deny it, and insist from "unimpeachable sources" that the first rumor is nonsense. Others say, the program is to be split—part Boston, part Waltham. The Dean refuses to comment. So there you are. We don't even know where we're going to live next year, if rumors mean anything.

But since rumors so far, good or bad, have generally been total busts at the end, you can see what we're up against. Certainly no lack of interesting topics for discussion. I have no doubt that next year, we—the junior class—will be taking our 21 lectures a week in the same Newbury street Building in Boston; while the seniors will get some, inadequate clinical instruction. Even that is a step forward, as Middlesex students heretofore never got any kind of official clinical instruction. At most, they received clerkships, where a kind doctor told them something.

I pass on the rumors, to give you some picture of the turmoil that is Middlesex Medical School. Actually it would be really much easier to talk about the ever present "latest rumor," have no end of excitement thinking out its possibilities, if you were close enough to talk to. As is, I have to write them down.

Really darling, any kind of a birthday gift will do. "It's not the present…" If you want to send me slippers, do so by all means. My size is 7 ½. Don't you think you're pushing the pipe and slippers motif a bit early, tho. Really, I'm only 25!

What you wrote about religion ties in pretty closely with my comments on adults acting very much like children in needing the security of those he thinks are stronger. In religion we see another aspect of the same thing. It's a definite need to be able to get on the good side of someone strong and big (father?) who will solve our problems: being a son back home safely, cure a sick child, having a better job…Also there is the superstition (fear) of the possibility of Hell. Prayer is a little insurance. Finally, the social implications of not being a respectable Joe…

Good night darling
Aaron

Tuesday 10/19
1:00 am

Darling—

Once I get beyond 10:30 or 11:00 o'clock I can stay up pretty late—particularly if I don't try to think too hard. It's getting by that sleepy period that's so hard. Eddie has been up till 4 or so every night—he's taking Mid-Years this week—so that the example has kept me up somewhat over my bed time. There's so much to know. And I just can't get my teeth into it all…

Right now, I'd give a great deal to be able to hold onto you, talk to you, and make love to you…But as with all things, the things we seem to want most, are so difficult to get. I'll come in to New York if it's at all feasible, Darling. Really, I want to see you a great deal.

Sometimes I feel a little lower than usual, and wonder what it's all about. Am I really learning Medicine as I study the Pathology

Text; will I graduate; will I be able to practice;… I "love" the stuff; in a sense. It's an interesting way of spending time. But the terrific grind would be easier with a purpose.

This year I'm weakening. I'll not go into work this week-end, and probably not the next either. We have finals on Friday and Saturday of both those week-ends. I'm just becoming a sissy. Yet I really ought to be more cautious of throwing my potential earnings away like that. So far we've gotten no word about that $200 loan coming thru, and I don't know anything about next year; living; job…But the site of piles of notes to be gone thru for 8 exams thru me into a bit of a panic, and I succumbed—as usual to the immediate necessity; letting future contingencies go. Very bad.

Your week-end was pretty active—and very nice. Only I should have been along (modest little fellow-- no?). Seriously, your getting out to the ballet and to lectures will do no harm at all. And if you decide to lead a group at the settlement—do so. I'll love you just as much whether you do or not. The experience, if it's a new one, might be interesting and valuable, tho. Who knows, you may have hidden talents!

As the night goes on, you can see, that my ideas get hazier and hazier. That's why I generally stop studying pretty early. From this letter, you probably can see that it's a very good idea for me to be in bed by 10:30. But then it just wouldn't be cricket to do that. I'll feel awful if I flunked an examination without even staying up late.

Anyhow, the consoling fact of these next two weeks is that they will pass. How, I don't know—but they will.

Incidentally—is my semi-lettered script any more legible? I adopted it when I couldn't read my own handwriting any more.

Good night dear,
Aaron

Friday 10/22
2:00 pm

Gloria dear—

Two down—1 to go. Wednesday afternoon we had our practical exam in Laboratory Diagnosis, where Dr. Singer found out whether or not my playing with blood and urine finally got me anywhere. It was all very simple: Each student received 1 cc of blood in a little bottle and had to go thru the routine analysis of Red Count, White Cell Count, Hemoglobin determination, and Color Index. What with the limitation on time, the coldness of the weather, nervousness…Then we received a urine sediment to read and report findings: pus cells, crystals, bacteria…Thirdly we got a stained slide and told to make a differential count of the white cells. Finally we were to pick a neighbor and make a smear ourselves, stain it, mount it, and hand it in. We had 3 hours. All in all, it is of course the routine things that every intern must do. When we were thru, I was tired.

This morning it was Pathology. I'm still tired. I'd like to put my head on your bosom, and sink as far deep into you as possible. But 'til I can do that, I'll have to go on wishing for you…

Your choice of presents was charming. The items and the thought. In fact, your taste is so adequate that I'm completely resigned to your buying my clothes…for me. When Eddie, Joe, and Mrs. Ellis saw the pipe and slippers they said that I was a marked man. But then I like being "marked" if you're doing the shooting—so everybody's happy.

So far we've heard nothing about next year. Tomorrow the Dean is making some announcement. I believe he'll tell us to go get rooms in Boston during the coming week, as "He's still working on something." Or something to that effect.

So you know—as of Wednesday we walked out of our last laboratory period in Medical School? Assuming I pass finals, and the school keeps on running, I'm thru with my so-called "undergraduate medical school days." No more microscopic work, animal experiments…Either we get clinical training from now on—or we just get lectures.

I can put my lab coats away and return my microscope. In a grade A school I'd be looking forward to the next 2 yrs. of clinics where I can really apply what the theoretical courses taught me. Here I'm sorry to leave the labs. Just lectures will be a terrific bore.

Actually, I learnt more from our laboratory courses—inadequate as they may be—than from all the lectures which were so profusely poured at me.

Until later darling

I love you very much.
Aaron

Wednesday 4:00 pm

Hello dear:

The days are passing apace. I'm making very good (or at least, intensive) use of the pipe and slippers. I parade around all day muttering all sorts of gibberish about babies being born, how much to feed a 3 mo. old at each feeding, the average adult dose of Acetyl B-methylcholine, 6 liver function tests for differentiating between intra-hepatic or extra-hepatic jaundice, the pathology of Weil's disease, the functions of a Public Health Department; what to do in a Typhoid epidemic; how to treat a second degree burn…I'm so dizzy that if they push the wrong button on the exam, they'll get a swell answer for a totally different course! Did you ever feel like a sponge? Well, now I can sympathize with the poor things. Sopping up all you can hold, giving out, then sopping up again; Ouch…

The weather should have told you that I'll be in for vacation. You can expect me at our usual Rendezvous—the Capital Terminal—Sunday night. I don't have my ticket yet, so if I can't make it for some reason you'll get a special delivery or air mail. To make things more interesting, we won't be going back by Dec. 1. I'm becoming more fatalistic every day. Look at the newspapers for me, darling. I want to go out and get a suitable job right away. Remember, my conscience is going to bother me considerably if I can't get one—as I'm going to tell the manager of the Super Market tomorrow that I can't work for him next month, having some very urgent business in New York.

The way I feel now, all I want to do is go someplace where it's quiet, with good merit, nice pictures, soft lights and you (like Omar Khayam, no?) By Sunday, I'll be absolutely desperate.

I'm enclosing two Interne excerpts. Both are pretty good. They are not for broadcast, tho, as other people might not understand what is taken for granted by the Medical Profession…

Until Sunday, darling

Love

On second thought, I'll only enclose the article on "Female Strategy". "How to do a Pelvic" will go to New York by courier.

Monday 9:20 pm

Gloria darling:

Well I'm here, dear…I miss you terribly…I've said that before in letters, I'm sure, but the intensity was never as great, or the need as strong as it is now. Probably adversity brings with it the awful, haunting quest for security, somewhere, anywheres. And the arms and bosoms of those we love, are very potent refuges. I wish you were here, darling; and yet it would probably be even worse to try to give you the warmth and security in me that you deserve when I'm so insecure and shaken myself…

Joe got us a pretty nice double room. It is called the "penthouse" euphemistically—or the attic I guess. It's a huge place, lots of windows and a wonderful view. We're alone on the 5th floor of a large rooming house in a pretty snazzy section, pay $10 a week for it, and have no cooking privileges. Probably, it will be a temporary set-up. Very temporary. The news at school is black. Even worse than we thought. It looks almost positive that we'll be dropped and the school closed by the end of this year. Altho Hershey hasn't apparently given any reply to Rushmore as yet, he is not looking with favor upon our plea. Apparently, the AMA has notified him that we will definitely not be allowed to take State Boards. So legal technicalities are not impressing him particularly.

The set up at school is like a ghastly comedy of some kind. It's the worst I've seen since coming here. We sit in a small lecture hall and physicians, who are very unimpressive, come in and talk very uninspiringly about a lot of rubbish. Our first two years was like Bellevue compared to this stuff. Particularly now, it looks ghoulish…

Living costs are very high. So far I haven't done anything about looking for a job. I'll have to snap out of it and do something about it by the week-end.

Good stuff; no? I really want to write to you, in a more cheerful vein; but it just won't come out any other way. My pen seems to write along almost without my volition. You'll have to accept my outburst as a necessary release to one who will understand.

Do you know darling, I've been feeling all day, just as tho it were before breakfast…

It's going to be a little difficult getting adjusted to live with someone. Actually, this is my first experience of sharing living quarters with anyone but my family. But probably it'll be over pretty soon.

I'm dreadfully sorry you're mixed up in my mess, darling. Very deeply runs the need in me to make you happy; not frustrated and sad. My fatalism is growing. And dangerously so. Don't let it get you. I'm beginning to feel that there is little in store for me but frustration…It's a terrible feeling, dear. Don't let it get you, darling.

I love you very much,
Aaron

Thursday 12/9
10:30 pm

Darling:

Joe and I have just gone over a case history we picked up; it was very interesting mental gymnastics. I think you'd like it. It's almost like doing cross-word puzzles. You remember, don't you? They give all the symptoms, and you try to answer the $64 question"—"What is it?" Even tho both you and the Doctor giving the case, don't get within miles of the right answer, it is very interesting mental exercise—probably for both of us.

So far I haven't gotten into a routine yet. The situation isn't one which lends itself to routine very readily, you know.

On Tuesday I went over to Waltham to pick up my books from the Ellis's. A sophomore that I met in Waltham had a car and brought my books in for me. Nice, no? Not everyone is a louse, apparently. At any rate, Mr. Ellis did have pneumonia. Do you remember that I diagnosed his case as pneumonia, and then my prof said it was pleurisy. Well, is Mrs. Ellis impressed now! You ought to be proud of me. I'm better than my teacher's stuff already (Tsk, Tsk)!

Maybe I would have made a good Doctor…

But the finale is approaching rapidly. Yesterday we learnt that the Army has stopped granting Commissions to Graduates of Grade B schools—even if they took and passed State Boards. There goes our very excuse for being; our "raison d'etre." Nice stuff… Hershey issued a statement today that several hundred thousand men would have to come from 2A classification—and I guess we are among that little group.

So far I haven't found a job yet. I've looked in several places, but find that like all ads, the Help Wanted ads, are a gross exaggeration. The jobs aren't nearly as desirable as they say. I begin to realize too that I don't know anything useful. I may possibly be a nice guy, sterling character and all that, but I don't have any useful skills to sell. (At least you are a useful citizen—and know something). It won't be very nice, after the war, to try to find work with the same lack of skills. But…

What are you doing with yourself darling? Do you play with little kids in the settlement house. And is your fur coat on the way?

Good night dear,
Aaron

Tuesday, Dec. 14
7 pm

Gloria darling:

I'm alone now so I'll try to type this letter; Joe won't stand for my pecking away while he's trying to listen to the radio or reading a Reader's Digest.

Your letters are coming regularly, and are finding a very appreciative audience. You understand without my writing very much about it how much I want them. You can type them at the office if you like, but somehow they can't be quite as satisfactory as a personal, written one that you compose at home. In any event, finding letters from you waiting for me when I get home from school is a bright ray in an otherwise awfully dismal day.

The situation is as atrocious as ever, dear. I guess it's going to get worse rather than better. I was a little startled when you wrote that I had already been at school a WEEK. I still can't believe that I was in New York, kissing you good night only a few days ago. As we've noticed before, a multiplicity of new experiences rushes one along the present tense, and feels like a million years in the past. The school situation is—No news. Whatever that means.

So far I have heard nothing from my draft board—ominous sign. A few fellows in my class, and about 15 in the sophomore class were reclassified to 1A. Study is out of the question. We've gone over a few case histories which we found interesting but so far have done no original studying at all. I am completely demoralized, I guess. The thought of opening a Pathology book and memorizing the histological picture of Influenza horrifies me. And everyone else in my class too, probably.

Joe has a very good friend who just graduated from our school and is interning in a small hospital in the vicinity. He has been going over pretty regularly in his free time, and taken around by the visiting men who think that he is just another doctor. Very interesting. But I want a little glimmer to hang on to before I can put forth any real effort. It's almost remarkable what a goal—any goal will bring out. While I was feeling that the clouds were breaking and that I was going to be a doctor willy nilly, effort not only meant nothing, it was actually keenly enjoyable. It's good to put forward effort and feel that you're winning the fight. But now, I just don't seem to give a damn. Possibly, I'll get over it if the situation lasts long enough. Work, any kind of work, feels annoying. Wow—some state of mind…

Last week-end I worked as a busboy in a restaurant-night club nearby: Friday, Saturday, Sunday. Earnings were low; meals fair, work not difficult but extremely boring and distasteful. (imagine!) I don't like the idea of doing this for the next year, but probably I won't have to much longer. You know just what I did so I won't have to give you a description of my duties and obligations on this job—I guess.

Now that you're earning so much money, I will have to propose to you. After all, you are becoming worth marrying now. But don't you start snubbing me just because we are now almost in the upper bracket income tax payers.

This afternoon we were off at 2 o'clock, and I went to see Crazy House—pretty fair entertainment for Boston. It'll furnish a couple of laughs if you go to see it. Don't expect much tho.

There's a meeting at the school tonight—at which we'll probably get some more rotten news plus an appeal for funds. I'll go over since we live only a few minutes away.

By the way, I don't know exactly when Solly is being confirmed, but it's probably this weekend. I won't be in. If you have the time, you might drop over for a few minutes to offer our felicitations or something.

Good night darling,
Aaron

Friday 1:10 a.m.

Gloria darling:

There is certainly something psychic about us; a few days ago I wrote saying that I preferred your letters written at home, bringing me a more intimate experience; and even before you could get it, you write to me that way. (Now don't come back with that crack about "anticipating my every wish.")

It's kind of tough having everyone at home sick. You remember my brothers were ill last month, and I was right in the middle of a very upset household. My professor of Medicine, who has a very active practice, is constantly telling us that he fears a bona fide flu epidemic. I'm not so sure whether he fears it, or would welcome it, as medicine men are far more interested in the money and importance a situation gives them than the amount of misery it would cause. This chap, Dr. Levinson, is young, tho, comparatively highly intelligent, and very busy anyway. So he might not be so guilty. But the chap who teaches us "Chest Diseases", and our "Dermatologist" bewail the decrease in Tuberculosis, and the comparative lessening of violence of the Trepanema pallidum of syphilis.

Perhaps my cynical bitterness about the medicos is a product of frustrated hopes and sour grapes; in another situation I might see the noble part that is medicine.

As you know, I bussed at the High Hat last week-end, and got practically no sleep at all. On Wednesday I spent the evening getting a Christmas job at the Boston Post Office, and worked yesterday and today. So you see, I am pretty busy. Not in the way I want to be, but busy none the less. Living is very high out here, and I can't regulate life quite as rigidly for Joe & myself, as I did alone. And without almost military routine, my cost of living soared.

Probably it'll make little difference. I'm about certain that Hershey's position will be that "he'll leave it up to the local Boards." Thereby sidestepping the hot issue, and passing the buck. We'll know what the local Boards will do.

As far as studies go—I haven't even bought my books; nor has Joe received his...If we stay, I can pretty easily catch up, I think (providing I get work to take care of my expenses which won't be too time consuming): if not...

Darling, I want you pretty badly. The situation is such that I can give you very little, but I'm selfish enough to want to hold you close enough to almost assimilate you...

I'll go to sleep now; tomorrow we have classes 'till 12, and then I'll work as long as they let me.

Good night dear,
Aaron

Monday 1:30 a.m.

Gloria darling—

I've just come home from 6 hours of being bored to death in the Post Office; Joe is fast asleep; even the alarm clock can't be heard…Your letter was waiting for me when I got in; we're both victims of "Postal inefficiency"…I love you very much darling; want you with me very intensely; and we can get married, as soon as either we grow big enough to tackle the rotten situation, or the situation gets small enough for us to tackle. I'm totally helpless in improving the situation…

Yesterday, Joe, I, and another chap in my class, Jerry Weinstein were day-dreaming out loud. Or at least Jerry was dreaming, Joe was agreeing, and I was trying to punch holes in the air castle.

Jerry was thinking about China. China has asked for doctors, apparently any kind, to come and live there during the present and post war period, probably indefinitely, on a governmental salary, to practice the sorely needed medicine. Jerry felt that he could be very happy in China, for the rest of his life. Not alone of course. His wife, Shirley (who is going to be his wife, soon) has already agreed, so she'd be along; and he'd also need 4-5 other compatible men to go along and form a white, American nucleus amidst the "Barbarians." He doesn't expect to, or want to be assimilated in China. He wants to retain his identity as a White, American. But he feels that all one has anywheres, in China or Brownsville, is a small group of friends; the other people, even tho they speak your language, are not part of your personal life at all…The 5 intimate friends in China, together with a chance to really practice medicine, and to live decently with his wife and children would be a good life…

In Massachusetts, as a Grade B doctor, and a Jewish one, you are not only an outsider, but an intruder. You're not wanted. In China, Jerry feels, you are an outsider, too, but are wanted very much, and would be accepted as a good, sincere, responsible individual.

In China, Jerry feels, there would be advantages, which even an ethical AMA practice on Ocean Parkway, wouldn't equal. The chance would be present to feel that you are really doing something constructive; that you are helping to build; that you could practice medicine, in other words, the way he would like to practice it. In Brooklyn, you are primarily a small entrepreneur who must develop a good sales talk; you sell medicine, or a reasonable facsimile thereof; you take no responsibility unless absolutely necessary for fear of losing a customer; you stick to the traditional, because it has apparently sold very well for years; you engage in the same "ethical competition" as the grocer on the corner; and you live a harassed life trying to keep up the trappings of your social position, "___M.D."

There you are, darling, the eternal search for Shangri-la. My objections seemed rather feeble against the enthusiasm which the Utopia brought forth. Can you give me some brilliant & mature thoughts on the matter? Don't worry; the whole thing is very academic, but it made a swell evening. The three of us, in our big room, coffee brewing, pipes and cigarettes going, and Spaldings' rendition of the Beethoven Concerto as a prelude…

I should have gone to work Sunday night, but didn't…

As to Christmas. We're off on Friday, and have 9 days; 'till Jan. 3. I want to come in…, but there are a lot of reasons for my staying here and working during that time. So many reasons that my head whirls as I try to brush them all off. (Now don't offer to sell any of your bonds for me!)

There is really only one reason for my going in to N.Y.—you. I want you, and need you. I feel kind of starved.

So I'll see what shapes up by Thursday & let you know. Probably, I'll compromise, as usual. But don't count on it. You'd save me a lot of headache, if you'd come up here for 4-5 days. You could even have one of those gorgeous rooms. The boys are leaving for the week…

It's terribly late now, dear.

Good night.

Love
Aaron

(So far no news of any kind at school. We're marking time…)

Tuesday 12/30
4:00 p.m.

Darling:

Now you know why you didn't hear from me. But it's the only one I misaddressed.

The meeting was as I expected. The administration promises to do something.

I'll call you Friday night between 9-11 p.m. if I can get to a phone.

Better send me your number, tho.

Love
Aaron

1944

Tuesday 1/4
2:30 p.m.

Gloria darling—

You're right. It is snowing and blowing up here now. But not last night or during my ride in to Boston. In fact, I was so sleepy, or so used to the trip by now, that I slept most of the way in, 7 of the 8 hours. We're back at the silly routine again: lectures, lectures & more lectures. But such poor ones! We have a few profs with an I.Q. of 90-110—and it's a relief to even hear them. A really good man would kill me.

But Gideon Trimmer the student who saw you off on the BMT Sunday night is not typical of students—even Middlesex students. So although, I still don't have any love for the profession, it's not as bad as all that. Actually he was in my class last year and flunked out, so he's repeating the second year. His draft board is not too keen on the idea and is going to induct him no matter what happens to the school. So don't take him as typical of the medicos.

Nevertheless his information is essentially accurate, I find. He quoted that letter pretty accurately. It did say Feb. 1. So maybe we'll know more by then. That fatalism is getting stronger every day. It's getting so one can't plan to do almost anything with any assurance of next month being by and large similar to this one. Oh well…

Did you notice tho, that Solly said rather disparagingly, that there isn't a student in Bellevue that he'd like to introduce to a girl he knew? Can it be that the kids in Bellevue are scrubs too? Bright boys certainly, but future doctors. And if most doctors, to my way of thinking are scrubs the stuff that they are made of must be pretty terrible, too.

Sour grapes?

At any rate darling I keep my heart warm loving you, and my hands warm with your lovely gloves so all's not terrible in this world. Thanks darling. Write often, at great length, and very warmly.

Actually you don't even have to send me a glamour picture of yourself. The one of you that's on the wall above my desk is very much you. Any picture could do very little more than bring back the emotional complex that is you to me. Like a familiar theme bringing back a splendid symphony to the one who is very familiar with, understands, and loves the beautiful work. So send me a picture if you take them, but don't go out of your way to do so.

Darling, I'd like to get you the Sibelius Violin Concerto for your birthday. But I don't know how to mail it to N.Y. without getting some extra cracks. Would you buy it if I send the money?

All my love dear
Aaron

Thursday 1/6/44
11:45 p.m.

Darling:--

To the stirring harmonies of the "Eroica" I'll try to write to you. Joe went out, it's teeming out, and I was thinking of how nice you'd fit into this place right now. Hmmm…

It's only 4 days that I've been back; gosh! It feels like a year ago that I was in New York…

Yesterday, I tried something interesting. One of the boys is working in a shoe store selling lady's shoes and doing very well. As I don't like the restaurant business at all, he suggested I try to get into his place. So he primed me for about 2 hours—how to read sizes, most popular sizes, how to switch a 9A for a 6 ½ B…Kinds of heels, kinds of leather, shape of toes, heels, styles, how shoes are arranged in a shoe store, how to wait on a customer, how to pack shoes…

So we went down. I told the manager that I was an old shoe salesman who decided to go in for medicine as a side line, and made a pretty good impression. Then he took a box of shoes and dumped the shoes on a chair, and asked me to put them back—I did—after five minutes of struggling…It looked so easy when Malcolm, the other student, did it. So he said, politely, that he'd send for me if he needs me. And that was that. I'm working as a Bus Boy this week-end…

I just don't have any ability to bluff at all. But any rate you won't have to worry about my ever hiding anything from you. Even if I didn't want to tell you everything—as I always do—you'll be able to see it right away. Isn't that awful.

Don't worry dear…I don't love you exactly like a sister…And you don't need perfumes, creams, or warm negligees. You do all right as it is. I've never loved anyone so happily before, and can't even imagine wanting to love you in any other way.

But do take care of yourself, dear. You're not the immune thing you thought. I didn't "take" apparently. All those germs you implanted did die in the heat of transference. Of course, my catching cold in this weather won't be any trick. On the other hand, you try to keep well. After all…

Happy Birthday darling. You're legally an adult now. How does it feel? Do you realize that we are both pretty much free agents (free, white, 21…) and can get married at any time we decide to? Very nice…I found a music shop that has the concerto I'm getting us for your birthday. I'll mail it to you soon. I'm told I can insure it against breakage. I like what I feel is the deep passion which is put forth in a continuous vein of understatement. Sibelius is one of the few moderns I care for.

So many happy listenings, darling, for both of us together.

Aaron

Joe sends regards—happy to greet you in the ranks of the adults.

Tuesday 1/11
9:00 p.m.

Darling:--

By now you know that I haven't forgotten your birthday. I do hope the records got to you in toto. If not, we can make the Post Office get a new set, as they are insured. Strangely enough, I heard the Sibelius Violin Concerto this Sunday night. I liked it even more, and was very glad that I got that one. What with the art books you got me, and the records I got you, we ought to have a very cultured home.

Last weekend I worked as a bus boy again—only Sat. night and Sunday. It won't be enough to cover all my expenses, but I can't bear the thought of being so near working again as soon as I get thru with the weekend. As is, I can look back Sunday night on the laborious job done, and a long ways to go before I have to go back to work the next Saturday. Oh well…

How are you darling? I'm getting disturbed receiving all your letters written from bed. Incidentally, did you have good regular period yet? That disturbed me even more…Get better in a hurry and come up to visit us. We'll entertain you royally, make coffee in a good Bohemian fashion and look like real medical students (or Philosophy students, perhaps) living in that attic I always told you about.

Life goes on up here. I've often felt that one either adjusts to a situation, or cracks up. Given food, warmth, fairly good health the situation looks more palatable. No real reason. Just waiting for another blow to make it look humble again.

What am I studying now anyhow? Actually the basic theoretical stuff is over. True, I don't know it as well as I could. Right now, I could no more give the origins and insertions of 5 muscles of the forearm, as play the Paganini Violin Concerto. So really, I should be reviewing that material and really get it down. But the prospect of learning old stuff isn't very thrilling. In fact, I've been thinking about it, but not too seriously…

I did buy a book on Medicine, you remember, and since then I got the Host (Pediatrics). Actually those are the two Sig. courses this year—except for Surgery! I'll get the surgery book later if we stay. But there is really very little surgery, or medicine, to be learnt from books alone. The theory interests me, of course, so I'm spending time going into the "Why's" of the various diseases. I don't need patients for that and it's good mental exercise, too. Like an Ellery Queen story. Only, very often, they don't know who the murderer is, or when they do find out (at autopsy) it isn't quite clear, how even the most astute would have talked him down.

Happy birthday again, dear
Aaron

Saturday 2:00 p.m.

Darling:

You've been taking it easy for quite a spell, haven't you? By now you ought to be pretty tired of staying in bed, and ready to find working even more interesting. But take it easy, never the less. Stay put until 48 hours with no fever. That's the standard rule you know.

Maybe you ought to take cod liver oil every morning, too. I don't really know whether it will protect you by its Vitamin content, but it tastes so badly that it assures you psychologically that it must be awfully powerful—and that you can roam around with impunity.

Since I've been back I've tried to do some real studying. I find it difficult to do the same kind of exhausting, concentrated work (even when I want to) when I have another person in the room. In a way it isn't bad. I have to get used to learning with others, not up in the clouds. Mostly one's information must be of a readily available kind in medicine, easily talked about and applied. Furthermore I can't resign myself to being a recluse.

The courses are very poor. I am more depressed during school hours than at night when I'm at home with my textbooks. At least the men who write the articles in Cecil or Hart are intelligent and well informed. That is a far cry from the men who lecture to us about the subjects.

Our professor of Medicine, Dr. Levinson, is a young chap, early thirties I'd say, who came out of a good American Medical School not too long ago, was among the top in his class, and now has a very fine Boston practice. He comes in three times a week, about 15-20 minutes late, speaks rapidly, and, apparently extemporaneously, very superficially about Pneumonia, Typhoid, Encephalitis…and dashes out at 10 minutes of the hour. I'm grateful for his intelligence, and keen mind; very dissatisfied by his total lack of interest in teaching us. Probably the deferment from military service, due to his being a "Professor" in a medical school, is his reason for wasting his valuable time with us at all…Of course at best, teaching medicine without patients is like learning carpentry from a printed book…But there could be a sincere effort, I suppose!!

Dr. Singer, in his course in Clinical Hematology, keeps trying. It's too bad he isn't teaching medicine; hematology is such a small part of the whole. Yet he gets case histories printed up, each illustrating a point, goes over the material, helps us in making the diagnosis, and finally discusses the particular disease from all its aspects. I think he's tired of it, tho. There isn't much response. The class is passive. No sparks anywhere. Apathy is the most enervating situation for the sincere teacher…

Be good darling—and let me know when you can visit.

Love
Aaron

Tuesday 1/25

Darling:

Your letter today charges me with only "lukewarm" longingness. Nonsense, darling. If I were to stay in the perpetual state of near hysteria that I was in just before Christmas vacation, I'd be in a good hospital very soon as a patient. No dear, I love you and want you with me; I have your picture pasted up on the wall above my desk, the only pin up girl on my side of the room…The problem of maintaining myself, as well as the constant thought of the ominous gray future keep me so fully chained down, I can do little else.

For the past few weeks we've been writing to the local non-affiliated hospitals asking about clinical clerkships. It is a pretty good idea that hospitals have the arrangement of keeping a few students in the hospital, and give them room and board for the services they render in the evening and week-ends. Theoretically, the student acts very much like an intern; learns some medicine and in turn relieves the intern present of such routine work as doing physical examinations, emergency laboratory exams, taking histories…In practice, this is true in the better, larger hospitals. It's a pretty good set up. Beth Israel is one of the best hospitals in Boston that is not officially connected with a school; Malden is a small good hospital. So you see by the replies I got that you're either completely in—or completely out. My colleagues in Tufts get Tuition paid, books free, \$50 or so per month to play with, are paid for room and board, and then save the money by living in Hospitals…Last week-end I worked at the Hi-Hat as a bus boy. One of the parties was a group of ASTP medical students who tried to make the waitress…

We do have students in the small hospitals. Mostly seniors. One of them, Revere General Hospital, asked us to come down. The set up there is a little different. Revere is a small place of about 55 Beds; privately owned by an Italian doctor who found running a hospital more lucrative than practicing. And is he making money! His daughter stayed in all day as his secretary ostensibly, and watches the business for papa.

As are nearly all these small hospitals Revere is essentially a place where people come to have operations done, or have their babies. There are no "service" cases i.e. charity or ward patients upon whom medical students practice. Everybody comes in under some doctor's care, who is fundamentally responsible for them. The operating room is used every day for appendectomies, tonsillectomies…and two or three babies come squawking into the world every night. Occasionally some unfortunate gets into an accident, lacerates a finger, gets a boil…and wanders into the "emergency room." There is an X Ray room, a very small, inadequate laboratory for blood & urine examination housing a microscope Leeuwenhoek wouldn't have used, and no library…

There are two seniors living there now. Their room is the attic, but not a big, clean roomy one like ours. I wouldn't have a pet dog live there. The room is apparently never made; the two cots they are supposed to sleep in look distastefully fragile. There is one rickety desk piled full of books, not enough closet space, and very poor lighting. Perfect set up for study! And they offered us space in the same room if we wanted to go!

The boys practically never sleep. They are probably learning something. Minor surgery, and hospital routine. As medical cases do not go to these small hospitals, they learn very little. The heart, kidney, liver, lung…cases go to the big hospitals where facilities exist for diagnosis and treatment. The boy in the small surgical hospital is just for labor. He is one of the most exploited persons I have seen. He is up all night giving anesthesia to women giving birth; or being second or third assistant during the morning's run of appendectomies. As no one is going to let him do anything, he learns very little after the first few. He has no time to study his books, or any stimulus to do so. And it's all glorified under the name "interne" and the pretty white coat he wears. Those seniors aren't going to be good doctors. They hate the patients already. Their goal is to get out and make as much on their patients as possible.

When we realized that it would cost us almost as much to live in the hospital as at present, we are deciding not to go. We have until February 15 to decide.

Wow, did I go off!

Good night darling
Aaron

Friday 1/28
10:30

Gloria darling—

Tolstoi was very impressive. Surprisingly, tho I remembered nothing about the actual story of "War and Peace", this section was very familiar. I remember being impressed by his general philosophy of history when I read it, very immature tho my outlook was at the time. (Tsk, tsk) Do you know, his conception of history is fundamentally, Marxism. History is a predictive science, with world events progressing inevitably along to the goal which natural laws dictate.

In my chemistry and physics courses there was the concept of Mass Action in working out gas laws. That is, a gas is a collection of molecules all running around madly, bumping into one another and the sides of the container, and totally unpredictable in the path any molecule was going to take. But in working out formulas for what the result would be if we average all these individual motions, the whole concept of our present understanding of gases was worked out.

Similarly Tolstoi—or Marx. The action of any particular individual and its influence on the great events of the time cannot be predicted—but by and large, the general result of a lot of little Homo Sapiens trying like the devil to get ahead, can probably be understood in the making of history.

Fatalism? Yes, I think so. Only there is this, too. We are not all identical molecules. And it is that difference which may give some basis for changing the history to come to suit our needs. Once an event happens, we can say with Tolstoi; millions of little causes, [probably infinite in number if we go back to ascertain what caused each person…] were instrumental in shaping the event. But before it happens, we can be part of those causes to try to influence it for the way we see it.

Oh well…I am confused. You dope it out and let me know. You'll have to bring in the terrific power which the Lords of the Press, Radio, and Channels have now. Or the power a modern army gives a small group at present, to enslave a much larger group.

How do you like your work at the settlement? If the girls will both like and also respect you, you'll have really accomplished something…

As for Thelma…she's probably trying awfully hard to drown a deep ache…She can use sympathetic company…You might try to help her build up some of that ego she lost.

You know, I never did send you the diagram to our "Penthouse." Well, you'd go up to the fourth floor of a very respectable looking house on Beacon Street, and open one of the doors leading out to the hall. Then you go up our private flight of stairs and enter one of the largest rooms you've been in:
(DIAGRAM)

The diagram is probably self-explanatory. But there you are. We could rent out ½ of the room and still get along.

Last Wednesday two other fellows came over and we went over two clinic-pathological cases in the New England Journal. Very interesting. The Osler Society is defunct, so we're just doing it ourself. If time permits we'll try to make a little seminar of it. If time permits…

Now that you know all about this place, you can start planning a trip up here. I really can't remember when I saw you last…It must have been two or three years ago…It's remarkable how perspective changes in Boston and New York. Up here, the problem of your coming up to visit me sounds like a ridiculous "problem." That of being able to support us, very real. It was just the opposite when I was at home.

Good night darling. Don't get sick again.

Love
Aaron

Thursday 1/30
6:30 p.m.

Gloria darling

I guess I've been neglecting you this week. It's not that I've been so busy, but living with a roommate has changed my way of life considerably. We talk a lot, listen to the good music on the radio whenever there is any…and it's always two o'clock before I get to sleep. The result is a very sleepy fellow during lectures…I've been doing very little formal studying, but do select topics of interest as they come up, and spend two or three nights on them. What with my week-ends gone, I don't really know where the time disappears to…

Since I brought up my big frying pan we've eaten most of our meals in. Beware young woman! Altho I am more convinced than ever, that cooking and keeping house is a wife's job, I am going to be a very good critic of your efforts. If we keep it up, I ought to become a pretty good cook. So far we've made nothing very fancy, but I'll know good cooking when I see it…I discovered, for example, that when pork chops are stewed they taste just like chicken, and when fried they taste like pork chops. Some day I'll write a paper on it.

Interestingly enough we are doing all our cooking stealthily. We lock our door before starting to eat, put all garbage in bags and take it down every morning; bring food in at night very carefully avoiding the landlady...Did I ever tell you of the Social Investigator I knew who very "painfully" and carefully practiced meticulous contraception for 9 years, and then found out, when they wanted a baby, that his wife was sterile right along? We're probably in the same boat—our landlady undoubtedly knows all about it and is amused at our clumsy attempts at fooling her...

I've bought my third book this year. A surgery book. That is all the books I expect to buy in Medical School. I have about ½ of the required books; but I think they are the basic minimum. They are all I can afford and think that they'll do. In any case, I'll be the best theoretician in medicine if I know what there is in the books I now have. As you see I'm going along on the assumption of staying on. There is no basis for the assumption, but it's the only way to keep going. If we stay, I need the book. If we don't stay, I won't need the $10 it cost. Very neat, no? But not very satisfying.

I don't know what to say about Sylvia, dear. It doesn't look good. Not knowing anything about psychiatry I can't do any judging or make prognoses. As a layman, I'd say she was going to have a "nervous breakdown" one of these days. Her problem isn't simply an unholy fear of staying single. A lot of girls are single and make the adjustment to a tolerable life. Rather, her deep rooted personality problem is even more seriously threatened than ever by the feeling of inadequacy that not being able to "get a man" gives her. I don't think getting married would solve anything. She would probably find that situation difficult, too. You know that I believe marriage makes no real change in the two people. Happy, solid, people continue to be so afterwards...

If you can skillfully steer her to a psychiatrist you may be able to give her a chance; otherwise, she'll simply have to go along until she's so unhappy, finds life so unsatisfying that something cracks. At that point she'll come to the attention of somebody. Of course, she may never get to the stage of developing an incapacitating neurosis. Miriam or Thelma could probably give you the names and telephone numbers of agencies to whom you can refer her. They are listed in the Social Service Directory to which they both have access.

Tonight we're having another student meeting. I live so close, I'll go over. The deadline is approaching and the boys are nervous. There aren't any good rumors even…

I don't know what you could get Solly, dear. I asked him when I was home; he wanted some game. My mother thought any gift he got ought to be practical. But pay no attention; mothers always say that.

Until later darling
Aaron

Monday 1/31
10:00 p.m.

Hello darling:

I'm a telephone girl!

Well, just a minute, and I'll explain…

You know, in these very swanky professional buildings, they have frequently all night phone service for the doctors. And they generally have some arrangement of having 2 students watch the switchboard on alternate nights, in return for an apartment.

While Joe and I were knocking ourselves out about Revere General Hospital, and a similar one, Allenton Hospital, we got word of one of these jobs about to open up. So we got the introductions, saw the boss on Friday, and we're here today.

Boy, oh, Boy! Sometimes I think that I go to school as a side line…

But to be more specific. On alternate nights, one of us goes "on duty" at 10:00 p.m. That means, he brings his books into the room where the switchboard is located. Then he studies, and when the buzzer rings, goes thru some complicated motions with cords and keys, says "Dr. Singer isn't in" or "Appointments at the Lahey Clinic can't be made until 8:30 tomorrow." Very interesting. Joe has been "on duty" since 10:00 this evening; he's had one call during the past half hour. Are we in touch with Boston's organized medicine! The best specialists in town depend on our switchboard. When Middlesex is closed, I'm going to get all their calls mixed up, and really get them all confused.

As to the physical set up. Our place isn't as pretty as the Super duper attic we moved from. But I'm slowly learning the comparative superiority of prosaic essentials, eg 3 burners and an icebox, even petty non-essentials, eg a gorgeous view. We have a two room apartment, in the swankiest section in Boston Bay State Road. [The place is literally infested with doctors.] I guess you can say that we moved from Park Ave. to Central Park West. The two rooms together are probably not as large as our attic, but one of them is a kitchen. Dishes, pots & pans, 3 electric burners, a toaster, ice box, sink, kitchen table…All very primitive, but present. The other room has 2 beds, fixed up as studio couches, a soft chair, desk, lamps…We're much more crowded for space here: closets, dressers…But we're getting things settled.

Upstairs, there is the switchboard in a large room, and a very nice office next to it. The office is for us, too. It can be used for a study. And the fellow who is on duty sleeps on a couch there, so if a call comes in at night he's right near the telephone. We're told that they don't often wake you in the middle of the night—we'll see. Weekends we go on at 5 pm Saturday night, 'till Sunday; and the other at 7 p.m. Sunday night. Since Joe is making a fortune at the Fox and Hounds Sat. night, I promised that I'd let him have that night off. Will I have time to write you letters!

Well that's the story temporarily. Oh yes, we each get $5 a week also. That will almost cover expenses. I'd prefer not to do any more bussing, but I may have to go in, if I can, once a week. Actually, I've seen all that I want to of the inside story of night clubs.

Wow I really will have to learn to cook and keep house…But I reiterate, it's a woman's job…

The situation, of course, boils down to a means of making more time (I hope) to do Medicine. In the past two months I've learnt nothing. Not even the things I'd like to know about. I was working all week-end, found it very difficult to study with another person in the same room, etc. Now I'm in our apartment when Joe is working, and will be up in the study when I'm working. Actually, I haven't really been alone as I am right now, and so free to be close to you in spirit, since I've come to Boston…I like solitude, occasionally…

I wish you'd really come up, darling. I'd give a lot to see you. I don't think, I could stand having you live as primitively as two fellows; but there is very little I could think of that I'd rather do than have you near me now and be able to love you very actively.

Willy-nilly, I'm learning, the rudiments of housekeeping.

Interestingly enough, one fellow drove us back and forth in his car so we could move—and wouldn't let us pay him; another two chaps in our class ran their legs off helping us carry bundles down from our 3rd floor "penthouse"—and wouldn't let us take them out to dinner. So we moved, and got settled in one evening. It'll take some time to make the place livable, but I can do little things such as write 2 hour letters already.

As you noticed probably, today is the 31st of January. We expect some word from Washington as to our selective service status any day. But never-the-less we proceeded on the assumption that we're staying. It's the only way to keep sane.

Good night darling
Write to:
15 Bay State Road
Boston, Mass,

Yours,
Aaron

Thursday 2/3
12:50 a.m.

Darling:

I'm on tonight. The house is very still. I'm studying in a small office…[Oops—someone just called for Dr. Harriet Jones. How do I know where she is at this hour?] As I was saying I'm in a small office, a few yards from the switchboard which is in the next room. Joe is downstairs in the apartment, presumably studying or sleeping…[So far neither of us has been awakened during the middle of the night by some worried father calling a doctor—but maybe I will be tonight...If I am, I'm supposed to get the facts about the emergency from the person, and if I think it is serious, call the doctor at his home.]

Slowly, the routine is settling in. I've cooked some dinners in...Eaten some out. The school is about 10 minutes away, so that coming home for lunch is really no problem.

When I get tired of studying tonight, I'll go to sleep on a cot in this office. There is a loud bell hooked up to the switchboard. It rings loudly enough to make any alarm clock absolutely blush with envy. So, if any call will come in, I'll jump clean out of bed, and be at the switchboard before I really know what I'm doing. It's a good idea, because if I really knew what I was doing, I'd stay in bed where it's nice and warm.

Tentatively I'm going to work Saturday night, so that Joe can be a waiter at the Fox and Hounds; and he'll take Sunday, so that I can be a busboy at the Hi Hat. I need about $10 a week to live on, over and above rent. One day a week bussing, together with the $5 I get here, should pretty nearly cover it. Right now, I don't know whether they'll want me to work if I can only put in one day a week.

Of course, all this is on the assumption that we stay in school. There is no word. I'm still unclassified. The school goes on as usual.

In fact even more so. During the week, one professor who has been very obnoxious all term long, finally broke the camel's back by announcing an exam for today, threatening to fail anyone for the course, if they couldn't pass this one exam. He was pretty nasty about it...

Dr. Feldman, our physio-therapy instructor (Diathermy, Massage, Electric Shocks...) is a very successful man. He runs a factory, where paid "assistants" give credulous patients all sorts of treatments for real or imaginary ills with a very expensive, and impressive bunch of machines. [After two months of the Course, all I can see is, that no matter what the treatment, Massage or Static Electricity, it kind of warms the part and stimulates circulation]. At any rate, he is a doctor, can move among his patients dangling a stethoscope, and look very professional as he takes their pulse while they bask in his super-duper ultraviolet machine.

For the past two months he has been coming in twice a week and read us some mimeographed material he has, in a manner and tone you'd expect of a prosperous contractor at a Ladies' Garment Convention.

He talks down to us, repeats constantly that he must simplify the very, very complicated physics behind his treatment; and obviously knows less theory than a high school pupil.

His attitude towards his assistants, as being minimal; of all doctors having to band together against a public that is constantly ready to "get" them, all help…

As you can gather, I detest the fellow…But to get back…The class met, decided to simply cut the exam in a body; both as protest against a course which is really superfluous, a teacher who is obnoxious, and an exam many were afraid of. The Dean was notified. Today Rushmore came down to speak to us.

He warned us that insubordination would result in expulsion of the whole class, if necessary. And in an elliptical fashion told us that it might be a good thing for the school if they did get rid of a bunch of Jews…

The instructor postponed his exam to next week, and life at Middlesex continues as usual…

I'm glad you're continuing at the settlement and are going back to school. You know how I feel about it. I don't want you to stagnate; but to build yourself up to the highest point your potentialities can reach. I want you to be as big, and complete a person as possible, in your own right…

It's very late now, darling. So good night…

Love
Aaron

Thursday 2/10
12:15 a.m.

Gloria darling—

Yesterday they posted for our edification:

["Brigadier General Hershey, Nat'l Director of the Nat'l Selective Service System, today notified Middlesex University that students of the school of Medicine will be given the same consideration for deferment as is given to students of Medicine in other Medical Colleges until it has been definitely determined under the Massachusetts law that graduates of the Medical School are not eligible to take the examinations for licensure in the state"]

So there!

Along with it we were told unofficially that the order keeping our graduates from getting commissions has been rescinded—they are now to be judged on "individual merit". We are told of several of our doctors applying and getting the commissions…

You certainly are psychic dear. Your letter this morning said that you were feeling fine—and wondered whether there was any basis for it in the situation up here. Well, I'll be in Boston as a civilian until July or August 1, 1944. For which I am duly grateful.

But what does it all mean? Frankly, very little, I think. By a legal fluke, we are getting a reprieve. I have spoken to several doctors, and some members of the faculty. They all feel that our closing down is just a matter of time. Legally we stalled it off. But the day of reckoning comes in August—and with no clinics, the State Board is definitely going to turn us down.

So we're back in status quo. There was a disquieting ruffle for a while; it blew over; and the tragic farce continues…

"We met the enemy and successfully forced him back"—but he's solidly entrenched, and we have to attack to win…

During the week we joined the YMCA. It's a 15 minute walk from the house, and is a good one. It's not so much that I have the time or money to spare; rather, as our living quarters don't include the facilities for bathing—well, we can bathe at the Y several times a week. A necessity you see. Of course, since we are members we're going to try to make use of the athletic facilities. There's a pool, gym, handball, billiards, music, fencing etc, etc. Good stuff, but I'm both lazy and busy. There is so much that I don't know…

Which reminds me, you get that scale to read 120 pounds again—or else! And how did your pictures come out?

Tonight I saw "Old Acquaintance" with 2 of the fellows in my class. I found it swell. Of course, I could almost do Bette's scenes with her, but I enjoy seeing her do them anyway. It's like seeing a good play over again; the acting is enjoyed more with each performance.

If you've seen it you'll know what I mean by a real person, and one that is so covered over by mechanisms (rationalization, projection, sublimation...) that one can hardly find the real person underneath. Unfortunately this latter-group person really believes in the role he is playing. Tho people are usually not at such extremes as Bette Davis or Miriam Hopkins—yet they both certainly represent valid types.

So your feeling of maturity, of calmly knowing what you want, of self analysis to see whether you're not behaving in response to a mechanism, your attempt to be sensitive and really understand others—their mechanisms and subterfuge—are all to the good.

I've been getting 6 hours of sleep a night at the most lately, so that my eyes are about to close.

Good night darling,
Aaron

Sat. 2/12
4:10 p.m.

Gloria darling:

I just got thru an hour's handball and a shower, so I feel human again. Passing by the little desk with stationery set me down to write to you. There are a lot of nice things to do—if they let you. I'd like us to do them together.

There's a swimming pool here, and a nice gym, too. So far I haven't gone into the water. Probably the snow on the ground psychologically deters me.

My handwriting is worse than normal, as my hand is puffed up like a little balloon, and my arm feels as tho someone had pounded it with a hammer. But it's a good feeling. Not like being tired after a hard day's manual labor. Rather the luxurious tiredness of a hard day's play.

Yesterday I got a telegram from my mother asking about my not writing for a week! Today I got your letter telling me about all the other guys still in Brooklyn!...Is that nice?

I'm going on duty at 5:00 p.m. this afternoon, so until later darling.

Yours
Aaron

Feb. 13, 1944

Darling:

I don't love you more on Valentine's Day than any other day but sending cards is a tradition that's probably here to stay.

This is not an excuse for one of my letters. Rather another way of gently hinting that I'm in love with you. I'm too bashful, you know, to just blurt it right out. What's more it's not refined. Or is it?

All my love darling,
Aaron

Tuesday 2/15
12:00 Midnight

Gloria darling:

I'm "on" tonight…Altho I'd like to stay up until 3:00 or so, to avoid being awakened, I'll probably succumb to my tremendous proclivity for sleep and drop off as soon as I finish my letter to you.

Today is St. Valentine's Day, I take it. I received a very pretty one, from some girl in Brooklyn. I wonder who it could possibly be. Surprisingly, she knew my address, too. I'd like to phone you dear, but I'm not at all sure about your schedule. So let me know when you're at school, at the settlement…And I'll try to call you up to tell you that I love you—even on St. Valentine's Day.

And how is your course coming? It sounds good. I'd like to be discussing and reading that kind of material. I'm pretty far away from the world of ideas now; pretty much restricted to learning a lot of facts. So pour out…there is so much to know, you feel insignificant just thinking about it. I think, I'd like to be a Leonardo da Vinci—master of all fields of knowledge. But I'm afraid I'll be master of none.

School is just one depressing day after another. It's when I get home, and start reading, that the depression I've built up all day listening to the incompetent, uninterested, unintelligent lecturers, is dissipated by the magnificent clarity of thought and expression that our good American Professors give forth. It must be magnificent having men like that teach you…

Actually this is not a third year of Medical School. It's reviewing, with some added detail, the material I learnt in the first 2 years. If I can go along and study, I'll have a better understanding of the theoretical material, after 8 more months of studying it.

What is the general scheme this year?

Fundamentally we study Medicine. No, I'm not being facetious. I mean diseases, as separate entities. During the first two years we took up general subjects: Anatomy, Physiology, Bacteriology, Physiology, Pathology…During the third year, the idea is going over all the diseases described for man, and learning their Etiology, Pathological Changes, Physiology involved, Symptoms of the disease, How to recognize it (Diagnosis) and treatment. To do that, the subject is arbitrarily divided into segments: 1) Infectious diseases, kidney diseases, and a few more= Internal Medicine; 2) Diseases of the Lungs=Chest Diseases; 3) Diseases of Heart=Cardiology; 4) Diseases of the blood=Hematology; 5) Diseases of the Eyes=Ophthalmology; 6) Ears, Nose, Throat=Otorhinolaryngology; 7) Diseases of female urogenital system=Gynecology; 8) Diseases of male urinary system=Urology; 9) Various diseases in the abdominal cavity (eg ulcers, appendicitis…)= Abdominal Surgery! [Since he can't teach us to do operations, we take up these diseases here]; 10) Diseases of the joints, bones—Orthopedics; 11) Diseases of the Nervous System—Neurology, Psychiatry; 12) Diseases of the Skin—Dermatology; 13) Special diseases of children—Pediatrics. Then throw in some

Toxicology, Physical Therapy, Obstetrics and you have most of my courses.

How does that picture look?

Actually, you see, all that it is, is a division of all the diseases by regions, tacking a name onto each and thereby calling it a specialty.

This isn't the "Practice of Medicine"; of course. I'm becoming familiar with a lot of names. But I'm no more a doctor than you are.

As you can see, the amount of material I'm supposed to cover is terrific—there are a "lot of ills man is heir to…"

I wanted to take that course in organic chem. As you suggested. But the only course given at night was at B.Cl. and it was a second course, the first course being given in the fall…

By the way, do you remember how easily I got the addresses of the Lifshits, William Miller, Aaron Braverman and Herman Dolgea? Well, I lost them! So if you can get the addresses for me thru Sollie I'll get around to writing.

Good night darling,
Aaron

Thursday 2:00 a.m.

Hello darling—

It's kind of quiet at this hour, but not very disturbing. Actually, I always feel most in need of writing, in these early morning sessions, when I can really feel alone…

I received your 2 page letter today. It's unfortunate that Manny couldn't stay in the states. You can imagine my sympathy being very real and sincere. Will you wish him the best of luck for me? Hopefully, we'll all 3 be living normal lives again—soon.

How is your stuff coming at school? I'm really dying to know what goes on in the world of thought once more. You're stuck. You'll have to read a great deal of extra material to satisfy my "insatiable" curiosity. Maybe someday I'll be content to stop going to school, and just enjoy living the simple pleasures.

But so far I'm the original sponge. I've been taught since I was 6 years old. So now, you can go right ahead and pour out your views on Kant, Spinoza, Hegel…I'm all agog.

We'll get married when Middlesex is recognized all right—but that isn't really tying me down to much. I'm very much afraid that it won't be. Nothing much is being done; there will be no clinics for next term either—and the boys come up for State Boards in July. We got a reprieve—not a pardon.

[Sorry, darling, I'll have to finish this tomorrow. I can't keep my eyes open—Good night, dear…]

Friday 8:30 a.m.

Good morning…

No calls last night. Thank goodness. Somebody woke me at 7:30 or so—but I might as well get up anyway. We don't have any classes 'til 11:00 o'clock today. "And thereby hangs a tale…"

It seems that nobody wants to teach us obstetrics. Starting back in our second year. The first semester Obstetrics was scheduled but they got no instructor—so after 2 months, of coming in to school to find no class being held, we got the office to admit there would be no course that term. The following semester they got someone, an old, decrepit refugee from Germany. He was so bad that the class just quit. He was fired at the end of the term—still no obstetrics. This year they acquired a competent American obstetrician, who simply came in and read the book to us. But, after all, one must be thankful for little things. At any rate, he came in for one lecture and quit. I suppose he's too busy to waste his time with us.

Nobody wants to teach us obstetrics…

We're doing a minimum of housekeeping—you understand. About once a week there is a brief flurry of activity with vacuum cleaner and broom, attempting to tidy up. Our cooking is pretty simple: steak, chops, halibut, salmon steak, omelettes, salads with vegetables and soups coming out of cans. Any simple recipes glady accepted. Our contention is that cooking, eating, and washing up not to take much more than an hour. And how about those cookies!

Until later darling
Aaron

Wed 1:20 a.m.

Hello darling—

I suppose, to be perfectly accurate, it's Thursday. But until I go to sleep and get up again—no matter for how long (or short) a period, it's still today. Joe is "working" tonight. That means he's upstairs in the office either studying or sleeping. I'm alone at a desk, lamp cascading light over my desk as I write. At this moment I'm getting some music—Victor's Classical Album—coming out of the little radio. Reception isn't very good, but Marion Anderson is Marion Anderson.

It's not that I've been studying so much that keeps me up to these un-Godly hours. Rather a lot of time is killed. Making supper, talking, cleaning up, talking, chasing visitors home so all of us can pass courses…I really don't know where the time goes to. Last year, I sat me down at 5 or so, and studied right thru 'till the hours that I started to write letters. Not so now. The semester ends March 21; finals in six courses start then. Right now I haven't even started them. Since I don't like the way we're getting Physical Therapy, Dermatology, Chest Diseases, Orthopedic Surgery, or Toxicology, I don't even have good notes…

Each night we try to "get down to work." Last night, Joe and I made a pact not to talk to each other in the evenings. That's the only way we'll get the necessary memorizing done. Because we don't see any of the diseases, memorizing clinical pictures is really tough.

[The music at this hour is wonderful, darling. I just got another program when the last one finished. Beethoven…]

But to get back to memorizing the symptoms of diseases. Can you imagine learning that in Uremia, the terminal stage of kidney disease, we find the patient with:-- 1) Low urinary specific gravity; 2) Albuminuria; 3) Probably oliguria; 4) Azotemia; 5) Anemia; 6) Leucopenia; 7) Thrombocytopenia; 8) Epistaxis; 9) Melena; 10)

Pallor; 11) Coma; 12) Asthenia; 13) Convulsions; 14) Nausea; 15) Vomiting; 16) Dyspnea; 17) Cheyne Stokes breathing; 18) Uriniferous breath; 19) Pruritus; 20) I'll take vanilla.

So given 1003 diseases, or so, you get the idea. Also while we're at it, there's the etiology, pathology, treatment…

Of course, those big words are meant to impress you. They are Medical Jargon for symptoms. Yet, if I had seen just one case, with the patient lying in a stuporous state, breathing very heavily (dyspnea); bleeding from the nose (epistaxis)…I'd be in a far better position to remember it.

More later on, when I can think a little more clearly. At 2:00 in the morning, all I can really do is feel. And I feel like holding on to you very tightly and going to sleep. So I'll go to sleep.

By the way, we heard a news bulletin about the Army calling up first year Medical Students for active duty. What do you know about it? Probably just a big mistake.

Good night darling
Aaron

Friday 10:00 a.m.

Good morning Darling—

We don't have any classes this morning (you remember our Obstetrics professor quit) so here I am. Not as fresh as a daisy tho. In fact, I probably won't wake up until 12:00 or so. Somehow, I just don't get to bed before 1:30 or 2:00 any more, and can't sleep much beyond 8:00. One of these days there'll be a collapse. With finals in 6 courses only 3 weeks off I have to start some real formal studying. So far, you know, I've been "enjoying" my studies. Instead of memorizing the lecture of the day in about ½ an hour, and going on to the next…(10 symptoms of Measles; indications for Pneumothorax, Contraindications for Peptic Ulcer Operation…) I've been picking up topics of interest and just reading along about them. Very interesting. But in medical school, that is really a luxury. The fundamental aspects, pathological physiology of disease, is all very interesting; but what is required is that you know the facts.

It's very funny, these facts vs. explanations. Medicine is largely a compilation of facts. Men knew that Tuberculosis was manifested by chronic coughing, spitting blood, ematiation, low grade fever, night sweats, flushed cheeks...long before the Tubercle Bacillus was discovered, or the microscope made the details of lung destruction understood. The involved theories, some based upon experimental work, as to the mechanism of operation of the Bacillus in the body, do not fundamentally alter the facts about the disease which were so well described generations ago.

I find very frequently that different men, even different textbooks, will give different explanations. But all agree about the facts of the disease ("Most common in younger people; characterized by...")

So that, really, is our job. Brute memorizing. Of course, seeing the disease many times, doing the examination, and watching the treatment, makes the study a livable, more palatable thing. Brute cramming is my bugbear,

On that basis, I've been spending nights doing just what isn't required; reading about explanations. More interesting. Not too important.

This week and part of last, I've been studying kidney diseases. Very good stuff. Yesterday I bought a back issue of the New England Journal of Medicine with an article by Thorn, professor of Medicine at Harvard, on "Treatment in Kidney Diseases." Away from the stupid meanderings of the average doctor, one sees that there are good men working in the splendid field of medicine. The man writes with directness, clarity, and intelligence. I take it all back. The medical profession isn't composed entirely of dolts and blackguards. As in every other group of people, so in this one. Most of them are stupid fools; some are magnificent, clear minds.

There is only one solution. Socialized medicine. Where the doctor is not God, and is answerable to a supervisor for ability, intelligence, and information. Where the profit motive is removed from curing the sick. Where entrants to the field will be interested essentially in Medicine, instead of fleecing the public.

Better I should stop raving,

Love
Aaron

How about those cookies?

Tues. 2/29
1:00 a.m.

Gloria—

I'm on duty tonight, darling. So before I put the alarm on and hopefully go to sleep, I'll write and tell you that I still love you—even at 1 in the morning.

Today was a manic day. We cut class at 1 o'clock, theoretically to go to the Y and get some exercise. Instead, I was inveigled to go to Jordan Marsh's (a la Wanamaker's) to help one of the boys buy records for his lovely record player. So there I was—buying records that I liked with someone else's money. I had a grand time.

I tried to get him the Sibelius Violin Concerto (no imagination, you see), but as it wasn't in stock, compromised for his Second Symphony, Beethoven's Fourth Piano Concerto, and the Red Army Albums.

As Victor might have made a mistake in the recordings we naturally had to listen to them. Very nice. It was only that I was getting awfully hungry, or the poor fellow would have gotten stuck with a couple of Beethoven Quartets too!

There is one radio program which I indulge in nearly every night. A local station plays symphonic music every night from 11:00 to midnight. Very good stuff, too. Tonight my soul was fed with Chopin's First Piano Concerto. Gorgeous stuff. Rubenstein is magnificent. For about half an hour, I made no attempt to follow the themes or structures of the work, but just let the notes, cascading up and down the scale, pour over me. As soon as I have some extra money, I think I'll invest in getting it for you. I still feel good about it, and it's more than an hour since I've heard the music. Probably it's too bad that I like the music so much without being too familiar with it. Possibly, I'll get tired of it later. Yet, tho Chopin doesn't seem to know what to do with a man-sized orchestra, he gets the piano to do things, even Beethoven (sacrilegious?) doesn't do.

Fine talk for a medical student. As you see, going to Medical School, without having a Medical School to go to, drives one to many distracting pursuits. Since I can't go in for wine (as I don't like it) and women (because), I take the song and let it go at that.

I'm enclosing the article by Deutsch, which you might have overlooked. I once tried to make the same point, but not being able to say it as well, was literally hooted down. Do you remember? I felt very strongly, at the time, that there is a strong difference between being at the front, or being related to someone who is. And that the people back home, had no conception, of the Hell that the fighting men are going thru. That putting them all in uniform, and subjecting them to some of the hardship to which the soldiers are put by our "immoral population" would either conclude a peace in a hurry, or wake up to reality and really try to finish the war and make a lasting peace.

Maybe they would. Or maybe they're too stupid and selfish to do anything but perish. The more people I meet, particularly away from that Spring of the Intelligentsia, New York, the more pessimistic I get. Stupidity, bigotry, and ignorance really prevail. The only hope I see, is a progression similar to what the U.S.S.R. is going thru. Dictatorship by the "Vanguard of the proletariat"; wholesale revision of the present set up, both economically and socially; wholesale liquidation of those who obstruct; with hopes pinned on the new generation to be educated to live for the good life for everybody. I'd say, those beyond early childhood are hopeless.

Pessimistic? Yes. Every philosopher who looks at man's problems from Olympian heights and, does nothing, is pessimistic, blaming mankind's stupidity…

At any rate, Deutsch ought to be interesting.

Ouch. You ought to see what time it is!

Good night dear
Aaron

Friday 3/3 9:00 a.m.

Good morning darling—

Someone wanted a doctor, so that I'm up bright and early, with no class 'till 11:00.

You're really getting some activity in, finally, aren't you? Pretty soon, I'll feel like the stay-at-home, early-bird.

I'm glad you're going down to the settlement house and like it. It's interesting and valuable experience. But I think you're a little wrong about the value of Thelma's job. Good, bad or indifferent, the fact that the job lends itself to a real challenge; that she even reacts emotionally to it; is all good. Good for her growth. There is little growth actually without challenges to grow over. Of course, if it's too big for her, failure won't help any. If she learns (emotionally—by actual contact) what people are, how they react to situations, and develops poise and maturity, she'll be much further ahead.

A couple of days ago, incidentally, something brought up that trite thought of: no learning being worthwhile unless it were very difficult to learn…There's probably a very practical, present day slant to it. Only those things which are difficult to learn are worth learning—or else everybody else will go into the field, too, and competition will force you down. The force of this realization has resulted in what we see all over, as the groups that do "know" something (Doctors, Printers, Dentists…) attempt to make the learning of their trade as difficult as possible for others. The "difficult" is rarely in the learning at present; rather in being given the opportunity to learn. In some cases, eg Typographers union or Medical School, admission is the all important hurdle. In most other professions (Law, Medicine, Engineering, Social Work) having enough money to spend a few years leisurely. In either case, it is fundamentally restriction of new people entering the profession. Making it "difficult to learn", so that it, therefore, becomes worthwhile.

Getting philosophical again, eh?

Is Manny still around? What is the story exactly, anyhow? And how does he know that he's going anyplace?

So your father is finally back, and your mother's vigil over. Darling, I'd really like to see you much more emancipated. It's a little awful to feel that she stayed up in this rotten weather for a couple of months to keep an eye on any impulse you might have to see me. In New York, it looked a little exaggerated, but fundamentally natural to me. Up here, with the people we meet either away from home or very much on their own; it feels very strange.

Tomorrow morning I have to give a talk on surgery. Every student delivers one. Since I've never seen an operation except in the movies, I'll be able to be very authoritative. So far I've done very little preparation. Tonight I'll see what I can dig up. Hopefully, I won't make a fool of myself…

I think I'll go up and see whether I have any letters from you—long & loving.

Love
Aaron

Saturday 2:30 p.m.

Hello darling—

Saturday afternoon; La Boheme is on; no one is in…I didn't go over to the Y this afternoon, as I strained my shoulder a bit playing handball and it twinges when I swing at the ball. So I'll give it a rest for awhile like a good boy.

This morning I gave my speech: it went over all right. We were supposed to select a subject in surgery (Burns, Fracture of the Elbow,…) and talk about it. After some preparation I just couldn't see myself killing a few nights studying some rare & surgical condition that hasn't been given for this paper. Instead I tackled the problem of the differential diagnosis of the "Acute Abdomen." It's a terrifically important subject as you can imagine. You walk in on a patient who is in bed with agonizing abdominal pain (such as your mother's gall bladder attack) and you must <u>do</u> something. What saves most diseases for the doctor is that if he's not sure of his diagnosis (Grippe, Pneumonia, Typhoid) you treat "conservatively"—that is you don't do anything and wait. Then either the patient gets better or the disease will manifest itself some way as it progresses. After a while if still stuck, there is always a consultant, laboratory tests, X-Ray, Electrocardiograms…

But in the acute abdominal condition that doesn't hold. Doing nothing in a case of a perforated gall bladder means that the patient will die; operating in the case of Acute Pancreatitis or in Coronary Thrombosis which can look very, very similar—also means that you kill the patient. The big idea is that doing nothing may rapidly prove fatal. Diagnosis is then pretty important.

Of course, only real honest to goodness experiences can teach adequately. But not having that, and being comforted by case histories that had just this problem, I was interested in studying it theoretically.

The only other condition where a similar situation confronts the doctor—Coma. Again doing nothing is impossible. And not giving insulin in a patient with Diabetic Coma will be as fatal as giving Insulin to a patient who is comatose due to a hemorrhage in the brain.

About that Deutch article…Let's see if I can make myself a little more clear.

Suppose I were an eminent AMA doctor, a "specialist", with a good practice, and fancy prices. Now you know that I'm very strongly for socialized medicine, and think that the only sane form of medical treatment is to have the patient, any patient, taken care of when he is well. The Doctor being independent of collecting fees on his patient's misfortunes and with unlimited facilities can really do his best to practice ideal medicine—namely, keeping people healthy. It would be patently ridiculous for me, in that situation, to give up my practice as it stood, make contracts with 100 people who would pay me a lump sum for the year. Even if the AMA would allow it, I would starve and not make a ripple in the whole problem. On the other hand, I would vote for a system of socialized medicine, with "Health Centers" where people could really get modern medical care, even if it meant a severe cut in my own standard of living.

As to the war. My enlisting tomorrow wouldn't change the situation an iota. The immorality of our people lies in the set up as a whole. Putting me in uniform, making me work twice as hard, sleeping in barracks, strict army discipline, getting the information into our heads in half the time,…no matter what the hardships, it would still be nothing compared to what Bataan meant to some fellows.

However, beating the people as a whole over the head, real hard, would make them all acutely aware that there is a war on, and make of living, during the war period, as grim—not pretty tolerable business. With the suffering would come realization of war crime. Do we have any, or don't we? Is the war worth fighting? Is this suffering worth enduring? If it is, then production for the war comes first, living for oneself second. And how would the news be received that we are being robbed by our own Colonels and Commanders? That powerful lobbies are able to kill a renegotiation clause in Congress to enable big companies to make even bigger fortunes? That big farm groups and politicians are so little interested in winning the war that the subsidy program was killed, threatening a severe runaway inflation? That the vote was denied to soldiers oversees because the politicians are afraid of their reelections? That with a country giving those sufferings, the State Department still is Reactionary-Fascist minded and plays around with Argentina?

No, darling, I do not mean that I think my program is "good for someone else." I feel that the people back home are too comfortable. And, that comfort makes it possible for the disgusting spectacle splashed over PM every day to go on. I want to wake them up. Make them feel that there are damn few things worth dying for, and if they decide that honesty, decency, and the good life for all is worth it, to kill the hypocrisy, corruption, and Fascism in their midst.

Of course, I don't know whether it would help anyway. We may be too stupid and immoral to be denied. I don't know. At any rate, maybe it's my feeling of impotent rage against the selfish hypocrisy so prevalent in nearly everybody, that gives rise to my plan for wholesale torture.

I didn't really know that this was going to be as long as this, darling. It just happened. I'm awfully long winded sometimes—no?

You'd better write two letters a day for a week to make up for this one!

All my love, dear
Aaron

My telephone: KENMORE 2270

Wednesday 3/8 9:00 p.m.

Hello darling:--

My morale is pretty low today; I better write to you early.

More and more, I think we have less and less chance of being approved. By now it's almost certainty with me. I, for one, if "on the outside, looking in",-- would close the school!

What am I beefing about now? I don't know, really; it's just an accumulation. There is such damned stupidity and indifference on the part of the administration that our collective blood boils.

Today, the exam schedule was posted. We get exams from 3/27-4/1, and the next semester starts 4/3! Not a day in between semesters. I'll try to come in for a few days anyway, but the stupid planning gripes me as a symptom of the rot of the disease which affects our school. Two months ago the students discussed this vacation-finals problem with the Dean to avoid just this situation…Oh well…

For a while, right after the boys started getting "A's" big plans were afoot. Now all is quiet again. I suppose, that about June 15, a few weeks before the deadline it'll start again. But by then it'll be too late.

It's leaking out that Rushmore is a big, slow-thinking dope. Imagine! He has an awfully good front, hasn't he? One of our elected representatives to the "Faculty-Student Council" talked. Rushmore, who is running the show, is just slow-witted. So nothing is being done. And to extricate us from this mess we need extra bright people at the helm. Nor is there any way of getting rid of him. There are some little things that would change our present limited facilities enormously, but nothing is done. You know that we're getting oodles of lectures in lieu of clinics. The most obvious thing would be an epidiascope with which to throw pictures of the cases on the screen, and movies. Films and pictures are very plentiful. It's so obvious that only a moron would let us do without it. We're doing without. Maybe he feels that we are absolutely unimportant. It's the school that counts. If the school gets clinics for its upper two years one of these days—good—and no machines are necessary. If not, it won't make any difference. And the fact that we're getting an atrocious training is of no matter to the "school."

Phooey!...

Spring is probably on its way. Very soon my fancy is going to turn to many things besides Cancer of the stomach, and acute Pancreatitis. The Esplanade, a walk along the Charles River, is beautiful in the Spring; and the Boston Symphony plays a few minutes walk from here right thru the Summer. Why don't you drop over for an evening?

I'm dying to hear those pearls of wisdom that you're growing in your philosophical oysters. So give forth. You know that I get no chance to read that kind of stuff. You don't want a dope for a husband, do you?

Incidentally, Saturday isn't set aside for the Y. We generally go during the week, and again on Saturday if convenient.

Love
Aaron

Friday 3/10 11:00 p.m.

Hello darling:

My hour of classical music is on (-something very light and pretty—I missed the announcement. Here it is:-- no they didn't...) What with all the gabbing that goes on here, washing dishes, making food...we never get to work before 8:00 p.m. or thereabouts. Since my efficiency is about 10% after 10:00 o'clock you can see that I'm rapidly going to the dogs. (This did it; it's a medley from Carmen; you can't fool me with the Toreador!)

This afternoon we cut classes to go to the Y. So you can see for yourself. Can't be helped. I just can't be good in the face of almost universal agreement that the situation is quite hopeless; no State Boards even. Memorizing the so important signs and symptoms of Secondary Syphilis just doesn't look very enticing when being out of it altogether looms so large…

I've developed another bunch of neat little cards. I'm just in or out, I guess. Can't do anything new. When I was at the Laboratory at the Museum, I worked up a very respectable batch of cards covering the work that I was doing—I hoped to give them up to Lester, but salary and security won. Going to the New York School with plans for a career as a brilliant social worker, I worked up a nice bunch of cards—you remember. I discarded those with a little bit of a sense of futility in going to Middlesex. Now I have another neat pack; just like the others, on 8x5 cards; these list symptoms of diseases--: one card to a disease. If I were at all superstitious…

Medicine is a grand field in and of itself. Dr. Singer, as cynical as ever, keeps poking at the Medical Profession in general, and the rest of the faculty in particular. And do they hate him for it!

(Bach's Violin #1 now. Hmm…)

He keeps on hinting at the disorganized teaching we get. He feels that clinics are more important for the staff than the students. He wants the teachers to realize that their "preclinical" courses are part of medicine. And to teach with their eyes on the patient, not the textbooks, or History of Medicine.

During this semester I've been attending classes held by Dr. Singer for the senior class—cutting my own lectures if necessary to do so. And he's so right. The boys don't know anything (including myself). Since the group is comparatively small, he runs it as a conference rather than a formal lecture. Stalks around the room, jumps on some likely-looking student and rips questions. Soon answers are coming from all over the room, mostly very sad; Singer gets disgusted and goes over an elementary topic that every Junior should know cold.

Mass education by the lecture, or lecture-demonstration method is terrible. You're never sure of anything. Nothing stands out from the grey mass of constant lectures & textbook paragraphs. "Hemochromatosis" (an enormous rarity) stands forth just as clearly as Cirrhosis of the Liver (a very common disease). Yet that's so ridiculously ineffective. The major diseases, those which the doctor in New England actually sees, should be gone over very, very carefully; should be discussed in conference, pictures, movies…all to make the symptoms, lesions, treatment…part of you. Dr. Singer says if he were to awake us in our sleep, the "Differential Diagnosis of Coma" or "Blood Groups" should pop out correctly. Yet, to me, having memorized, but never really used (even in repeated discussions) medical lore, I hesitatingly grope back to that little cubbyhole in my mind where those facts are; packed under a host of irrelevant data.

Dewey was right. "Learn by doing."

It's getting way into tomorrow, so good night dear (and take care of yourself).

Love
Aaron

Wednesday 3/15 10:30 p.m.

Gloria darling:

Once again (as they say in all good books) we are presented with our everlasting problem—two alternatives…At any rate, I have an appointment for an interview with an Army Lieutenant for consideration in regard to the Japanese Language Course I applied for. I go to see him this Sunday or Monday. Now, the question before us is—do I take it, or don't I. And if I don't, I must tell him now.

As you know, I've been thinking about it in my customary fashion—at a distance. But when the situation actually hit, I went wild for a little while, trying to decide what to do.

There are lots of pros and cons:

<u>If I accept the offer:</u>

1) I leave the horrible uncertainty that is Middlesex, for the certainty of a year or so of peaceful quiet.

2) No more fuss about money; working as a Bus Boy; wondering how I'll meet expenses during my fourth year—if there is a fourth year.
3) I can forget that vexing problem which is just beyond the first one of recognition—what do I do if I can take State Boards? How start a practice…
4) I wouldn't be faced with the prospect of living my whole life, considered by my colleagues as a second rate—constantly taken aback by the simple question, "What school?"
5) Middlesex may well fold up this July or August. I'd be left hopelessly stranded. The Army would get me as a Buck Private. In the case of the Japanese course, I go to the University of Michigan for a year or so, paid and in uniform, and graduate as a Second Lieutenant in the Military Intelligence Corps.
6) When (and, if) the war is over it'll be very important to be a veteran. I don't think anyone else will have a chance: Civil Service…
7) Disquietingly, too, two Unrecognized schools just closed: Kansas & Oglethorpe. Both left their students high and dry. Kansas was taking examinations in class. And the same law that was applied to us is applicable to them. They didn't even fight it…

<u>To stay in school:</u>

1) I want to practice medicine. I don't think I'd be happy translating Japanese. And I can't forever keep preparing myself for new professions. If you want to be respectably married and raise children, I'll have to be gainfully employed in the near future.
2) By this point I've invested a lot of money, time, and energy. I've worked hard. It'll be a strong blow to give it all up. On the other hand—"no point throwing good money after bad…"

3) A lot of our boys did pass State Boards, have successful practices and are apparently happy.
4) What do they do with Japanese interpreters? Waves and Waacs can do the paperwork in Washington.
5) This is my last chance for a professional standing. The circumstances which pushed me there—or may be able to do so—won't be repeated. The war situation has enabled me to pay tuition [incidentally that last $150 for the balance of the third year has come thru; that's all there will be]; and man shortage enables me to get odd jobs to pay my expenses, more or less.

So there you are. No clear cut answer, is there? If I stay, and am drafted when the school closes in August—pretty bad. If I go, and the boys take State Boards—I'll be learning Japanese hieroglyphics.

What do you think, darling? I've pretty much made up my mind as to my course of action. None of the fellows envy me, the situation. None gave any advice—saying they didn't know.

So write soon. I'll tell you what I think.

My best wishes for Manny's safe and uneventful crossing. Let me know as soon as you hear from him.

Good night dear
Aaron

Friday 3/17 8:30 p.m.

Gloria dear:

Your last letter is pretty thought provoking. You can't talk to me about Politics or philosophy and get away with it, you know…

On Russia…There seems to be a little confusion there, somehow. Maybe I can help. First, I believe now, and have believed for a long time, that Russia was being run for the Russians. And even exceedingly well. Start with that premise and you may be able to judge and understand many of their actions. I believe it was the fundamental question of whether the Russian Communist system was going to spend itself trying to develop Marxism all over the world, or to build it up in Russia—which made the great rift between Trotzky and Stalin. These are big issues, and a lot is at stake on which policy is adopted. At any rate Stalin won, for good or evil, and the Russian policy is to develop socialism and the good life—for Russians.

They have expected nothing from the other countries, and have gotten it. They have very simply, and very directly followed a policy of self interest—using every weapon possible. So goes the Soviet-German treaty, the original war in Finland to get bases…

The Russian policy has one thing that other countries don't have: there is only one policy. The policy for Russia is the policy for the Russian people.

In all other countries where class distinctions are so very important, there are two Loyalties for each person: National Loyalties & Class Loyalties. That conflict makes for some very disastrous results: Chamberlain should have stopped Hitler if he had listened to his National Loyalties; German growth wasn't good for the English people. But his Class Loyalties called on him to build up Hitler to fight Bolshevism, which was a greater menace to his Class than Fascism. Remember, the big Factory Owner still is comfortable and wealthy under a Fascist set up—maybe more so, in so far as labor is regimented. But he is thru under Communism.

Finally, Russia is considerably more Marxian than we are, darling. We aren't at all. They are building Socialism in Russia. Before the war they were going ever higher. We were going continually lower. The only reason for the comparatively high standard of living in this country is its fabulous natural resources. Russia is probably the only country that can compare. If not for the war, I think they would have surpassed our standards in much less time than it took us to achieve them.

As for Mill…That concept isn't so simple. Think about it some now, particularly applying it to specific examples. I think it's pretty good as to personal relations. But for Government-Citizen relations, it's not going to be easy to define "conduct which concerns others." Does exploitation of one man by another concern us? Does teaching children superstitious nonsense so that they are biased all their lives concern others? Try to think of what things we can do that don't concern others and maybe his simple philosophy might seem a little more complicated.

Now look at what you've done!

Love
Aaron

Tuesday 10:30 p.m.

Hello darling:

Yesterday, I saw the Lieutenant, and as you surmised, told him I couldn't take it. Too bad, tho. I'll probably be sorry. The set up is quite nice. A year at Ann Arbor studying Japanese and Military Tactics [they're turning out officers, as well as Japanese interpreters, you see]; Then six more months at Camp Savage, University of Minnesota, for advanced work, mostly application of the language to Military Intelligence. Then you graduate as officers in Military Intelligence Corps. Kind of a quiet life for a year and a half. And at the end of it, I think it's still a far cry from a Lieutenant who interviews Jap prisoners to a private on active combat duty—even in the Medical Corps.

Oh well…

Sunday night I saw North Star, finally. You're right about it. It was only a few moments from start to end—and it wrung some tears out of my cynical soul. All of it was beautifully done; the director certainly knew his business. The continuous underplaying—my favorite mode of expression-- struck me very forcefully.

But I disagree pretty much with what I've heard about the movie; the so called "idyllic exaggeration" of the first part. I don't think the fundamental idea was exaggerated at all. Of course, details are over played. All is not new and shiny; and it probably rains occasionally in the Soviet Union. Also people have bunions, are occasionally grouchy, and probably sometimes don't like their relatives.

Yet that isn't the significant thing to me at all. It isn't comforts, let alone luxuries, that make for the good life. But the knowledge that tomorrow, and tomorrow…will be here with relative security for ourselves and loved ones. I don't know how many times I've said the same thing. Security is the all important concept for me in forming any kind of milieu for man to live in.

I think people would sing, and laugh, play accordions, and go to enjoyable picnics—if at the end of the day they didn't have to "spend their time usefully" in making as nearly sure as possible that there will be a tomorrow…

So all of us are constantly grinding in our attempt to push ourselves into some niche of the ladder from whence we can look down at the others and hope then to relax. But "then" never comes…

Every small entrepreneur is constantly busy planning expansion of his business, planning to beat his competitors, watching for their attacks on him. Not that he needs more money to live—but for "tomorrow." No matter what his position today, he cannot feel secure. And so it goes, up to the big businessman, and down to the laborer. A girl spends a lot of her time planning for, and going thru the motions of getting, a "good catch." The student tries to push to the head of the class, to get the appointment.

Every neighbor, every newcomer, is a potential competitor. And where can there be true warmth, friendship, music, singing, laughter, relaxation—with these potential enemies.

How often have you heard your mother really sing—singing that just welled up because she was glad? Or yourself? Why don't our parents go to folk dancing groups with their friends, enjoying being with them (not just to impress them, or kill time)…?

Your father has to make all he can now, he'd tell you. You'll never know what next season would be like…

So the basis, I think, is force. With the day's work done [and one needn't work to the point of exhaustion who's not competing with anybody] with a reasonable assurance that tomorrow will bring the same situation as today, the whole community can relax, can exude warmth, can sing, dance, and be happy.

Possibly the best example I can give you, is the difference in the relationships in a civil service job—and in most private industry. I think it speaks for itself. Maybe you don't squeeze as much work out of the civil service employee. But he lives a far better life. And it's the people we're thinking of; it's the better life we want.

Are you getting tired of my philosophical discussions, darling? I ought to be writing about medicine, I guess…

Incidentally, you wrote last week that you'd been having some pretty regular quarrels with your mother. It comes as a bit of a shock. Are they about me? I'm very interested, as you might expect, and you ought to keep me far better informed about stuff like that.

Try to guess what time it is?

Good night dear,
Aaron

3/24 Friday 10:30 a.m.

Gloria dear—

I'm writing early this morning. We're cutting most of the day, to try to do something about those finals starting Monday. "Something" is right. Once a day—like vitamins—we're taking exams in Toxicology, Physiotherapy, Diseases of the Chest, Hematology, Orthopedics, and Dermatology. Except for Hematology, given by Dr. Singer, the other courses are punk, the teachers are rotten, and not having patients, movies, or even slides for demonstration, you can imagine what I get out of it. Well…

I received your pussy-cat poetry yesterday, darling. Also your rather broad hint that my letters lack—passion. Tsk! Tsk! They probably do, dear. But that is because I write completely instinctively, and take for granted our love…I do not like, and so couldn't emulate, the swarm "who protests too much." If I needed to convince myself, I'd write very impassioned letters. But I don't. My future planning is very simply, almost casually, built up taking you with me for granted. And sometimes, the problems of just how to manage it give me quite a headache.

How goes it at home? Have you heard from Manny? Is your father better? Do your folks still plan on travelling? How is Thelma's love life coming along? I wrote to Aaron and Esther, you know; they were the ones we left in the most precarious position. So far, no reply. I'll probably write again, & if I get no reply see what's up by writing to Allan.

Incidentally, drop over to my home and give my mother my love when you get the chance. I won't be in for at least three weeks.

Medicine and I are in a very funny position. Theoretical medicine, I mean. There is so much that I want to know, it almost hurts. It's very difficult to explain that feeling, but it's like being given the first few bars to several magnificent symphonies, and then left with the records and record-player. You are dying to play them all, over & over again, get the themes, see the form, the method of development, follow it with a score…but you aren't given the time. Wouldn't that just about drive you mad?

So it is up here. I have the books. Magnificent books on Anatomy, Physiology, Pathology, Internal Medicine, Surgery. They are all tied-up together, so that reading one, and really understanding it, makes each of the others, that much more significant. Yet I can't do anything about it. The school kills about 8 hours a day for me with lectures I must attend, tho I play tic-tac-toe or something to stay sane while some asinine M.D. raves on. Then I have only the evening to get something from the text.

It's really awful. All that I ask is to be given time to learn the stuff…On the other hand, I'd probably never do anything as boring as physiotherapy if left alone.

There just isn't enough time to learn anything in this school. If the day were spent seeing patients, so that my reading is clarified, it would help. But to have it all wasted by a bunch of stupid lectures, it's criminal.

Beefing again…

Incidentally, I couldn't get very far in Whitehead. If you want to read Modern philosophy try Morris Cohen's "Philosophy and the Scientific Method."

Love
Aaron

Tuesday 3/27 1:30 p.m.

Gloria darling:

Two exams over—4 more to go! So far they've been pretty simple. The instructors gave us the questions to the exam just before finals to make sure that nobody fails. Some school, eh? The next four are going to be harder, as we don't have the questions and answers…Tomorrow, Singer's Exam in Hematology will probably be a lulu. He doesn't believe in making any concessions to anyone. There is pride in his teaching, and a knowledge of a job well done. He, and Dr. Levinson (Professor of Medicine) are the only saving features of this year's work.

That is why you haven't been getting weary letters telling of my killing myself studying. I read along—doing as much as I can in the time left after a day of lectures, listen to some music, drink a lot of cocoa and coffee (how about those cookies you've been promising me!), and go to sleep pretty late.

There is a kind of dull apathy at school. Nothing seems very important or significant. There is a vague hope that we'll be allowed to take State Boards. Exams are best; a necessary inconvenience…

I wish you were with me. Time goes by. Time that we could spend together…I'll be coming in to New York the weekend of April 15—if nothing turns up to stop me.

I don't want to go in this weekend as we have an exam Saturday morning, so that I'd only have a few hours in New York. The following weekend is Passover; both Joe and I wanted to go in—he won. You know one of us has to be on duty. So I come in the following one—barring accident.

Send Manny my sincere hope for a speedy return home. England may be lovely; Brooklyn is where he'd be happier. Maybe I'll even write to him, if I feel full of energy. Or can you do that for both of us?

I got a letter from Allan. He is put out at my silence but "Won't let a friendship of so many years be affected by my lack of cooperation…" I'm going to assure him very soon that the only reason I didn't write was not having his address. I hope he believes me. He's still in Washington, kind of dissatisfied with his dull life after his brief sojourn with the army.

I'm enclosing a letter from our team published in the Norfolk Medical News, a branch paper of the Boston Medical Society. This paper has been rather favorable to us as evidenced by its publishing the letter. There isn't much in it, but will bring you up to date "on the state of the school."

Good afternoon, darling
Aaron

Incidentally-- I want my letters hand written.

Love
Aaron

Thursday

Gloria darling:

After all the pros & cons, I'm going to come in this Saturday. I was half thinking about it all along, and we finally agreed that nothing much will happen if I take Monday & Tuesday off. So I'll come in on the Train leaving Boston at 1:00 p.m. and due to arrive at Grand Central at 5:45 p.m. If you meet me at the train, I'll meet you at the main information booth. (I hope there is only one).

It's very miserable in Boston now; cold, wet rain. I hope it's not as bad in New York. But I'm expecting the worst.

So take Monday & Tuesday off and we'll see how best to spend the time.

Four exams gone, two to go. Gosh, is this boring. Today we had Dr. Singer's exam in Hematology. It was typical in being the only intelligent exam so far. Unlike the profs who either give us the questions, or whose exams are "Write all you know about Anatomy", he gave neat, concise, selective questions which in one hour told what you knew.

I have the two most disagreeable ones to go, Toxicology & Physiotherapy.

Until Saturday

Love
Aaron

Wednesday 4/5 9:45 p.m.

Gloria darling:

Well, I'm up here again. The trip was uneventful, unexciting, and unsatisfactory. Some kids insisted upon singing all the way up. I got no sleep at all last night.

Up at school there is no turmoil at all. Apparently only a few were affected by their local Boards. Most know nothing about it. I saw the Registrar today who advised my sending in a letter of appeal, and said that the school would send one, too. We'll probably all get preinduction physicals—and then, it's in the lap of the Gods—or somebody. Things are very tight and very confusing. I'll pass more information on as I get it.

The new Program looks pretty good considering we have no clinics. So:

	M	T	W	Th	F	S
9	Medicine Clinical	Medicine Surgery	Medicine	--		
10	Obstetrics Conference	Surgery Pediatrics	Obstetrics	Surgery		
11	Surgical Path Movies	Medicine	Gynecology	Med	Conf	
12	--	--	--	--	--	
1	Medicine	Medicine	Surgery	Medicine	Trop Med	
2-4	Surgery	Clinical Conf	Legal Med	Clinical Conference		

Until tomorrow dear
Aaron

Friday 4/7 11:30 a.m.

Gloria dear—

It was very nice talking to you last night. We should have done that before, too. But, of course, not very satisfactory. I couldn't tell you that I was coming right over. Nor could I give you any decent news about the school situation. I'm just waiting.

It's quite lovely out today. I've really an awful urge to tuck your hand under my arm and go strolling along the Esplanade with you. Then we could come back to the apartment and behave like little animals. Disgusting…

I've been reading some of The Apostle—and maybe Eliot (a classmate) is right about the book. There appears to be more than sympathy for a teacher in Israel who was killed by the Political and Social forces of his time; or for an attempt to explain Christianity's birth as a result of those same forces.

Instead, he seems more mystical, more in sympathy with the Divine Origin of Christ, and of his spirit imbuing his Disciples. I'm not going to go thru the whole book, as it is so long, but it's very well written. So if you get a chance to read it, let me know what you think.

Since we were given Good Friday off [but not Saturday, despite our being 80% Jewish] most of the class left for New York Thursday.

It's so quiet I'm about talking to myself to liven things up a bit. With my draft status so uncertain, I can't get up much incentive for study; I've just finished PM; there's nothing on the Radio…Maybe I will read The Apostle after all!

About that prescription:

Use the wash as I told you. Get several drops into the scalp with a dropper along a part; make another part, & repeat—until you have scalp well covered. Rub it in. You don't need to shampoo the stuff out immediately, but don't leave it in indefinitely. Repeat the treatment every night; shampoo at the end of the week. Tell the druggist to make up half as much as the prescription calls for; there is far too much listed.

Let me know how it works out. I saw it do the trick for Joe who had a terrific dandruff.

I'll take my fee out in kisses. How many do I get for a visit, anyway?

I don't know whether you realize it or not, but your handwritten letters are better—at least more satisfying—than typewritten. You figure out "how" and "why." It's not just a whim of mine, darling, but the personal letter is more "you", and I want as much of you as I can get.

Well, I'll throw together some lunch; and then probably go for a walk. Walking along by myself, I can let my reveries go on unchecked…

Love
Aaron

Tuesday 4/11 11:00 p.m.

Sweetheart:

I think I never miss you as much as when I feel in trouble. Then, like a little boy I want to run to you, and bury my head in your bosom…I'll talk to you tomorrow and tell you the "latest" about the situation. But despite daily variations in detail, the general picture is pretty gloomy. You can see what the latest draft rulings are in the papers; we're waiting for "final word" from Hershey "on Middlesex." You can probably imagine. Today I received a reply from my draft board on my appeal, simply stating that the forms sent in by the school should have been stamped by the Nat'l Router, so that I have to be kept in 1A. Mr. Smith, whom I called up, told me that at the moment there was no sense in sending out any more letters or anything; he doesn't even know whether, under the new regulations, we are entitled to deferments…

Very helpful.

Yesterday I went down to the Chelsea Hospital, to visit an interne (recent Middlesex graduate) who is a close friend of Joe's. It's a small place, but not nearly as brazenly mercenary as the Revere, I wrote to you about. It's approved for internships by the AMA.

I saw my first delivery. There was no connection between that unconscious woman whose perineum was stretching, and extruding a bluish mass which turned out to be a healthy boy—and a nude, young girl. So you'd never need to worry—even if I become a doctor. Strangely enough the delivery was a remarkable lesson. The doctor did nearly everything our professor tells us not to do. And for the reasons we are warned against. The doctor is a busy man; nor does he give a damn about the patient. When called, he pointed out to us that one should take it easy—"let nature do it…", then proceeded to pull the baby out in 5 minutes. The patient was under ether. She suffered some minor tears (4-5 stitches); the baby looks all right, but will never know what the forceful yanking did to the head & brain—or might have done. I wonder what he would have done if there had been some delay; his office hours started in ten minutes.

Arthur, the interne, was one of the most sensitive fellows you ever saw; so Joe tells me. He's still a very good egg—but treats patients as tho they were stray dogs.

We walked thru the wards and stopped at a patient's bed who was complaining that her arm which was broken & in a cast & sling hurt. She was crying. Arthur took off the sling roughly; told her "she wouldn't die", as she kept on crying-out; made an ineffectual attempt to feel her pulse; made sure she could move her fingers; and "treated" her by telling her to be quiet & go to sleep—it wasn't hurting at all! He told me, loudly, in front of her, that he rarely pays any attention to her as he knows she's an old souse…

The woman in the bed next door was very shy. Delirium tremens, Arthur said. She kept her head under a sheet. Arthur had the grandest time yanking the sheet away from her face many times, for Joe's any my amusement…

These are the Ward or "Service" Cases. They're not getting anything for nothing.

Nor is it Arthur's fault. Dr. Arthur, I should say. He recently passed the State board. He is one of the most sensitive medical students I've seen. He writes sentimental poetry & short stories; comes from a very respectable, loving, New England family. At 27 he is not childish in his judgment.

But where on earth is human dignity? Where the sensitivity to another's suffering? Of all times when man feels small, lost and afraid—it's when he's sick, in pain; and afraid to die. And the person who tends to him at this time is apparently the last person on earth to be able to really feel, understand, and comfort. Patients to doctors are "cases". For the interne, interesting cases from which they can learn something—and routine cases. For the doctors they are paying-cases—or cheap cases; the duller, easier, less interesting—the better.

Yet, why not? Where was Arthur supposed to have learned that people are basically alike? That they suffer, are in pain; and are afraid? That his approach to his patients as an incipient healer should be with a great deal of humility, and prayer for understanding? That a broken arm hurts even in a service case, and a sedative might help? That even prostitutes have feelings, feelings that he of all people in the world ought to respect?

No one is born with this understanding. And rarely, is it taught in our society. Of all people doctors get probably the least of this kind of education. Social workers, teachers, even Historians get far more.

There is only one solution, darling. The solution that will be fought tooth-and-nail by all the Arthurs, and the great bulk of the profession, who are far, far more cynical, and mercenary in their role as "healers."

Doctors should be paid salaries, and closely supervised by competent men. If the top men have the sympathy, knowledge and understanding; it's only a matter of time before the run-of-the-mill employee (M.D.) either shares it, or will leave the service and go into poultry slaughtering. Doctors should become members of society; work normal hours; get regular wages; have paid vacations; and advance to superiority and specialist positions on absolute merit—medically and personally.

Until this happens, medical care will continue to be the disgusting farce it is today.

Good Lord—Look what I've written. A thesis?

I meant to tell you how very beautiful the Rembrandt is. I'll keep it in good condition for us. I've shown it to about a dozen people already, and they all think you're wonderful. The pictures are magnificent. Can you imagine what they're like in color?

Good night darling
Aaron

Thursday 4/13 12:00 Midnight

Gloria dear:

I only had the chance to say "Hello darling" last night, before our time was up. You must have paid a fortune last week, particularly if you made it "person to person"...It was very nice hearing your voice tho, so very close...

Morale is nil. I haven't done any studying worth talking about.

Today we went over to Leo Hochmin's, the son of a Rabbi, who is in my class. They must have been sorry for two Jewish boys in the wilderness, and fed us good Passover food, until we were ready to burst.

I don't think I've ever really come into close contact with the orthodox Jewish life. For the first time I ate with a skull cap on, and said Grace after the meal...

Rabbi Hochmin is a venerable man, with frock coat, Bernard Shaw beard. Every inch the "spiritual leader" of his congregation. They really live in Chelsea, a small city just across the river from Boston; more Jews in Chelsea...

Leo is pretty fortunate. Just what did it, I don't know,-- but he blissfully goes along not having any religious crises. Another one of the boys, who stem from a similar background is continuously on the defensive about his religious customs. Not smoking on Saturday, not eating Pork, going to Synagogue regularly...all seem to require a lot of apologies. Not so Leo. He is a very quiet, likable, inoffensive chap who observes most of the customs without saying anything about them; if asked, points to his family's position; and is taken for granted. Peculiarly enough, he went to Boston College (a Catholic school) in trying to crash Medical School.

You remember that I suggested the records for Leo. Well, we spent the evening listening to a lot of them. New records on a pretty good phonograph, are good listening…

So goes another day. Yesterday we spent the whole afternoon at the Y…

I miss you a lot, darling.

I'm tired again; and want to escape into you. A strange expression, I suppose. Yet it's true. I don't think I'd be much of a source of emotional support these days. Probably, I'd drain you dry.

On the other hand you undoubtedly have an unlimited reserve of warmth that I couldn't exhaust no matter how hard I'd try. Willy-nilly, I'd like to have you with me for a while just now, anyhow.

It's pretty late now, as you can probably guess. Tho I'm not studying, I don't get much sleep anyhow.

Good night darling,
Aaron

Monday 4/17 1:10 a.m.

Gloria darling:--

It's pretty late, I dare say, but I'll be able to get a letter written to you before turning in. There is music on from 1 o'clock on now-a-days, so something pretty is playing now…

Your letters are present and very sweet, dear. Keep up the good work. I'll expect letters even if your work piles up, tho. You still have some time when you're not working, you know…

Funny, but life goes on in the most difficult situations. Tho I don't know what's going to happen to me or to the school a month from now, I started to work as a waiter on Friday. For two days, Friday night & Sunday, I pretty clumsily carried dinners to people, put plates down in front of them and collected the bills. For which I was duly tipped. Kind of silly. Yet the work is considerably easier than bussing (even my kind)—and pays more. I don't want to spend more than 1 night or day a week at it, so I don't know just how I'm going to arrange it. So far the manager thinks that I'm going to be a waiter on Friday night, and a bus-boy on Sunday afternoon—"till I learn how." It's really not very important, but interesting in that daily problems just keep on coming up, asking to be solved.

You know, even if I can ever afford it, I'll probably never take you to a night club. I've seen too much of it. I'd like to eat in a place where the food is good, the environment is very quiet, dinner-music played by strings…Now just think of the perfect opposite and you get a night club…

Oh, well. We'll face that very important problem as we get to it…

Which reminds me, darling. You better call on Thursday. I'll probably be working Friday night. So then I'll be expecting you Thursday, or Wednesday at about 10:00 o'clock. And don't call "person-to-person." Get <u>Kenmore 2270</u> in Boston. I'll be at home both evenings. See how faithful I am?

Probably by that time I'll have more information about the school situation for you…

About that inscription. I'd love you if you wrote "Violets are blue, roses are red…" on the fly leaf, I guess. But if you want to make them as satisfying as possible, just write what you think, don't get them from a book. No matter what you write, it will be appropriate, dear. A very clever epigram may sound forced.

I'm never going to be able to get up for a nine o'clock class tomorrow. It's awfully late.

Good night darling,
Aaron

Sat 11:15

Hello darling:

I've been trying to get a letter to you written, since Thursday night. And this is actually my first chance. After I talked to you Thursday, I studied for a little while, Joe took his girl home during the interim, and we got to work on a case research. Well, it was 2 o'clock before we finished & I went up to go to sleep.

Yesterday Sammy got in all right. Joe met him, took him out to eat, and made him comfortable. Today we found him a very pretty room in a building about ½ block from here. Three of the boys from school share the floor with him. His luggage is all moved, and for all practical purposes he's all settled.

He's a pretty interesting egg, but he'll have to find something to do with his evenings. I have so little time, I'm afraid I'll be able to keep him company for only very short periods. Anyhow his landlady is very young and pretty; I almost took a room there myself…

So much for Sammy. Since he cost your father about $2 for my talking to you, I had to give him some time, no?

Spring is here, darling. The Esplanade is lovely. The grass is green, water is rippling, boy and girl ducks are swimming all over the place—and you ought to be here. This part of Boston is pretty nice in the Spring. I say it very grudgingly…

A couple of days ago I got off onto a long reverie on my favorite subject, lately. The evils in the present medical set-up. Why should a system of free enterprise, which apparently works, after a fashion, in other similar "professions", be so bad in the medical profession. No one is making any great to-do about Socializing Dentistry, Watch Repairers, Radio fixers, carpenters, plumbers…There are dozens of service trades in which the set up is very similar to Medicine; you pay for a job done as a service. What's all the fuss about the Medical profession?

Well, I don't know whether you've noticed it, but I've built up a straw man in order to knock him down.

There is <u>no</u> similarity between Medicine and any of the other professions, except very superficially. In every other one you pay the Dentist, Lawyer, Electrician, Radio man…when he has produced. The tooth is filled, the contract written, the bell fixed, the radio is playing. Only to the medical profession, do you pay for "advice" which in 90% of the cases has no bearing upon the course of the disease. Nearly all the patients who are "cured" by practitioners, would have gotten better if they had never gone to the doctor. Most of the time a diagnosis is not made and "symptomatic" treatment is given. As you know this has really no effect upon the illness.

Frequently the wrong diagnosis is made, and the patient recovers despite treatment!

There is, then, one fundamental difference, at least, in the Medical profession from all others. There is no check on the doctor's competency. The greatest fraud in the country is probably being perpetrated by the Medical profession—legitimate medicine or its illegitimate branches…

Is competency so very important, anyhow? Terribly. Let alone the general monetary swindle; -- correct, early diagnosis is the only hope in most serious treatment. Incompetency is yearly killing many, many patients. Nor will the truth really ever get out—Medical ethics forbid a doctor testifying against another, nobody is the practitioner's superior and can even tell him that he's wrong! The insufferable, stupid docs are very jealous of their sovereignty; without it they'd be peddling magazines, a lot of them…

What is the minimum that is really required from this unique profession? Competency; Honesty; Willingness to have the patient's health as their sole aim in treatment.

In the present set up, you can see there is no way to ensure the first. The "personality kid" is the most successful usually. And if he loses a few patients—nobody knows. Supervision is practically mandatory to achieve competency. Very close supervision. A doctor must keep on learning all the time. Medicine as practiced 50 years ago is criminal negligence today. How to correct this? The patients, as I've said, are no judge of the MD's knowledge or ability. Only constant supervision by MD's superiors will keep the practitioner learning.

The second two are inexorably linked. It is a tantamount contradiction, I think, to expect a body of very ordinary men, to want to be honest and try to keep their patients healthy, even to the point of telling them that they don't know what to do at times—when their livelihood is pointing in exactly the other direction. The situation is so impossible, that the profession, by and large, looks upon the public as a victim—rather than as a patient.

Finally, I think the public has a right to have the best "medical practice" available, practiced. Disregarding competency for the moment, Medicine is practiced today in the Horse & Buggy stage. Practice is so far behind the "best practice" as taught in school, it's not even funny. And the reason is that medicine has evolved to the point where it is so complex, and so dependent upon laboratory findings (rather than percussion or praying with the family), that it must center about very expensive equipment and very trained personnel. No individual doctor can afford it. The only real decent laboratories, X-Ray equipment, electrocardiograms…are in the huge hospitals. The price for individual tests is prohibitive. So medical science goes on, but only the discoveries which can be put into pills and given every 4 hours are really of use to the profession. Our professor of medicine told us recently that mortality statistics for Cancer of the stomach haven't improved at all. Early diagnosis is possible at present with an X-Ray series. But it costs $25-$30. And since early symptoms are so few, who is going to pay $30 for an X-Ray, when he only has a mild belly ache? Yet the X-Ray men keep their prices up, and make fortunes. Also a lot of people die who might have been cured with an early X-Ray…

Maybe you can see what my solution would be for insuring Competency; bringing into the profession men who love Medicine and are in sympathy with the sufferings of their fellow men; giving another motive, but maximum fee for service rendered; and bringing all that Medical Science has to offer, in a coordinated fashion, to the people…I feel, that of all professions, medicine needs a profound reorganization most badly.

I went off again darling.

As I said on Thursday, by now you ought to know everything I think of. Am I repeating myself?

It's almost one now, two of the boys just dropped in.

Good night darling.
Aaron

Thursday 12:45 a.m.

Hello darling—

Like talking to you; but not quite. That was very nice last night, but I'll have to talk less—on my salary. I suppose I talk too much anyhow…

Sammy was over this evening. Things look pretty smooth for him, so far. He thinks they are saving him for <u>after</u> the invasion. When the Germans are licked, the army is going to cancel a lot of its orders with these defense plants, and they'll need accountants to check up on the Cancellation Agreements. So that sounds very nice, if it works out.

So far I haven't received any further word from my draft board. Forms or no forms, I'd feel more secure with a 2-A classification instead of a 1A…

That overwhelming discussion I keep on making anew constantly, has hit me again. I don't know anything—even in medical theory—compared to what I'm supposed to know. If I don't sleep at all, and don't go to work anymore; I can't learn the stuff. I've been doing nothing else except reading Cecil this year—and I've done very little by the looks of it. There are acres of print not yet underlined! I ought to get someone to underline the book for me, while I'm in school, so I won't feel so badly. My goal in life right now seems to be to put as many lines in my Textbook of Medicine as possible. Since nearly everything is important, I underline nearly the whole page. Very silly…

About Laski. I really don't remember a thing about his books. I do know that I read some of his stuff and thought that he was magnificent but can't really remember what he wrote about. I think his stuff isn't too light. It requires a good deal of thought. Go to it, and pass it on.

To get any grasp on World Politics, modern thought…you'll have to "read it all." No "one book a month." There's an overwhelming amount to know. In politics, sociology, philosophy, modern history. Without being familiar with Modern thought, & having some solid point of view, one cannot be called "Cultured" today. You literally have to devour the stuff. Beard—"America in Midpassage"; "Middletown in Transition"; Morris R. Coblen's "Nature and Reason"; Beard's New Book—"The Republic";

Laski…I haven't read a fraction of what I want, & need, to read. So you become as intellectually sophisticated as you wish, and pour your ideas out to me.

I'll take my head out of Cecil long enough to pick up any thoughts you pass on—and I'll be very grateful.

Incidentally, darling. I'm not nearly as good as you apparently think. If I were half as good—I'd be pretty wonderful. This enforced separation keeps things on such a "high plane", you're getting an "idealistic picture", I'm afraid. I'm just an ordinary guy who wants very much to live & let live—and who happens to be in love with you very much…

Good night dear,
Aaron

Sunday 9:30 a.m.

Gloria dear—

I was in the mood for the longest, warmest letter you ever received last night, when my previous housemate Eddie dropped over at about 10:00. He stayed 'til 2:00—and I went to sleep. Always being frustrated…

But you know that I'm in love with you. Why waste time & paper telling you things you know about?

I'm enclosing a letter from Esther. As she says, "All's well…" From what I've been reading about Fibroids, she is a very lucky girl at this point to be healthy, and capable of bearing children.

Do you notice that everyone, far and wide either thinks we're already married, or are going to be very soon? Some time ago, one of the boys, returning from a trip home (his wife is in Sea-Gate), told me he heard that we were married and wanted to know why I hadn't let him know! I don't know what it is; there must be an organized propaganda drive on. Yet I'm making no effort to squelch these rumors. I just tell my assailants that I wish we were married—and they keep their peace.

I've been pretty tired lately. For the past 3 weeks I've been a waiter all night on Friday (until 3 am), a bus boy on Sunday, and on duty at the switchboard Sat, Wed & Thursday. Since we go down to the Y twice a week, approximately, it just doesn't leave me much time to do much else. Nor am I making a fortune! The now 30% tax has made night club business hardly worthwhile. I'm lucky if I make $5 on either of the two days I work. As soon as I can arrange it, I'm going to drop the Sunday afternoon. I'd rather sleep and take walks on the Esplanade than make money…

My mother wrote that Solly broke an arm last week. This kid sure is getting all the breaks! Drop over to see him, will you, and bring him something to cheer him up. I'd like to go myself, but it's really impossible just now. At any rate, I think he likes you and will accept you as my representative. I'm a bit worried about the kid. I think his Ego is so small that he'll never be able to find it. From all the signs (and I'm no diagnostician, certainly) he's going to get himself into an awful emotional tangle. Nor am I able to do anything about it. My mother would be totally impervious to any suggestions along those lines. So don't try to make any…

I'm half asleep, before I'm even dressed to get up. I can't take these 5, 6, and 7 hours of sleep at all!

I love you very much darling,
Aaron

Sunday 9:30

Gloria darling:

I didn't plan writing to you tonight—but I just can't help it. The night is so beautiful—and I'm very lonely.

All our windows are open to the night that is seeping in. As you know, the Charles with the Esplanade is just beyond our house. It's very beautiful out there. I was going to go out and stroll along for a while, but so much nostalgia hit me, I had to write.

You ought to be out here now. Or I be in Brooklyn…

Sometimes, I feel overwhelmed by a feeling of inevitable constant frustration. As tho I don't have a firm grasp on reality, and am not able to make the situation adjust to meet my needs; but rather that I constantly adjust to meet changing situations. Situations which are constantly changing and pushing me around. No solidity from which I can do as I please.

Gosh darling, I need you now. Need solidity on which to rest; warmth and acceptance in which to nourish myself…

I guess it's the weather, dear. The weather, and my feeling of utter helplessness in fulfilling the call of the night.

Good night, darling
Aaron

Wednesday 5/3 1:05 a.m.

Gloria darling:

It's so beautiful out on the Esplanade tonight, it's almost unreal. Something like a movie of Spring & love…The indirect lighting of lamps more or less hidden behind trees, the Maple trees and Forsythias in bloom, the Charles flowing by very quickly, the half moon; the very gentle breeze; and boys and girls all looking very quiet and a little subdued by the beauty…

Sammy was over and we took the walk. He must have been thinking about Mary; as I was thinking about you. Yes, I guess it's spring…For me, May is the beautiful month of the year…

I received my draft deferment: 2A until Oct. 13…So life goes on. Of course, the date of expiration really doesn't mean anything. The next crisis is sometime in July, I suppose. The State Board will rule us not fit for approval. What happens next is Anybody's guess. You know mine…The whole "crisis" didn't raise much of a ripple up here. I suppose we're getting pretty much inured to the situation. Most of us are developing a fatalistic outlook.

Work, of a sort, is piling up. There are at least 10,000,000 diseases that man is heir to. They all have very interesting, very long names, like Osgood-Schlatter's Osteochondritis of the Tibial Tuberosity, or Wilsons Progressive Hepato-Lenticular Degeneration. And by the end of the year, 3 more months, I'm supposed to be pretty familiar with their names (which is enough), pathology, symptomatology, etiology, diagnosis, and treatment (if any). While

I'm at it, I'm also to know the essential points of every operation performed on the human body, Legal Medicine, & the whole subject of Obstetrics. Very silly. And all this without seeing a patient or an operation (even by movies), or knowing whether memorizing the stuff is worth anything.

There I go griping again. Maybe I'm just sex starved. Keep writing, dear; picking up your letters in the morning has become practically a necessary habit. Since I don't smoke, I indulge in the habit of automatically reaching out for your letters in the morning.

I'll be expecting your call tomorrow. You'll probably get this after I've told you all the "news" by phone. But, you say you don't get tired of reading or hearing me call you darling.

So, Goodnight darling
Aaron

Friday 5/5 9:10 a.m.

Good Morning!

I still have about an hour before my first class this morning, so while waiting for Joe I can't think of anything I'd rather do. It's very lovely again today. The wind is coming in from the river and just about caressing all it hits. Very lovely.

You'll do better calling me at 9:00 o'clock instead of 10. I'm generally home evenings—and if I know you're calling I'll be at the telephone. You see, if you call before 10, I take the call in our study, and I'm not distracted by bells ringing and lights flashing—people apparently trying to get me and whom I ignore blissfully…

It's good that you went over to see Solly. I'm glad he's getting along O.K. And he'll enjoy not only the book, and the fact that someone, unsolicited, had gotten it for him. You'll be his favorite if you keep it up. Believe it or not, I forgot all about Arthur's birthday. I'll drop him a note this morning. I see where you're going to be a very busy girl keeping me in touch with what's going on…You're starting pretty well now.

I've told you about the Draft Situation last night; there is little to add. We can count on three months anyhow. Morale, as I've said, is still pretty low—or at any rate unchanged. Nobody anymore feels that we're going to be recognized, or get clinics. It's all pretty much resignation. Maybe we'll have a fourth year; maybe not. At any rate I'm doing some studying.

My working at the Hi Hat isn't working out the way I planned. I had expected to be allowed to work only Friday night, as a waiter. Instead, the manager told me that he needs me far more as a bus boy on Sunday—and is only letting me work Fridays as a favor to me. So I'll probably stop going in Friday. One day a week is all the night club work that I can stomach. As you put it, there is no point killing myself, if I don't know whether I'll be getting anything out of it. Studying is very enjoyable; working in a night club distasteful.

So as to meeting me in Hartford for lunch…It's a good idea. But try to make it for any day but Sat. or Sunday. I'm on duty at the switchboard on Sunday until 12 and then at the Hi Hat from 1-8. Tho I could probably get away with the latter, I don't think I could do anything about the switchboard. Of course, if there is no other day you can get, I'll try to get Joe to take over Sunday morning (he works 'til late at the Fox & Hounds Sat. night you see).

All very complicated. No? So take a Thursday or a Friday off one of these days & just let me know. It'll probably rain.
School's on, darling

Love
Aaron

Tuesday 5/9 12:15 a.m.

Gloria dear:

I've just gone over the two letters I received today. Very sweet…You must be just revelling in the mass of ballet you're gorging yourself on. You're right, tho. The combination of music & dance is pretty miraculous.

Mary and Sam were over tonight for a while. This Thursday, Mary's going to try to make supper for us. Considering our facilities—or lack of them—she'll have to be good to cook up something good.

She's a pretty good person. Politically quite sophisticated, she has very definite ideas. One of them is that she hates Communists; but really hates them! Her background, particularly that of her former husband's would be very, very interesting. I don't say much, just listen. Mostly because I really don't know enough to argue with anybody really informed about current politics. Where does Sammy fit into the picture? She practically has to push him into the conversations—where he obviously doesn't belong. Sammy is a pretty nice egg; but they don't seem to have very much in common, do they? Oh well, I really don't know very much about either of them…

Upon your suggestion, I got my mother a Mother's day card. Now I really don't believe in them, you know. But I am going to get one anyhow. It's really a lazy man's way of getting out of saying something nice originally. I wish the cards weren't so awful tho. I did pick out the least offensive that I could find, yet I'd be ashamed to be caught vomiting such sentimental stuff.

Lately I've been getting the queerest urges. Do you remember Arrowsmith leaving medical school in his 2nd or 3rd year to go to his girl friend's home out west? Well, I don't think I'll do anything so drastic—just yet. But you'd better come up to see me soon…Those urges come and go. I'm very restless…Maybe it's the quantity of sunlight I'm absorbing these days…In any event I'm missing quite a bit of the surgery lectures these days, as my day dreams take me far afield…

I'm enclosing another "Interne" classic. You'll soon have the most complete collection in existence. You ought to get them together; they're really very good. Someday, I'll want to go over them. At least, I will if I'm a doctor. If not, I'll probably never want to see a Caduceus or a stethoscope again.

Good night darling
Aaron

Thursday 1:00 a.m.

Gloria—

Tho it's really tomorrow, I'll still call it tonight—a little late at night. And you can't find time to write to me since you got home at 9! Come now young lady, you're a big girl. At least, I think so.

If it weren't so expensive I'd like to call you once a week, as well as have you call me. As it is, maybe just once a week will do. Incidentally, darling, why did you change your mind at making all the calls. It's not that I can't afford the half dollar—I'm just interested in the situation. Did your father object? Is your "pride" hurt at making all the calls? Give out with it…

Mary and Sam, as you know, were over for supper. Mary got here at 4:30. What she doesn't know is that we spent at least an hour yesterday, cleaning up the house for her. Maybe two hours. The place will never quite look the same again, I'm afraid. She ought to stay around for a few months; the apartment would benefit marvelously. Since she only made a salad, I can't really judge whether she's a better cook than we are. I'll just assume so, on the basis of her longer experience. Mary's a charming person, as you say. She has completely captured Joe. I haven't, tho, tried to be personal in speaking to her as you must have been. We've talked about everything from PM to Medical Ethics. On the whole she's very sound in her points of view and basis for them. Tho I may disagree with what she says…

I don't suppose she can transfer any of her "charm" to Sam—but it would help. He's a very nice guy who can use a lot of "savoir-faire."

As I said, don't expect anything good to come out of the school, dear. I'm staying on because I've come this far and don't have anyplace else to go. It's a rotten situation for you, but I don't want you to build up to a letdown. Wishful thinking won't help…There is an excellent possibility, conceded by everyone up here that the school will fold up this summer. As soon as it does I'll be drafted. There is really nothing necessarily wrong with my eyes; nothing that serious.

So I think you ought to meet me in Connecticut this Friday. I don't like to copy lectures, and only have a limited number of cuts, but it'll be worth seeing you—even if it isn't as satisfactory as I'd like it.
It's terribly late darling

Good night
Aaron

Wednesday 9:30 p.m.

Gloria darling—

I didn't write Monday or yesterday mostly because I've been in a psychological turmoil during the past few days. All I can attribute it to is Spring, Sunlight, and living on the Esplanade.

Just imagine, darling. Living inside of Prospect Park! Only the Esplanade is much more a mating ground than our beloved park. And there are still plenty of persons of both states in this Fair City to do justice to the grass abounding here.

I don't think you need worry about my fidelity, tho, dear. Just my peace of mind. I love you very much. And my personality is so put together, that I can't make love to a girl unless I believe that I'm in love with her. Whether I like it or not, my actions and words must pretty closely reflect my inner feelings. You'll have no trouble knowing how I feel about anything at any time, I think.

The situation has pretty much overwhelmed most of the boys. They are to be found lolling in the grass, roaming the parks most of the time.

The whole situation is very demoralizing.

I hope you are strong, darling. As I become more and more demoralized I'm going to lean on you increasingly…Talking to you tonight was very pleasant. It'll even be better seeing you Friday. Tell your parents, by any means.

Mary and I had a talk just before she left about "breaking away from home." She kept on maintaining (speaking in general, of course) that it wasn't necessary to make "small breaks" if they would cause a rumpus; rather wait until a big issue comes up. In other words cutting your hair, going to see me in Boston, or what have you, are best acquiesced to. When we're ready to be married, the big decision is made, and the big break is made. I disagreed. In a subsequent talk, of which a student having supper was the main topic of conversation, we all (students) agreed that from the Modern Psychological point of view, Mary is wrong.

Growth is a slow process, and goes by steps. And since "the break of the adolescent from the home" is the most important, second only to "Achievement of Heterosexuality", in maturity (Frank Williams), achievement of that kind of maturity must be by steps.

There must be millions of small points on which you and your parents disagree. Not obviously stupid ones. But yet, not vital. Deliberately, have your own way. Cut your hair; buy lots of clothes that make you look like a woman, not a kid; read a lot of nonfiction; grow disgruntled with the status quo of the world, your situation, your progress, your knowledge, other people's ideas; learn to hate smugness nearly above all else…

Sounds like Polonius, no?

Forgive the tempest of advice…

I'm enclosing an editorial you might have read. Do you remember my inarticulate ravings several months ago, about how I'd like to put everybody old enough, man & woman, into uniforms and make them feel, as closely as possible, what soldiers are getting. Everybody—even you—was startled. Doesn't everybody have a relative in the service? Doesn't everyone want the war over?

Probably I have identified myself very closely with the service-man. Maybe it's because I'm constantly being faced with the possibility of soon being one…

But Bernstein is saying, as I would have liked to have said, that there is a vast, an immeasurable difference between soldiers in Italy & Civilians in the War Department. People are fundamentally very small, weak & ignoble. Rationalization is the primary function of our "thinking" brain.

The bitterness in the fighting troops will turn to deep hatred. And I fear for our "Democratic Institutions" if that hatred is channelized along Fascist lines after the war.

I apparently can rave on and on. Right now, I need a lot of quiet, with your hand on my brow, and prospect of being able to stay that way indefinitely.

Good night darling,
Aaron

Friday 5/19 12:30 p.m.

Hello darling—

I'm somewhat better now—From my last letter you could probably judge that my state of mind wasn't in the best possible condition for mental health. With a couple of good nights' sleep; less sunlight, due to the cooler weather; & an afternoon at the Y, I'm more tranquil. Not that I still wouldn't give a lot to have you pop in on me right now…

Imagine darling. The year ends in about 7 weeks! Considering what I'm supposed to know—even in theoretical medicine—and what I do know at this point, it's absolutely impossible. Yet the situation doesn't concern us too badly. If we take Boards, I think we'll pass. Most of the last class to take the State Boards passed, and they didn't particularly do any more work than we do. The only problem is to be allowed to take them…

As you remember, I wrote about our courses. They are all based on exactly the same plan. All medicine really is. We keep on studying disease after disease. If it's in the stomach, it's in the Gastrointestinal Course; if it's in the kidney, it's Urology; in the female reproductive set up it's Gynecology. So that except for the region of the body, it's pretty much all the same pattern: Etiology, Pathology, Symptoms, Treatment…

I've been studying Gynecology this week, darling. So go ahead, ask me. I know all about WOMEN now. At first I thought that the material would be very interesting. But, no! Only the pictures in the book were good…Give me "Internal Medicine"…

There's really a good reason for my predilection right now for "Internal Medicine."

It's the only medicine that is based to a large extent on theory. You see, in every specialty, the specialist is primarily a technician. He cuts, or takes X-Rays, or inserts tubes into the male urethra (Cystoscope) & looks around in the bladder, or he does pelvic examinations on women very well. But, no matter what else he does, (except for the Radiologist & Psychiatrist) he cuts. Therefore, there is very little in these specialty fields which can interest me, in-as-much as I don't have the patients for demonstration or practice. The only other field is, so called, internal medicine. This is the job of making the diagnosis. He is the practitioner, or on a higher level, the "Internist" in a big hospital. Since he can be the biggest faker of them all, the internal medicine man is looked down upon by all the "specialties."

But in this case, the problem isn't one of manual dexterity. It's greatly knowledge, intelligence and experience. The patient presents symptoms: Intense pain in the abdomen, for example. It is the internist's (doctor's) job to make a diagnosis. This is like a puzzle, & therefore interesting even on paper. He has to think of all the possibilities: Gall bladder, Appendicitis, Gastric Ulcer, Perforated Ulcer, Acute Pancreatitis, Mesenteric Thrombosis, Acute Intestinal Obstruction, Acute Salpingitis (Fallopian Tube); Tabes Dorsalis; Lead poisoning…Then he must be able to elicit symptoms, physical signs, and order enough laboratory tests (blood, urine, spinal fluid) to make the diagnosis. It's a lot of fun. Those case histories you saw are based on just that idea. The doctor is given a bunch of symptoms…and the question is "What is it?"

The gynecology text, therefore, was mostly concerned with what to feel and how to operate for the various pelvic disorders. The specialty is essentially surgery. Since I can't go ahead and improve my skill by practicing; the stuff, offering no food for thought, is comparatively dry. Can you beat it? Oh well, if you have any "personal problems" just pass them along and I'll look it up.

At any rate, darling, I'm looking forward to seeing you Friday, a great deal. Since you have to get leave,…I'll let you arrange for when you're to meet me. You'd better check with a timetable, tho, to make sure that a train from Boston will pull in to

New Haven when you arrive. Make it pretty early in the morning; 10 o'clock at the latest.
Good night dear,

Love
Aaron

Tuesday 5/23 12:30 a.m.

Gloria dear—

Altho I'm going to speak to you tomorrow night, I'll write this letter anyhow, or else you may not receive a letter from me until Saturday morning. Imagine!

As you probably know, I won't believe you'll be in New England until I see you. I hope the weather clears up by tomorrow. Considering all the marvelous weather we've had wasted on us, it'll be a shame to be stranded in New Haven in the rain…

I received your picture this morning; and some of the boys passed it around as I looked it over. They all agreed that you're getting plump! I think you look like a fat little girl! Tsk, Tsk! It better be a poor picture…

Tonight we heard Beethoven's 9th. The music, you know. All would have been fine if the radio played even in a mediocre way. But all I could get out of it, were the familiar themes. There's no getting away from it; nothing like a nice little Capehart.

This afternoon most of the class attended the annual convention of the Mass. Medical Society. It's staged just like any convention held by Automobile Salesmen would be, I guess. The affair runs for three days, at the Hotel Statler. Big meetings with speeches, little meetings with speeches, several dinners with speeches, and some exhibits. We went to see the exhibits and a couple of medical movies being run off.

All the drug houses, medical supply shops, and miscellaneous entrepreneurs were represented by little booths advertising their products. As you go along, detail men explain to the Doctor (or prospective Doctor) the merits of their vitamin tablets, laxatives, condensed milk, eyewash, gargle, machines, iron lungs, office equipment for the Modern Doctor…the drug houses give away free samples of pills, lotions, tablets…the medical equipment booths give out literature. In fact, one advertiser was thoughtful enough to give out Shopping Bags, in which to hold all the accumulated trash.

"Now doctor, there is nothing milder, more scientific, more efficacious than our new super-fine Peristal laxative. There is nothing like the personal test, you know. Just try our free sample, and you'll see what Peristol (for Peristalsis, you know) will do."

A country fair in Boston, for yokels who also happen to have M.D.s so there was no skill game or Fortune wheel, tho.

Joe tells me that among waiters everywhere, the doctor is considered the cheapest person on earth.

I'm a little hard on the meeting, tho. The movies were good; the state labs had some legitimate exhibits; some of the talks were probably excellent.

Until tomorrow, Love
Aaron

Wednesday 5/24 9:10 p.m.

Gloria darling—

I spent the day at the Mass. Medical Society. Classes were conveniently called off; as the profs either felt we'd learn more there; or they wanted to attend themselves.

Yesterday my reactions were considerably different than they were today. In the morning we attended a Symposium on Gall Bladder Diseases. Twenty minute talks were given by the Chief of Medicine at the Mayo Clinic, Rochester; by a Harvard Professor of Radiology; and by a Professor of Surgery of Boston University. The men were keen, intelligent and spoke with understanding and authority.

A great many doctors filled the Hall for this symposium. The other lectures of the day were probably not nearly as well attended. Very intelligent of the audience, too. Later on we went to a talk on Abdominal Pain, by the Mayo Clinic chap. And in the afternoon saw about 3 hours of surgical films. In between, there was always some roaming around to do, among the "exhibits"…

As Joe said this morning "They're not all jerks." No. It repeats probably what I've said dozens of times: The subject matter, the science of medicine is marvelous. It probably outranks any of the other callings. But of the men in it, so few are really any good. The good men, the men on top, the Harvard profs, (and probably the Bellevue profs, too) are marvelous. They are intelligent and keen. The bulk of the profession—if the ones I'm meeting is any criterion—is composed of dolts who wouldn't make intelligent shoe salesmen; there is no reason in the world that they make any better doctors. Singer calls them the "Medical Laymen." I don't like them as people, or as doctors. They aren't particularly cultured, don't read, don't listen to music; in short, know little else but their iota of medical lore. They are politically unconscious, and therefore generally reactionary. By virtue of little knowledge, but a livelihood depending upon it, they assume a perpetual art: the bedside manner, combined with a Christ complex, which becomes part of them but makes them insufferable.

The good ones, tho, the people who are making medicine. They deserve all the respect and reverence granted the profession; they are very good men. And our greater well being, medically speaking, is a tribute to them…

Supervision. Supervision. So that the good men can train; and watch the rest is the only solution. In fact, such a system would raise the standard of medical personnel to an unheard of level…

It looks as tho I always get back to the same topic. Stop me if you hear me starting it again.

Love
Aaron

Wednesday 6/1 3:00 p.m.

Hello darling:

I'm just over a nice, cool shower. But as soon as I go out into the street. I'll be reduced to a sweltering mass again.

Yesterday, right after school, one of the fellows took us riding in a very pretty car (Leo Hochman, the Rabbi's son). We stopped off at the Charles and went canoeing. Right after supper I fell asleep & slept for 14 hours! Joe is amazed, but you won't be, I'm sure.

The only thing about our trip to New London that was bad, was that there wasn't enough of it. Also, we should have thought of it two years ago & done it about every 3 weeks right along...You're very, very sweet darling, and I love you very much... Tomorrow, our new library is being opened with the usual dedication ceremony. We saw it yesterday, as the automobile trip went by the school in Waltham. Very nice building—but no books! Very impressive.

To add to the confusion, the Mass. State Board is due to come down very soon. They will turn up their August nares; the case will be brought to court, and... I've been doing a terrific amount of cutting. But so is everybody else. There is rarely half a class present at any one time. It's very hot, the lecturers are atrocious and obviously don't give a damn; the Esplanade beckons; and nobody knows whether the school will be open next month...Are we learning medicine?

Do you notice in recent PM's the fight being waged by organized medicine against the Government's granting aid to wives of Service men who are going to have babies? The Government's plan (now in operation, but up for continuance) grants $50 to a reputable obstetrician for the delivery. I don't know if you've gone thru all the arguments...but fundamentally they are opposed to the ceiling price! The Medical Profession, as saviors of mankind, wants the Gov't to give the women the $50—and let her do her own bargaining, throwing her to the wolves. Where on earth do they get their gall! At present, a great many doctors are organizing to boycott the whole plan. So the private, or corporal in Italy, whose allotment isn't enough to buy expensive obstetrical care, is going to be mightily uncomfortable thinking about his wife's predicament, as our Noble Profession refuses to treat her as they wallow in the fat fees the private is making possible...

I'll call you tomorrow night darling at about 9:45.

All my love

Aaron

Friday 6/2 12:10 a.m.

Gloria dear:

I've just finished listening to "Gaite Parisienne" and Paganini's Violin Concerto. I thought of the ballet, and so of you, and missed most of the Offenbach…God, I'd like to go out with you, to the Ballet perhaps, and feel that we can go out together tomorrow, next week, and the week after…With no deadline to meet. As it is, as soon as I get to see you, time starts to pass and we start getting closer to having to part again. That reminds me of the chap who said that as soon as a child is born it begins the process of dying. Very sombre tonight, no?

On Wednesday, Joe and I visited a senior whom we know, at Robert Breck Brigham Hospital. This darling, was my first visit, professionally, to a really first-class hospital. It's exclusively Harvard, Lahey Clinic …Recently (this year) a Middlesex Resident got in due to the manpower shortage.

The Brigham smacks of wealth, and long medical tradition. Nurses stand when the intern enters the room…The laboratory is extremely well equipped; boasts a technician in charge & 3 assistants, gorgeous microscopes, centrifuges; chemical apparatus…

Rooms are enormous, ceilings vast, screened porches all over the place for convalescent patients.

The operating room knocked us for a loop, tho. You remember my attending an operation in Chelsea Memorial; there it was in a small room; the surgical team and a few observers seemed to crowd the place; equipment was available for Ether, or spinal anaesthesia. At the Brigham one enters a huge room, half the North wall is a sloping corridor to give maximum, perfect illumination. Cabinet after cabinet of instruments; apparatus for any kind of anaesthesia the surgeon's little heart can desire…The only other place you'd think of such an operating room is in the movies.

The cases here are limited to Arthritis and, along with it, Rheumatic Fever. Since arthritis is a chronic disease, with no specific treatment, the whole emphasis of the hospital is different from the typical General Hospital. A patient going into a hospital for Maternity, or Appendicitis, or even Meningitis, eg, will be well probably, inside of several weeks; the main idea is to keep him someplace where very active specific treatment can be instituted: operation, giving transfusions, giving Sulfa drugs or Penicillin. The hospital-diet can be meager as the patient will probably eat little anyhow, and will convalesce at home. You can see how the economics will work out...

In the Brigham, tho, the story is entirely different, I think. The arthritic comes in with a disease that has been treated for years by various doctors; cause not known; treatment uncertain. He will probably stay for 3-6 months—maybe longer. Since no specific cause for Arthritis is known (eg, a bacterium), a complete workup won't be done to rule out any disease. Blood, urine, fever, X-Ray, teeth, eyes...The patient must be built up with food, sunshine, fresh air, operations where necessary. Physiotherapy, occupational therapy...all around the same patient. Drugs, like Gold salts, are used when indicated. A complete & careful history is kept; you can imagine what they're like...

Whether they get results, I don't know, of course. But that is the method of present day medicine. Terribly expensive because done on such a small scale, and not Governmentally financed.

It's very late now darling. Your letters are coming in—and are very welcome. I hope my constant harping on the philosophy of Medicine doesn't bore you.

Good night darling,
Aaron

Thursday 12:20 p.m.

Gloria dear:

I've really wanted to write to you Tuesday or yesterday, but you know what happened. I spent Tuesday afternoon and evening at the Chelsea Memorial Hospital; slept over; cut Wednesday morning (for which I hope to be excused) and fell asleep last night before I could write. I'm really not ungrateful for your daily letters dear…

What did I do at the hospital besides wear a white coat, and try to look important?

In resume:

Spent a while talking to Arthur Schiff, the interne I visited;

Went along with him on his "rounds" done for my benefit at that late hour;

Was shown a patient suspected of gastric ulcer; listened to her story; felt her abdomen for "masses" which might indicate some reason for her pain. (I knew nothing was there, but felt anyway for practice);

Talked to a patient who was in for Continuous Uterine Bleeding; a comparatively young woman, who had an interesting case history available; and who is getting hormone treatment for it;

Saw Arthur do an intravenous, with very careful explanation of the technique;

Helped take blood for a transfusion, and then watched it being given to the recipient;

Saw the site of an interesting skin graft on a kid who had a severe burn; Arthur changed the dressing so I could see it;

A kid arrived in the Emergency Room who had fainted after hemorrhaging from a tooth extraction; Arthur did a blood count as the Technician was gone by then, scratched the area with adrenaline, and kept the girl in the hospital overnight just in case…

In the morning I watched several operations in cap, mask, and gown, so I could stay right at the surgeon's elbow…

Vaginal hysterectomy (removing uterus),
Caesarean section,
Tonsillectomy,
(Delivery, too)

Finally, I was allowed to do an intravenous injection (i.v.) which I approached like a major operation, and was probably very clammy. Never-the-less, since the vein was very prominent, I got right in with no trouble.

Probably sounds like a lot, doesn't it? Well it really doesn't mean anything. There are a few things that I really must know in order to be able to handle myself in the hospital, on the technical end: i.v. (intravenous); passing stomach tubes, passing catheters, operating room procedure, suturing up wounds, reducing a fracture or dislocation, putting on a cast…Most of this, tho, has little bearing on my practice of medicine. To learn to be a doctor, I need a hospital where people come in who are medically sick: pneumonia, meningitis, kidney disease, heart disease, asthma, ulcers, diabetic coma; I need to see kids in Scarlet fever, measles, Rheumatic fever, heart disease…; I need women presenting themselves with gynecological complaints so that I can learn to do pelvic examinations and know what I feel…I need obstetrics where I actually take the babies…I need outpatient departments of General Medicine, Cardiology, Ear-Nose-Throat, Dermatology…where I'd see ambulatory patients as they would come into an office…And with it all, I need Training; supervised instruction, so I know what I am doing, & what I am looking at…

And these things, we don't have at all. God knows where the boys learn it…

Brigham is a good thing. I'm damn glad to be able to tell you something nice for once. Right now I don't know many more details than you do. I'll pass information along. The previous boys (who are House Officers now) are crazy about the place, so I guess it's good to go there. I ate there once; at least the food & service is good.

Of course, it is all pretty contingent upon my being allowed to go to school for the fourth year. Some contingency…

It's extremely late now darling.

Good night dear,
Aaron

Saturday 6/10 1:30 p.m.

Gloria dear—

This morning the letter from the Robert B. Brigham came. "This is to inform you that this hospital has given you the fourth year student appointment beginning the last week of July. You will be notified of the exact date later."

So we're officially in…

I'm very happy about it, of course, but there are still an awful lot of problems.

First, and most important, is being granted permission to take Boards. There will be no fourth year, or at best a very disheartening one, if no Boards are in sight. Morale is terribly low. As the deadline approaches and no Boards seem imminent, less and less studying, attendance…goes on. The present freshman class is down to 50—students dropping out weekly. There is an incoming class of about 50. So upon the decision of the State Board, the Governor or the Courts depends the entire course of my (our) future…

Then comes some thoughts of meeting my expenses. So far, when stuck, I've drawn on my reserve. Right now, I have about $25 less than is needed for my Fourth year's tuition. Living at Brigham isn't going to be as expensive as at 15 Bay State Road. They will furnish us with quarters, good meals, & laundry. Since I have school every afternoon, which is mandatory, car fares are present; together with all the million things we call miscellaneous. To make things even more complicated, we, as well as all other students, will be assigned to Brockton City Hospital for 3 months. Now Brockton is a city, about an hour's drive from Boston. Somehow we'll have to get up in the morning, do whatever has to be done at the Brigham, go to Brockton, & come back to Brigham in the evening. There will be a lot of squeezing there I'm afraid. To add to the difficulty, it'll probably cost $1 per day for car fares alone…[Incidentally Rushmore has announced that 15 students are going to be assigned to Brockton during August—so losing their vacations.] At any rate the financial picture is, at best, hazy.

Finally, what next? What does one do with an M.D. from an unapproved school assuming that he is allowed to practice in Massachusetts? Residencies, particularly wartime are out, Commissions are out, Public Health Service Appointments are not being granted us, Federal Jobs are not possible. I'm enclosing Dave

Ausubel's letter to give you the picture of what the "successful" graduate feels like…

So there you are Darling. What I'm looking for is the path to a fairly normal life; a house, kids, you; weekends in the country, mutual friends, concerts, plays…But from here, I don't even see the path to that state; it's all just haziness.

Oh well. I'm not really kicking darling. I'm not comparing my problems with the doughboys in France. But I'm just taking cognizance of the barriers between (1) where I am, and (2) where I want to go…

Incidentally, you can see that I really don't know when I'll get off. If you must give a tentative date get the third week in August for your vacation. Maybe I can get that off. It'll be my fourth week at the hospital.

I've given you quite a chockfull of my problems to worry about, haven't I?

It's largely because I want you to know just what I'm doing & trying to do at all times. I'll never be a mystery to you…

I love you very much,

Yours,
Aaron

Wednesday 6/14 5:15 p.m.

Gloria darling—

I'm writing now, rather than in the wee hours, as I want to get to you in time to remind you that I'll call tomorrow at about 9:30. Probably, you'll get this letter on Friday, tho…

Monday night, I and two other students went to a Hospital to see Dr. Konrad, our OBS professor, do a normal delivery. He was marvelous. Since I've only seen 2 others, I really have no way of comparing various techniques. The other two were butchers; Konrad was a master.

It's very difficult to explain what makes one Obstetrician good and another one mediocre or terrible. The result is impressive, tho. Dr. Konrad's patient was a young girl of 18; this was her first baby. [For a normal delivery, you understand, it is much easier if the mother has had children before; the baby will just pop out; tears are less common]. The child was delivered without a single tear to the mother! A rare thing, indeed, now-a-days.

He gave the mother a couple of drugs to induce twilight sleep. She wasn't unconscious during labor, but it did kill a lot of the pain, & she'll remember very little of it later.

When things really began to get going, she was brought into the delivery room and, at the actual birth of the child, given ether.

Konrad is a specialist. He has no immediate office hours with a lot of people dying to pay him $2 for his sagacity. So he gave the patient no drugs to speed up labor, didn't use forceps, delivered the kid (a girl) without even a slight tear to the mother, and then oiled and cleaned up the baby himself. Only then was he thru.

As are a lot of experts, Konrad is a "therapeutic nihilist." "Leave them alone," is the plea. But only an expert can "leave them alone." He has to be able to intervene, & quickly, if things don't go right. For the average, treatment of some kind right along is far more feasible.

Today he showed us a movie. A Caesarian Section done by—Dr. Konrad. He's really neat! Other men are undoubtedly as good or better, but after some 40 years of obstetrics, this man is good, sure, and confident.

So I rave on. This taste of medicine is really a shame. The chances grow more probable daily that nothing will come of it! Will it be like my teaching experience; Taking the entire "education series," doing very well as a Pupil Teacher in Lincoln, and not being given a chance to teach?

Love
Aaron

Friday 11:30 p.m. 6/15

Gloria dear:

Hello darling. Three minutes is apparently the time it takes for me to say "Hello" and you to say "I'm fine." We could use a direct line & be able to talk for a little while.

Your letter was very sweet, dear. You must feel very strongly in sympathetic vibration with my own feelings. I'm glad you love me, and want to tell me. Tho I really can't help it, I'm sorry that I can't manage to carve myself that niche in which we both could be happy…

Financially, there is no problem at this point. I won't need any money at all if things go as I expect. But I know that you'd help if you could; never fear, I'll call for help when I absolutely need it…The offer and your way of putting it was very sweet & thoughtful, dear…

Finals are scheduled for about July 15. Just around the corner. We're getting a break, tho. Instead of 15 exams, as was given in the past, 4 case-histories are being given. For each one we get 4 hours in which to answer 10 questions, asked about various points in the case. This type of exam is much more intelligent, in that it avoids simple regurgitation of lecture material. Also, it is much harder to fail one of these. Yet, between now & finals, I have to learn an awful lot, and review a year's work in Medicine, Surgery, & Obstetrics! You can imagine my zest for cramming with the school in the present state.

I was supposed to go to work tonight & have Sunday off. At the last minute the manager told me that I was to come in Sunday—one of his regular waitresses wasn't coming in then. So I'm stuck. I had counted on Sundays to go to the Chelsea Memorial Hospital to prepare for my debut at Brigham, & to see you once or twice before exams. Now, I'm not certain when we can make it. I'll try to cut one day in order to see you in New London. With the ruling on Cutting being enforced, I'll have to watch my step a bit. Until the school closes, I'm giving them no excuse to throw me out, if possible…But I'll arrange it somehow & let you know soon.

You are "running around," aren't you. Plays, movies…every night. Tsk, Tsk. No moving, absorbing interests—or anything.

I'm enclosing another Chapter in the "Textbook Never Published." You'll have a complete Medical Library in this vein pretty soon.

Good night darling,
Aaron

Incidentally, I sent my dad a card.

Tuesday 12:40

Gloria—darling:

Apparently my despondency last week carried over to you only too well. Don't worry too much, dear. All we can do is wait for a few more months to see what will happen. Medical school, or no medical school, if I can earn enough to support us, and you'll want me, we'll be married—for better or for worse…

As you know by now, I'm working Sundays again. I went in this Sunday as a waiter. Possibly I'll be able to continue doing so for next year. It would help a lot, financially. I do want to see you soon. How about this Friday morning? I'll cut the day.

Call me up Thursday night at 9:30 p.m. & we'll make arrangements.

Classes are going to begin again soon, so I've got to rush back to school.

Love
Aaron

P.S. Joe is getting some wires pulled getting into B.U. Med. School. It looks good. I'm a little jealous.

Aaron

Wed. 6/21 11:30 p.m.

Hello darling:--

Schumann's "Spring Symphony" is going on now, but it looks more like "A Night on Bald Mountain" tonight. I don't know whether you'll be able to make it this Friday, of course, but the weather better change if you can!

Yesterday's letter was inadequate, I know, but I was being rushed to get to school while writing it. At night, now, with no one in the whole house, I can write at my leisure. How is your cold, darling? Sometimes I think you need attention & supervision more than I do. And here I am living alone in the wilds of New England; natives definitely unfriendly.

Joe right now is "cooking" like mad, about getting into B.U. I hope it really works out O.K. for him, but living with a B.U. man for the next year isn't going to be easy on my delicate & pretty frayed nerves.

With finals only a month or less away, I really ought to get down to business. Yet I'm really not able to do very much studying. Very, very bad…

Yesterday, I went over to Chelsea Memorial again. I wanted one more day's familiarity with hospital routine, so that if I get into Brigham before any drastic changes occur up here, I won't be too green. We told the superintendant there that we were "experienced." I didn't get very far in my visit. It was a very quick afternoon. I tried to put a needle into an old chap's vein 4 times—and had to give up. The interne made excuses & put it in himself later. Boy, do I have manual dexterity! I probably ought just to be a "brain"—Psychiatry, for example. At least, I couldn't do any harm.

During the afternoon, I walked around in a pretty little interne's coat, with a stethoscope around my neck, and examined several patients. Theory is O.K. in its place, darling. It's a lot different when the patient is in front of you. And since I'm the timid type who can't put on the bluff of knowledge & self confidence it's a riot. I started examining one chap's heart who had a nice murmur. Very majestically I pull up his shirt, adjust my stethoscope, & plunk it on his chest. As I listen intently with a look of—I hope—deep understanding, he ups with, "I always like to help the students. Maybe you'll be able to do some people some good one of these days." I'll have to grow a moustache again, darling.

Tomorrow night, I'll talk to you, I hope. You'll get this Friday, but I don't think it'll be dated. It says that I'm in love with you in every line; and you said that that never gets dated.

Good night darling,
Aaron

Tuesday 6/27 12:30 a.m.

Gloria dear—

Your call tonight was obviously a surprise. I'm sorry about Manny. Sometimes I forget that everyone else in the world aren't Medical Students, to whom injuries and disease are daily conversation. Try not to worry too much, tho. Fracture of the Ulna isn't serious at all. By now it has probably all healed up, and the cast is removed. In a young man his age, there probably will be no residual disability at all…

So I'll meet you this Monday. Barring rotten weather. If you can't make it, let me know, and we'll set some other date…

Tonight we went over some more cases. Reading thru them, the point struck very forcefully, regarding Healthcare as it should be practiced; as compared to Medicine as it is, and must be practiced, of necessity.

You know that most of our present day diagnostic criteria are laboratory findings: X-Rays, blood analysis, Urine analysis, Spinal Fluid Analysis, and looking into every possible part of the body (stomach, bladder, bronchi,…) with special tubes. Barring these aids, the doctor can only look wise, give Aspirin & Sulfa drugs, and hope the patient isn't really sick & gets well.

Serious illnesses, early Cancer, early Kidney damage, liver disease…don't get well by themselves. And are diagnosed too late frequently, not because the doctors really couldn't do it, but that very few can afford laboratory diagnosis.

In a hospital, if the patient is a "service case", and is being used for study, many tests are done routinely. In either of the cases we read today, the laboratory fees, if the patient were to pay for them (as you, your mother, or I would have to do) would amount to $150-200.

Money like that can't be spent "routinely." Only when you're desperately ill, and then it's too late.

No general practitioner can order "Blood Chemistries" while giving Sulfonilamide (very imp't, too) at $10 each; no patient would do it...

Yet it is all so preposterously ridiculous. A technician, earning $5 a day, can do 100 bloods a day for Sulfonilamide, very easily. At $10 each, everyone is making money; & no patient would object. With our present set up there are a few private labs equipped to do work, & no mass production methods set up, it would be $5-10 very easily.

Similarly for all X-Rays ($40 for a gastro-intestinal series; probably $1.50 in mass production with better diagnosis) & all other lab data.

So long as organized medicine prevents mass medicine, and maintains "pioneer day" individual entrepreneur methods, the advances made in Harvard will never reach the public.

Good night darling
Aaron

Thursday 6/29 12:30 a.m.

Gloria—

Tho I'm probably in one of the coolest spots in Boston, I'm just managing to keep from crawling into the icebox. This certainly isn't time for finals...

Your letters are coming promptly & very sweetly. I'm so used to picking one up every morning, I'd feel very queer (and disappointed, too) if one weren't waiting for me each morning.

I'll probably be going to the Y every day now for a swim. Nothing like a pool to cool you down. But I'm hotter when I get out. Are you going to continue your equestrian endeavor? Riding a pony is pretty hot work, isn't it?

The school situation continues to grow progressively worse. I haven't been given my program for next year yet, so I can't pass it on. I'll do so very soon tho. Yesterday, another one of those parents' meetings was held in N.Y. It was probably as bad as the one we attended. Very cheerful affairs. My father probably attended; I'm waiting for him to let me know what went on.

Oh yes, I meant to ask you about Thelma. The last I heard she was planning to marry the errant boy friend after all. Well?

I hope it's nice this Monday. It'll probably be the last time before finals that I'll be able to take a whole day off. And you'd better make sure there's a beach there. Or else we'll have to rent a couple of seats in an air conditioned movie for the day…I'll put a bathing suit into my pocket just in case we can really find water. Yesterday, I heard Dewey's acceptance speech. His fine speaking voice annoyed me. I have to think of him as a possible rival against Roosevelt. What I think of Dewey and the Republican platform is very ably expressed by PM; Max Lerner has the knack of putting our feelings into very powerful language. The only bright point in all the "news" around me is the Red Army's march towards Berlin. Thank God for that!

Until Monday dear
Aaron

Thursday 5:30 p.m.

Gloria darling:

Yes. Monday was very lovely. I'm going to try hard to come in to see you soon. Actually, since I've been able to see you twice this term, I haven't made the strenuous efforts to come into N.Y.—my family probably has forgotten what I look like…

When are you going to convince your mother that coming up to Boston for a few days isn't too damning? Particularly with an uncle around to chaperone us. I'm sure Sammy wouldn't mind at all. If I can't get time off in August you ought to spend your vacation in Boston, I think…

You're very sweet and lovely, darling. I'm pretty sure that I didn't say so Monday, but I meant to indicate subtly that I love you a great deal. It isn't just that I need a good audience for any dissertation on "Gall Bladder Diseases."

Your picture is going the rounds now. See how vain I am. I'm showing it to all the boys, saying "Ain't she cute?" Yep, it's very cute, too.

Interestingly enough it didn't rain in Boston, either. I'd like to know just what significance our mutual prediction has. It's a good thing I'm not superstitious. From now on, I carry a rain-coat any time I'm going to meet you. I deliberately checked on the weather report that day, and it was "Fair & Warmer" for Connecticut. If we can guarantee rain, we'd be a great boon to farmers, tho.

Since Tuesday morning, I've been trying to study. By now I'm going frantic. Tuesday was supposed to be a day of "grinding." We went over for a dip in the morning and Joe injured his knee a bit. Since this was a good chance to get an official record of his knee disability, we went down to Boston City Hospital, where Joe gave the internes the easiest diagnosis they ever had. His symptoms "were just like a medical textbook."

As we got home, Sammy dropped in. When he left, a student in the neighborhood dropped in-- & stayed for supper. As he left, Eliot Korim called up telling us he was coming over from Chelsea (his home town). So we did cases 'til 2:00 a.m…

I'll call you Tuesday, dear at 10:00.

All my love
Aaron

Sunday 7/9 11:15 a.m.

Hello darling:

I know you're probably exhausted trying to keep cool in this heat; but you'll have to forgive my not being able to write a cold letter. (Gee, I couldn't help that lousy pun!) At any rate, I'd suggest swimming. I'm doing quite a bit of it myself. We go down to the Y for a dip nearly every day now. It's swell while it lasts; only it doesn't last very long…

We told our "boss" that we're leaving the 21st of this month. So that's that. On Monday, I'll get in touch with the Hospital to find out when I'm to report. If I can get any more than the weekend, I'll come in. So ends my career as a telephone girl!..

This morning I'm studying neurology. Altho our exams are going to be like the case record I read to you, the 10 questions going along with each case, makes it a free-for-all. It is pretty much the same as the individual exams were required.

Neurology is a mess of big words, and in some parts, without much understanding. As always there are dozens of diseases with symptoms, pathology, etiology (usually unknown) & treatment (nearly always unknown). Tabes dorsalis, syringomyelia, Amyotrophic Lateral Sclerosis, Subacute Combined Degeneration, Infectious Neuronitis, Syndrome of Guillaume-Barre, Epidemic Encephalitis of von Economo,… millions of them.

I'll undoubtedly never see 99.96% of these conditions. Even if I have a busy general practice. And to make things even more helpful, most of these diseases have men's names attached to them as well: Spinal Progressive Muscular Atrophy of Adults or Aran-Duchenne's Disease; S.P.M.A. of children=Werdnig-Hoffman's Disease…

"For better or worse," finals start Monday. Do they mean anything?

I wrote to Manny yesterday. I don't really know what to say that you're not telling him, but I asked him to reply. If he does I'll keep up a correspondence with him as long as I can.

My congratulations, best wishes…to Thelma. As you see, the essentials of a marriage are two people with enough money to live upon & a draft deferment. The "higher things" probably follow. They'll undoubtedly be very happy; as two intelligent, modern souls should be.

All my love darling,
Aaron

Wed. 7/12 9:30 p.m.

Gloria dear:

So time rolls on. I wish I knew where it was rolling…About 10 minutes ago I came in from a walk on the Esplanade; very moody & lonely. It's enchantingly beautiful out there. And lots of couples are taking advantage of it. There is certainly a breeding season in man, too. And this is probably it…

This afternoon I finally had my eyes examined by a specialist in our building. For 2-3 days I've been unable to read, as they were so "strained." Just looking at a book hurt them.

But apparently they're quite all right. No pathology. Even my glasses, which are about 6 years old are still practically a perfect correction. He didn't advise new ones. So all I can do is to "take it easier." I just can't read all day long & expect to get away with it. Well, I'm glad I don't have something terrible which would require dropping school. I've heard of such things, as probably you have, too…

No, I'll drop out of school as the Army drafts us. Not, of my own accord.

Situation to date: Everything they've tried has failed. The school is broke. In fact, rumor (semiofficially) has it that we cannot even have Brockton City Hospital next year! The present freshman class is composed of 33 members—whose combined tuition probably doesn't pay Rushmore's salary. The State Board apparently turned the school down, as the public hearing (duly provided by law) is scheduled for July 17. The school will take the matter to the Superior Court in October, when it convenes; then, probably, to the Supreme Court of the State. If nothing is done by the Army, in the way of drafting us out—we'll probably get a final decision next year. It's bound to be negative.

I don't know why they don't give up the ghost, & arrange for us to take boards. The school is doomed. According to the new Army program, there can be no more entering classes for the school…So finals start Monday…

There, darling, is your periodic summary of the "situation in Middlesex."

Otherwise we're pretty comfortable. It's considerably cooler on the Esplanade than in the City. The only cooler place I can think of is the movies.

I'm going to try to do some studying. Joe is so tied up with B.U. he can't do anything.

Love
Aaron

Thursday 7/13 11:15 p.m.

Gloria darling:

How are you tonight? Right now it's very lovely out here. There are cool breezes blowing in from the River. All the lucky swains and their girl friends are out on the benches or on the grass; looking at the sky, water, or each other…I'll take a look at your pretty picture soon, so I too will be fitting in with the season & weather.

(I'm trying to manipulate the paper so my lines will come out straight; the results so far are pretty disappointing…)

Today was completely wasted as far as studying is concerned. Altho I was going to cut all day—both to keep up my morale & to do some good hard grinding—Arthur Schiff called up last night to tell Joe that a post-mortem was being done this morning at the Chelsea Hospital. So off we went, bright & early to see a teacher of Pathology at Tufts Medical, do the autopsy on a 65 yr. old man who "came into the hospital the day before in coma"—and died yesterday. The Post mortem isn't something I'd have you see before dinner, darling. I don't think I'd like to be a pathologist, no matter how essential they are.

As you probably know, the autopsy consists of a very detailed & routine, methodical, dissection of the cadaver to determine the cause of the death, & incidentally any other pathology of interest. From certain key places such as heart valves, lung, liver, kidney—particularly if pathological changes are visible in the gross,-- pieces are taken for microscopic examination.

All findings, both gross & microscopic are listed objectively, & finally put together to make the diagnosis.

For example, in this case, he found a large heart; slight arteriosclerosis in the arteries to the heart; some old kidney damage, now healed & scarred; some pneumonia (inflammation in the lungs)… But all these are just of academic interest. It was when he went into the brain & found a hemorrhage, nearly destroying half of the left side of the brain that it told the story.

From the big hypertrophied heart in otherwise good shape, & the small areas of arteriosclerosis the evidence of hypertension (high blood pressure) was obtained. The picture was pretty clear, & typical, of the constant high pressure in the arteries over a period of years; the heart hypertrophying in its attempt to keep the blood pulsing; the small blood vessels going arteriosclerotic & weak; until one gave way in the brain…

The autopsy started at 11:00; at 10:00—an hour before—we saw a delivery…(there should be a good quote at this point, but all I can think of are very trite).

Until later darling,

Love
Aaron

Wed. 7/27 12:00 N.

Gloria darling:

This is going to be very short; as for this time, on this swanky paper in order to properly impress you. I'm absolutely dead. Practically no sleep last night on the Bus; running around like mad all morning at the Chelsea Memorial & all night at the Robert Brigham. We haven't even had time to unpack. The Lord knows whether I'll be able to do all I'm expected to adequately. But I'm going to try.

For what it's worth, we heard today that Middlesex men are being commissioned by the Army again. The ones that have passed State Boards, of course.

I'm too sleepy to say more dear. I'd very much love to have you with me. I miss you already, although I've been with you only yesterday.

Love
Aaron

Saturday 7/29 1:20 p.m.

Gloria darling:

I've been so rushed, that the letters I wanted to write all week aren't yet written. I'm now on duty at the Hospital waiting for the telephone to ring 3 times. That means me, you see.

Well what is it like? To be very brief I'm scared to death. You know me, darling. I'm no good at doing things. I am at my best in figuring things out; when talking to someone or all by myself. In our job now there is no figuring to be done. It is just—do it!

I told you about the Robert B. Brigham. It's a pretty spacious place. Two wings: one for private, very swanky operative work. Mostly orthopedics, tho at present the Lahey Clinic has been doing almost everything in this hospital; as good operating rooms, or hospital beds on their standards are kind of rare, today.

Actually we are responsible only for work on the part-force side. "Rounds" are made at 7 in the evening by the House Officers (me) to see if all is well. [of course the real Rounds went on in the morning with good men doing them]. Usually nothing is wrong. Tho occasionally something comes up. Yesterday, eg, one kid in bed with a bad hip began to run a temperature, cough & feel very sick. He was getting Sulfa pills for his hip already. We examined him; decided something was doing in his chest & called up the Resident. He told the nurse to do something. Now whether he came in to see the boy & what he decided it was, I don't know. I'll find out later, I guess.

Our two main jobs, tho, are to do emergency lab work when necessary, & certain "emergency routines" such as giving intravenous injections, taking blood for Wassermans, doing catheterization…It seems as tho everything except doing a urinalysis depends on getting a needle into a vein. And am I rotten at it! I blush to tell you. Yesterday, I missed getting in twice & had to be helped out both times by the interne or Joe. I better improve!

Another part of the job is to do examinations on all incoming patients. Probably 5-7 a week. We were left with a backlog of 6 to do. This part I will learn to do adequately in due time, I hope.

In the evenings, I'm at the Chelsea Memorial watching better medicine. Another post-mortem was performed yesterday. (Not that that part is so lively, darling). Babies are born…

I'll try to write more frequently, dear.

Love
Aaron

Tuesday 8/1 11:00 p.m.

Sweetheart:

I've been outside for a while going over your past few letters in my mind. It's gorgeous out, with a heat quenching breeze, Lazy moon…You ought to be up here with me.

I think I would be all right getting married in response to the court decision— pro or con. Although I think I'd feel very badly about marrying you with no "prospects" at all if the decision is negative. I think you're old enough & mature enough to know what you want to do. I'll try to make you happy, tho I'd wish for more propitious circumstances.

Interestingly enough, I promised— more or less— not to get married while I was in the Brigham. The superintendent, Mrs. Cox, a wise woman realizes from long experience that young men just can't stay away from their wives. As it is, I can sublimate; if we were married & sleeping together several times I don't think I could.

I wish I were able to talk to you instead of write, about anything as important as our getting married soon. I'm all for it. It's just the practical aspects that concern me at all. Try to think them thru, darling. At any rate give me a call— at the hospital of course. There is a central switchboard with extensions to the various sections. One phone is in our cottage. You can call at any time up to about 10:30 p.m.; the switchboard closes at 11:00.

Let me tell you something about the set up so you'll know what goes on.

The Brigham is a pretty big, 2 story affair set up on a big hill. Lots of trees & grass, so it feels like being in the country. I need a flashlight to get around with…

This is the general layout. It is pretty spacious, being built low & with a view toward giving a lot of air and light.

In its field the hospital is one of the best in the country— and it deserves its reputation. Money is spent lavishly on each patient and with no differences: free, part free, or nearly private. Nobody is making money, so everybody involved gains. The resident told us today, e.g., that the laboratory work in this hospital (for 150 patients) is bigger & better than in Boston City (several thousand patients). They have facilities for doing everything.

The East Wing is private & very, very expensive. Lahey Clinic patients are put up there. West Wing is "staff": free, partly free…depending on ability to pay. There is a social service department which works it out. The Residents and House Officers (us) are concerned primarily with this West Wing.

Patients usually come in for weeks to months. Bed rest, good food, vitamins, sunshine may be the only treatment for the rheumatic kids; Rest, graduated exercise, physiotherapy for the old arthritic.

What do I do anyhow?

This morning we got up at 7; went to the small lab where 4 urines were waiting for us to "analyze." This takes about 1/2-3/4 hr. for 2 of us; entering the findings…then to breakfast. Dash down the hill to get the trolley to Chelsea.

At the Chelsea Memorial things are very quiet. I examined a patient for one of the doctors routinely; he was in for Epididymitis which gives him a red, swollen scrotum, but was otherwise O.K. These routine history & physicals are required tho & give us some practice. Then I watched a Paracentesis— a big hollow needle was pushed in to a woman's abdomen & 10 quarts of fluid was drained/gushed into a pail; I went over the chest of an asthmatic; watched Joe try to strap a strained back. Times at the Chelsea.

I did a few errands & got back to the Brigham to take a shower, eat, and do a complete physical on a Rheumatic Fever patient.

Some ping-pong, coffee; & here I am.

Of course, this is unusually quiet; usually there is a great deal more to do: i.v.'s, catheterizations, emergency lab work…

So far all is quiet…

I'm swamped by my lack of knowledge, technique, & ignorance of the future.

But in it all, I am secure in the knowledge, that we love each other. Don't worry about nurses, darling. I'm completely yours.

Good night, dear

Aaron

P.S. Don't forget to let me know exactly when you call. Or better still, I think I'll call you & reverse charges occasionally. Before I do that, I'll try to get organized. You see, if you call here, I might be out on an emergency just then.

Love

Aaron

Friday 8/4 9:30 p.m.

Gloria darling:

Beethoven's quartet is going now. You know, the one with the very beautiful slow movement you've got. It's magnificent. Slow, sad & very, very beautiful. If you didn't have it already, I'd get it for you as soon as I had the extra money…Every time I listen to something good I make a mental note & determine to get it for you. It's pretty selfish, tho, since as Joe feels it, it's like getting you a good pipe that I'm going to enjoy.

The article I'm enclosing about the State Boards action is another step in the relentless march forward of "Der Tag." Apparently no compromise was reached, & we're completely out so far. Now they're going to court. Your guess is as good as mine…

So with complete frustration facing us, just as it seemed to finally be so near, playing "Doctor" isn't easy. All day long I'm "Doctor" to patients, nurses…Every time I'm addressed like that a little twinge goes thru me, I think.

Yet it's a very fascinating field…I'd probably go nuts if it weren't.

Gradually, I'm becoming acclimated. Yesterday I passed a stomach tube in the early morning & sucked up some gastric juice. Then in the laboratory we analyzed it for degree of acidity. We ran off a series of urines & dashed to Chelsea. Things are very slow in that hospital. In the summer time there isn't as much pneumonia, falls…I strapped up a kid with a fractured rib, examined some patients routinely,--

12:30 a.m.

We were just called into the East Wing to do a routine blood & urine analysis on an emergency basis. The patient was operated for thyroid some time ago by Lahey Clinic & is coming in for a checkup. These routine tests are being done tonight, tomorrow morning she gets a BUN. Lahey Clinic practices real medicine. But at exorbitant prices. The tests should normally take me an hour. It took both of us 2 hours since we dropped in the dining room for coffee, and killed time…

Last night, the night supervisor woke me at 3:30 a.m. to catheterize a patient who was unable to pass water & was in severe pain. This morning I passed another Levin (stomach) tube at 7 o'clock, & ran the gastric analysis (patient probably has gall bladder trouble; I'll find out if I'm right when the X-rays are developed and read.).

There was very little to do in Chelsea. A kid in a post Epileptic attack was admitted.

Back in Brigham I examined 2 kids with Still's Disease. A very crippling & widespread rheumatoid arthritis of children, it strikes without warning for no apparent cause, & as it progresses it leaves these children stiff & deformed, unable to move hands, feet, spine, neck, & even jaw. I saw one pretty bad case today in a 14 year old boy who in 4 months had progressed to where he could hardly bend his wrists or ankles; his neck was stiff, & I couldn't examine his mouth or throat as he couldn't open his jaws more than about ½ inch…

Rheumatic Fever and rheumatoid arthritis—etiology unknown, treatment unknown, prevention unknown. The utter hopelessness of it all can drive one desperate…

There is so much I could write, darling. I'm terribly sleepy now, tho, so Good night, dear.

I'll call you next Thursday at 10:00 p.m. if at all possible. We'll make arrangements for other calls then. You'll be able to get me at any time before 11 I believe. Ask the switchboard for Doctor Kelman (House Officer, if she asks)

Love
Aaron

Saturday 8/5 3:00 p.m.

Darling:

I wrote last night, I know, and right now, lolling around in shorts, hot breezes blowing thru the cottage, I miss you enormously & want to tell you about it. I'll probably be able to take days off pretty soon, having Joe cover for me at the Brigham, & we can meet in New London. Better wait until it cools down a bit, tho. I'm warm enough when I see you with the temperature below 90 degrees F. in the shade!

I miss you a lot, darling…

Since you're working so many hours a week, I guess you'll be pretty tired now. Particularly in this weather. I know that the more tired I get, the more I feel that I want to bury my head in your bosom & relax. Maybe you feel that way, too…

I've just finished going into town to pay school tuition for the next third. (The games go on). It leaves me about $25 short. However, I'm continuing to work in the HiHat, so in due time I'll make it up. Inevitably some Doctor or Nurse is going to meet me in Waiter's uniform. Will I be embarrassed!

You know, darling, when I feel like this I am completely sure that we should have been married— let alone, should be married soon. Not that our union is particularly and peculiarly blessed in heaven. I'm a cynic, you know. I think that our love is the same beautiful thing that men & women have experienced for generations. I am perfectly sure that I want you to be with me all my life, & feel very complete in your love.

All I'm trying to work out now, is some way to ensure our relationship flowering into an even more beautiful thing. I'm very conscious of the effect of bad environment on the most promising growing organism. Being together, making love, reading poetry…won't flourish very long I fear without the stability & security that a "respectable" position, adequate income & good health (no bullet wounds) will give.

Your being happy— for any cause— makes me very happy. Seeing you unhappy— particularly if I thought I were to "blame" for it— would make me far more unhappy than anything that could happen to me…

This is a pretty strange letter darling, isn't it? It comes from my missing you, the heat, & simply needing an occasion to tell you I love you.

Aaron

Friday 8 pm

Hello darling:

Your concern about Joseph and his family is evident and very understandable, dear. My lack of real emotion is only due to my not even being able to visualize the boy or his mother. I don't even know whether or not I have ever seen him. So the tale is that of a tragic illness. To you, being in the midst of it, the situation is that of a horrible tragedy.

I'm not really working very hard, darling. It only sounds that way on paper. You're working much harder. I run around a lot to be sure, but it doesn't mean much in terms of real physical or mental effort. I'm learning a little, tho nothing compared to what the boys get in other schools.

This morning, the Harvard boys came over for a lecture in orthopedics. Joe and I stayed home from the Chelsea to sit in. It brought home with a bang all the things I've talked to you about before. Good medicine and bad medicine; good schools and poor schools; intelligence and stupidity…Twelve nice boys in Navy uniform sat around comfortably in our Day Room, a lovely large room in keeping with the rest of the luxury of the hospital. Six interesting orthopedic cases were brought in, described, had their cases gone over, the entire history brought out, the X rays were shown and explained, and the boys were able to examine the patients. The lecturer, Dr. Kuhns, is one of the leading men in the hospital, a master in his field. He talked for two and a half hours giving a very pretty discussion of the whole field in an elementary fashion, using plaster models, charts, preserved specimens, typical X rays…for his purposes.

The facilities of an entire hospital for a two hour lecture for 12 students.

Joe was impressed (and thereby depressed) by the instruction given to the Harvard men as compared to ours. These third year students get similar instruction in medicine and pediatrics, for example. We get nothing.

I was impressed far more with the students, the professor and the relationship there. Maybe I have a bee in my bonnet that is always buzzing. Yet again and again, the situation presents where I find another example of the terribly trite dictum that people are what their environment makes of them. Everybody mouths that phrase, nobody believes it apparently. Nice people are nice people, stinkers are stinkers. [The important thing about Harvard isn't that they give such good training that all their graduates are thereby good doctors. Given just the chance to live and go into medicine I'll learn nearly as much as most of them. It is being selected by Harvard to be one of the chosen few— a Harvard graduate— which is the prize. Being a Harvard graduate, an Oxford or Cambridge man, an MIT man…means that your credentials have been reviewed and passed on; that you are of protestant religion, of an old american family, of professional or very wealthy lineage. In short that you come from the ruling stock and therefore are fit to carry on in the capacity of ruling. The university has in this way taken over the job of perpetuating the rule of the chosen few. This is all by and large of course. In a democracy some exceptions are bound to crop up.]

To get back to the students, darling. What I meant was that everybody was relaxed, nobody fell asleep, nobody read the comics, no games of battleship went on, no spit balls were thrown…The boys were extremely polite, very affable…All was sweetness and light. I couldn't help contrasting it with a lecture in orthopedics in Middlesex: a second rate, down-at-the-heel orthopedist, obviously bored with his job of giving us of his knowledge, talking away about stuff that neither of us really understood, resentful of the fact that he has to lecture to a bunch of oafs for ten or fifteen dollars; the students fifty or sixty strong, bored to death, some not interested in medicine in the first place, some feeling that they can't practice giving up the ghost and annoyed at being bothered; lots of noise and talking during the lecture, every once in a while a scuffle breaks out in some corner as the bored students find something to do, no exhibits, no models, no pictures, nobody cares. Dull droning of meaningless words going from the teacher off into the cosmos someplace. The students don't get any of it.

Most of our students aren't nice I guess. No. They are little, and pushed around and beaten over the head. A good clerkship is a prize, or an internship…Fight for it.

Nice people are made. They have leisure. They go to school where nobody fights for grades or anything else, as there is no real point to getting them. They don't need to compete. They learn to enjoy the arts by having it brought home to them and have the leisure to absorb it. They learn manners, table manners and sweetness and savoir-faire since they have the leisure to practice manners. Above all they can be sincere and ingenuous and charming. They don't have to be thinking all the time about how to make something of the situation. The situation will be made for them…

So our resident twists the residentship, the draft situation, the school, his practice, us, the hospital doctors…for everything that he can make of it. He has to make as much as possible to survive. Arthur Schiff, is constantly planning and trying to turn every situation in the Chelsea to his advantage. The boys at Brockton all scrambled like mad, plots and counterplots, in attempting to be the fortunate two who would be allowed to stay overnight and possibly learn a little more. Our seniors have opened each other's mail trying to steal internships from one another…

Baby, is my bee buzzing!!!

Well darling, with that off my chest I can relax and tell you that I'm very lonely. Don't say that I'm wonderful in your letters, dear. I get worried every time I read them. I know better. I'm a good egg, who loves you and is very content to let it go at that, but I will never be able to measure up to your imaginings.

Good night darling. This is my vacation, all right, but I better not sit up all night writing to you anyhow.

Incidentally, I think you are probably right. About the physical. I still haven't sent out the letter. If I get very discouraged maybe I will.

Love
Aaron

How do you like my typing. I love you very much.

Aaron

I'll expect your call at 9:30 Monday.

Monday 9 pm

Gloria darling:

I'm trying to use this typewriter to spare you some of the eyestrain of reading my handwriting. But I still insist that I like your letters in longhand; it's more intimate.

You win. We get married anytime you say. But not because of your arguments, dear. Only the first one: we're in love with each other and need each other. Let's just wait the few months to see what the court decides. I'm terribly afraid that the decision will go against us. And if it does, well…The situation will be pretty sad, but we'll still be married if you want the poor investment I'll make at the time. At any rate there is no reason that we can't see each other in New London during the next few months several times if you can get the time off on some pretext. I can take any day off I choose. Also, the telephone set up can be on the same basis that it was at my previous address. So long as I know at what time you are calling I will be in the cottage and ready to receive the call. So we'll continue to call each other regularly. I'm becoming acclimated…

Everything that I do at present is pretty new, of course. There is really no medicine without patients and cases. Yesterday, after the Hi Hat I went to the Chelsea to stay over. There was one patient there in complete coma, breathing very heavily as tho each respiration would be her last, pupils fixed, sweating profusely, blood pressure soaring to 170-180-190, and every once in a while she would have convulsions. She will probably die, leaving behind the baby she gave birth to Friday night, and two older children. Her only sin was being unlucky enough to hire a stupid, negligent practitioner instead of a competent obstetrician…You've heard of eclampsia. This disease of pregnancy, together with several related diseases dealing with the kidneys, fairly shout their presence to the doctor who will listen. During the 5,6,7,8,9, months of pregnancy it is absolutely criminal to neglect the signs of warning. They are so simple. Rising blood pressure, excess gain in weight, Albumin in the urine, headaches, spots in front of the eyes…signs that every medical student is taught and any tyro can recognize. Well, this woman, from her relative's story, presented a pretty typical story of rising blood pressure…but her doctor never even tested her urine or tried to make any effort to prevent complications. So in all probability her blood pressure really went way up during delivery, she burst a vessel in the brain, and is now waiting to die. All the nurses are furious, the relatives sit in the waiting room all night deploring this act of God.

I was awakened at 6 when she had several convulsions. There was nothing for me to do or suggest. I know so little; there is so little that can be done for her by the good men who are now treating her.

At 8 I was awakened to give a few babies whiffs of ether while a surgeon did some minor surgery. During the day I watched a fracture, which was very similar to the one Solly had, set. I examined several patients, trying to distinguish between what is really there and what my imagination makes me hear and feel in the patient.

From 4 to 6 I gave ether anesthesia to a young chap who had badly mashed up his hand so that this very prolonged operation was indicated to try to suture back into place the various muscles and tendons. It was pretty exciting and nerve wracking giving my first anesthesia. One hand holding the ether cone, and cupped under the jaw to prevent it falling down and so permitting the tongue to fall back and choke the patient; the other hand poured ether into the cone as required, took the pulse in the neck every five minutes or so, watched the respirations, and the pupils so as to keep the patient in the correct level of narcosis. The intern and other student both congratulated me on a very good job. So there! I can do something. Of course, I've made it sound much more impressive than it really was. You know how vain we get. (Probably tomorrow I'll be unable to take out some sutures and have all the wind taken out of my sails.)

I got home at 8; was immediately called to pass a catheter in a man with pretty severe pain (strangely enough darling, there is no therapy giving such prompt relief of almost intolerable pain as passing a catheter into a man who for some reason or other is unable to pass water; it is pretty simple, asepsis is observed, and relief is, of course, immediate; The patient is very profuse in his thanks for the doctor, the medical profession in general, medicine as a science…)

And here I am….

Gosh darling, would I like to curl up in your arms and hug you. I'm tired.

Tho interesting, the whole thing is probably for nothing. I've typed out a letter to my draft board requesting a pre induction physical. It's not mailed yet. We discussed it in New York. Do you think I ought to? I'm holding it until I hear from you.

Good night, darling. I'll try to write as often as I can, and time permits. Right now I'm not studying formally— I'm on vacation. So I have more time comparatively.

Love
Aaron

I'll call you Wednesday at 9:30 p.m.

Monday 8/14 11 pm

Hello darling:

I'm not really awake right now, but I feel that I want to continue the conversation that was so rudely interrupted tonight. It's gorgeous out here tonight. The air is balmy, a light wind is up, crickets are chirping and there is the promise of rain in the air. Very romantic, dear. But aside from a little nostalgia, it doesn't affect me very much. I don't feel very sexy lately. Either I'm getting old or I don't have the only adequate stimulus around. So don't worry about the local girls dear…I do miss you a lot. Last night, very tired, I went to sleep wanting to hold you in my arms very badly. Thinking how this situation is ever going to clear itself up so that I'll be able to do it, Relaxed, not trying to beat a time limit…

I was at the Chelsea Memorial most of the weekend. Last night there were four deliveries; I saw three. If one doctor hadn't come in just as he did, I probably would have been the accoucheur willy nilly. The girl was so fast that all the doctor did when he got himself into the delivery room, was to make a grab for the baby's head which was already out. I'm slowly becoming used to the cries of a woman in labor. Just so much more noise on the second floor…Again I saw the difference between the punks who are pulling babies out by the dozens and making a fortune, and Dr. Konrad who does a delivery as a work of art. Of the three I saw, he was the only doctor who was waiting for the baby. He carefully supervised the preparation of the mother, slowly took the baby from her, was at all times completely the master of the situation, called out the steps of the delivery as tho he were demonstrating a text book case, and finally delivered the mother of her first child without a single tear. One of the other men who also delivers babies decides by the time of day (office hours in fifteen minutes) when to put the patient under ether and make an incision in the perineum thru which the baby can be forcibly delivered with Forceps.

I've written an awful lot about medical shortcomings. It must be atrocious in the office of the practitioner—I see how terrible it is in the Chelsea. This is a small hospital to be sure. But as a Grade A hospital it is immeasurably better than the office work of even a fairly good general practitioner. The one big glaring defect in the hospital—so big that it stands out in very bold relief against all the little shortcomings of the place—is the lack of anybody in charge. The superintendent, as is true of most hospitals apparently, is a nurse. All she is fit to do is worry about the cost of the menus, the clean uniforms of the girls, the financial peace of the place. There is nobody in the hospital who assumes responsibility for the Medicine that goes on.

Patients can come in as "private". That is, they belong to their own doctor. He books them for severe pneumonia, for unknown pain in the abdomen, for severe diabetes, for an appendectomy…The doctor gives some orders and, until changed, these orders are carried out to the best of the ability of the nursing staff. Usually, the doctor visits his patients in the morning; sometimes the morning may be too busy for him to come down. "Staff patients" are those who are too poor to be able to afford a private physician and are left at the mercy of the internes and those doctors who are "on staff". The latter are, in Chelsea, two local practitioners who look at the medical patients and have as their guiding principle: "get the patient out of here somehow": and a young surgeon who is out to complete his required number of operations for his FACS as soon as possible…All sorts of medicine is practiced under these conditions. On the private patients, the job is to impress him with the doctor's benevolence and wisdom, and to milk him of as much as possible in visits, consultants, unnecessary diagnostic procedures…The staff patient, not having the good taste to be able to pay heavily for his contact with the "profession" is simply fair game for anything any of the men might want to learn. I've been told by very nice men to go ahead and do as many vaginal examinations, rectal examinations, lumbar punctures, caudal punctures…as possible on the "staff patients". We're waiting for a good drunk—supposedly ideal material for learning technique…

The hospital keeps case records by requirement of the AMA or somebody. To show that a decent history and examination was done when the patient came in and the operation justified. Most of the histories I've done were on patients who were about to be discharged. I sort of prove that the patient really did have gall bladder disease after the operation. Noble stuff, no?

Even at that, some of the orders written are definitely wrong by present day standards; some of the doctors show less knowledge than the students, far less interest; the old nurses or internes are frequently instrumental in starting treatment which they later get approval for.

Nobody is present who is watching all this; or who reviews the treatments ordered, and the diagnostic procedures thru which these treatments were finally reached. Nobody spot checks case records to see whether they are really being kept in an honest fashion—or kept at all. Nobody questions decisions to operate when no operation is indicated except the financial affluence of the patient. Nobody assumes responsibility for the condition of the 100 sick people in the house during the greater part of the time when nobody is around but a disinterested and ill informed interne.

In brief there is no supervision. Each doctor is God. And he can kill, maim, and bleed his patients as long as he likes provided that he can convince them by the cheapest kind of "confidence game" that he is doing them good. Good medicine could cure millions now simply being bled by the parasites; it would save fortunes by eliminating the unnecessary medicine. But good medicine requires supervision, and supervision is what the practitioner is fighting and will continue to fight til it is forced upon him by an enraged public.

Great Lord darling, what's gotten into me lately? Fine love letters to be sending my girl friend. What would Rosaline think? If Tuesday works out I'll tell you how much I love you much more personally.

Aaron

Thursday 8/17 11 pm

Hello darling;

When your letter came telling me that you poor little girls were going to work something like 54 hours a week, I remembered the many times in welfare when the mayor decided we were needed desperately by our clients and were to work all day Saturday. It never lasted for more than 3 weeks. I think that somebody has to present a report and wants to show some activity. Once the report is in, it makes no difference if the department goes back to its normal schedule. Maybe not. At any rate, I hope you're allowed to take vacation again. I'm looking forward to seeing you for a few long evenings soon. Give your General a talking to, will you?

Tuesday is fine. I'm sure that we won't make it on Tuesday. I don't think we ever did meet on the day we planned, did we? But for tentative plans then, it's Tuesday. Do call me Monday at 9:30 and we'll discuss the weather and why it would be better to postpone it to Wednesday. And I'll make it on 10:30. It means my leaving the hospital at 7, but I'll try. For you I'll even get up at 6 in the morning. Who said chivalry was dead. I don't promise to be clean shaven tho. That takes time…

I'm still no good at putting little needles into veins; at least into little veins. But I did pull a lulu last week which sort of discouraged me for a while. Twice I found that I had to give up when the patient had perfectly large easily visible veins. The interne just picked up the needle and put it right in. What was going on anyhow? In both cases I did get in apparently, since blood welled up into the syringe. But instead of the saline solution coming down from the bottle and going into the vein like all good intravenous drips should, the blood simply stayed in the needle, clotted, required some poor tired nurse to change the entire set, and left me feeling very unhappy. Finally it dawned on me. I forgot to take the tourniquet off! So the saline had no place to go. The blood which we draw up initially to make sure we're in, simply stayed in the needle and clotted. Was my face red!

Incidentally darling, medicine at the Lahey Clinic also had a lot to be remedied. Last week a circumcision was performed on some man who apparently could afford good treatment. It was done as a major surgical procedure under total anaesthesia! It should have been a small job done in a doctor's office or in the minor surgery room of a hospital under some local anaesthetic. Instead it was done under big lights with a full surgical team, for at least $100. That's the dirty side of "good medicine". If my stuff comes out garbled tonight you'll know that it's just lack of sleep, dear. I need a lot of it but just can't even seem to get a normal share. Now that I have to get up around 7 each morning I am in great difficulty when the clock starts calling out 10:30. But so far I haven't thought seriously about going to bed before 12. Time just seems to disappear around hospitals. God knows where it goes, but since there are so many people around, a lot of it probably goes up in conversation. Some waste of time, no?

Today was pretty hectic, relatively speaking. At Chelsea, I examined a chap who came in last night with a fever, stiff neck and about 70 years behind him. He couldn't speak anything but Jewish so Joe acted as interpreter. Later on there was a fetal heart to hear on a woman in labor who delivered about 1:30; listening with a stethoscope on the abdomen one hears the rapid beating of the baby's heart. From there we were called down to watch Dr. Callen set a Pott's fracture (of the ankle); X rays taken before and after showed a very good job done. The radiologist then came in to read a bunch of plates taken the day before by the technician; he examined one chap under the fluoroscope while we stood around him in the dark and marveled. You can see the chest wall with the heart beating and the lungs moving up and down; the patient swallows some barium mixture, which is seen on the screen sliding down the gullet into the stomach, outlining the stomach and showing the peristalsis of the stomach and duodenum as it moves along…One woman suddenly became wild and the nurses had to strap her down. Another woman became ornery so we gave her a sedative while waiting for her private physician to get to the hospital…The valve on the oxygen tank feeding a cardiac patient got stuck and there was a few hectic minutes of trying to fix it…Suddenly a post operative appendix case, began to get shaking chills so badly the bed shook; his pulse began climbing from 70 to 100 to 120, 140, 160! His temp went up to 105, his respirations to 40. The internes were scared. We all examined him and decided it was pneumonia…I did a history and physical on a patient with textbook rheumatoid arthritis when I returned to the Brigham…and here I am…

Now I know where all my time goes…Writing letters. I won't tell how long it takes me to type these thoughts (!) out.

Good night darling. Get into a little part of the house by yourself and write me warm long letters.

All my love
Aaron
Good night, dear

Saturday 9:30 pm

Gloria dear:

I've practically just gotten to the hospital since I left you darling. Friday morning we went to the Chelsea and I stayed over last night to get to the Brigham about 6 tonight. Yesterday and this morning were pretty busy. Altho I really don't remember what went on I did run around an awful lot, and dropped off to sleep for about an hour right after supper tonight. When I got out this evening it all looked very much unreal. Probably a combination of my state of half awakeness, the dim lighting of the hospital grounds and the general atmosphere. Do you ever feel that somehow you're dreaming and will wake up to find reality? Every once in a while I get that peculiar feeling. Tonight for instance. Clear cold stars and a crescent moon, dimly making magic in the gardens of green grass and flowers, everything quiet and hushed, croaking of frogs or night birds somewhere off in the distance. Even my reflection, all in white, looked somewhat imaginative…

Yesterday morning I did my debut as first assistant at a major operation. I assisted Dr. Kallen at an appendectomy. So there darling. We're so good we simply skip over the job of being second assistant, you see. If you read that Interne article I sent you you'll realize that to the lowly second assistant goes the duty of holding a retractor so that the wound gapes open, and the surgeon can see what he is doing.

Also included among his duties is the job of cutting the suture after the surgeon or first assistant makes the knot. Well I held the retractor and cut the sutures like a good boy. There just wasn't any second assistant. As Joe once put it, being an assistant in surgery is very much like helping his father put up screens or paint the woodwork. The surgeon says "Hold this" as he hands you a hemostat—and you hold it until he says "All right, doctor, let it go, will you?" and – you promptly let it go. The only major difference is that if you are of my timid temperament, you are so nervous at being in on the operation and under such awfully close scrutiny that the simplest manual operation becomes very difficult. You remember that I practiced tying knots all over my room last week anticipating this occasion. I really got very proficient and was able to tie a string around any chair in the room with one hand. Well, at the actual operation I tried desperately to tie a neat little knot with two hands—like tying a bundle—and found my fingers just got very much in the way. The string kept slipping out of my gloved hands as tho it were out to make a jackass out of me.

The procedure is pretty interesting. Notified that I was going to assist, I went to the Doctor's room adjoining the operating room. There I changed into a completely fresh set of white pants and loose white shirt. With mask and cap on I began to scrub. Since Kallen was in the same room scrubbing, I scrubbed diligently for a full ten minutes using a stiff brush to try to take as much off my hands as possible without removing any skin. In the operating room, a nurse puts a sterile gown on you and then slips on gloves. From this moment on life is just one long series of don'ts. You are sterile; the rest of the world isn't. Ergo there must be no contact between you and the hostile outside which is just swarming with bacteria eager to pounce on the sterile team. I must touch no one, keep my hands above the level of the table, not turn my back to the operating table—in fact I mustn't even try to scratch my nose when it starts to itch under the mask…The patient is ready, the surgeon cuts, Blood flows, the surgeon clamps the bleeding vessels and says "Sponge the area doctor"; the assistant sponges; if he does nothing else, he at least has to sponge. I grab a piece of gauze and dab at the oozing blood. It doesn't seem to help much so Kallen stops being proud and does some sponging himself. Eventually the appendix is exposed, clamped, cut, the peritoneum sewed up, and then the skin closed. Since it was such an easy operation I was allowed to put in a few of the skin sutures. If I were more experienced, it would have been my job to sew up the skin altogether. As it was Kallen was actually doing the operation himself, teaching me what every first assistant should know.

When it was all over, they said that I did a very nice job…

I was just called to pass a stomach tube into a chap who is very distended. If I can get the tube down I'll hook it up to suction. Here's hoping I don't have too much trouble and have to call up the Clinic…

Good night darling. I was going to use the pen to show you how beautifully it writes but there was so much to say that I thought I'd be able to do it this way more easily.

All my love
Aaron

It wasn't much trouble at all darling. If nothing clogs up, I'll be able to sleep right thru. So far I've never been awakened I think but there is always a first time. Let me know when you see my parents.

Love Aaron

Sunday 7:30 pm Aug. 20

Hello darling:

By this time the mystery of the missing letter will undoubtedly be solved. Why I persist in writing to 507 is really a mystery tho. Maybe, it's because I wrote so much to 202. Who knows? At any rate you know now that I really didn't simply get tired of writing to you or decide to spend my evenings more profitably in the nurses quarters…

It was gorgeous up here today. So lovely that I called up the Hi Hat and didn't go in to work. There were other reasons too, but you know those already by this time (Tuesday). I sat out on one of the porches with the sun beating on my face, my view unobstructed for miles, no sounds but crickets and the occasional voice of a nurse somewhere off in the ward, reading in a very leisurely fashion my book on Physical diagnosis. It's a quiet life up here all right. I'd love to have you in it and part of it. I don't see just how that would be possible without you becoming a lab technician or student nurse. But hospital life is in some respects very interesting; and for the doctors in a good hospital, very comfortable. I don't really belong either. A lot of the time I feel something like an imposter. Not that the superintendent didn't know my school, but that everybody takes it for granted that I am or will shortly be a doctor…

Can you imagine what it is like to feel like a coiled spring? Well that is very much like what I feel like right now. I have so much to learn and a great deal of opportunity of learning if I really applied myself. If I could really let go I could exhaust myself each day learning and learning some more. But I can't. I can't release the little piece of wire which holds the spring taut. Just think darling. Hundreds and hundreds of case records; electrocardiograms with diagnoses written on them; millions of X rays with descriptions of the findings; a magnificent laboratory equipped with marvelous microscopes and slides ready for study; all my textbooks waiting to be read or reread in the light of new knowledge and experience; all here and just being allowed to go to waste. I don't know whether I'd do anything about it if I could take exams. But right now there is that feeling that I'd uncoil like that wound up spring and come out of the hospital tired but knowing a lot.

I don't really have much to say tonight, dear. It is that I love to write to you and let you know that I'm thinking of you. It was probably the terrible difficulty I had writing that kept me from writing to you more often. As soon as I'm psychoanalyzed I'll be able to write letters to you regularly and very frequently. But I sincerely hope I won't have to write to you by then. I don't expect to be analyzed in the near future.

Incidentally how do you like these letters all typed up? Just say the word and I'll write them out again…They won't be so long of course but if you prefer them written, as I do, they may make up in quality what they lack in volume...So don't be bashful and let me know.

I'm going over to the Chelsea tonight. I probably won't learn much over there but Joe has a date tonight and I will be very much appreciated out of the hospital. Since we've been up here I've been sleeping over at Chelsea on Sunday. It gives me the chance to see deliveries which occur that night. So I'm not just being a good egg, you see. I don't expect to see anything interesting but if I do I'll tell you about it on Tuesday.

Something terrible happened dear. I put my raincoat in the cleaners and can't have it before Wednesday. Now I know it is going to rain on Tuesday. Isn't it terrible? I tried to explain to the cleaners about the urgency of the situation: how I had to have my raincoat to prevent it raining when I go to see my girl friend. But it was no go. I'm not sure he even understood or believed me...

Good night darling. This letter will probably sound funny when you get it as I will have told you all about what I wrote when I see you, but I just wanted to write to you, and since I did I'll send it on.

All my love darling,

Aaron

I'm not sure which is worse, my typing or writing?

Wednesday Aug 23 9 pm

Gloria darling:

Just as with my last letter I really can't write intelligently since I don't know whether I'll be seeing you tomorrow or not. I'll simply have to write in an ambling sort of way...You get the general idea that I'm fond of you I dare say, but in this mixed up state of affairs, I can do so little about even telling you myself.

School was to have started for us officially today. One of us (Malcolm) went down to see the Dean and fixed it so that only one of us need attend any one lecture. That would mean that for the next two months each one would be required to attend one afternoon a week. Not bad. If I do see you tomorrow, this will be old news, of course, but like everything else I've been doing lately, all I can do is go along. If I had counted on seeing you on Tuesday there would have been no point in writing my last letter when I did.

This morning I got up real early to apparently assist at one of the operations. I don't want to assist, particularly, but since I was requested to do so had really no alternative. Well it turned out that they really didn't need me; so I watched a bunion removed by a pretty good orthopedic surgeon. It took about an hour and a half to do both feet. Orthopedic surgery is a difficult and not very thankful field. It is difficult to get excited about that brilliant operation on a bunion—or a hammer toe. Even the big operations in orthopedics are rarely thrilling in that they are not life saving as are the thyroidectomies, and acute abdominal conditions. People just don't stand around with baited breath waiting for the outcome of a repair of a hip joint. Yet the field is very difficult, and very few men are able to qualify as experts in orthopedic surgery. I understand that my prof was one of the brilliant men in the field, but the death of his wife, followed by an attack of arthritis sent him down very fast. He now is completely thru, a has-been and an object of pity in the profession. For years he was continuously drunk, and would even come to lecture half-sober. But nevertheless, he must have been pretty good to have earned the admiration of the tough bunch making up the medical profession.

Right now my biggest trouble in working with patients is my overenthusiasm in finding diseases that aren't there. One must learn to distinguish between a belly ache, and the real acute appendicitis; vague discomfort after meals, and peptic ulcer; a little dullness on percussion with pneumonia; patients who complain of being in severe pain and say they are going to die, and those who really are emergencies and will die…If somebody threatens to die I believe him and get pretty excited. Actually, most symptoms are a big mystery to the medical profession as well as to the patient. Pains come and go. Pains in the back, in the muscles, in the abdomen…You've probably had some yourself. Medical knowledge doesn't try to diagnose them; largely because the effort involved, even if it could be done, wouldn't be worth it. Well, the thing that is done as a routine measure is to see whether the temperature, pulse and respirations are elevated. If they are, it is a sign that there is something the matter, which isn't functional (functional being something medical men don't treat). Whereupon the story resolves itself down to "Is it an acute emergency, or can it wait?" If it isn't something demanding immediate operation such as terrific pain in the abdomen with high fever and very rapid pulse, the thing to do is to get the patient to bed. From then on he is watched. This is called "expectant" or "conservative" treatment. If he complains of headaches, nausea…drugs are given to take care of the symptoms. So far nobody knows what is the matter with the patient. Frequently the temperature (under sulfadiazine treatment) drops, the patient feels better and goes home. Your guess about what was the matter with him is as good as mine or any of the other doctors in the hospital. In other cases the patient just doesn't get better. Severe symptoms develop. Pains really are pains. Coughs really wrack, wheezes in the chest really are unmistakable, and the full blown picture of a typical disease as described in the texts manifests itself: Tuberculosis, cancer of the lung, amebic dysentery…

Of course a lot of medicine is pretty obvious routine. Fractures usually don't require a brain to diagnose them; lacerations are clearly evident and the only consideration is whether to put in the three sutures he needs, or the six the students want for practice; sudden acute urinary obstruction in the old man is obvious, with the equally obvious catheterization for treatment until a urologist takes a piece of prostate out; the asthmatic is given a shot of adrenaline; the big tonsils are removed; the normal delivery done preferably by waiting and catching the baby as it comes out…

A lot of this routine is what I have to learn in the hospital. And the better I learn it, the better doctor I'll make. These things are skills which have to come easily and without effort when needed. It is the bulk of the general practice. Most of the practitioners I meet know only this routine stuff. They have long since forgotten the finer aspects of theoretical medicine. But they serve the community by doing this routine medicine in a fairly satisfactory fashion. That they are terribly overpaid for this pretty simple job is obvious; they are capitalizing on the knowledge that is possessed by the good men in the field that can also treat really sick patients. But the routine stuff is essential of course. In my system of medicine I'll have certain men devote themselves to this material as their job, and keep at it by virtue of their limited abilities.

Another discourse on medical practice. I don't think you'll ever want to go to a doctor now, darling, will you. I repeat, one of these days I'll surprise you and break out with a real torrid letter, But at the moment I'm surrounded by so much that is new and not part of daily experience that I must tell somebody about it. And I can't tell anybody else…

Good night darling
Aaron

Thursday Aug 28 8 pm

Gloria darling:

No darling, I won't divorce you if you don't set the world on fire with startling discoveries in Medicine, or learn to play the Brahms concertos beautifully. I love you very much for whatever things that go to make you up. I'll accept your delicious concoctions with alacrity whenever you learn to prepare them. I have an insatiable drive to learn. Learn about almost anything. Maybe it's just curiosity. At any rate, I just naturally assume that everyone else has that same compelling impulse. So I'll undoubtedly keep on pushing you in the direction of more and more knowledge as long as my interest in learning and my love for you hold out…Unless my yearning for information gives way, it looks as tho you are going to be studying for a long time…

Yesterday I did my first transfusion. There were two of them to be done at the Chelsea and only one interne was present all day. So Dan let me do one. It was all very simple. I just took the big needle and put it into the fellow's vein…Actually it was a big job for me. It all is the first time, isn't it. I took blood from the patient and the donor; spun them down in the centrifuge; did a cross matching with their respective blood cells and sera; prepared the patient by starting an intravenous of salt water going; prepared the donor in the small operating room by going over his chest, taking his blood pressure, fixing up a transfusion outfit with anti coagulant in it; and when everything was ready, put the huge needle into the donor's vein while the interne held the bottle (and shook it to prevent clotting while the blood drips in)...Finally the bottle full of blood is substituted for the bottle of saline, which is going into the patient, and it's all over...Believe it or not, I was all in. For any experienced fellow it is very routine. Particularly as the vein I went into was as large as Manny's best. But to me, it was major surgery.

This morning we had one of those rare dramatic incidents that you read about. A patient came in in semi coma. When I saw him he was quite restless, tho one half of him was pretty well paralyzed. His doctor, the Medical director of Chelsea Memorial, came in to go over him, and finally decided that it was a stroke—a brain hemorrhage. There was some question of Diabetic coma as the patient was a known diabetic—but after testing the urine and looking him over, the doctor did a lumbar puncture (which was perfectly normal), and watched the patient go deeper into coma, go completely paralyzed, go cold and clammy all over, pupils become fixed and pinpoint; and told the family that he would probably not last the day out. There was nothing else to be done...This fellow was as dead as any other cerebral I've seen go out in the past two months. The only question was how soon he would die...

I dropped by the laboratory to do something else and asked the lab technician whether she had found sugar in his blood up high. Very casually she said that it was only 37 Milligrams. 37 Milligrams! The normal level is 100; at 26 the patient is on the verge of death from hypoglycemic coma; and this was 37 two hours ago...I grabbed the head nurse looking like a nut; had her set up an intravenous of glucose in a hurry, and called the interne. Within two minutes after the sugar was dripping into his veins the corpse was sitting up talking to his relatives...

His life was saved just as surely as if I had pushed him out of the way of a speeding locomotive...

The doctor looked like a fool of course. And tho I did nothing at all but just happen to get the lab report as I did, and do what any third year student would do, I couldn't help feeling a little smug. Anybody would pull the paralyzed child off the tracks, but the feeling of saving the life is still there. [The doctors in Chelsea are going to hate me. By this point I've made an awful lot of them annoyed with me I guess. Both internes owe me banana royals, and I am unable to listen to tripe with equanimity—even if the fellow is a graduate from a good school…]

It doesn't make any difference I suppose, how well or poorly I do, I still remember very vividly the other pupil teachers coming in to watch me teach in Lincoln; my teachers were proud of me; I got the highest rating for pupil teaching given by the school; and at the crucial point—I failed the interview…

So don't expect me to set the world on fire either darling. I mean well Lord knows, but I don't expect to be able to put it across…

Good night darling. Your letters are very satisfying, and altho I don't say it as often, I love you just as much.

Love
Aaron

Tuesday Aug 29 11 pm

Gloria darling:

How are you dear? It's cooler out now, in fact, it looks as tho autumn were on the way. Altho I think that it would make love-making in the park more remote, the cooler weather still would allow for a lot of things we could do together…It's the time for hiking, and bicycle riding, and being active in any way at all. If you want to do the same things that I do (as you do) there are a lot of things that could be made so much more enjoyable in the doing of them together.

I'm continuing along in a way. By Sunday the crisis of whether to go to work or not asserted itself again. I went, after wrestling with my soul a la Hamlet for a couple of hours. You know all the pros and cons. I felt after a while that I have more to lose by having to pinch pennies than by risking the probability of someone coming in and seeing me. I'd be constantly in need of clothing replacements, and other small items that would be constantly annoying and distracting. So I went and did pretty well. I don't know of course that one of the many people who came might not be one of the nurses or doctors. But I'll try to keep my emotional state of mind in line and force it to do what my better judgment tells it to. You're very sweet, dear. I know that you'll let me have the money if I need it. But I'd rather not take money until I absolutely do need it. So far I've managed after a fashion. How, I still don't know. Probably in the back of my subconscious was the thought that if "worse came to worse," and I were in a difficult spot, I could always count on you. It's a very comforting feeling. It's very important in the present economic and social set up to work at least in pairs. The lone wolf finds it difficult to get by. It is of basic importance to feel that somebody is keenly interested in you and in your happiness, apart from any of the emotional ties that blood relationship entails. Oh well, if it sounds like a lot of nonsense, it boils down to my being very happy that you love me and that I love you; that in all our relationships I try to make you as happy as I can, and by so doing, am happy myself; that I feel your efforts are directed along the same channels and am very glad about it…

Yesterday I registered as a blood donor at the Baptist hospital, across the street from our place. This morning I was called for an emergency transfusion. I got there all right, but by the time that they opened up the patient's abdomen they found that she was too far gone with metastases to waste good blood on. So they paid me five dollars for "waiting" and said that they might call me some other time. I don't mind giving the blood; I do hope tho that I don't catch cold just at the same time. Altho living in a hospital, I'll get expert medical care if I do fall sick.

We're considering plans for the Jewish holidays. Will you let me know as soon as possible whether or not you can get those two days off? On that little point depends my going in you know. Or how about the Yom Kippur holidays?

I'm enclosing the editorial from PM, although you've read it probably, because it reflects so very well what I've been trying to say so very poorly in many of my letters. That the basis for discrimination, as for many of our social problems, is economic scarcity. Whenever any kind of problem comes up, if you look to see who is making money on the deal, you'll invariably find the alignment of forces and a good understanding of the problem. As everything else, it is a concept easily mouthed, but not easily appreciated or emotionally accepted. It isn't even applied too easily even by those who say they accept the doctrine of economic motivation. Apply it to the social problems you find darling. To unions, to discrimination against Jews and Negroes, to the Middlesex problem, to the Philadelphia transit strike, to the machine politics, to the rise of Fascism, the building up of Hitler by the "Democracies"...It strips man of a lot of "civilized" coverings. But I'm afraid that there is very little that is noble in the creature that is struggling for survival. Civilization can only arise with freedom from want. Culture does not grow with cut throat competition...If you come across any major problem that doesn't seem to open up when you apply the reasoning set forth in the editorial, send it up. I'd like to see it.

I'm practically dead on my feet now. I was awakened at about 2:30 last night and had to get up at 6:30 to report for the transfusion which didn't come off.

Good night darling,

Love

Aaron

The pen writes beautifully darling. I'll have to be psychoanalyzed or something before I can write easily and legibly tho. So as long as I can do so I'll probably use the typewriter.

Aaron

Thursday 31, August 10:30

Gloria darling:

I'm more than just a little sleepy tonight darling. Somehow I don't seem to be able to get to sleep early even tho I don't do anything all day. Then getting up at 7 or so, leaves less than seven hours of sleep as against my required nine or ten. Half the time I'm going around in a semi state in between wakefulness and sleep. Lord knows what I do to my patients.

Your letter today painted anything but a comfortable home environment at the present time. It sounds almost as noisy and hectic as the Chelsea, but with no Robert Brigham to go to where it is quiet. I think I can imagine how you feel. Except that I don't imagine I could stand it. Somehow I have a great need for privacy. I must have someplace where I can be alone, and not have to answer to even unspoken questions for my thoughts or actions. It was some time ago I think that I tried to tell you how I feel about that kind of privacy; I don't know whether you fully appreciated what I was trying to say then. But you certainly know what it is now! Altho I'm thinking of coming into NY for the holidays, I'm almost afraid that we'll have no place to be. I don't want to be polite to people I don't know in the few hours we have alone together. It would probably be far better if you could come to Boston. But it would undoubtedly be easier for us to get married than for you to come out here for those few days. Anyhow, bear up under the company for a little while longer, and see whether you can't assert yourself to the point where something is done (such as your friends getting a new apartment, or moving back into their old one) if nothing happens to alleviate the situation soon.

I'm still running around as you are imagining me to be. I'm either on a train, trudging up a hill to a hospital, or running around in the hospital doing the little things that take up so much time.

There was a gem here this afternoon. You know how an IV is given. Once the needle is in the vein, you regulate the rate of flow with a little clamp so that it runs in at about 40-60 drops per minute. There is a little glass arrangement in the set up so that you can see just how fast the solution is going in. Well yesterday I gave an IV on one of the patients over on the East side. It was pretty easy, as she had good veins. This afternoon Joe went in and the nurses greeted him warmly, saying that I was a wonderful IV giver. Joe was a little amazed, he said, but contained himself, thinking that my getting in with one stab had impressed the nurse. But that wasn't the reason at all. I was wonderful, she said, because the IV given by the Lahey Clinic (!) that morning took four hours to run in; mine only took two!!

This afternoon a nine year old boy came in with a pain in his belly. He was somewhat tender over the place the appendix is supposed to be, had a little fever and a moderately high white count. After talking it over, we all decided that although it might be acute appendicitis, it probably wasn't—and that the best treatment was to wait till the morning. Since the case was in tho, it was only cricket to report it to Dr. Kallen, the staff surgeon. The interne was to tell him, tho, that it was only a formality and that we really didn't think the kid should be opened as yet. As soon as he heard about the case, Kallen began giving pre operative orders. He was coming over in an hour—not to examine the patient—to operate! He was going away tomorrow on a short vacation and wasn't going to have us calling him up then. He came up and operated. The appendix looked a little red...

Joe took that pre induction physical today that he asked for. They put him into 1A, saying practically that he was faking the whole thing being a medical student. You were right about it this time darling...Actually, it doesn't mean anything to Joe except some annoyance. He really does have the bad knee with a long record of it at the Israel Zion hospital. He is sending for the records and will appeal the decision with an ultimate reversal, and classification of 4F, I believe.

The Baptist called me up tonight to say that there might be a transfusion required sometimes tonight on a patient with a bleeding ulcer who can start to hemorrhage without any warning. So I'm apt to be called at any time tonight to stagger over to the Baptist to give blood...

I'm ready to fall asleep at the typewriter, dear. I love you very much darling—miss you enormously when I'm very sleepy and want to fold my head in your arms and go slumbering off...

Good night darling,
Aaron

Monday September 4 11:00 Pm

Gloria dear:

Here I am again darling. Another week end gone by. Mostly wasted. I'm not doing any studying at all practically. So far I haven't attended any of the lectures at school, so that I hardly feel that school is going on. This evening I began to do a little reading but soon found it more pleasant to discuss a case with Joe and then start this letter to you. At this rate, even if I could take state boards, I wouldn't pass...But the prospects of taking them are so slim that it doesn't bother me much.

I'll call you this Thursday evening at 8:30 darling, unless something ties me up in which case it'll be a little later. Not seeing you for a whole week makes me miss you a lot. Not seeing you for several weeks is going to make me miss you even more, so I'll come in for the Rosh Hashona holidays. In all probability, I will let Joe work that Saturday night and come in Sunday. But since that is at least two weeks away there is no point in going into details at all. For all I know I may not be able to leave. But I really must see you in your new black dress. I bet you look pretty cute too. Are you going to wear it to Thelma's wedding?

I guess you told my folks that I would probably give some blood to the Baptist as a donor. At all events, my mother picked it up and let her fertile imagination run away with her. Last week I received a check for $10 with strong warnings about giving blood and earnest advice against it...You see, my mother evidently thinks that giving blood is a terrible thing, a major catastrophe. She therefore must picture me as veritably destitute and needing the money terribly. Maybe she already sees the lines on my face and patches on my clothes. I thought of returning the money, feeling that she probably can use it as well as I can, but didn't do so largely for fear of hurting her. I'll try to explain in my letter tonight that giving blood is simply a very easy way to find $25, that Joe has given blood once and is only sorry that they are going to make him wait at least two months before letting him make $25 more. Don't let the incident bother you at all, dear. For the past five years or so, I've found that because my major contacts are so different from my mother's, that

I've often been misinterpreted, and would then have to explain the best way I could…

About Germany. I don't pretend to be able to give even a lot of the answers, dear. Let us see what can be done with this problem tho, in the light of the economic interpretation of history. First, I think that the only understanding for the present status of the German people and the German situation is only achieved by realizing that post war Germany was one of depression, unemployment, & destitution for a great many people. Something to what hit us in 1929—only worse. A lot of little business men like your father who would have been the backbone of a democracy were wiped out by the post war inflation (just as your father would be) and found themselves declassed. They didn't belong. They weren't of the proletariat, they weren't simply laborers; yet, they no longer had the means to continue in the middle class life to which they had become accustomed. Well, be it as it may, the great body of horribly insecure people were ready for any way out. And it was to them that Hitler addressed his call. And they answered just as the same group of discontented, unemployed, bitter, post war veterans and war workers will answer in this country if things go along "normally."

Of course this discontent was channelized, and was led. It didn't just happen to turn into the Nazi party and war machine which nearly conquered the world. The angry mob always is. But just as the Roman mob was used by the Caesars, the masses of lost souls were used by the players of power politics. You can read in a great many sources about the rise of the Nazi party with the financial support of the big Factory owners in Germany; and of the rise of Hitler Germany with the backing of the English government acting for its class interests—essentially afraid of the influence of a strong Soviet Union upon their private property rights—instead of the English national interest…

So you see darling, it isn't the little phrases of "have nations" against "have not nations." Those are cute words but really explain little. It is within a nation that there are haves and have nots. Germany had enough resources at her worst time, I am sure, to take care of her population. Instead of producing so that everyone would have enough, we find that there was an enormous amount of unemployment in Germany before the war began.

There is enough for everybody, and nobody will want to slit his neighbor's throat for more, if we produce for use. I don't know the answer of what to do with post war Germany. The enormous amount of propaganda poisoning the children may well have been enough to produce pathology which will not be eradicated for decades. I'd like to see the Soviet Union take over and force socialism upon Germany, killing off those who led the present holocaust, and those who would obstruct their program. There would be no Germany. Just another Soviet republic which would never again threaten the safety of the world.

Of course, I don't expect to see anything of the sort happen. The most I hope for is that the Soviet Union has a large share in policing the future Germany. I'm sure they won't forget. Pieces of paper aren't used to becloud the issue in Russia. In their country the diplomatic policy is simply an expression of the national interest. And it is very much to their national interest to want peace; peace for a long time…

I'm sure I haven't come near to answering your questions. There is an awful lot you ought to read to be politically sophisticated. Go thru Strachey for example. You'll find a lot more. At first it'll all sound so good you'll simply accept every word of it. I'll expect you to get to the point tho when you'll be challenging even the great.

Good night darling.

All my love
Aaron

If you do read all of Strachey, you'll have to do a lot of answering of my questions. My political education stopped several years ago…

Love
Aaron

Wednesday 9/6 11:00 pm

Gloria darling:

Yesterday, speaking to you only seemed to last a moment. I'm sorry now that I told you I wouldn't call this Thursday. I'd like to talk to you tomorrow very much. As is, I'll call you on Tuesday instead (9:30 p.m.).

Right now, I'm all alone. Joe is staying over at the Chelsea tonight. It would probably be much more valuable for me to do some studying for a change. But I get a greater kick out of writing to you, so I compromise and write to you instead.

Do you approve, darling?

This morning I gave (sold) Blood at the Baptist Hospital. I was called up last night & came in this morning to be "tapped." No sequelae at all. My pulse was from 56 to 57, I think! The chap who took the blood is Dr. Evinole, chief anaesthetist of the Lahey Clinic. A transfusion is treated like a major operation. Everything but the general anaesthesia. It probably costs the patient a fortune. But it is swell for the donor. As I left, I was given my check for $25. Very easy money. And if I don't catch cold or anything, it's pure "extra."

This afternoon I saw "Lady in the Dark". Very good. Interestingly enough your letter today dealt with psychoanalysis—"my poor handwriting & what it means." I'm no analyst darling, but I don't think your analysis is deep enough in this case. It is too facile. If my poor writing stems from a neurosis (which it probably does) the underlying problem is far deeper than my rebelling against taking useless notes. I'm sure I'm a little neurotic; darling. But so are most of the people we know. In this case it may manifest itself in my sweating so profusely under embarrassment & writing with great difficulty at times. But if they are my sole difficulties in maintaining a stable, warm, secure personality I'll be among the more fortunate.

You remember our discussions of personality & what makes it. The big concepts of depth psychology is based upon a "primitive" personality we all have which is a product of our powerful emotional experiences. It is in the feelings of this part of us, in its struggles at trying to find security, that the personality manifests itself. The scared, tiny "Id" is constantly in fear. And fear is the basis for the personality pathology seen. In the mechanisms derived by the individual to pacify the terrified primitive personality (Id), the surface personality we know is formed.

Now, what forms this Id. It varies with the author. Freud puts our primitive instincts into it. Adler says it simply is the struggle for existence. Call it what you will. Primitively there certainly is a struggle for existence. And this is threatened by severe emotional trauma. But severe trauma of this kind is pretty hard to inflict upon the adult. There is very little deep emotion connected with his life's activities. In the early growing stage, tho, when experiences are new, then emotion is present & plays a big role. Rejected by mother, called ugly by a big brother, physical deformity (strongly stressed by Adler), clumsiness, stood up "on a first date," being a wall flower at a dance, not being sexually well developed, mental infirmity, not being able to find emotional security in mother as a child, because mother is as insecure herself,…these go to make up the things in a child's development which will shrink his primitive personality until it is tiny & scared. And in its struggle to bring itself peace & security the "goals" of that person thru life will be manifest: the jobs in which he will be happy, the mate with whom she will be content, the kind of clothes, almost (flashy…) will be dictated.

This is the "normal" person darling. Real neuroses develop when the situation is such as to threaten the elaborate structure & expose the subject's "inadequacies."

Good Lord, don't let me rave on like this! I've gotten so, that even when I don't have a typewriter available I go on & on & on…I'm not very clear, I know…Mostly because I'm not clear myself about the subject. Try "Neurotic Personality of Our Times" by Karen Horney. Then the others she wrote, & some of Adler's stuff. It's very good reading. It will also be good preparation for understanding your husband & children—but don't look for psychoneurosis as I do for "Cushing's Syndrome."

I'll probably have access to the typewriter by my next letter darling, so it'll be more legible.

Good night, dear

All my love
Aaron

Thursday 9/7 9:30 p.m.

Sweetheart:

It's so lovely out tonight that I just had to write you a short note telling you that I love you very much and miss you a good deal. I run around a good deal now; so that these very brief periods of being all alone with the stars & my thoughts are precious & reserved for you…How are you darling? I'm looking forward to coming in for the holidays. I'll in all probability let Joe work that Saturday night at the Fox & Hounds so that I'll come in sometimes Sunday. If you have any preferences just name them. Do you want me in Sunday morning, or evening?

Probably more so in the past month, I'm very much tensed up. Maybe it's because of the tension a hospital puts one under. Whatever the reason, I want very much to bury my head in your bosom and let the tenseness just ooze out. I hope it doesn't just ooze from me to you. That isn't my idea of fair play at all…I don't think it does tho. In fact we'll both feel better for it…

As I've said before so many times, I love you very much dear—and am very happy that you love me, too.

Good night darling,
Aaron

Tuesday September 12 7:30 pm

Sweetheart:

I'm tired…Sunday night after working at the Hi Hat, I went over to the Chelsea Memorial and just got back…It feels as tho I haven't been at the Brigham, where everything is quiet, and peaceful, for weeks…I slept over, you see, Sunday and Monday nights, in a room that was vacant.

This afternoon when I was asked about treatment given a patient, I didn't know whether it had been given last week—or yesterday. What did I do anyway? I really don't know. All I remember is the constant moving around , greeting and being greeted by dozens of nurses and doctors, helping to move a patient over for the X ray technician, putting in a catheter that came out, putting in an

IV, taking blood for a Wasserman, doing a White blood count in a hurry, doing some blood smears, examining patients as they come in terribly sick, running down to the accident room and suturing lacerations, listening for heart sounds in the abdomen of pregnant women, watching the deliveries, going on rounds, answering relatives who want to know how their boy is doing, trying to get into veins, doing more catheterizations, making a vaginal smear and looking for Gonococci…

Gosh, I can't even tell you straight.

At any rate, I've learnt my internes generally really like that. It's a very exhausting life, particularly if you want to see and do everything. It's a constant round of activity with very little let up at night. Last night I was awakened two times. Arthur probably got no sleep at all.

What does one need to learn anyway? As I've written several times, I guess, the body of theoretical knowledge which is most easily exemplified in that case we did together, is only one part of the equipment of the doctor. It is indispensible, I suppose, but pretty useless without the other two parts of his equipment. By that I mean, first, the skills which go with medicine. It is easy to say that given cyanosis, dyspnea, cough with rusty sputum, P2 greater than A2, ascites, enlarged liver, pitting edema of the extremities, enlarged heart, systolic murmur at the apex, moist rales at the bases of the lungs,…it is heart failure. But it takes definite skills to be able to get those findings from the patient. Is he cyanotic or just a little blue in the finger nails, can you get sputum from the patient, can you really make out by listening to the heart in certain areas whether the sound is louder or softer, does the patient really have fluid in his distended abdomen or is it just gas, can you really outline the heart by percussion and determine that it is enlarged, do you really hear bubbling rales at the bases of the lungs or don't you???

It takes a lot of skill and a lot of experience to make anything out of physical diagnosis. Right know I don't know whether I'm feeling liver or not, whether I'm feeling gas or water in the belly, whether the funny noises I hear in the chest are "asthmatic wheezes" or "pneumonic rales"…

Not only me, darling. All of us. This evening, a little boy came in breathing very heavily, very rapid pulse, coughing, and looking very sad. We found a lot of interesting noises in his chest. The internes were all ready to start Sulfadiazine. Masters came in. It wasn't pneumonia, he said, but probably asthma with a little cold superimposed. No sulfas at all for the present. Try adrenaline instead. And he gave some very good reasons too…

The second part of the armamentarium is the ability to treat. A needle must be gotten skillfully into veins and into the spinal canal—even in the hard cases. Suturing of wounds and lacerations in any part of the body. Application of dressings anywheres in the body. Catheterizing. Taking babies. Taking a simple X-ray and then setting a simple fracture. Reducing a dislocated shoulder. Putting on and taking off a cast. These skills must be part of any doctor. They must really be "skills."

So there you have the triad of: theoretical knowledge and diagnostic skills in recognizing pathological signs, and Treatment skills. To all that comes the additional feeling for what a person will most probably have, Perspective. It is absolutely impossible in most instances to make a list of all the possibilities and then do all the work to rule out all but one diagnosis. It just can't be done outside of Mass General. And even then some sort of diagnosis must be made in order to start treatment while all the tests are going on. So the doctor must know from seeing a great many cases in his locality that a big liver is probably Cirrhosis and not Wilson's hepatolenticulate degeneration; that a kid with joint pains and fever is rheumatic fever and not Sickle cell anemia; that a pain in the belly is probably appendicitis and not Acute pancreatitis. Certain things simply happen; some are very rare.

One woman was in the hospital bleeding very profusely from the uterus. I thought at once of the rare blood diseases Singer taught me, and went running for my slides and needle. I could just hear Singer telling me what a smart boy I was for digging up a case of Idiopathic Thrombocytopenic Purpura, in which the patient just doesn't have any platelets worth mentioning so she doesn't stop bleeding readily. I did "bleeding times," "clotting times," and made lots of smears. All were perfectly normal. I was thinking of having the laboratory do actual platelet counts, and maybe take some of her serum to the Brigham to get "prothrombin times" tests done. Masters came in to see her today. He asked at once, and found out, that she had missed one period before the hemorrhage started. He diagnosed induced abortion. Very simple. It happens every day…What he was interested in finding out was the method the woman used in causing the abortion…

Good night darling. By the way, the picture you sent was very cute. But then you wouldn't have sent it if you didn't come out well. So I'm making no commitments on the new hair-do til I see it. I think it's good in the picture.

Love
Aaron

Friday Sept 15 11 pm

Darling:

It blew so hard yesterday, that we used it as an excuse to stay at the Brigham and sleep late—at Chelsea we said that we had to be on call for emergencies. Actually, I'd call for one of the experienced nurses if anything happened…

By this point I'm getting a little understanding of how medicine goes on at the Chelsea, which is pretty representative of the middle sized general hospital. I've been keeping small abstracts of the cases I see, indicating what the complaints were when the patient came into the hospital; what the diagnostic tests showed; the diagnosis if made; and the therapy given; finally, the disposition of the case at discharge.

Today I went over the group I have so far who have been terminated for one reason or another. The results were not encouraging. A great many ended by dying. One little girl came in severely burnt—Over half of her skin was gone. She was kept alive for nearly a week by a continuous drip of plasma. But she finally dies as everybody expected. I don't know whether or not any kind of treatment would have been of any use. Her doctor, Dr. Masters, knows what he is doing…

One old man, was brought into the hospital after an apoplectic stroke. He was in coma, half of his body was paralyzed, and the prognosis was grave. He represented what his doctor could have prophesied twenty years ago, the result of a high blood pressure. The continuous strain on his blood vessels caused damage to his arteries which finally gave way at the weakest spot. A hemorrhage into the brain as one of the little arteries could no longer withstand the ever rising blood pressure—and the man's life came to an abrupt end. Why the high blood pressure in the first place, and what to do about it—totally unknown…

Aside from such cases, there are a great many where the man comes in with pain in his abdomen someplace. The symptoms he gives aren't enough to make a diagnosis. The routine which is followed is almost never varied no matter who the doctor is. He gets X rays of the gall bladder, stomach, large intestine, and finally kidney—hoping that by this routine looking into the belly the xray man will find something wrong and thereby make the diagnosis. Unfortunately the X ray very often shows nothing. I've been down in the X ray department nearly every day now, watching the weird dark shadows move around on the fluorescent screen as the radiologist examined the internal organs. Usually he finds nothing and the report comes back—"stomach shows no evidence of disease". What next? I don't know. I've seen case after case come in like this, go thru the whole routine and found negative, whose pain eventually cleared up with rest and a light diet at the hospital, who were discharged "improved", no diagnosis ever being made…In fact this group seems to comprise more than any other single group in the hospital. It is really a tragedy that the greatest group to enter the hospital is really given no benefit by the stay. It brought to mind very sharply the dictum of Singer—the American doctor treats mostly patients who are going to get over their attack anyhow; that is why he is able to achieve some "cures" and make a living.

I have seen very little in the way of "cures". The essential is to maintain the patient—and let him cure himself. Symptomatic treatment. If the patient has a high fever, sulfa drugs are given. Maybe they will help. If not, Penicillin is tried. Enemas are given for constipation, paregoric for diarrhea, IV fluids for dehydration, Sedatives for pain…and one waits for the patient to get better. In the meantime the lab reports are watched. If the hemoglobin goes down too low, a transfusion is considered. Right down the line. So you see, to some extent I could probably be a doctor right now…

Of course, this group of men and women who really can get nothing from the hospital as the X ray man just refused to find an ulcer or something that can legitimately be taken out—they are really in a fix. They go from doctor to doctor, hospital to hospital, osteopath and chiropractor, hoping to find a cure. Maybe this group is the group where the emotional life is playing the big role in the etiology of the disease. Maybe it is here where Thoreau really is right in seeing the psychic as the big thing. Maybe psychoanalysis is what they need instead of antacids. I don't know. Maybe in a better hospital, with better equipment and better men, a pathological lesion could be discovered and therapy instituted. I don't know. I've seen so little.

Except for the infectious diseases and a few other diseases such as diabetes, Medicine can only stand by and watch. By and large, most of the ills to which man is susceptible come and go without any known etiology and no known treatment. Cancer, Rheumatic fever, Rheumatoid arthritis, Peptic ulcer, High blood pressure, Arteriosclerosis, Kidney disease (Nephritis)…It is quite an exception of course. The infectious disease comprised a big chunk of the suffering and death of humanity. Public health and preventive medicine is based upon the advances in this field. But I have the feeling that in most of these other diseases, that do not respond to investigation with the methods used by Pasteur and Koch in working out the secrets of the infectious diseases—that new methods along totally different lines will have to be used. In other words, that something new will have to crop up in the medical world with which to tackle the problem of these other diseases. Looking for bugs on agar slants—or even chick embryo media—won't work. It'll have to be something along a totally new takeoff…I hope the big discovery that starts it off comes soon…

Another discourse darling. Just stop me anytime you've heard it before. You can really prove my repeating myself easily enough. Just produce the fifteen letters which say exactly the same thing and I'll be quiet. Of course if they imply that I love you, it doesn't hold. All my letters are supposed to say that in some way or other. But aside from that incontrovertible fact, you have a right to as little humbug as possible.

This letter will get to you, I hope, after I'm in New York and with you for a while. Barring accidents I ought to get to see you Sunday afternoon. We were going to call New York to see whether the storm had done any damage to the people whom we loved, but all lines to New York are jammed.

Good night darling.

All my love
Aaron

Sat. 9/23/44

Gloria darling:

I'm dashing this letter off so that Joe will take it down with him & mail it. I want you to know that I definitely resent the weather! It is so beautiful out today. I particularly resent having weather clear up just as soon as I leave. Of course I don't really know what I'd do with gorgeous weather which we didn't do with our semi-fluid around us all the time. It's just that on theoretical grounds it is rank discrimination.

Today, I wished you were up here badly. It's sunny & warm & quiet…We'd make love very beautifully in this environment…

All is quiet again up here. Mrs. Cox never asked for me and presumably didn't know that I was gone. In a few weeks I hope we'll be able to ask her for time off to go see our families. Tho, maybe she knows more than she is letting on.

More later dear.

I love you very much.

Aaron

Tuesday Sept 16 7:30 pm

Gloria darling:

The letters you've been sending since I left New York are very, very sweet darling. They echo a lot of my own feeling. I too wish that I were in New York or that you were in Boston. Of course I'm terribly jealous of all your friends who are getting married and have their respective wives or husbands with them. But I have been running around so much, as usual, that the sheer activity has served as some sort of sublimation…

As you know, nobody missed me at the hospital apparently, so I'll try to take a week off in the near future and come in. By then I want you to take time off or there will be no point in going in…I arrived Friday evening, to find a case history waiting for me. I did that one as I was already in the red to Joe for his coverage of my cases during the week. (We work it fairly by having Joe do the odd numbered cases and I take the even ones) Monday morning we went to Peter Brigham to listen to the Medical rounds. They are swell. A patient was brought in with high blood pressure and a long discussion waged on the efficacy of treating the condition with a drug now under investigation. After the clinical man gave his impression of how well the drug works, they were able to call upon the pharmacologist who is currently investigating the drug to talk about it. Very snazzy. They discussed the literature and bring it right up to date—a lot of the literature that is going to be published is of course being prepared right in Harvard.

The other case discussed was a blood disease. And they had Minot there to talk about it. Minot is the fellow who discovered the cause and the treatment for Pernicious Anemia; Thereby turning what had until then been a truly "pernicious disease" into one which is very amenable to treatment. A great many people owe their lives directly to him. Well, his talk on hematology wasn't anywheres as good as Dr. Singer's, but it was nice to have him there for atmosphere…

Sunday was spent working at the High Hat. Do you know darling, what makes going to work Sunday morning so tough is probably the contrast of staying at the hospital. Particularly Sunday mornings, the hospital is so very quiet, the sun is hitting a certain part of the porch where I come to sit and read while the sun bakes my face. The only noises are very distant—a nurse talking to a patient, a door slamming on the ward…all around are open fields so that the eye travels out unobstructed. The sky is blue. A couple of small clouds just bring out the contrast. My God, I'm starting that rotten poetry again! At any rate it's very nice just then, at about 12 o'clock Sunday morning. And I have to prepare to leave for the Hi Hat. At that point all my mental agility is working hard to cook up reasons for not going to work. If you hear suddenly that I've quit, you know that I've finally succeeded in finding a really good reason. So far I haven't quite been able to kid myself.

Well, Sunday afternoon came and went and I found myself at the Chelsea. Nearly all the patients had changed and I was faced with starting to build up a new batch of notes. At any rate Sunday night wasn't altogether wasted—at about 2 o'clock some drunk came in with a laceration over one eyebrow. The interne was very sleepy so I went down and put in two sutures all by myself! Nearly a major operation. At least I worked as hard as tho it were a Miles resection. As I've told you, the most important thing in surgery is confidence. You could undoubtedly put in a much better stitch on any dress you have. My mother could hem stitch it. Yet going into an open wound, going into living tissue anyplace is considered such big stuff, and puts such a strain on the operator, because he feels that he is hurting the patient, causing a lot of pain. I can't quite put into words the idea in my mind, which tries to explain the difficulty experienced in doing simple manual operations on people. Every plumber does much more difficult jobs every day, yet he would be terrified if he had to go into a vein. Our laboratory technician at the Chelsea who is pretty new does all sorts of intricate tests, yet won't take blood from a vein…

Joe went home Monday morning, leaving me at the mercy of circumstance in the Brigham. I hope that nothing turns up I can't handle. As is I always felt that if I couldn't get a needle in or something, I could call on Joe who has somewhat more dexterity than I have. This week tho, all I can do is keep my fingers crossed. There simply isn't anybody around...He won't be back until Saturday evening I guess. I'm sorry now that I didn't take the whole week too. If you could have gotten time, I think I would have done so, even tho I didn't know that it was all right...

I'm sorry about Solly and will write to him. In fact I had thought of doing so ever since I came back and will do so today. It's remarkable how well you know me, and how similar our thought processes are. Usually that happens only upon close living over a long period of time.

Good night darling. I'm going back to the wards and do a history. I have to finish by 9:30 if I'm going to get your call.

Love
Aaron

Tuesday 10/3 11:30 pm.

Gloria darling:

As you can see I'm writing comparatively late tonight. I got pretty sleepy, so we made our usual nightly journey to the dining room for coffee. It's a pretty good idea, but it should only take 15 minutes—not an hour! People talk too much!

All except our telephone conversations, I don't know where the devil the time goes to. It just goes tho I only said "Hello darling" & that was all...

I'm very pleased you enjoy your course. I'd like to take it myself & so would Joe after I got thru telling him about it. I ought to get a job as publicity man for some school. It seems as tho I'm forever selling education to people...So don't forget to give me all the gory details. Not only your lectures, but of the books you read. If you read a lot, the course will be very good. It'll leave you a better person than when you entered. You'll have more understanding of people, or at least, a profound respect for their complexities; & reserve judgment on social questions. If I were in New York with nothing to do evenings—imagine!—I'd take the course, too.

I'm sending along a cute article—testing one's self for marriage. I marked up all the answers, so you won't be influenced by my answers. You do have my totals, so you can compare…I think that will probably be all right…The big emphasis in this series is similarity in background, interests, & essential personality, isn't it?

I'm relieved that your musings about my vacation…are only whimsical. I was getting worried. You know I'm not anything as good as you say in your letters, nor can we have as hectic a time as you're "planning." I accept them as the stuff of allegories. Poets in the old days wrote stuff that wasn't meant to be taken literally. O.K. darling, I love you; you love me…

It's very late now dear, so I'll go off to sleep. I'm to do a gastric analysis tomorrow at 7:30 a.m. if I can get into the patient's stomach with a tube. Early to bed & early to rise—pass days away very quickly.

Good night darling—

Love,
Aaron

Friday 11 pm Oct 6

Gloria darling:

You're getting this fancy paper, not to impress you, but just that I didn't bring any with me to the room where the typewriter is. It's way beyond the stage, I think, where I would try to impress you with letterheads or fancy accomplishments. I'll bring to you anything good that I do, because in your pleasure in the achievement, my satisfaction is more than doubled…

Today was a busy day at the hospital. One of the acute emergencies which you read about actually happened. That is, read about in peace time. In war medicine, the average case is one of the acute emergencies. At any rate, a fellow was struck very forcibly in the abdomen by a piece of lumber flying at him from a circular saw he was running. He was brought into the accident room by one of his fellow employees, who left him and ran. The patient simply knew that he was in terrific agony; he had severe pain in his abdomen;

please do something. It was difficult even to get his name. Pulse was good, blood pressure stayed up, no shock was evident. The abdomen was extremely tender and pretty rigid. When the doctor on the case finally arrived, the question before the house was to operate or not to operate. Like Hamlet. Did he have a perforated viscus, or was he simply in pain from the contusion—and in which case an operation is either absolutely essential in the former or detrimental in the latter…It isn't an easy decision. X ray was not helpful. My choices for the condition was first, perforated stomach; second, perforated intestine. Operation was performed in about an hour from the time the patient arrived. There were some ghastly rents in the small intestine. Not operating would have been absolutely fatal. While operating, plasma was dripping into the patient's veins, artificial respiration had to be given by the anaesthetist several times when the patient stopped breathing—regular war surgery…It is dubious about the chances for survival, but at least the patient has a fighting chance…

Do you know darling, the more we stay at hospitals, the more we realize that one of the really exploited groups of the population is the nursing profession. Joe and I discussed the fact this afternoon, that it is really surprising that no one has as yet done a muckraking job on the subject. There is very little that is glamorous about nurses or nursing. The girls are very ordinary; they have a job which is at best difficult and dirty. To achieve the distinction of wearing a white uniform the girl who meets the qualifications of high school graduation, required courses, fitness physically…goes thru a three year period of training that has a nunnery beat a mile. For the first six months, they work like drudges, cleaning up the floors, making beds, washing masks, mopping up the post mortem room after a messy autopsy is all over, and doing the work without let up for stretches of twelve hours a day! And then they go up to higher things: prepping diets for the patients, taking temperatures (mostly rectal), carrying bedpans, taking urine samples, giving patients baths, cleaning up the patient who is incontinent, or who has an attack of vomiting…Finally there is the real noble work of scrubbing in the operating room—giving the surgeon the instruments as he barks "snap girl, don't you know anything?"…Maternity work—working every night giving women in labor enemas and holding their hand as they groan with the pain. All the time living in the nurse's home with the regulations as strict as in the strictest boarding school. Lights out by 10:30; no smoking except in the "recreation" room; the only place allowed for movement is the short walk from the hospital to the home and back; in every night, but one, by 10 o'clock…Regimentation as severe as the Army…Finally the nurse, disillusioned and pretty tired of it all if bright at all, graduates. And after passing state board examinations, she may get a job as head nurse on a busy floor—for which she receives the remuneration for being the doctors' little helper of 25 dollars a week for Lord knows how many hours…The doctor is God, the nurse is taught that he can do no wrong, that she is to take all the blame if he makes a mistake, that she is to take his rotten temper and stupid boorishness as just, and she is to give the patient the nursing care for which the doctor will collect a very handsome fee. I wish you could see it from the inside. Maybe you could do the nurse's "Citadel"…

I guess I don't like anything, do I darling.

Only you…

It's midnight now dear. I'm getting pretty groggy. In my next letter I'll try to discuss some of the social work problems that you are throwing out. Try is right. At this point I'm no longer able to lecture to you from the height of my superior knowledge. I'll tell you what I think. But you have the basis for opinions which will be just as valid. I'll undoubtedly change my mind plenty if you pound at me, as you no doubt have been influenced by my opinions poured out over all this time. Your letters are interesting reading. Pour out all you can.

Good night darling.

I love you very much
Aaron

Monday 5:30 p.m. Oct. 9

Darling—

I've been feeling a little "under the weather" for the past few days. So far I've done nothing about it. This afternoon I got back from Chelsea early. Do you think I ought to call a doctor??? Actually, I'll probably start taking Cod Liver Oil again…

I'm very anxious to see you in your new coat. It better look gorgeous! I ought to be coming in during early November. Do you think it will be ready by then? I really didn't expect to see you in one this year. See? Maybe we'll be married just as unexpectedly before too much longer. I don't really expect to wait until I can support you. Tho I certainly would like to. But if you're willing, we'll marry before I'm making enough to keep you in the style to which you're accustomed…I'd very much like to know that I can take (& pass) State Boards, tho…

Incidentally, last week I did see a dentist. He filled 3 teeth, and wouldn't take my money! Strangely enough, I no longer have a toothache…

[Do you know, if the Dentist won't charge me; you keep on insisting on taking me out; & my father paying for my clothes I need in the future (he hasn't insisted yet) I'm going to quit working & just loaf…I'll sit out on the piazza & just sun myself…]

I'm very glad you like your course & books. You're absolutely right in finding a lot of material for identification. A lot of us do. I've noticed two types of people, "generally speaking." The soft type, sensitive, shy, easily hurt, introverted; generally cultured & lovers of the arts if presented with the opportunity…The other type is stronger & harder; more extroverted; very sure of themselves, their ideas, their beliefs…; they make the politicians, the good businessmen, the successful doctors. They are the Babbits & the Elmer Gantrys…The former make the neurotics; when the latter go, they become psychotic. It is in the first group that we find tired, sorry, hurt people coming to Social Workers, pouring their stories out in big self revealing torrents, & asking for help. The second would never go; would never admit unhappiness; never admit personal inadequacy; would never show the insight required for therapy.

I'm making very big generalizations I realize. And you know there really are no such absolute groups, of course. But see whether the people you know don't fall into one or the other. [In fact even "physical status" has been divided into "types" by many authors. They describe the big boned, short-necked, small-headed, plethoric, big eating, beer drinking type; who gets hypertension, cirrhosis of the liver, arteriosclerosis & "strokes." And the tall, thin, lanky, pigeon breasted, anemic, intense, irritable, worrying type who gets TB, bronchitis, ulcers, colitis, rheumatoid arthritis…]

To get back to what I started to say, you & I are both of the "neurotic" group, I think. If things go tough we'd tend to develop a psychoneurosis. So having the "tendency" we can see in ourselves the "neurotic symptoms" which if present to a degree which <u>would prove incapacitating</u> would be "neurotic." Now what makes us this type—that is quite a problem. Karen Horney talks it up, I'm sure, in childhood development. I don't know the answer, I'm sure. Generalities can be easily understood on the surface. But, as in clinical medicine, confronted with the patient it is not enough to know that almost anything can happen—specifically, what happened in this case…

I received the cookies today, dear. I've gone thru quite a few already. They're very good. No excuses now you can make good cookies.

I just got a call to go over to do a white count & do an i.v. I hope I don't run into any difficulties.

All my love
Aaron

Wednesday 8 pm 10/11/44

Gloria darling:

Your gift came today. It is "gorgeous." I too hope to be able to use it on a honeymoon soon. The sooner the better. It's going to make me nervous on my first trip in with it. I will be afraid it will be stolen all the time. Just as with your pen, I go into a cold sweat if I don't find it where I thought I put it. Your gifts are so lovely, I'm very concerned with someone else wanting them…

Your letter was interesting. It ought to be answered before I forget the gist of it.

I think you've made one of the mistakes so common to people entering a new field. It is inevitable of course. But it is very difficult to apply what one learns in the first course to actual situations. It is difficult to find "easy situations." In medicine, I'm up against the same thing. I only know "easy cases." But the patients who come in refuse to conform. They are frequently very hard cases.

Rosaline was legitimately upset when you told her that her love for her husband was nothing but "self aggrandizement," an "ego building device"; a mechanism for making her "feel better & more important"; "food for her ego"... If I didn't know you better, I'd be concerned that you thought those things of your love for me.

No darling...

To feed my ego, any girl would do. All she would have to do is to think I were very good, look at me with big blue (or brown) eyes-- & I'd be in love with her. Why do people choose one, instead of another?

It is much more complicated than that. I don't know what love is, to be sure. It is a very big thing. It is sex, & warmth, & tenderness. It gives a great deal—as well as receives. Thoreau (?) called it the "Sun—shining with the warmth of health."

What about this ego-builder? It is there of course. Some people are more adequate in themselves than others. Some are very insecure. Insecurity is the basis for a terrible search—which never ends—for more & more proof that the personality isn't really so inadequate. Being loved is one such proof. It is also a bulwark against the barbs of being rejected by the opposite sex in some advance; not having "dates"; not getting married...These are terrible blows to the insecure personality...Being loved is good protection. But this person cannot love. He (or she) doesn't have the ability to open up, to give off "radiations." He can only take. And take only with increasing dissatisfaction. He will need constant increasing proofs of love. For it is the proof which helps splint the poor personality.

So there is "the illusion of love" as a neurotic man. Just as there is a paralysis which is a neurotic symptom. But don't attribute the "illusion" to all lovers, or "neurosis" to all paralytics.

The stuff is very stimulating. Keep on reading. I can't promise to write long replies to each chapter in Freud. You know I don't go the whole way. I'll do my best tho. It would be interesting if you could get the lecturer or some author to tell you what love is. It is really a big question in psychiatry. Keep sending me your definitions. It must explain why one loves one girl, or at least one type. Why its highest expression—sex—is so gratifying with loved ones. Are there real differences in loves of mothers, mates, friends…The role of sex. Is platonic love possible? Is it love? What do we mean in saying we build a relationship?

So, all my love
Aaron

Thursday 10/19 11:15 a.m.

Gloria darling:

I feel as tho I've been in a football game, darling. My back muscles ache. I'm all tired & I'm slightly trembly. You see, I assisted at an operation this morning…One of the surgeons forgot to show up apparently, so a hurry call was put in for a house officer. As you know, that's me. I finished breakfast in a gulp, changed into O.R. (operating room) clothes & scrubbed for ten minutes. Then with very, very clean hands, gloves, gown, mask, & cap I held two retractors for 2 ½ hours while the surgeon hacked, sawed & chipped at the bone…

Am I tired!

All sorts of problems arise in surgery. Mostly of a personal sort tho. The end of your nose starts to tickle-- & you can't touch it. It really isn't cricket to ask a nurse to scratch your nose either. Very annoying…Or in my case, for instance, I sweat. The little drops just collect one by one on my forehead, eyebrows, & roll onto my glasses. The operative field looks very queer thru little drops of water. But there is nothing to be done about it. My glasses aren't sterile, so I can't touch them…Or sneezing. I think Lister or somebody would suffer untold agonies in Hades if I were to sneeze at the table. But you just try to hold a sneeze back for 3 hours…So you stand there, a retractor in each hand, wondering how long the damn operation is going to take, anyway. In case you're not sure about what my noble work is, I've drawn a little sketch. You can see that the retractor pulls the skin & muscle apart so the surgeon can work & see what he is doing within the wound made by his incision.

Of course, the big value in second assisting is that you're right on top of the operation & can see just what is going on. Looking on from the sidelines, never gets nearly as good a view.

Enough of surgery.

I'm very glad you weren't upset about my forgetting to call you on time. So long as you know that slips like that don't mean anything; that I love you just as much even if I am absent-minded, we'll never have any major personal difficulties. You may have to remind me about birthdays, anniversaries, appointments…but you'll never have to remind me that I love you very much.

All my love, darling,
Aaron

Monday 7:00 p.m.

Your past few letters are so full of questions that I better get down to work & answer some of them. Almost like taking an exam…

First, Thelma's "tipped womb." If the physician is competent, he means she has a retroverted uterus. Normally the uterus sits so (drawing). As you see the uterus is tipped forward & enters the vagina at an angle.

Now, in some women, usually after childbirth, the uterus tips over backwards, so this is a pretty common condition, & right or wrong, is blamed for a lot of symptoms. If asymptomatic, it is left alone. If she has "bearing down pains," trouble with the regularity or painfulness of her menses or conceiving, it will probably be necessary to do a "ventral suspension." That is, opening the abdomen & stitching the uterus to the anterior abdominal wall. It is not a dangerous operation; on the scale of an appendectomy…

So that's that…

About Freud. "There is no neurosis with a normal sex life." The interpretation you heard, i.e. "there is no normal sex life with a neurosis," is probably something I said. I still believe that that is the truer statement. I think that the personality is the center of the organism, & that the various facets, including sex life, are simply manifestations of that central personality.

It isn't that the child who is constipated later is to develop into a skinflint because of "sexual arrest"; but that the insecure baby who uses his defecations as attempts to gain attention, or as valuable property, later may be the adult with the same insecurity, same inadequacy, who uses money as his way of achieving prominence & pushing his ego. So the person who can't really love, may find it difficult to enjoy the partner's excesses.

I don't think that that is what Freud said. I think you hit it pretty well. But so far, I don't agree with his interpretations. I'm sure there are, & were, many Catholic-Protestant Nuns who tho Celibate—did not develop a neurosis. It's a good line to use at an intelligent girl—she doesn't want to get a neurosis, does she?—but I really don't think it's true. What do you think? Do you think that you'll go whacky with shear frustration if your sex life doesn't pick up soon? Or Rosaline?

Registration was tough up here too. I spent three hours in line last week to be told to go somewhere else. We finally did register today. If they don't discover that we're not in Boston for a year yet, I think we'll be allowed to vote. But I'm not counting on it. Something is bound to come up. You'll see. I was sure they'd want birth certificates, rent receipts, & affidavits from school. Pretty soon you'll have to bring a lawyer with you to the registration booth…

Your letter today sounded as tho you were lonely & empty, darling. I get that way too, particularly when I'm tired. And I want you badly. I'm very glad tho, that at those moments I want you so badly. Rather than just feel tired & alone…Your searching self-analysis is a good sign. It is not much more happy to say "I'm a jealous little bastard"—but yet the more we do know & bring these things up into the open, the less harm they are likely to do. Be careful tho, darling. Don't let the cold Freudian analysis make you decide that you & your friends are a bunch of no good hypocrites. At the beginning you're bound to go overboard. Just realize that people are pretty small, are full of weaknesses & in their own little ways are trying to get along. There is little true nobility—but probably little horrible wickedness.

All my love
Aaron

Friday 12:00 Midnight

Darling:

Today was officially our last day at Chelsea Memorial; "officially" tho won't mean that we'll stop going. I spoke to Dr. Musgrave, Chief of Staff today, who said that Joe & I could come in anytime we wished. We're told from several sources that the Superintendent of the hospital thinks we're the best bunch she's had there. And just to crow a little more (you don't mind darling; I've got to be modest with everyone else)—Miss Aronson, the superintendent mentioned me by name to several people as being a good student & probably a fine doctor.

Ironical, isn't it? There is absolutely nothing at school to even give us hope for boards. So I'd probably make a good doctor just as I'd have made a good teacher (everybody said so), a good research man (everybody said so), or a good social worker (everybody said so). I'm tired of almost arriving, dear…

I just finished reading some chapters in Karen Horney. It's a good book. I think tho that it can be simplified in essence. I picture the situation of the personality of today—"neurotic" or not—as "floating in equilibrium of forces: some tending to lift" the personality to greater feeling of care, sincerity, happiness; while the others drag it down deeper into anxiety. The PERSONALITY/Ego/Inadequacy/Insecurity is bred of neurotic need for affection; money, position; "Success"; Power; Conquest; Work; Drugs, Alcohol; attention getting mechanisms; and leads to Structures of the Neurosis (Inhibitions, Rationalizations) as well as Symptoms of Anxiety (Palpitations, Diarrhea, Ulcer, Gastritis, Headaches, Fainting Spells, Urinary symptoms, Sweating, Terrible "Emotional Feeling.") Situations which increase feelings of inadequacy include Rebuffs, Criticisms, Loving someone, Asking for a job, Attempting to do something which is not familiar & not certain of successful accomplishment, Competition, Reflections on physical deficiencies.

The personality is the circle at the center *(diagram).* We'll start with its being to some respect insecure with the feelings of inadequacy. Probably this originated in childhood experiences when the parents were unable to give the child the warmth & love it needed to develop "normally."

At any rate, there is the personality, feeling somewhat inadequate. If its own inner feelings are very strong, the forces below will have greater effect. Well, as the personality runs across situations which reflect his inadequacy his feelings will increase. Anxiety is the term we use for this feeling. It is manifested by a lot of clinical symptoms. Some of which I listed. There is also this terrible, lost, sinking, fearful feeling which is so painful the personality will do almost anything to escape.

Now what can he do. First, he avoids those situations. These avoidances are "Inhibitions"; and if these inhibitions are explained in some more acceptable way we have "Rationalization." So, a girl doesn't go to dances as she is afraid she'd be a wall flower (inhibition) & says she wants to be true to her soldier boyfriend (Rationalization). Loving someone is dangerous for the weak, scared personality as it leaves one wide open & very vulnerable. Therefore, first, is avoidance of anxiety creating situations. Usually, the person can lift himself out of the anxiety state by findings props, supports for the personality. Getting affection, sexual conquests, being the best ping pong player in school…are all props to the thirsting little ego. So going in for these "pick ups" helps too.

Now, I think you'll be thinking at this point that this fits all the people you know pretty well. That's right. I think it's only a matter of degree. If the inadequate-feeling ego is able to become a high school principal, with prestige & security & is happy in his work, he'll probably not need to avoid the forces causing anxiety, or go in for any more of those support mechanisms. He will live out his life very "normally."

If the basic weakness is great, those destructive situations must be avoided at all costs & we get all our fancy psychological mechanisms—rationalizations, projections…& secondly the need for the "lifting' experiences are so great, we get the "compulsions." When we reach this stage we have a neurotic. He has been unable to make a fairly satisfactory adjustment.

From this point on, one goes to the reasons for the basic insecurity & anxiety in detail; the detailed description of destructive situations & of "lifting situations." Finally to the unraveling of the threads of specific neuroses. As in clinical medicine, no two cases are absolutely alike. This is already in the domain of professional psychiatry,

It's frightfully late, darling. What do you think?

Love
Aaron

Tuesday 10/24 11:30 pm.

Gloria dear,

Just because it's costing your father 15 cents a minute is no reason to cut in on interesting conversation, is it? You tell him that we won't let him treat us to a day at the races if he isn't more careful…

I think I'd better go in Monday morning, leaving on the 8 o'clock train from Boston. I detest working; I can't think of anything I'd rather do than be with you; But I've got to see myself thru, darling. Don't you see, darling. I'm not thinking of this day, or this $7-8. I never do. It's in terms of many weeks. In terms of hundreds of dollars. Of more weekends. I know you'd be glad to replace what I'd earn. I'm terribly glad you are. But that is no solution. If it's true that we're being stuck for $100 more, it means 20 weekends just to raise it…

Nor is there any encouraging news to help along.

But, to get away from these morbid topics.

I took pictures for internship applications…I think they came out well, so I'm sending one along to you. If you don't think it's any good don't tear it up. I'll probably be able to use it on one of the applications. I think the picture is better looking than I am. It certainly shows more hair!

In regard to internships. We made a list of about 13 New York Hospitals which are approved by AMA for interne training (So is Chelsea Memorial), and wrote for applications saying we're from Middlesex. About 6 sent us applications; the others sent "regrets." Now we're just going thru the same sort of process as in applying to Med. School: pictures, transcripts, letters of recommendation ("I know somebody…") If I get any interviews I'll have to make trips to N.Y. I really don't mind of course. So we're going along "as if…"

I'm very sleepy. Leo Holbraun was over, back from Brockton Hospital last night. I'm just about falling asleep over this letter. Can you imagine what I'd like to do right now?

I miss you a great deal, dear

Love
Aaron

Friday 10/27 10:45 p.m.

Darling:

I got back to the Brigham at 6, ate, & then "took a nap for an hour"; I got up at 10:30. I don't know why I'm so sleepy lately. Do you think it's because I'm thinking of seeing you soon, and getting sleepy just by wishful thinking? You can work out the chain of association yourself, I think.

As you know, I'll leave Boston at 8 a.m. Monday morning and arrive at Grand Central at 1:00. If you miss me at the platform,

I'll meet you at the main information booth. I'm dying to see you, darling.

You're very sweet dear. I know that if I'm stuck for $100 I can get it from you. But it's like an army—its reserves. As long as you have your last defenses still intact & unused it is a great comfort. They do an awful am't of good in just being there in keeping up the morale of the fighting army. If the morale stays up high & the army fights well enough maybe the war is over before those last reserves are ever brought into action. They did their job, tho, very effectively just by being there. So when I no longer have any reserves—I'll draw on my reserve, dear. You've done plenty. By "being there"—an ever source of reassurance to my spirit in this distinctive period. So hold on dear. If things go well (& probably, if they don't) we'll need all our resources to make a financial go of it.

I'm not sure, of course, that the rumor is true. Maybe it's just another rumor. Tho bad rumors have a tendency to come true…

I hope you do get Sylvia's job. It'll be more interesting, probably, & give you the sense of responsibility of having a little girl take dictation from you. It's also a good thing that you asked the officer in charge. I don't know whether it will do any good, but I know how difficult it used to be (& still is) for me to ask superiors for favors. Yet forcing oneself to do so is probably a good way of getting over it…I'll be proud of you, dear…One of us would be doing something useful.

It's a little unfortunate about Thelma. I don't imagine it really means very much, tho. I've read again & again (in Doris Blake's love columns, eg) of the "period of adjustment" at the beginning of married life. So I don't know. I do have two generalities, tho, which you might like to toy with:

First, a girl's first intense sexual love affair is her deepest. She really never quite gets over it.

Second, reconciliations, if the break was serious, don't work.

More Monday.

Love,
Aaron

Monday 12:30 a.m.

Gloria darling:

I'm back writing again. Don't mind the late hour; Elliot Karim was over to see us tonight & the gab kept going pretty late. I'm very sleepy now, as you know…

Last week was simply a chapter taken out of a lovely poem. It almost wasn't real, was it? Even the weather was unreal for this time of the year. It started as I went to N.Y. and ended as I left. For most of the time I was in a haze. Almost like a dream…

Nothing terrible has happened yet in retribution for the gorgeous week. I'm expecting thunder & lightning momentarily, tho. The scales ought to be adjusted. Altho the mere fact that we can't be married right now is so aggravating it is retribution enough.

Seriously, Gloria, it was one of the loveliest weeks I've known…

More tomorrow, darling.

Love
Aaron

Thursday 11/9 10:45 pm.

Gloria darling:

I'm very much alone now, darling. Joe is in N.Y. right now, the lucky devil. So I'm really able to feel good & lonely & full of longing. It's been quite a while since I've been alone for any length of time; you really can commune with me in spirit very nicely.

I don't know who gave you the idea of getting massages for your legs, dear. I doubt their working, nor do you need gorgeous underpinnings to keep my love & affection—but go right ahead. If it works you'll have all the kids in Brooklyn & in Boston whistling at you. A very pretty thought—no?

So I'll remember to call you on Thursday instead. You'll have to tell me whether it was a masseur or a masseuse, tho. Your curves are only worth so much to me, you see.

Tuesday & Wednesday I went to the Chelsea. Today I was so swamped with lab work up here & with a lecture scheduled in school at 1:00 p.m. that I stayed in.

Interestingly enough, yesterday I diagnosed a Carcinoma of the large intestine in an old lady who was lying in bed for a week—on Typhoid precautions! It didn't require diagnostic acumen, dear. Just willingness to look. Arthur had seen this 70 year old woman come in with vomiting & diarrhea. I don't think he touched her, but took his order sheet up into his room & neatly typed out his orders for keeping her alive: Vit A, Vit B, Vit C. Also stools to lab for Typhoid investigation! As soon as I examined her I found a large mass in the right upper quadrant which was apparently not liver or gall bladder. So what else but a Ca of the Hepatic Flexure could this be? The surgeon came in. A nurse & I pulled her over. It was Ca, all right…We really won't know until she is opened up for operation—or autopsy. Nor does making this diagnosis save the patient. But it should easily be made, & is made, if anybody at all is interested…

Singer talked to us today. He's very discouraged about going into private practice. He hates it. He's a teacher, is cynical & bitter. It is difficult for him to reconcile himself to the bedside manner & the Diathermy machine…

Rumors are very bad. "Reliable sources" say we don't have a ghost of a chance. Maybe—only maybe—our class will graduate before it's all over. Boys are discussing what they can possibly do with an MD-- & no license. Tuition is up all right: $175 for next payment; $200 for the last. Brockton Hospital, it is rumored, will not be available next year (imagine!)

I told you that giving you rumors is just depressing. Yet it is peculiar in how very accurate bad rumors generally have been.

So it goes.

Good night dear,
Aaron

Sunday 9:30 am Nov. 11

Darling:

This week was pretty active; lots of medicine even if I'm not going to be a doctor. I'm much too tired to get down to any serious work now. I'd rather tell you all about it.

Yesterday there was something in the way of real drama quietly taking place in Chelsea Hospital. A young fellow of about 35 got a "cold" several weeks ago which apparently developed into pneumonia—at least that is what his doctor told him. After a few days of non response to sulfa drugs the doctor did what all good men should do—sent him in to the hospital for penicillin treatment. I saw him on Tuesday for the first time, He was probably in the place for a few days. The boys were telling me that he had a nice murmur to listen to. He did. As soon as I listened to his chest I knew there was something very wrong present. It wasn't the little murmurs that I've been hearing so often in kids at the Brigham. The possible diagnosis was pretty terrible. Subacute Bacterial Endocarditis has been invariably fatal within a year. Recently a few have been saved with Penicillin…His doctor had thought of the same thing he told me. It looked rather dubious just then—No history of rheumatic fever which nearly always precedes this awful disease, no little hemorrhages under the skin or traces of blood in his urine which very often accompanies it, no bacteria found in the blood which really makes the diagnosis. Just a low grade fever, a pronounced heart murmur, and a pale patient…On Friday I did a Hemoglobin determination to see whether it was falling as I should expect—it had dropped from 86 to 65…Yesterday I looked at his urine under the microscope…-- there were red cells present wherever I looked—there were two Red Cell Casts—little ominous structures which are pathognomonic of bleeding in the kidney…I think the diagnosis is pretty definite. If true, I feel like God. The patient feels pretty healthy; is planning on going home to his job very soon; has no history and therefore no anxiety about his heart. I know that he will probably not live very far into 1945…

By the way, on Friday Dr. Hall, attending physician here and professor at Harvard told the resident that one of my Histories was excellent. Imagine!

Last night this hospital almost looked like a general hospital…While I was leisurely examining a patient and asking him (73 years old) what his grandparents died of, I was called to the East Side for an "emergency." It really was. A patient who had a thyroidectomy several days ago was bleeding from the incision. The bedclothes and the patient's nightgown were all full of blood and the woman was panicky. So was I. The doctor on call at Lahey Clinic had already been notified and was on his way over. A very intelligent nurse asked whether a shot of morphine might not be indicated—when I thought it was a very good idea, she produced the injection all ready…I tried to catch the bleeder thru the incision in her neck with a hemostat with no success at all. While I was trying, a nurse had gotten in touch with the surgeon who suggested applying pressure and forgetting the fancy instruments. So we applied pressure to the neck. Just enough without choking her. It didn't work. When the surgical fellow arrived, he gave more morphine and applied more pressure. By the time the surgeon got here, she was really bleeding. They did some tall rushing getting her up to the OR where a major surgery was performed, opening the incision and trying to tie up the bleeding vessels. The big one couldn't be found even then. All the surgeon could do was pack the area—thereby applying more pressure. Nobody is really a genius, darling…

Incidentally I was allowed to scrub up with the Lahey clinic team on it. Isn't that wonderful. I'm really improving; Instead of two retractors I held three this time. Who knows, one of these days I might be allowed to cut the suture for the first assistant…I do have to assist a few times tho, to be serious, dear. If only to get the knack of putting on a gown in the right manner; and to have the operating room procedure become part of me. Since I can't think of more than one thing at a time, I have a great deal of difficulty keeping out of the millions of little don'ts which go with sterile technique. The last time I assisted I nearly drove the OR supervisor batty as I blithely violated the sacred rules to which all operative personnel automatically adhere. These things must be a part of you. And there has been developed a right way for doing the most minute thing in the entire procedure. It is supposed to work with absolute machine-like regularity. One puts on the mask and cap; then scrubs for 10 minutes in a very definite way; then rinses in alcohol in a definite way; then the gown is given to you folded exactly the same all over-- and you unfold it and slip into it in a very definite manner (when I put it on just as I would any old kimono last time the OR supervisor nearly had a stroke); powder is put on the hands just so; and then gloves are put on with a very elaborate procedure which requires a lot of dexterity…Instruments are always arranged in the same order, are handed to the surgeon in a definite position, are always used in only one way…Just imagine what happens if you aren't drilled to the procedure!! There is just no room for the rugged individualist in this business.

Gosh I'm tired this morning. I'd be fairly comfortable if I didn't have to go to work today. Just thinking about it spoils the lovely morning…

We both know how wrong the set up is which keeps you in New York and me in Boston on a lovely Sunday. You think of something dear, I'm tired.

I love you very much darling.
Aaron

Tuesday 11:00 pm.

Darling:

I really oughtened to write to you tonight. I'm sleepy & depressed. A bad combination. No there isn't anything new to be moody about. It's probably the same situation just giving rise to one of its periodic downs…I'd have phoned you, but I guess you're getting those gorgeous leg treatments tonight; very commendable (If it's a masseuse!) So I'll call you this Thursday, if I don't forget for some reason. At 9:30 pm.

Nothing of interest happened since Sunday. Rumours, good, bad, & very ridiculous are flying around. Mostly bad. The Junior class is up in arms. They are getting all those rotten lectures and see nothing but despair. So as we did, you remember, they are having class meetings, seeing Rushmore, talking to teachers about "what they think is going to happen", & getting to feel worse all the time. Rushmore apparently told them that the situation was pretty hopeless; the Courts won't even listen—or something. As they did last year. The school is going to ask the legislature for an extension. Last year it wasn't even brought up as a bill. This year the legislature is still Republican in Mass…

The court case is apparently scheduled for Nov. 20. I may be home for Christmas after all!

But enough of Morbidity.

The weather is very lovely, I feel fine, & extremely lonely (I suppose the hospital novelty has worn off), & miss you terribly. I'm doing no studying, although I'm learning some medicine by examining patients. This afternoon I read two Golden Books. Pretty good short stories at that.

All sorts of problems come up. Shall I study? Can I study formally? Shall I try to get a clerkship in New York for Jan.-March 1945? Shall I stay at the Brigham until July 1945 when my internship begins? Shall I go to the Bronx Hospital right after graduation (May 1) and get a head start by being a Junior Interne until my regular internship starts? Is there going to be a 1945 in medicine for me at all?

I don't know any of the answers dear, just now. I've also to plan to raise the last tuition payment somehow.

In my sleepy condition I don't know any real solution. As I get more wide awake I'll think of some answers for the easier questions.

What do you think?

I love you a great deal,
Aaron

Friday 11/16 4:30 p.m.

Gloria darling:

Your letter this evening was very, very sweet, dear. It's a very good thing for me that I do have someone who is as interested in my "rise or fall." It makes the good so much better, & the bad, not so terrible...

This morning I got up at 6:30! To do a gastric analysis at 7 a.m. By 9:00 we were at Chelsea; didn't do very much; but did get into a discussion with a Dr. on the "state of the school." When it was over Joe & I went to the movies...I'd have gone to any movie, but luckily "Ballerina" & "Carnival in Flanders" were being double-billed in the neighborhood. You know both of course. It was a repeat for me too. I felt better...Supper, two cases from the W.F. Journal; an i.v. that wouldn't stay in; & here it is 9:30 p.m. Days just whiz by. I reckon time from Sunday to Sunday. Tomorrow is Saturday already...So both our times disappear into the limbo of the unknown.

Incidentally, I've hit a new snag in my medical technique. Lumbar punctures. I'm still not so hot in getting a needle into a vein; not certain about getting a rubber tube into every stomach or urethra; but I've been totally unable so far to get a needle into the spinal canal. I've been given two tries, one at Chelsea & one up here. In both cases all I did was sweat & give the patient unnecessary pain. In the first instance Joe put it right in for me. The other time our resident did. So they weren't intrinsically hard. Just my lack of manual dexterity. You might be interested in the technique. Briefly, the spinal canal exists inside the vertebra. It extends right down to the "tail" or coccyx. Inside this canal lies the spinal cord. It however doesn't quite go down to the bottom of the canal. There is therefore a "safe space", of canal but no cord, into which a needle can (by a lot of people) be put in order to withdraw some of the spinal fluid in which the cord swims. It's just a manner of putting the long needle in between two spines of vertebrae right into the canal. Or, so they tell me...A lot of dope is obtainable this way about Meningitis, Syphilis, Brain tumor,...Oh well, maybe if ever I get the chance, I'll learn to do this, too...

We wrote to Kansas. I don't know whether we'll get any offers, but it means laying out $300 if he'll offer to do it for me. It's a lot of money which I don't have. If it gives me permission to take boards tho, I'll try to borrow it from your father or mine...But only on a guarantee of being able to practice, & thereby being able to pay it back. But I don't think the fellow will answer, be able to do anything, or that I'll be allowed to get my degree…Rotten set up, no?

By the way, darling, take care of yourself. I shouldn't have taken your Vit. D pills. I think Vit. D is good for you. And if you don't listen to me, can you imagine any patients doing so? So no matter how you do it, stay well.

Good night, sweetheart,

Love
Aaron

P.S. Can you read this?

Tuesday 11/23 10:30 p.m.

Gloria dear:

The case is on. It's very hard, no—difficult isn't really right. It's absolutely impossible for me to realize that in a room in town some words are being passed around which are deciding the whole course of my life. I know it's true, of course. But I don't really believe it. It's one judge listening to testimony from the school & from the State Boards. He is going to decide—or already has decided—whether the school goes on, or folds up. You know the consequences for us, of course…

Don't expect anything, but a flat refusal, darling. I know that hope will spring eternal—it is keeping us going up here—yet all the probabilities are against. Rushmore is a big dope. I understand he made an ass of himself on the witness stand today. Maybe he plans on coming out of this mess as an apostle of the AMA who dropped over to Middlesex to see if it couldn't be set right or closed up. It couldn't be set right, so it's being closed up. That may be his line of reasoning. In any event, as our Dean, he's proving a very formidable obstacle.

In any event, this court procedure won't mean anything at all. The loser will automatically take it to the state Supreme Court where it will be tried all over again; God knows the final answer…

No matter what happens up here I'm very glad you're with me. As I've said over and over again, I'm sorry the situation is so tough for you. Yet, I'm glad you love me—happy I can love you so freely. It's one of the major sustaining features of my life right now—has been for several years. In actuality, I can't remember—emotionally speaking—to pre-Gloria days. When my emotional self wasn't a little closed package—neatly labeled "Gloria." Tho I don't feel that this lovely relationship is unique or unusual, I'd like to descend from this "high plane" of feeling engendered by periodic long absences & get down to the normal level—humdrum as it might be—of everyday connubial living…Yet until I know tentatively where I'm going I can't start taking you there…damn it!

My letter is probably more jerky tonight than usual. It's difficult to maintain a routine without knowing that it won't suddenly become meaningless.

That I love you, & you love me—is the only permanent rock in my environment. I'm very grateful for it.

Good night dear
Aaron

Thursday 11/23 7:00 p.m.

Darling—

It's Thanksgiving. A tolerably good Thanksgiving, I suppose. Joe went to work & made a fortune. I decided to stay in & try to be thankful. The Hospitals were in Holiday spirit, of course. The clinicians were busy for days. The dining room was darkened, an open log-fire was working in the fireplace, tall red candles were the only source of light. It was a very gala dinner in point of food & preparations. But no Holiday spirit was present. People at the table weren't old friends—just people who happened to be working in the same place. It was all very quiet. The candle light kept people talking in whispers—even tho they had nothing very intimate (or rash) to say. I had a far better time eating by candlelight at the Silaka & saying "I love you" in Russian with the prompting of the waiter…There is a similar affair, Christmas, I understand. If you're up here at that time, I'll try to invite you to dinner so you can see for yourself.

I know you're anxious about school. I'm very nervous, too. The enclosed articles may give you some idea as to which way the wind is blowing. Certainly the papers aren't giving us a break.

Yet I don't emotionally really believe it, I guess. Medicine, its concepts, its great multitude of facts, its language, its associations, have all become a part of me. I can't really realize, I guess, that it may soon be all over. That a few men will soon decide, without considering me at all, that I'm not to be a doctor at all…

Earlier this week we had some interesting & sloppy medicine. A 50-60 year old woman came into Chelsea with vague GI symptoms (Bellyache, loss of appetite…), & jaundice (yellow color to the skin & whites of the eyes). She was very distended. I examined her on Monday. It was pretty obvious that there was a lot of fluid in her abdominal cavity & that the pain was down near her ovaries, not Gall Bladder. The diagnosis her doctor had written was Gall Bladder disease. The distention he attributed to "gas."

Now this isn't as shocking to you as to a pupil of Karl Singer. The favorite symptom, I think, of his is jaundice. He brings the whole armamentarium of medicine to bear on the problem. And a very important problem it is, too.

Briefly, Bile is brought by the blood to the liver. Liver cells then excrete it into very tiny ducts which coalesce to form the Bile duct which empties into the intestine. If the Bile duct is obstructed, eg Gallstone, the bile backs up into the blood & we get jaundice. This is called <u>Extra hepatic</u> jaundice. The obstruction is <u>outside</u> of the liver & can be reached by operation. However, if the tiny canals in the liver are all plugged up as in Cirrhosis of the Liver or Cancer getting to the liver, it is called <u>Intrahepatic</u> jaundice. The effect is the same, but operation not only is useless; it is very dangerous.

So in this case, a very, very serious attempt should have been made to make at least the basic diagnosis—Intrahepatic or Extrahepatic. To do so requires a little brains, some Knowledge, & a lot of lab work. None were available.

Joe & I rode home with the surgeon Monday. He was sure it was a Gallstone; her distension was just air; & he was going in

Tuesday to fix her up. [Water in the abdominal cavity would mean Cancer or Cirrhosis.]

We were at the operation. As soon as the scalpel punctured the peritoneum, yellowish fluid just gushed, it poured out, over the table onto the surgeon, & dripped on the floor…It was cancer all right. The operation was unnecessary, expensive, & shortened her life…The doctors were from very, very respectable schools…

Good night, darling.

Love
Aaron

Tuesday 11/28 10:00 p.m.

Darling—

You'd better come up to see me soon. Very often I can lose myself in some phase of medicine. More often, particularly recently, I've wanted you very badly. It's like an ache. A tightness in my chest that won't thaw out, unless I can bury my head in your bosom, stretch out beside you, and feel that I can stay that way for a long, long time…

About the school. It's washed up I guess. Yesterday, the opposition brought out the kind of stuff that even I didn't know. Apparently, out of a total budget of $190,000 per year collected in tuition—Rushmore (or the school) couldn't account for $100,000 per year! Someone (probably Smith) is making that much profit on this ostensibly "non profit" organization! Beyond that, of course, $120,000 or so put down in writing, more than ½ went for "administration"—very, very little of the money I paid went to teach me medicine. It's as good a swindle as the shell game. My figures may be a little off, but the impression is right…The State brought it up while cross-examining Rushmore—he denied none of it…

You know, I always felt that there was a big broad injustice being perpetrated on us by the AMA; that justice was on our side; & that a sympathetic judge or legislature might, therefore, give us a break. But it's apparently a whole lot worse. The school should be closed; there is no question about it. I see no reason for an extension to allow them to swindle a new bunch of suckers…

So that's that.

I don't like your getting sick worrying about the situation. You are, comparatively speaking, very well off. You'll undoubtedly have a lot of really bad situations to face—of more difficult problems. Think the situation thru, if you can, & pass on your ideas. You've probably noticed that I ask for, & want to use your suggestions more & more. As we get closer & you get older, you're at least 50% of the corporation. I don't know the answers to many things. Be as independent a thinker as you possibly can, & stick to your guns. I'll argue with you-- & then probably agree with you…

Good Lord—How did I get off on that lecture? I guess it was your headache.

Oh, incidentally, the scarf is a swell idea. And the symbolism of keeping me all warm: slippers for my feet; sweater for my body; gloves for my hands; scarf for my throat—is very good, very romantic & very, very sweet. I won't be able to get dressed without thinking of going to bed with you. You'd better cut such talk out. I've enough trouble sublimating as is…

About your saving money. It's a good idea, but don't deny yourself to do so. I see no value in your being unhappy now, to be happy later on. But you're right. I don't know what we're going into. I don't know whether the Army & the War will allow us to go into anything for very long; but whatever we do money is a marvelous lubricant to smooth our way. And money in the post-war world may be hard to get. The only reason that I'm in school & not in France now is that I saved $1000 during my earning years. I never dreamt that it would go for what I did, but the beauty of it is that it is convertible into nearly everything. It gives one a freedom of motion—or better still, lack of it gives paralysis & makes one the victim of every circumstance…

There now, you have a lecture on "The value of money," too. If I don't get over this pedantry soon, I'll tear the letters up & write about nothing but EKGs,..

Good night darling.

I love you very much.
Aaron

Thursday 11/29 10 pm

Sweetheart:

Saul Freedmen, one of the third year men, just left after a session in which "the fate of the school" was thrashed out at great length. There is very little to add to the general impression that you have. Little incidents, crop up every day in the courtroom which make us feel better or much worse; but I don't think that they have any real effect upon the final outcome. All sorts of witnesses are testifying, from the Dean of Harvard to show that we don't quite come up to standard, to the former treasurer of the school to try to show that they really didn't embezzle all that money…Our lawyers are very competent apparently. Still, making a monkey of an opposition witness doesn't materially alter the facts about the school. The present case should be over in about a week; the decision should be forthcoming by Christmas. Altho I hope it is favorable (and believe it will be decidedly unfavorable) it really won't mean very much as the Supreme Court may do anything…

Last night there was some pretty active medicine. You'll probably be interested. For the first time I had my ability as House Officer at the hospital tested. The resident isn't around you know. Well, last night at about 1:00 am, I was awakened by a nurse for an emergency. Getting over, I was told by the night supervisor that an old fellow of 62 who had recently been X rayed for some gastrointestinal disorder, had vomited about 15 ounces of bright red blood and had passed out. She had given him some stimulant by hypodermic and sent for me. There I was, just chuck full of all sorts of miscellaneous information about all sorts of medical problems. I could have given all the reasons for generalized itching, or jaundice, or maybe even vomiting of blood. But nobody asked me. At any rate the old man was in a semi reclining position in bed, in semi coma, cold, clammy, beaded with perspiration, pulse racing, blood pressure nearing zero…There was no time to grope thru my pharmacology notes. Nor did too much theory help. I tried to remember what I was told should be done for internal hemorrhage…and for shock…Funny, I knew pretty well what to do for each; but not very sure about what to do when they were combined. Also I was just aroused from a very deep sleep…I ordered "shock position", extra blankets, morphine gr. ¼ and atropine gr. 1/150 by hypodermic immediately, and an IV of 5% glucose in saline. We called the resident who confirmed the orders. With the patient's patron saint guiding the needle I got into his only possible vein…By the time the resident arrived, an hour or so later, the patient's color had improved, his pulse was better and his blood pressure was up. He is still alive now.

It was the most common occurrence for the interne. Handling this situation is absolutely routine for him. It was just that this was my first contact with a situation where a deathly sick person and I are the only ones involved. I had to make some diagnosis and institute therapy. There was no interne around to call on. The nurses were absolutely helpless. Tho in hospitals for 20 or 30 years, the lack of a theoretical background left them out on a limb, waiting to be told what to do…

Your constant threat to send me money is very sweet, darling. It is so sweet that I would refuse to let you, just so that you would keep on offering to send it. But seriously, there is no point at all in sending money to me which would simply lie around in my drawer, when it could be gathering interest for us in your savings bank. I've told you lots of times, dear, that if I'm stuck I'll probably call on you. My parents might rather have me use them as resources, but that isn't too difficult a problem. I don't think I'll ever get very sick worrying about having too many resources. So just hang onto your money until I send out an SOS.

You aroused my curiosity about those lectures on sex for which you made copies of your notes for the girls in the office. I hope they aren't simply using your course as another way of getting vicarious thrills—like dirty poetry. In any event I'm interested in the lecture material. Send me a copy and I'll give you my impressions.

My eyes are practically closed by now even tho I did sleep late this morning. There's a lot more that I could write about, but I better hold off til the next letter.
Good night darling.

Love
Aaron

Tuesday 12/5 12:05 a.m.

Gloria darling:

Three minutes go like blazes, don't they? Living in a state of suspended animation, hoping desperately that something good will happen, tho expecting nothing but bad, I need you for comfort more than ever. (You can probably get some idea of my status from my handwriting; I practically can't read it back myself, dear...)

As for the latest developments. You can get some idea of what is going on by following P.M. (It's a damn good paper anyway & you ought to be digesting it...) They give it more space than the Boston papers do up here.

Last Friday morning, I went down to the court. The session simply confirmed my former impression: We have a very clever lawyer (Colt). He can make almost anybody look like a "jackass" under cross-examination. I saw the Dean of B.U. Medical School, go red, squirm, & perspire frequently on that stand. The judge is young, was probably a good lawyer, and apparently admires Colt's technique very much; he was smiling throughout the entire cross-examination. Yet, I don't think anybody is fooled. They have the facts. No amount of clever questioning can take away B.U.'s clinics or Harvard's libraries.

Yesterday, the Judge is reported to have said that he must take the decision of the State Boards for a lot of weight, & although Colt has attempted to show they were wrong in their decision; he hasn't done so, yet. Not so good, is it? Yet, there is always some uncertainty about the decision until it is over. Gosh, I'd give a lot to get any sort of compromise to let me take Boards. It would, of course, open up a host of new problems; lots of very different ones, too. But I'd like to get a crack at solving them, with you…

Yes about Dr. Kildare…Don't feel in any of the things I write about my "medical experiences," that I'm mating—very dramatically—unusual circumstances in alarm. I'm displaying unusual acumen as asked. Not at all! A great many Juniors in our school, living in small Hospitals like Revere General are taking babies, sewing up scalp wounds, and are getting ready to do tonsillectomies. It's just that in meeting these situations for the first time I'm very impressed-- and I pass my feelings on to you automatically.

I'm fighting to keep my eyes open, darling. I'd probably fall asleep even if you were here (Awful, isn't it. But you'd probably be asleep by now, too)

[Incidentally, Joe saw me making up that diagram on the neurosis. He wants a copy, if you want to make it up]

Good night darling
Aaron

Thursday 12/7 9:00 p.m.

Sweetheart:

I saw "Frenchman's Creek" this afternoon, at one of the local movies. It is very dashing, full of swashbuckling romance. Everything is fine except that the Hero doesn't get the girl. She is true to the Hayes Office & goes back to her husband—very commendable. I'm sure I couldn't ever make love with the verve of the hero—but I miss you terribly none-the-less…You are nearer to me all the time, as I keep on living the days, thinking of you as part of me & feeling very, very close to you in moments like these. [Incidentally, I'm all alone in our quarters; 3 good rooms, books, furniture, a radio—all going to waste…]

Just think how we could spend the time if you were up here…Yet I think I'd still feel unhappy if you were here only for a day. I do so crave that feeling of permanency. Tomorrow & tomorrow…Lord knows why I can't just accept today. Letting tomorrow be. Still, I'd be so very much happier to feel while I'm holding you in my arms, that we won't be interrupted, that you'll still be there in the morning, & that if I'm to leave you it'll only be for a few hours…

You make something of it.

Oh yes, you've gotten me worried. I'm all agog over what you're picking up in your browsing thru psychoanalytical authors. Particularly "Psychopathology of Everyday Life." I'm going to be very worried about what you'll think now of my forgetting to call you, writing only a short letter, mixing up your key with mine, refusing to borrow money from you, not noticing a new hat or fur coat…Don't you believe it! I'm really very much in love with you! If anything does ever disturb you, tho, bring it up. We can discuss it from the basis of depth psychology & get it pretty straight. Keeping our feelings, beliefs…up on the surface is the best medicine, I think, for any good relationship. Knowing that fundamentally we know one another very dearly makes it easy to say or do nearly anything with complete assurances of acceptance…

The program goes on as usual. I'm going to Chelsea 3 times a week now, presumably to be able to study. But so far we've done only little with our free time as you can imagine.

I got a letter from my Draft Board saying they didn't as yet get a request for my deferment from school, & I will be in 1A if they don't get one by Dec. 15. I called school & was told they did send it out last October, & they'll send out another one. I don't know what's going on. If I don't hear from them by the 13th or so, I'd like you to go down if you could. Or just call up. I don't want to get caught in a mix-up of forms if that's all it is…

Tuesday, I went down to the Post Office to get Xmas work. I was sworn in, got an identification card & a lecture on "Being a Member of the Postal Service." Mostly, I'm going to be very careful & not steal (in lots of ways) from the mail. Or I'll be caught & very seriously punished. When the lecture was over I knew a great many more ways of gyping the Post Office than before. Plenty must go on… I'm to be satisfied about going to work. I'm not too anxious, &

they may not have work I'm willing to do. But I'll see then...By my next letter I will be a Postmaster General or something.

As you know, Xmas has been a very low point in the year for the past several years. Last year, it was just after the freeze. Things certainly weren't pretty then, were they? The Xmas before was just after the Army Navy program was announced; we all thought that this would finish us off; it was pretty bad; 3 years ago today was Pearl Harbor: If History repeats, & in my case it certainly does, this one won't be any better...I wonder what Xmas 1945 will be like...

This letter has just grown. I don't know how. You really don't have any reason to complain of the volume of my mail. With so little material, we both do all right.

By the way, if I don't call this Tuesday at 9:30 I'll be working in the Post Office...So don't worry.

I love you more & more
Aaron

Tuesday 12/12 9:00 p.m.

Gloria darling:

I'll call you in a half hour, but this is so good a time to write that I just can't resist. Joe & I have been going over those cases in the "Journal" for the past two hours & are "resting" now. I guess we've done 200-300 of those cases by this point. They're swell teaching material. The cases are presented & are then discussed very adequately, by top ranking Harvard men. I think I've learnt more from them than from anything else I've read all the past two years...It's like doing cross-word puzzles. It's very exciting watching the story unfold & seeing how close to the diagnosis you come. Of course as time goes on & the diagnostic acumen improves, one becomes better at hiding the real answer. I'm quite satisfied if I come out as well as the Doctor discussing the case! Very often, he can't hit the lesion picked up at autopsy. But so long as I can go thru the reasoning & reach pretty nearly the same diagnosis that a good Harvard teacher does, I'm satisfied!

Life up here (at school) is the nearest thing to suspended animation, I've ever seen. We're just waiting. Sol Friedman, the 3rd year student, was over last night. They've got finals next week. The class simply demanded the final exams from the profs-- & got them. Very few are doing any studying at all. Nor do I blame them. I don't know how anyone can study in this ungodly terrain—not knowing what is going to happen next. By this point I'm probably talking in my sleep, too. So if you learn anything bad about it just let me know. It's just pure chance that I'm not going around walking in my sleep…(I'd never know who I'd meet under those circumstances!)

Yesterday I saw "American Romance". It got 2 checks in PM, so we went. It's the story of someone combining Ford & Carnegie, who came to this country penniless & battered his way to the top of the heap. It had all the proper clichés & a lovely heroine. But what I thought about later & wondered if you see it, when you see the movie, is the basic character of the hero. I was uncomfortable with him all thru the show. What was it? Finally this morning I decided that it was his basic immaturity I disliked. It's very difficult to describe 'til you've seen the picture. But during the performance, I kept on calling the hero a "dope". Joe kept on pointing out that he wasn't dopey at all; he learnt to read & write under great handicaps, learnt all about automobiles, invented several very important parts…

No he wasn't a dope. In fact he was very bright. But bright as a child is bright. Very clever. Very quick in invention & adaptation. Quick in learning facts & skills. But yet so is any kid. I don't know how to define "maturity" very well. But my heros have to have it…

--later—

That was a remarkable coincidence. Both calls at once. It cost me $2.06 to talk to you for those few minutes that time. Of course, the operator normally shouldn't accept a person to person call for me while I'm trying to get someone else long distance. But both of us thought it was the same person. I couldn't imagine that of all the minutes of the week, my father would select the one reserved for our weekly phone calls. It probably wouldn't happen twice in a lifetime…

I'm going over to school tomorrow I guess to check on this. It's a damn nuisance! Just because Dr. Smith & his stupid secretaries can't send forms out on time. In case you didn't get the address right it's

[Local Board 195
1502 Surf Ave.
My order No. is 765]

Call here at 9:30 Thursday eve, if necessary. I'll call Joe at 10:00 if I'm working. (It's Dr. Eisenstein)

All my love sweetheart
Aaron

Friday 12/15 11:10 p.m.

Darling:

We just were shown the end of a letter one of the students received from her boy friend—"I love you & miss you dearly," he says…You'll have to judge that I feel pretty strongly, too, from the general tone of my letters, I think. I'll never learn to write that way. You've become such a part of me, so much for granted, taken so much for granted by all my associates who've never even met you that it is inconceivable for me to think of a set up without you…

Right now I'm all very confused. I'm all torn up—like this half of me keeps on wanting to forget all about medical school, Hate money, future…& go home & get married now. He's pretty convincing, especially when I feel it's probably all wasted anyhow, "tempus fugit", "Carpe diem" or something to that effect in English. The other half won't allow it. It wants to assure us of basic necessities for now & some assurance of a future. Right now (tonight) I think this prudent one is crazy…

The whole thing is so confused in my mind. I don't know what I'm doing half the time. This evening I went to the post office. (Incidentally, I worked for 6 hours per night on Wednesday & Thursday nights sorting mail.) I got there about seven & was told to wait a little while as they weren't just then pulling on a big group. I waited 10 minutes & went home…I just needed any excuse. Do you think I'm just fundamentally lazy, dear?

Life at the Chelsea Memorial Hospital is getting more chaotic. All the time. Nurses getting scarcer & scarcer, only one interne in the place (going nuts), the place pretty full right now, visiting men too busy to do anything—the place is cracking at the seams. (I'd draw you a picture of a hospital giving at seams if I could draw). Everybody is going crazy. Nothing is available & ready. Nothing much is done on time, or done right. And God help "staff" or free patients. Laboratory work is cancelled by the superintendent for staff patients as being too expensive.

The very peculiar situation exists where there is a tremendous demand for accommodations (No beds at all available right now!) & absolute chaos & lack of facilities in the hospital which gets worse daily. There are lots of reasons, of course, all of which could be corrected by group medicine. One of the big differences I've seen in several hospitals, is that the superintendent is not a doctor—a nurse or layman. That is ridiculous. I can see a smart business man being "business manager." But a doctor must run the place. A very good doctor who has the right in his own namc to criticize what goes on in the hospital, to criticize the medicine going on, to bring charges against incompetence or knavery…It would cost at least $7,000 a year to hire any good doctors full time, so except for NY Dept. of Hospitals & some group affairs, it just isn't done. This leads to the preposterous situation where the hospital is run by a group of nurses as well as they can for a group of doctors, each of whom is God in his own right. The only person on call, who lives at the hospital & knows all about it, its great weaknesses & possibilities, is the lowly interne who is in a very vulnerable spot and is able to criticize no one. He hopes someday to be able to take his place amongst his peers, The Doctors, be inviolate to all criticism of his mistakes & chicanery, too. There is here, then, the lack of any real possibility of growth. Nobody wants to be "president" or "chief of staff." What will it get me, but headaches? Dr. Musgrave asked us. No, staff like that can't be voluntary. Hospitals must be run, by good full-time executives who are medical men. They must be acquainted with all the patients, the doctors, the therapy going on, the facilities in use & available, the latest developments in medicine, & take part in active programs for the education of the staff. Research to as large an extent as possible (even correlating therapy tied with results, & post-mortems with symptoms) must go on & be reported. So growth in medicine would be possible on a scale as yet unheard of…To some extent this does go on in the larger "Medical Centers"—where these full-time men are paid by Med. Schools as "clinical professors."

I think that the great new stride for medicine in improving longevity will probably not come in a great, new discovery. But in putting what there is to use. More & more routine work must be done—spread to the great masses of the people. X-rays ought to run 15 hours a day--, not 2 or 3. Teeth X-rays, chest plates, GI series…ought to be done routinely—on some suitable schedule. Labs ought to run like well-equipped factories—a great deal of urine & blood work should be done routinely. Only in this way (by routine examination of "healthy people") is diabetes picked up today, & early Tb, cancer, bone diseases, blood diseases will be picked up in the future.

Any doctor worth his salt knows what to do with a given case. It is just that usually that is the least of his considerations. Expense for the patient, the "kick back" he can expect from the specialist, & actual facilities available are far more impt.

So that if good medical men were paid full-time to run our hospitals, & those hospital facilities run at full capacity—a lot of "medicine" could get to more people.

Isn't this fundamentally what is wrong with all industry? If profit motives were removed & all facilities used to capacity wouldn't life be made infinity more liveable? In medicine it is the practitioner who is the entrepreneur, & his "profits" determine medical practice.

This is going on terribly long, darling. Can you guess I love you from this letter? Since I might be working Tuesday call next Sat eve.

Love
Aaron

Wed. 12/20 4:00 pm.

Gloria dear:

I'm writing pretty early today, as getting home at 12:00 or 1:00 tonight leaves me in too sleepy a state to write any kind of letter, even an unintelligible one.

Vacation started as of today! Imagine!! It makes absolutely no difference, of course. I cut Monday & Tuesday anyhow, as I was too bored to go to a Path lecture for the fresh & it was too cold to go for yesterday's! School really isn't playing the role in my life that it should…

Monday & yesterday I put in about 5 hours a day at the post office. If it doesn't drive me bats I'll keep it up thru this Friday. It's a special Christmas unit, not very large, & not much to do. It's just that time drags so. There are about 100-200 high school kids (1/3 Bobby sox girls) who comprise the bulk of the personnel. For the past two nights I've been tying sorted-letters into neat little packages. A very essential job. Essentially I have been practicing the "one-handed tie", so urgently needed by any operator or first assistant. I just kept on making knots until the envelopes looked right. I'm pretty sure these knots won't give. I'm also absolutely sure it is the most inefficient procedure possible. But nobody gives a damn. In several cases I kept on putting in so many knots the letters looked like a fringed shawl…If I keep it up, my "one-handed tie" will be as good as Dr. Frank Lahey's.

Yesterday I received my 2-A, good, (barring further action) until April 13, 1945. It was 2-A, not 2-B; & the address is as I wrote. Half Moon Hotel is now a Navy Hospital. Are you sure you were talking with the clerk you called about the same person?

Judge Cabot has as of today, not handed down a decision, as far as I know. It certainly is due any day now…I'm very nervous…

Sammy Berson called last week. I wasn't in but he told Joe that Mary has been up here for the past 3 weeks. I don't know why you haven't been up here by this time, or why you didn't plan to spend Christmas up here. I can't see why your uncle & aunt can't be perfectly good chaperones.

Sam just called. They're going back to New York tomorrow—so that's out. I still think it was a good idea tho. [Since Joe didn't tell him I was at the P.O. I didn't go into any long explanations about not being in. I just said I was out.]

Incidentally, darling, what am I going to get you for your birthday! Please drop a hint. I can't think of anything you need that I can get you.

Love
Aaron

1945

Tuesday 1/2/45 10:10 p.m.

Sweetheart:

I'm glad you're better by this time. Somehow I had a hunch you might not be entirely recovered by the week-end. I'm really surprised at you. A supposedly very healthy girl who invariably gets sick every time she stays out past bed time for several days. It just doesn't make sense. Was your mother furious? If she wasn't I bet she felt like saying "I told you so"...

Yes, I was "night clubbing" this New Year's Eve. I made about $15 working from 1 p.m. to 4 a.m. with 3 hours off in the afternoon to go see a movie. Yesterday, I was so tired I slept all day...Actually I wasn't sorry that I wasn't a guest instead of a waiter, too much. I don't really see what they get out of drinking gallons of alcohol, doing their best to "get high" even if not really intoxicated. Drinking, drinking, drinking...Making noise with any kind of instrument available. Laughing hysterically. Trying to squeeze onto the jammed dance floor. With the rotten 4 piece orchestra booming away in a terrific attempt to make more noise than everyone else...Happy New Year...

The spectacle used to amaze me before. It was a little revolting in these war years. Why, for God's sake, try to be so hysterically & openly happy with your friends & relatives getting killed & suffering? Saying that being sad won't help them over there is no good either. I'd be a little disturbed at hilarity at a loved one's funeral—even if sorrow can't help the dead...

And in this case—waiters, bus boys, chefs, orchestra players, distillers...equipment of all sorts are wasted in utter disregard for the problems we're facing...

Maybe I'm just bellowing about sour grapes...

Laski's book is splendid. I'm thinking seriously of getting you a copy as soon as I can. I can't send you our library copy-- & I think it is well worth studying. [I'd get it as a birthday present for you, but I want to get something more personal for you.]

Laski is giving an analysis of the world today. A beautiful analysis. But the book really is only as good as the background & incisiveness of the reader. I'm pretty lost. Every chapter is full of allusions to things one must know to be an intelligent citizen today, that I feel like running to the books and reading & reading. There are so many questions we so smugly ignored. Every reference to the French Revolution, Robespierre, Puritanism, Cromwell, Bolshevism, Lenin, Mussolini… make me realize that I learnt nothing in College. How did these things happen. Specifically, what were the forces involved. How did the common man get into it. How did it really affect his life? Did the opinions of the masses influence the French Revolution? Or of Hitler's rise to power? And how could it? How does your opinion influence present policies? And did Rousseau's stuff really influence the store keepers, the peasant, the traders? Just how are great revolutions brought about? By spontaneous mass movements or by planned uprisings of small groups of conspirators who seize power? The American Revolution, Taylor, Marshal.

Gosh, I don't know anything. Yet it is vital to be politically sophisticated or else there is just chaos, ignorance, & one is floating about on the waves of opinion as promulgated by every clever journalist or propaganda agent…

Intellectual maturity today demands a lot. Reading Laski showed me how naïve I am. We need to know a lot, think it thru, read opinions, & develop a point of view. Then only can an intelligent appraisal be made of the volume of speeches, articles, pamphlets, movements…

Of course, the course of individual thinking, & of intellectual maturity isn't going to be realized by every gum chewing salesgirl—telephone operator. But you're going to, easily enough. Read a lot. Only a small amount will become part of you. More will remain if you go to the book not with "an open mind" (which means blankness)—but with definite questions you want answered. And if unanswered go elsewhere.

Another lecture!

Good night darling.
Aaron

Wednesday 1/3/45 8:30 p.m.

Sweetheart—

I wrote to you yesterday, of course, but this letter is to get to you before your birthday & to wish you a very happy one. It is meant to tell you that I love you & miss you, & hope we spend most of your 23rd year happily together…

I still don't know what to get you that will be suitable so your gift will be delayed. But the sentiment is all there.

I'm alone just now, & you know that it is just in moments like this that I become most conscious of my need for you to be with me. To be sure, I'd insist, if you were, that you stay in the other room, but even so, it would in some way be very comforting to know that I <u>could</u> go in & kiss you, if I weakened…

Your letter today about Hegel was fascinating. You ought to read the comments I made about the book upon those cards I typed up. (I didn't have anybody to write to about psychiatry, I guess, so I wrote on cards.) At any rate, your letter sounded like my comments of 4 years ago coming back. I suppose similar backgrounds & points of view make for similar "discoveries." Our "discussions" have, of course, been by mail 'til now (We can't seem to keep our life unoccupied long enough to say anything when we're together). But never-the-less a great deal of what we thought & felt has gone back & forth—repeated under dozens of different headings. In the near future, possibly, it'll get to the point where a great deal will be unsaid. We'll both automatically think of the same thing…At any rate, I'm very glad you criticized the book, & feel good that your opinions were so very similar to my own…

So tonight I'm "taking-off" from my usual type of letter—full of medicine, politics or something equally impersonal to tell you that no matter what I write about, I write to someone I love & trust very much. I pour out ideas without fearing rejection or cynical sarcasm. By their very nature, they say that the writer loves & is writing to someone he knows returns his love…

Good night darling
Happy Birthday

Love
Aaron

Thursday 1/4/45 10:30 pm

Gloria dear:

I'm deep in Laski—and there are so many ideas roaming thru my head, I just had to try to get them out of there this way…If I don't make sense, or repeat what you already know in a less intelligible fashion, just think of this as my talking out loud in a letter…

What does Laski say, anyway? First of all he sums up, not new but very well—what we know about the fundamental relations in our economy today and its effect upon world politics. You've heard the story often: Capitalism is based upon the profit motive; during the nineteenth century, in this country at any rate, continuous expansion of production was possible under this drive to make more and more money. As new sources for investment disappeared we arrived at what has been called the mature stage of our capitalistic system or the closing of the industrial frontier. This came to be in the European countries earlier than in the US and the problems which resulted started sooner in England, France and Germany. The basic problem these countries faced is very simple: they stopped increasing their production. The production curve, instead of continuing to climb ever higher and higher, started to flatten out, and then even to decline. At best there were far too few houses, automobiles, refrigerators, good food products, clothing, in the country. With the population increasing and the curve of production going down the situation becomes maddening. Competition becomes terrific. Unemployment [which is to some extent inevitable in a society where we are not going to produce more, but are going to find machines to replace workers and so do it cheaper] becomes a major problem.

In other words, when there is no continuous influx of wealth to the population from opening up new grazing lands and making lots of money, or going to India and exploiting the natives…there would be a decrease in the number of people in the community who could buy cars—and the production of cars would fall off to that number. So in every industry.

And that is the one big flaw in the capitalistic economy. Our industrial plants aren't run day and night to produce all that they possibly can in so far as the need for supplies by our people is nearly limitless. But they are run to give the maximum profit—which very often means turning out very few units indeed, comparatively speaking.

It is not important who owns the plants. "Government ownership" is the slogan, but it seems to me, that our present overlords of business would be quite welcome to a yearly annuity paid by the state equal to their present income, just so long as they turned over these same plants for "production for use." It is the "economy of scarcity" which is the big monkey wrench in the machinery. Not particularly who owns what, or the fact that a few people have big yachts. By virtue of the necessity to safeguard existing plants and profits, the well known and scandalous spectacle of patents bought up by big business—not to use but to keep off the market; why have to remodel a whole factory?

That this "economy of scarcity" is a result of our profit system with its planless anarchy is best demonstrated by the spectacle of how much can be produced by even a little planning in these war years. Our capacity is overwhelming. It has been variously estimated that the man-hours and materials put into one battleship would supply thousands and thousands of homes, so many schools…We probably could have housed half the country with the armaments already made. And this was a basically unchanged set-up and with 10 million of our best men non productive.

Therefore, the socialist hope lies not in some ephemeral idea of "government ownership" of some plants—but in putting <u>all</u> our productive facilities to maximum use; allowing and encouraging science to do more and more in order to enable us to produce still more. It is in the curve of production that the happiness of the society lies. With "enough" of the necessities produced more time is available for the cultivation of the arts. This is the utopia dreamed of for so many years…

Laski feels that as the crisis deepened, as the misery of the masses increased and they looked about for relief, the rift between Right and Left increases. They are able to get along only when there is still an "expanding economy" (as in the US of 1890) so that business is able to give more and more concessions to labor and still make profits. But as the set up grows tighter and unrest grows it is inevitable that one of the two tries to take over power—and democracy will be very sorely threatened. You know what happened in Germany; big business appealed to the gangster element to keep labor under control and we found Fascism. (It is important tho to see that Hitler could never have gotten anywhere without popular backing; but the unemployed, the ruined small business men, the business afraid of communism and loss of privilege fell into his party very well).

So there we were before the war, and will be after the war—with ever increasing problems of mass unemployment, poor housing, decreasing profits, lack of opportunity…Laski asks for "Revolution by consent." It is the core of the book and—the basis of Socialism. The owners of the means of production are asked to see the evil of their ways and to give over their property to be used for production for use. Very pretty. Do you seriously think that Revolution by Consent has a chance? No matter how many reforms we will get, the one thing not even touched upon is in property relations. We can make all the laws imaginable, pass a super Wagner Bill just chock full of Social Security and Health laws, but all it will mean will be more taxes on the profits made by business and less incentive for them to increase production. And if we are to measure the standard of living of the nation by that old production curve—that isn't going to be any answer, is it?

What is the answer? I don't know I'm sure. The Communist answer I suppose is for Revolution by Force. I don't think there is any real hope for that either. The French Revolution took place in a time when barricades could be put up in the streets and the sheer weight of numbers would win out. I wonder very much if the masses of a country, no matter how sincere in their efforts, could put up a fight against tanks and guns and planes in the hands of a good little army paid well by the ruling classes. No, I was never surprised that the masses of Europe did not revolt against Hitler no matter how bad their conditions. How could they?

The hope for the masses of Europe enslaved by Hitlerism lay only in the military defeat of the armies which enslaved them. But if it becomes true that we'll all inevitably become semi fascist—or will certainly resist any attempt on the part of labor to take away the privileges from the present owners of the means of production, how can the masses ever effect their revolution? It won't happen by consent, and I don't think there is any possibility of their being strong enough to get it by fighting…

I think (but don't really know) that the basic Communist Party premise is that the masses will have to have tanks and planes too. And the only well equipped army labor may have, is the Red Army. In its march across Europe and maybe ultimately across the rest of the world they will bring with them the change in the forces of production…If this premise is correct—the basic plank of the CP, of the primacy of the Soviet Union, follows. And all the ramifications of the involved "party line," always having as its sole aim the preservation of the USSR, becomes intelligible. The military-like discipline of the CP, with its disregard for getting popular support, is understood on the basis of their being a need for a well organized and disciplined group to take over if invasion or chaos should make opportunity as it did in Russia, or as may happen in Europe if the Red Army invades.

So there we are. Laski is a gentleman. And so are most of the Socialists. It's comfortable being a socialist. I think I would make a good one. One attends meetings, reads a lot, maybe does some writing, contributes some money, meets a lot of intelligent people, feels very noble, and keeps on voting the Socialist ticket. Two labor governments in England got no place. It's too bad because I'm psychologically set for that kind of political affiliation. The other is too tough for me, God knows, in the last analysis they may be right, tho…

Wow, can you imagine what time it is now? I've got to cut this out. This stuff may bore you to death, darling, even if you're too polite to say so, but just accept this as my need to tell you what I'm thinking about at the moment.

Love
Aaron

Tuesday 1/9 10:00 p.m.

Gloria dear—

I'll probably continue to call thru the pay station—only I'm stuck at the end of 3 minutes; I generally don't have that much change. If I get a lot of change together by next Tuesday, I'll call you up "in private." Otherwise, we'll take the telephone operator into our confidence…

Gosh, darling, could I use you here this week (particularly). I'm practically a hermit, not being very sociable anyhow—I'm very lonely lately. Particularly in this situation where I'm sick at heart anyhow & find studying nearly impossible. So, just about all I can look forward to is seeing you again—as soon as possible. Now don't you go "blue" on me; For 25 years or so, I've been having that trouble with my mother—I couldn't bring her my troubles or she'd feel so badly. In fact, it was up to me to protect her from bad news. For better or worse, I'm going to bring you all my woes, & triumphs—if I have any. So you better just develop a lot of fortitude & stability to keep on an even keel despite my precarious progress…

I miss you a lot, darling…

Last week a pretty exciting bit hit us up here at the Brigham. A young fellow (35) came in with a bad rheumatic heart a few weeks ago. While I was home he began to get shaking chills. On getting back here, I found him getting thru another chill & we suggested blood cultures to the resident by phone. You see, a chill generally means bacteria are being released into the blood stream & in a case of heart disease it is probably Subacute Bacterial Endocarditis. Now getting blood during the chill may give you the bug after 24-48 hours of incubation. The bacterial demonstration makes the diagnosis conclusive…Treatment is penicillin and prayer…

So night after night I was awakened at 3 or 4 a.m. to take blood during Mr. Martin's chill. One night just after I took blood (5-10 min) he sat up, began to breathe very heavily, turned blue, his eyes grew glassy as his pupils dilated, I couldn't get a pulse—he was dead…I gave artificial respiration, injected adrenaline & Coramine but no dice. I never felt so helpless in my life. The poor chap died in 2-3 minutes. We still don't know what really happened. I think it was pulmonary embolism; Dr. Feldman thinks it was rupture of the aortic valve.

I felt very queer; wasted; went over to the East Side where the night supervisor (who must have seen that I was upset) had the nurse make me coffee. I got to sleep at 5 a.m. that night…Sudden death is pretty terrible…

Oh yes, about your sick leave. I'm not really disappointed in you, darling. It is just that you manifest the same kind of weakness that I do. And it is very, very bad. I'm sore at it in me. There is probably nothing you can do, either.

Basically it comes down to "know how" to "savoir faire" & to that Baconian quote about "suspicion of evil." It means that (1) nobody (except me, & possibly your immediate family) loves you; (2) In any given situation which is at all competitive (& nearly every one is, even if only for the prestige & lift one person gets by socking a second) you'd be stepped on if at all possible; (3) Only by anticipating; & being in control of the situation can you remain "on top"—I think you can be as sweet as you please.

I'm always getting into trouble by not being able to follow those ideas. I try to be spontaneous, fairly sincere, & have people like & respect me, but it really doesn't matter at all. Nobody (but my close friends, I guess) is at all interested in whether I'm sweet, or kind, or good, or noble…If I'm harmless, good. That is all. But in any important situation—getting a job, promotion, fellowship, deferment, entering Med. School—it's the "power" you have in the situation: legal right on your side, transcript, Civil Service Exam, laying for the Bar,…

Do you understand what I mean, darling? I've been up against it so often that the concept is pretty clear to me.

Love
Aaron

Friday 1/12/45 10:10 a.m.

Gloria darling:

I only went into Chelsea once this week: it's been very cold, I finished morning lab work pretty late, & I just feel dreadfully lazy…So this morning, I get a chance to write to you instead of trying to concentrate on the Medical Textbook.

By now you've probably received the records. I really wanted to get you earrings, but reconsidered when I realized that you couldn't exchange them if they didn't suit. Records are records. And in buying them I have the entire vista of recorded music to choose from. I had quite a time deciding on the album. So even tho we don't own a record player now, we're going to-- & will want a good collection. Don't give your records to Solly, now! Actually I only wanted to get the B, minor suite; but as the album has both suites, I had no choice. It's very good, I think. Bach can get more emotion into one of his restrained works for a small group, than Tchaikovsky or Dvorak into their big symphonies.

At any rate, Happy Birthday, dear, -- may our love endure as does Bach's music…

Do you remember dear my emphasis at one time of one criterion for emotional maturity—in being able to look someone straight in the eye & tell him to go to the Devil, being not at all concerned with the hatred (hostility) he'll manifest? I just came up against another example of failure in one of my experiments. I couldn't do it. It probably would bear analysis some day.

At the end of last semester, I asked around school for chances of assisting during the term. The Dean was non-committal, sent me to profs who were glad to get an assistant but didn't think "funds would be made available." Last week Rushmore called & said an assistant was required in Rheumatology & for me to see Dr. Mauntner. I saw him & started to go to Waltham on Monday. But I began to hear very disquieting reports about salary being negligible. I saw Mr. Smith, Tuesday, fully prepared to be told I'd be paid 75 cents per hour & to tell him I was no bottle washer, that I was traveling in from Roxbury three times a week, that I wouldn't waste my time for less than my Tuition & graduation fees…He told me that student assistants get 50 cents per hour & that it would be up to the Dean to make further arrangements. I left without making my speech at all. I wasn't able to descend from my pedestal of untouchability & talk to him, man to man, about getting more money thru the Board of Trustees…

In the mean-time I could see that the situation was pretty bad in the Dept. of Pharmacology. It consists of Dr. Hans Maunheim (old, alone, a refugee from Vienna where he was supposed to be a leading pharmacologist & pediatrician) & one instructor, Dr. Navula (also a refugee who is trying to build up his practice pending collapse of the school). Maunheim is old, tired & can't talk English. Navula is busy with his practice. They really could use a third person to help give the course. Navula just about told me that the school was definitely secondary. I'd be doing all the work. Finally, I just didn't see anybody else, in my class who would be interested.

There, tho, was a perfect experimental set up. I really wasn't desperately in need of the job, I didn't see any competition, & the school really needed me. Here was the chance to assert myself, to argue with Rushmore, to point out my advantages…So I called him up Wednesday & told him that I was terribly sorry but I couldn't afford to go to Waltham at the salary offered & hoped he'd be able to get someone who could…

Use your Hegel on that, darling!

You probably have a lot of that too. We're very similar people I think. Did you ever tell a salesgirl or waitress that if she didn't hurry or change your order you'd call the manager? Did you ever tell an acquaintance to go to Hell? And all without getting flustered, flushed & emotional?

It won't be easy for us to change. Analysis would probably show up definite character weakness there. But I find it interesting to see the weakness, & work my inevitable struggle with it in recurring situations. Maybe we can act for each other in these situations, if we can spot them ahead of time. Since I'd only be emotionally tied up in the situation I'm a part of, & you with your daily contacts, we possibly could do a lot better together.

I'll unconsciously rip apart your weakness in a given situation—you can do the same for me. I don't really think it'll help. But if knowledge is strength & "know thyself" is the important maxim for personality fortitude—well, it can't do any harm.

Wow, my letters grow longer & longer-- & you can't find anything to write about! I don't understand it, unless you try to write in the office, which is a ridiculous place to concentrate or grow intimate. I'd never consider writing to you on the wards, or in Chelsea…

I'll expect your call on Tuesday dear.

All my love
Aaron

Tuesday 1/16 10:45 pm.

Sweetheart:

We just did some cases in the New England Journal to keep in practice. I'm doing some reading, too. Not in any concentrated fashion & in a planned way, which would prepare me for State Boards, but kind of rambling over cases, interesting materials which will be helpful for exams & useful—just in case. It is absolutely remarkable how little mere words mean in medicine. Going over a book on Pharmacology for example, I find that those drugs I've ordered, seen given, or only just handled are vitally interesting & important. Yet, 2 years ago, going thru the same book for a pharmacology course, they meant absolutely nothing to me. Just words to be memorized. And "Morphine Sulfate, Analgesic & Hypnotic, dose 10 milligrams" was practically memorized in the same breath as "Strychnine Sulfate, Central Nervous System Stimulant, dose 0.25 milligram." Obviously the first is foremost among all drugs, the Strychnine practically useless therapeutically.

I really think all learning is on that basis. John Dewey was an experienced & wise educator when he formulated his ""learn by doing." I learn more & more how right he was. Just think how far you'd get learning to type by just getting lectures on the subject! In more abstract fields, eg Philosophy, Math…it still is "doing." Doing problems, or thinking thru the abstract concepts which are presented…

Particularly in medicine, "doing" is all important. Even excepting obvious skills (suturing, tonsillectomies, I.V.s, obstetrics, physical diagnosis, bandaging, transfusions, laboratory work…)—even learning medicine is only possible by doing it. No matter how often I memorize the symptoms of Kala Azar (a tropical disease) I forget it at once. It just vanishes into the dull grey of all the other stuff I've memorized in the past 20-25 years. But given a case which I think <u>might be</u> Kala Azar, running to Cecil to get the symptoms, getting the lab to do the diagnostic tests-- & I'll remember it for a long time—even if it finally isn't Kala Azar at all. Some months back—that did occur with a case of Trichinosis. I still don't know if it was Trichinosis, but after spending 2 weeks doing blood counts, skin tests, & watching for the development of symptoms the book called for,…I'll know how to describe the disease, no matter what he had…Even doing cases is "doing" in some way. Getting the right answer before Joe does (or at all) is a challenge, & in trying to work it out, active thinking (of a kind) does go on, & some of it sticks…

I'm glad you like my choice of records. I had quite a time deciding. It's a big album, so I could have gotten any major work. Let me know how it sounds. I wasn't able to listen as the record store had no player! But any imperfection can be exchanged, I'm sure.

It looks to me that you are bound to become a very well educated young lady. You'll learn a great deal as time goes on because you'll approach books & lectures with active questions as you mentally try to see whether the author or lecturer can answer your questions, & how, you do "active" learning & the material is a part of you. Just reading or listening passively gives a little information which is soon forgotten. In the days to come you'll be able to teach me a great deal. After all I can only learn so much. You'll be far better informed in lots of topics. But, don't worry, I won't be jealous. You just go ahead & tell me all that you know &

I'll be proud of you. Unlike Solly I don't expect you to memorize the 10 essential amino-acids. I just want you to feel yourself on an intellectual par with anybody you meet…

By the way, that prescription was a very, very typical cough medicine. It isn't nearly as good as Terpen Hydrate with Codeine (but it looks much more impressive). So you see, I'm not kidding about the general level of medical practice…He just had to give you something…

Good night darling; a letter a day & talking to you for 3 minutes a week—isn't enough.

Love
Aaron

Thursday 1/18 11:30 pm.

Gloria darling:

I just got back from pronouncing another patient dead. I'm still not hardened to it. I'm learning, tho…

Mr. Hartman was a young chap—40 or so, who developed subacute bacterial endocarditis about 6 months or so. Pretty hopeless isn't it? Up until this or last year, the very diagnosis was equivalent to a death sentence. At the present time penicillin is apparently the white hope at the Peter Bent Brigham. They report cures of this slow killer using terrific doses of penicillin dripping continuously into a vein for 3-6 weeks. It is absolutely miraculous if they get any cures, as those people would have assuredly died 2-3 years ago.

Mr. Hartman went out with penicillin dripping into his veins…

I was called during 10 o'clock coffee. His breathing had just about stopped, heart was still beating, his wife realizing what was happening was crying. I was the doctor—what was I to do? I knew that I really could do nothing. He had no heart left; the ever growing "green streptococcus" had been steadily eating away Mr. Hartman's heart valves. Without valves no pump can keep going. By early tonight, I knew his heart was no longer able to push the blood around as fast as it was brought to it; fluid was accumulating in his lungs & making him very short of breath…

But still I called for stimulants to be injected, & I started artificial respiration. It was very, very hopeless…

All that stuff about heroic measures, like injecting adrenaline into the heart, saving a patient's life is a lot of malarkey. If you can't keep the patient from starting to die, you can't stop him from finishing the job. If anything would help, it would have been used before…

Brr…A very morbid topic to be writing to you, darling. It's just that it happened; I'm full of the situation & write to you just as I would talk if I had you here. Hopefully we'll do something in the near future to prevent hearts like Mr. Hartman's from developing. These major sources of heart disease are not at all amenable to any kind of treatment. We don't know what to blame for them & of course have absolutely no therapy. Rheumatic Heart Disease in young people & Hypertensive Heart Disease (high Blood Pressure) in older people. Arteriosclerotic Heart Disease is the third. Nobody knows what causes Rheumatic Fever, Hypertension or Arteriosclerosis; Nobody knows what to do for them…

On Tuesday we had some real major surgery here. An attempt was made to convert another fatal diagnosis into hope.

An old chap (65 or so) came in last week & we all diagnosed Cancer of the Pancreas. That is absolutely fatal. It's like telling the patient he's got 6 months to live…Recently, several surgeons have started to operate on the pancreas & a few cures—all too few—are reported. Lahey Clinic is in that group.

The operation took 7-8 hours! The finest surgeons in the country worked in shifts. The patient received 3 transfusions during the operation. The anaesthesia must have been extraordinary. He's still alive tonight. The whole thing was a "tour-de-force." It was a question of "can it be done?"

Both of the patients were Lahey Clinic patients; they did receive what medicine can offer today for pretty hopeless conditions; one medically; the other surgically. Both will probably not be cured. At least they're getting what is possible at this stage…

Some letter! Just to make up for it: I love you, I love you, I love you, I love you. Better? I'm sorry I'm not writing good hot love letters lately. Don't you worry. One of these days I'll simply be alone up here, nice quiet music, nobody dying or anything, & I'll tell you in words how much I miss you. As is, you'll have to guess. But you're a pretty good guesser, aren't you?

All my love, dear
Aaron

Tuesday 1/22 11:00 p.m.

Gloria darling:

I've been pretty busy for the past few days, as I said:-- but just relatively speaking. Friday morning I stayed at the Brigham to see the post-mortems of the SBE (Subacute Bacterial Endocarditis) who died, as I wrote, the night before. There was an interesting bit I'll try to explain—but I don't think I'm going to make myself clear. The previous night, when I had examined the patient I found him pretty suddenly getting very short of breath, slightly blue, & running a very fast pulse; in his lungs, were lots of bubbles, like blowing into the straw of your ice-cream soda. This is the kind of thing that is seen very commonly in people with Heart Disease due to High Blood Pressure & is called "Cardiac Asthma." It is due to sudden failure of the left ventricle & a filling up of the lung behind it with a great deal of blood.

In Hypertension, this sudden failure of the left ventricle is due to the high blood pressure straining against the Left Ventricle. As you know from your courses the Left Ventricle is pumping blood into the Aorta & is working against the blood pressure in the Aorta. Now, if a sudden strain is put on the Left Ventricle it may temporarily get weak & blood will pile up behind it in the lung, giving those very embarrassing symptoms.

But this chap had no high blood pressure at all. He had an infection of his Aortic Valves. And his "Cardiac Asthma" wasn't temporary & relieved by anything we could do. He died.

I suggested to the Lahey Clinic Fellow who came in that there was the possibility of the infection rupturing the Aortic Valve. You can see what would happen:-- a sudden terrible strain is put on the

Left Ventricle; every time it relaxes, the blood just rushes back thru the hole in the valve & smash up against the ventricle. The Left Ventricle would fail very soon; the lungs would fill up; "CardiacAsthma" would ensue; & the patient would die in a few hours. At autopsy there was a nice round hole in the Aortic Valve…

It doesn't mean anything in the way of reputation, prestige or anything else, dear. It's just that I wanted to boast to someone who won't mind. Dr. Rouzer, Lahey Clinic Fellow, was surprised, I think…

But what's the difference. There is no indication at all that I'm going to be a doctor…

This morning both internes at Chelsea, Kansas City School Boys, were notified that they failed their State Boards…Gosh were they sick! For both, it probably means the Army—as a Buck Private & probably the end of medicine…They felt, I guess, as I did, when I was notified I had failed the T in T examination. That finished a career for me, too.

Both are married; one has a child. Both solemnly warned me against getting married. They were sorry they ever got married, were going to tell their respective wives that maybe they ought to go get themselves other guys…All not very realistic, I think, & conditioned by a great deal of feeling of guilt about failure in the eyes of the wives and in laws…In fact guilt and resentment & they blamed their wives for "tying them down" & so for part of the failure…

Nobody was very happy…

I think we ought to get married anyway. Or to put it simply, we ought to legalize & make more convenient an already existing married state. I won't be any more "married" emotionally or intellectually if 10 ceremonies were performed…

I just present the evidence of what happens to Grade B men sometimes…No comebacks later…

I do want to know tho that I'm going to be home for a while before we can make specific plans. Right now I don't know whether I'll be allowed to accept an internship at all; or whether I'll be drafted as soon as the Supreme Court says—"No." So just hold on, darling. As soon as I know I'll let you know & probably come into New York to talk over the unfortunate details.

Since time is growing closer I'd suggest you talk the whole thing over now with your parents & get their reaction. Lord knows, I can't answer the question "How are you going to support the little girl?" Fundamentally, that really is the big problem. Both the internes would not be so messed up if they were supporting their wives; finding themselves unable to do so, is the big rub…So that is the big hurdle…

There you are—the ever present chain of problems:--

1. Do I get a reprieve—an internship—so we can count on being together for a while?
2. Married, with me an interne—how are we going to support ourselves?
3. What do we do—when my internship is over?

These are terrible questions. You've got to answer them, tho.

I was going to say that I'd like to have you up here so I could talk to you. But I mean to talk to you any-time I get home. It's no use. The only way I can talk seriously to you is by letter…

I love you a great deal darling. I'd do anything in the situation which would make you happiest. If you're sure you want to get married now & leave all those questions—just questions—we'll just wait until I know that I'm taking an internship & I'll come in to N.Y. and we'll get married…

In any event you'd better discuss it with your folks—on a grown up basis & let me know their reactions.

Good night darling

Aaron

Incidentally, if you take medical courses you'll know a lot more than I do, as I've written you all I know.

Aaron

Wednesday 11:30 pm 1/24/45

Darling—

I wrote to you yesterday. Tonight I've just finished running around the hospital doing odds and ends which go to make up being "on duty"; don't feel that I can get down to doing any real work; and am pretty lonely and discouraged…So this letter.

Time in the past tense seems endless. I can hardly remember back to Monday…I splurged and bought tickets for myself, Eliot and Leo Hockman for the Opera that is coming to Boston this week; by error I was given tickets for Tannheuser instead of for Faust; going down to return them I was asked at the Box Office when I bought the tickets and I said "sometime last week or the week before." The box office only put the tickets on sale the day before yesterday…Time just seemed to be so long. At any rate I did get the tickets changed so that I'll probably see Faust with the fellows after all. It won't be the Met; I may not like it at all.

Everything is just one big turmoil…Meetings are being held by the administration telling the students that they are to "voluntarily" contribute $300 more to "keep the school running" or else they will be forced to close down <u>before we get our degrees</u>. Nice job of blackmail, no? The graduates of last year have gotten together and hired a lawyer to submit bills to the Legislature which would cover them if passed; the parents and students of our class are getting together, I think, to try to get someone to submit bills to cover us if passed; the administration is trying to get the students to kick in for the fight for a bill to keep the school running and so cover all the classes…Each class with its own interest at stake, all semblance of cohesiveness or esprit de corps completely gone. Nobody even knows whether they will keep the school open for two more months…God, what a set-up!

It is in this sort of situation that the temptation to wish or to dream is great. I would wish that I were in some secure place and could be with you every day, that we could grow in our love for each other, that we could do the everyday things which make for the good life in modern cultured society, that we'd have leisure and ability to use it constructively…But dreaming or wishing is childish and very much a sign of weakness. I don't let myself do much of it. The facts of "what is" are much too everlastingly present in the front of my consciousness. After achievement, one can dream in retrospect.

I won't let myself go off dreaming then. What can I do tho to make something out of the situation?

Darling, you've been getting the mixed up kaleidoscopic thoughts that are running around in my head these days. Half formed, and not very clear. I'm thinking in writing. It would be better probably if I could think out loud by speaking to you, but it would be too expensive by phone or to come in to New York. So I think to the paper.

I don't have any answers at all, dear. I'm certain that you don't have either. Two or three months ought to precipitate the story and give us a few answers. I'd like to anticipate and thereby prevent some of the consequences. Yet, How? Just waiting passively, hoping that something good will happen to me never has worked and probably never will. Usually the "good" follows pretty active effort.

Oh well. I'm sleepy and temporarily depressed. If this kind of letter makes you depressed for any length of time you really oughtn't to get them. You know that I write as I feel at the moment without thinking at all of how you are going to react. Better let me know if they depress you and I can write more intelligently in my more lucid moments.

I love you a great deal darling.

Good night, dear
Aaron

Friday 1/26 10:30 p.m.

Darling:

Another week is gone by. Time is certainly passing, but I wish I knew what it was getting us to. I'm listening now to a "Symphonette" program in a very warmly lit "apartment," just after eating lots of dessert & coffee. Very, very comfortable. Yet I'm anything but very, very happy. It all feels so useless, so empty. And I'm pretty much incomplete without you.

Latest information from the administration—Smith told his class in Medical Jurisprudence that Selective Service has agreed to defer students of the school only up to May 1, whether or not all litigation is over by then. They are ready to go to town, I guess. I get my degree May 1, I think. But I don't know whether they are going to let me take an internship. Probably, I'll write to Bronx Hospital, asking whether they'll take me in May so as to cover me. I don't, of course, know whether even being in Bronx as a "pre-interne", will defer me. What a set-up!

There's an awful lot of good medicine going on here, but I'm just not very receptive at present. The Lahey Clinic gets very interesting stuff & handles it just as the textbook orders. Very, very pretty.

Interestingly enough an experiment was performed, practically, in the hospital. A fellow came in with Jaundice & was diagnosed as having cancer of the pancreas. At operation, this was verified-- & his pancreas was nearly all removed. The operation was a "tour de force" as very few survive. I wrote you about it, I think. But what is very interesting is that he has developed diabetes! Insulin is, of course, manufactured in the Pancreas & extirpation of the organ should lead to Diabetes. That was just how it was discovered: pancreatectomized dogs became diabetic. But this experiment, of taking out pancreases of people, isn't done in medical school to demonstrate the point! It is really fascinating to watch the development of the typical high blood sugar, acidosis…-- which is now being controlled by Insulin!

War news ranks very high on our radio listening these days. I hope, gosh how I hope, the Red Army does it. I suppose I'll spend my stint in warmer latitudes.

With the good news from Europe, we get, via PM, the rotten news from Wash. You'd never guess Liberals won the election. No real progressive step is being allowed, Wallace being beaten simply as he stands for liberalism.

Oh well. Good night darling. Better call any other night but Thursday as I'm going to see Faust then. But don't forget to call. I don't know what's going to happen to me; Yet, I selfishly demand your continued love, warmth & support…

I miss you a great deal, dear.

Love
Aaron

Tuesday 1/30/45 10:30 pm

Sweetheart:

It's comparatively early now, yet I'm pretty sleepy. Probably it's because I got up rather early and kept pretty busy. We're not going to Chelsea at present—maybe not any more. First of all it's because we're getting lazy and don't want to brave the cold weather; then the third group of students are in the hospital at present and we might be wearing out our welcome; and finally, as we learn more, there is less to learn at the small hospital—another pneumonia or cerebral hemorrhage isn't something new.

But lazying around is very bad for me. There is a direct relationship between lack of activity and libido I believe. I'm beginning to understand why there is always such a great increase in population during periods of unemployment. If the converse is also true—that a great deal of activity lessens the need for sexual expression—it's going to be awfully tough on you if I'm an interne and come to see you after having been up all night and run around all day…

Your letters are very lovely dear. They were warm, loving, and very comfortable. They were very flattering, which tho I know is not deserved, still inflates my wilted ego considerably. I should have spoken to you over the phone tonight of course, but we're getting our wires crossed this time. Unless I hear from you to the contrary tomorrow, I'll call you tomorrow night person to person. You see, I really must love you very much to spend money so lavishly on you! Seriously I really want you very badly now. July is such a long time away…As I've told you dozens of times I'll fight you anytime on who loves who more…

There is very little that is going on now. I'm reading along and doing those case records just the same way that you might do crossword puzzles. In fact to spur us on, Joe and I have organized a game with all sorts of rules so that either he or I get points for making the diagnosis: one point for making the clinical diagnosis, three points for making the same diagnosis which the professor who discusses the case makes, and five points for making the diagnosis established at autopsy; maximum points for any one case being five points. Fifty points wins, and the loser buys a cake for our evening coffee. Joe bought the first cake. I nosed him out by three points. We're deep in our second series now…The air in our quarters is filled with blue electricity as we think at a furious pace to try to make the diagnosis—after all there's a cake at stake: Anything for morale.

I'm very proud of you darling in that you're going to see Tristan—standing. It shows great fortitude and love for the music. I told Eliot Korim of our going to the opera among the standees—and he beamed all over. That was the picture of young love which appealed to him. Standing at the opera. Enthralled by the great music. Holding hands. Eyes shining. Hearts beating in unison. Ad infinitum. All kidding aside, I'd really give a lot to go with you this Saturday. The way I've been feeling lately I really don't need Wagner to spur on my passion, but unless the seven hours of standing and the great emotional vicarious experience washed me out, there would be trouble taking you home. So I better not come for it. Also, I can't afford it, I'm afraid. Twenty five dollars to stand up and see Tristan—too high. But I'll think about you all thru Faust. What would you like me to think of you?

Gosh, I'm practically asleep right now, as you can tell from my typing. (I usually make only one mistake to every two words) I'm going back to the quarters and probably drop right off. I mean to do a lot of reading but the time just seems to disappear. Tho what is the difference anyhow.

Good night darling
Aaron

Friday Feb 2, 1945 10:30 PM

Hello darling:

I really am becoming a sissy, dear. Only early evening and I'm sleepy. There is so much studying to do, but I just don't seem to get anywhere at all. Time seems to disappear with talking, eating, attending classes and a few conferences—by the time I get down to work my eyes are tired and I am ready to do anything but read.

We saw Faust last night. Today's "Globe," in the tradition of the small town paper saying nothing that isn't nice (except of Communists and Foreigners), ends its review by saying that the role of Margarite was sung as the reviewer had never heard it sung before. It certainly was. I have never heard anything quite as bad. It was like a bunch of kids seriously trying to do Hamlet. Except that poor singing is even worse than poor acting. And in the opera there was both. The orchestra was small and tinny; the principals were grossly inadequate; the chorus consisted of about 8 people who couldn't even keep together in unison (to say nothing of part singing); and Margarite—my God! The only explanation for using a fat, graceless, hammy, voiceless female for the part is that her husband is supporting thc show…The ballet was in line too. Mme. Rackasovska and her ballet school were featured. To the lilting music the little elephants cavorted on the stage without the slightest knowledge of anything even simulating ballet. They must have been the kids in the school. Down in the orchestra sat the fond parents, I guess, proud as hell that their Sylvia was already a Ballerina and on the stage—after two weeks of lessons. Finally Mme. R. flitted on, climbed up on her points, tried to do a pirouette, lost her balance and flitted off. Faust was a fairly good tenor who could only go so high and hold a note so long; when in difficulty he sobbed. Mephisto stalked around in a gorgeous red cape—trying to make up by stalking what he lacked in voice. Valentine had some possibilities; I think he was just getting old; Leo aptly compared him to an old Cantor, who, tho unable to sing with his former power, is still graceful and able to handle the material. And Margarite…

The Boston Opera Company and The Metropolitan Opera Company—Middlesex and Harvard. The analogy was very apt. The whole performance lacked professional capability. It all rang of the amateur—and the cheap amateur who really doesn't hope to get anyplace. A young singer of promise wouldn't try to go way out of her range. There are lots of good people available. Why weren't they singing? Why was the orchestra so inadequate? Why the whole shoddy performance? I think in both instances it is the lack of money. An opera company as well as a medical school cannot run on the basis of current intake. There must be financial security behind it. The staff must be ensured an adequate (and commensurate) salary which would be independent of the capriciousness of the public at any given time. It must be a big permanent affair. It must be able to give to the staff the chance to work together for years and to grow up with the company.

There are two ways of achieving this situation—for opera companies or for medical schools. Either we have an aristocracy which supports the institution. Or the government supports the institution. In our country now, both the opera and the medical schools are supported by some kind of aristocracy. The big drawback is that the facilities of these institutions are limited to a large extent for the benefit of their patrons. Art for all who could and would enjoy it, and education for all who can profit by it—can only come if supported by the potentially wealthiest group of them all: the people as a whole…

Something else came by which I think is interesting. I came across a reprint of a scientific paper printed in the Journal of the AMA, Oct 14 1933, entitled "Postmortem Examinations—Method of obtaining permission." Never was the fundamental insincerity, the hypocrisy of the medical profession in dealing with the public, put down so frankly in writing. The paper is an analysis of the ways to convince the relatives of the deceased of the advisability of the autopsy, the answers to their arguments and the "percentage successes," using the author's way. Let me quote just a bit—

"Request for autopsy is never made in the patient's room or the ward. Such a request is best made in a part of the hospital not too intimately associated with the deceased person and among surroundings calculated to lend an air of grave responsibility and dignity to the interview. Further, a white uniform is not an asset to such a discussion. To many it is the badge of immaturity, the mark of an undergraduate clinical clerk. The interview is more likely to be successful if the doctor wears a business suit with or without the long white coat associated in the layman's mind with the maturity of the attending surgeon.

"After a patient has died and the relatives have recovered from their first expression of grief, they are taken in charge by the nurse and brought to meet the resident surgeon at the office of the clinical director. (in the method being described by the author) In conducting the interview the doctor's manner should unite dignity, responsibility and sympathy. No reference to the purpose of the meeting should be made. The subject should arise apparently without premeditation, and in most instances the talk can be guided around to it so that it will be broached by the family. Their first question will be a desire to know why they have been brought there. The reply is: "I have sent for you to ask if I can help you in any way."…

"A few minutes may suffice to form a quick estimate of the psychological types among the members of the family. It quickly becomes apparent which one is the dominant personality, in the group, and it is on this person that one's attention must be concentrated and toward whom most of the conversation must be directed…"

Then he gives all the arguments to be used depending upon whether the relatives are Catholic, Jewish…

Some profession, eh?

Well I've spent another whole letter on anything but what a young man should write his girl. Maybe better next time.

Good night darling.

Love
Aaron

February 6, 1945 10:30 pm

Darling:

I don't have very much to write about tonight really. I said that I would get a letter out to you—and a Kelman's word is his bond…, so

Your call did surprise me of course. I was speaking to you from the office of the Men's ward, which affords no privacy at all. Altho no one was in the room, the door is open and in the quiet that always prevails in the Robert Brigham during the night my voice was clearly audible. So I couldn't tell you that I loved you even. Isn't that terrible? Money just absolutely wasted.

If you want to tell me something in a hurry, you can call me at the hospital at any time; I'm always in here after 5 o'clock. But if you want to spend the time just talking to me, you had better warn me in advance so that I'll be in my quarters waiting for your call.

An article came out in the latest New England Journal about the Middlesex Question. I'll enclose it tonight if I can. It can well be entitled The Middlesex Obituary. The only possible chance the school has for a reprieve is to have the legislature pass a bill extending it for some length of time. But if the Mass. Medical Society is actively working against it, there is practically no chance at all for one of the bills to go thru.

I did write to the Bronx Hospital asking him to let me begin my internship in May. The superintendent replied that he could not let me know about that now and would be able to give me a definite answer in the middle of March. So I don't even know about that definitely. I don't know about anything definitely. It's a good thing that I'm not studying social work where the concepts aren't even definite. That would drive me nutty. At least in medicine there is a solid body of information that is very definite—and until one knows that there is little mental anguish about the great amount of material that is still unknown or about the validity of the stuff that is currently accepted.

So there we are. Classes four afternoons a week—if I attend that often. Down at Harvard for lectures open to the profession several times a week. A minimum of hospital work up here in the Brigham. Some reading of medical texts. Two letters a week to you. Work on Sunday. Music over the radio. And that is last week, and this week, and the week before last. Very leisurely—not at all the way a fourth year medical student should be killing himself soaking in medicine thru every pore.

You go ahead and learn all you can about anything at all that interests you. You find out, just as I do, that there is so much you know nothing about it is beyond belief that one can even manage to learn all there is…The only saving feature is that we don't need to know everything, only a little…I feel that I'd like to know absolutely everything sometimes…From how to spin thread on a spinning wheel (they showed that to me this week in the occupational therapy department up here, but nobody could explain how the sewing machine worked) to how bridges are built. If man does it, it is understandable. The only sane approach probably is to specialize. Become interested in some field and spend what time you have in learning a lot about that. It need not at all be connected with one's profession. But the bigger and more important the interest, the bigger and better is the person whose interest it is; the more he can grow in pursuit of his interest.

I always feel that the best persons I meet are those who are deeply involved in something outside of themselves. Their major interest takes them out of the petty considerations of their own little personalities. They are no longer so concerned with little hurts and grievances. There is no longer the need to be constantly feeding upon life's daily little occurrences for salve to their thwarted egos. Probably because men are forced by circumstances to become interested in something bigger than themselves—their job—that they are usually so very much superior to women as people. When women are given the same opportunities as men to enter the business and professional world, I think the discrepancy will cease to be.

What on earth got me off onto that anyway? I don't know. I'm all for everybody having a purpose in life. Do you know that the slogan of the ICL is (or was) "join the party for life with a purpose"…A very good slogan. I think that everything will sooner or later grow dull except progress and growth. Given a purpose, progress and growth in the fulfillment of that purpose will always be interesting and satisfying.

I'm falling asleep darling—as you can tell from my typing—so I'll go to sleep.

Good night darling

Love
Aaron

Thursday 2/8 11:00 p.m.

Gloria darling:

So spring is here! Some prophet you are. Your other prophecies better hit on a higher rating. Funny. We started to go to school today (for me lectures—Singer doing a case) & decided it was too much like a blizzard out. Then after being cooped up all morning, decided that a movie was in order. Saw "Life & Love of Beethoven" (again) & "Three Waltzes." So, so…

You know that I'm proud of you for your initiative & aggressive showing. I want to see more of it. Pretty soon you'll be giving me lectures on "Being Quietly Aggressive"-- & I'll like it very much. Only in this case, don't be disappointed if nothing happens. I've seen Gov't agencies promise promotions & never come thru. It'll probably require a lot of perseverance. You remember that it looked pretty good when Sylvia left. So keep your fingers on the pulse of the situation & push your advantages…No matter what happens, I'm glad you did push out. It's very good for you. Remember my writing (or saying) that when you can tell a salesgirl to change the dress, a salesman that you want better seats which you're sure he has at the same price, a waitress to change the soup, your mother that you'll choose your friends…all <u>without any emotional involvement</u>—no anger at all—it's a definite sign of maturation; of an organism ready to fend for itself in our hostile environment. The baby can't bear the thought of somebody not liking him. It means hostility-- & to the insecure infant, that is terrifying. True adulthood isn't there, I think, until one is not afraid of arousing hostility, & of having no emotional reactions to most people at all. You just watch people full of protective mechanisms to everybody they meet from "friends" to local storekeepers to telephone operators—they seem to be eternally apologizing—or getting flustered & angry…I have some of this, you probably do, & so do a lot of our friends. Did you ever notice it? I think in noticing we "know ourselves" better, can understand others better & possibly (only possibly) change a little…

Some takeoff in your asking for a raise—no?

Beethoven wrote a very lovely letter to his girl in the movie. "My immortal beloved"—Now why can't I write like that to you? I can't compose you a little Sonata either…

There is very little change going on. Maybe it's because I haven't been to school for a week, practically so don't know the latest rumors…

I still go to work Sundays. It's just as bad, but I do need the money. Actually it is the only exercise I get…

You're getting me not only penniless—but in debt to the Gov't.

Good night sweetheart
Aaron

Feb. 12, 1945 Monday 10 pm

Darling:

Your letters are swell. It will be almost a shame to get married and have you stop sending them. Yet there are no doubt some things in the situation which will make up for it. Incidentally, the stationery is vastly improved too. All of it. That blue paper is really something, and the Russian border style is too pretty to write on.

Last Friday was a rather strange day. I went down to 15 Bay State Road to pick up a letter I was called up about, and found a check from the Federal Government for sixty dollars (60); reimbursement for income taxes overpaid for 1943!! I didn't even know that I paid any in that year. Maybe it's all a big mistake/ but the check was apparently good. When I got back to the hospital an emergency transfusion was needed—my blood type. So I made another twenty five dollars. My feeble arithmetic got 60 plus 25 equals 85. Funny, isn't it?

At any rate I paid tuition in full today (my last I hope) and have just enough left to pay graduation fee. You're still my final reserve, darling…

Karen Horney's lectures sound very good. I'd like very much to hear them. I don't think you are really going to get all that information on psychiatry, love, sex…just so that you'll make a better wife. That's much too calculating. You like the stuff. But about what she said about sex and neurosis. I think it is perfectly consistent with the facts and with my little diagram. If you recall, I said that sexual life can be either (1) experiences which lead to greater insecurity eg. Rape, a young girl being ignored by all the boys at a dance because she isn't sexy, lack of a husband or boy friend when old enough to have custom demand one, the young fellow not knowing how to go about sexual intercourse being laughed at by the girl he's trying it out on, frigidity, impotence…These experiences are very potent depressors of the personality into the stage of anxiety from which it is going to try to escape, come what may. These experiences are no different than physical deformities which I think play an enormous role in personality. Big noses, adiposity, shortness, baldness, buck teeth…Or (2) sexual life can be, in its manifestations, expressions of the neurotic personality. Can be. Not must be. As we have learnt in medicine there are a lot of physical manifestations of the so called Psychoneuroses: ulcers, heart disease, sweating, enuresis…But the patient doesn't have them all. In the psychological field, agoraphobia, hysteria, frigidity…may be manifested. All symptoms of the underlying anxiety or neurosis again. But again the patient doesn't have the whole book. So with the sex life. The neurotic may have a very crummy sex life—an expression of the neurosis. Or the sex life may be o.k.—some other symptom giving the clue to the neurosis.

There you are. I explained nothing. Just said "that it happens." Why one person gets into a cold sweat when climbing up a hill, and another is frigid, is completely beyond me. That, of course, is the real problem.

As for Thelma, I'm not at all sure that she is even moderately neurotic or that she is unhappy in her marital relationships any more than normal. In the beginning we all tend to find pathology where it doesn't exist. I do it all the time in medicine. Fortunately, the X ray simply rules out my tentative diagnosis of Tb. So I really didn't hear those crackles in the lungs. But in psychiatry there is no answer except the opinion of one with a lot of experience. I'm certain however, that the novice will call a great many more persons neurotic (including himself) than he should.

I've been pretty tense these past few weeks. Maybe you can tell by my letters or the quality of my typing. It may be "withdrawal symptoms." You're as necessary to my mental and emotional health as morphine is to an addict. There is nothing more that I can say. Nothing is more necessary. I'm love starved and sex starved and all tightened up. I would usually begin seriously thinking of going into New York at about this stage, but I don't think I had better just yet. First my total capital at this point is about 10 dollars, and then the way I feel now I won't be in any mood to go back to Boston…Very unsatisfactory. I can't study with you, and I'm too jumpy to study without you…

Good night darling,
Aaron

Thursday Feb 15, 10 pm

Darling:

I'm glad you liked the Valentine; tho, I really wasn't a bit worried that you might not like it. You see, I don't worry about you not approving what I do at all now. Particularly when it says "I love you" all over it. Actually I think that is a sign of softening of the brain on my part, giving in to such sentimental things as Valentines. Pretty soon I'll be turning the stamps on my letters upside down! Women are the downfall of even the best men. Aren't they darling?

I didn't realize what I said when I agreed to explain the Argyl-Robertson pupil. At the time it sounded easy. But here goes…

One of the ways of spotting a person who has had syphilis for many years is to notice that, although his pupils constrict when he converges them,-- as for example in close reading—they fail to constrict normally when a light is flashed into them. So, in a routine examination (and you can try it on yourself or a friend) I flash a light into each pupil and watch it constrict to a pinpoint size; then ask the patient to watch my finger, as I bring it up from a distance to the tip of his nose. As the pupils converge to keep my finger in view, the pupils will also constrict. This is the normal response.

Now what makes for these responses? Reflexes—as the patient has absolutely no control over them. As you remember, a reflex has two parts to the arc—the sensory and the motor. In the case of the pupil, the motor nerve is a very fine nerve coming out of the brain and going to the muscle in the iris which it causes to contract and thereby close the opening—constricting the pupil. The origin of this nerve in the brain is in a small island of grey matter given the very cute name of the Edinger Westphall Nucleus (E D Nucleus) But don't worry your head about it. This nerve then will constrict the pupil, then, no matter what the incoming stimulus is. Just so long as the proper stimulus gets to the ED Nucleus, the nerve will do its work.

Now how to get the proper stimulus to the Nucleus with the fancy name? If a light is flashed into the eye, the stimulus as we might expect, runs along down the optic nerve and heads for the cortical area of the brain which is concerned with vision. But on its way there, it gives off a little branch, which goes over the ED nucleus and stimulates it. Thereby causing a constriction of the pupil in the face of a bright light—a very intelligent procedure.

How about the convergence business? Here again a similar mechanism holds. The Third cranial nerve is basically a motor nerve which goes to the muscles of the eyeball—in fact to the muscles which cause the eye to converge. This nerve also has a nucleus, its starting-off point in the brain, very intelligently called the Nucleus of the Third Nerve (III). By chance (or evolution) this nucleus is situated right next to the ED nucleus. Also, it so happens, that not only does the third nerve cause convergence of the eyeball, but after it does it, it has some sensory fibres, which relay that fact right back to its nucleus. And in so doing, get over to the ED nucleus, which thereupon goes about its business of sending a stimulus along the constrictor nerve which constricts the pupil.

Are you confused enough? If not, let me add that I've left out most of the confusing details…*(diagram)*

But to get back to the syphilitic. We have then, in short, two ways to stimulate the ED nucleus: by a light stimulus coming along the optic nerve and sending a little offshoot, and by a stimulus coming from the eyeball muscles which have converged the eye and travelling along the third nerve. No accident ever occurs to the convergence part. So long as you can converge the eye, the third nerve is o.k. and the incoming stimulus will be able to let the ED nucleus know about it. But in syphilis there is very often a lesion at BB—in the little offshoot. The stimulus has no trouble going along the main nerve to the brain, so the patient can see perfectly well; but with the offshoot out of commission, there is no way of letting the ED nucleus know about it, and the pupil remains dilated despite my little flashlight shining away and wasting its good batteries. This combination of constricting to accommodation (convergence) but not to light is then diagnostic of syphilis. [Incidentally, if a lesion were to occur at A1 to the main optic nerve (as in an accident which severed it) the patient would of course be blind if it were on both sides, and as you can see, no stimulus could get to the ED nucleus either. So there is one way of telling if a person is really blind. Flashing a light into his eyes will not cause reflex papillary constriction.]

Finally, why the spirochetes will select just this little spot to destroy is absolutely unknown. So I don't explain "why"—just "How."

Did that make sense dear? Usually I don't give you anything nearly as technical as this. It's taken me an hour to put it down on paper. If you like this sort of thing I'll let you have "The Mechanism of the Electrocardiogram" next time. Or are you willing to read about it in a medical textbook when you really develop a passionate interest in the subject? But you just keep right on going to those lectures and I'll explain anything you don't understand (if I can). The more you know about medicine, the better will you be able to appreciate those articles from the Interne I sent you. That alone is worth the effort.

Good night darling. I can hardly see the typewriter. Gosh I miss you.

Love
Aaron

Tuesday 10:30 pm Feb. 20

Darling:

It's a little peculiar trying to write to you, knowing that I'm going to speak to you in a little while and not knowing exactly what I'll be able to get into the three minutes…If I'm repetitive it really doesn't matter; I call you up, not to get information across in a hurry, but because of the closer contact it affords.

This Sunday was probably the last of my sessions at the Hi Hat. Not that I decided that I had far too much money than was good for me, and that I was cut out for finer things, but that I bumped into a Red Cross Nurses Aid from the Robert Brigham…I had been afraid that something like that was going to happen, you know. Funny that it finally did—so abruptly. She was seated right next to the table I was at taking an order; in fact, at my "station," so that I would have had to wait on her. I kept my face averted, walked down to the phone, called Joe who called me back and said that I was wanted at the hospital at once, and to the admiration of all the personnel of the Hi Hat dashed out madly to go on my errand of mercy…I must have sweated bullets…

Right now I don't think that I can go back. Maybe by the end of the week I'll be able to reconcile myself to the situation and decide to brave it out. But I doubt it. Probably to a large extent I hate the work and needed a good excuse to quit. This was it all right.

To get to something better. We just learned that of the last graduating class, about 30 students took the examination for the Navy (as doctors of course,) and passed! The examination was very difficult and included an examination at the bedside to see whether the candidate had more than book knowledge. Even more interesting was the fact that some of these boys (most in fact) do not have a license to practice medicine—and don't need one for the Navy. So unlike the Army, if I get my degree and can pass the examination (if it's held again) and if I can get thru the pretty stiff physical requirements regarding height and eyesight, I might be able to be commissioned as a Doctor there. There are an awful lot of ifs, you see; Yet it is the first bit of encouraging news in a long time…

Your letters are pretty swell now with all that you have to tell about. I'm at a loss to try to answer very many of the questions that come up. They are all pretty stimulating, start chains of thought, but I don't know anywheres enough to be able to really comment intelligently. But just pass it on. I'll give you a free medical education; you can keep me up in the arts and social sciences. That way we'll both become the best educated couple we know.

First about Karen Horney's description of the neurotic. Dividing the tendencies into aggression, compliance and detachment I thought was very good. It describes pretty well what we see about us in the people we meet. Some few aspects apply to me I think. But there are equally good methods of making the analysis of the same personality probably which sound just as logical. She is good, there is no getting away from that. You'll learn a lot. Be careful of one thing, tho, particularly in relation to your girl friends. Don't attribute what Karen Horney describes to them. Thelma is doing that and it is very typical of all who begin in any field of the pathological. I can't tell you how to avoid it, because I do it myself. But I merely can warn you, so that you'll know the tendency exists. I'm worse than anybody I know of finding pathology in people up here when it doesn't exist.

I'll never forget writing down that a kid had greatly enlarged injected tonsils only to find out that they had been removed a short while ago. The little tabs I saw and took to be tonsils were just normal parts of the throat. But after seeing a few really enlarged tonsils, I'll never be able to make that mistake again.

In psychiatry too, the only way to get perspective and really understand what is normal is to be able to see a lot of neurotics. Clinical experience is the only real teacher. The theoretical basis is fundamental, so that one understands what one sees, but without clinical experience it means nothing.

Gosh I'm getting sleepy darling. I'll finish this, get some Journal and read til it's time for me to call you. By the way, the "withdrawal symptoms" I mentioned in my last letter or so don't refer to withdrawing anyplace. Rather it is the technical name given for the symptoms one gets if the addict has the drug to which he is addicted, eg. Morphine, withdrawn. The symptoms of restlessness, irritability, sleeplessness, loss of appetite, great craving for the drug, dreams about it, even hallucinations, are part of the picture. I meant that you and our love life were the drug; and being kept from you for so long I was manifesting these symptoms…

Incidentally too, what do you think about my quitting work? I don't want to be silly about it. Actually I can adopt the attitude of "Suppose they do know" and let it go at that, I suppose. Nobody will fire me for doing it. And I can earn about 5-8 dollars a week that way, taking it very easy, and not wasting too much time.

Also, as I will tell you tonight, I'm going to come into New York as soon as the weather clears up a little. In two or three weeks I think. I really can come in any time. With neither Joe or I working, weekends are anybody's. Do you have any preference? When does the Met close? Or wouldn't we go anyhow?

Good night darling.

All my love
Aaron

Friday 2/23 10:30 a.m.

Gloria darling:

You're not the only one thinking about getting married, dear. In writing to Bronx for starting my internship early, I asked to begin May 15. That gives us two weeks, if it works out…Gosh, I want to be with you very much. I just feel trapped by circumstances, dear.

I'll come to N.Y. early in March, if Spring is in the air, & we'll go over to The Hospital & ask him, if I've not yet received an answer. If things look favorable we can make specific plans for being married in May…

How's that?

Nothing is being done up here as far as can be seen. The hearing for giving us relief by the legislature was held sometimes last week, but the school decided to postpone their presentation until May 15. The opposition was out in full force; the State Board of Medicine, the Dean of Harvard, Tufts & B.U.; All the county Medical Societies in Mass. put themselves on record against any postponement for us; the Mass. Medical Society also. In short, all Medicine in the State was down at the hearing (by representatives, of course) & put themselves on record as opposed to doing anything but close the school now. As one member of the State Board put it, "Middlesex couldn't be recognized if it had 100 years so why give it any more time now?" It was pretty fierce.

We present our case March 15. It will be very small indeed compared to the power shown by the opposition. Obviously, what goes on at the hearing is nothing at all. Nobody cares for arguments presented, pro or con; it is the influence of the chap who is arguing that is at all significant. No matter what we say, unless the school can get some very powerful "patrons", it won't make a particle of difference…More later…

We have a very interesting case up at the Brigham at present. About 6 weeks ago a 38-40 year old woman came in with pretty definite signs of Rheumatoid Arthritis, some fever, & obviously malnourished. I did the History & Physical & therefore became interested. I couldn't see such high continuing fever & emaciation just from Arthritis. In my note I suggested Miliary Tbc. Despite the symptoms there was nothing to be found except her joints on examination.

After 2-3 weeks of this Fever with the Diagnosis of Arthritis, The Staff became worried. Lab work was finally ordered & -- we still have no diagnosis. I suggested Miliary Tb, only in that it is one disease which is notorious for its great prostration without anything found on examination. It's probably not that tho, as she's living too long & nothing was found by X ray.

A lot of lab work was done: blood cultures were taken, agglutinations were run for Typhoid, Paratyphoid, Undulant fever; X rays were taken of chest & Abdomen; Repeated bloods & urine only showed Morbid Anemia, sputum was examined repeatedly but no Tb was found…Just a high spiking fever 104 degrees, 101 degrees, 103 degrees…

Last week it was noticed that she was getting deaf; couldn't hear anything in 2 or 3 days. An ENT specialist examined her ears & opened one. He thought he got pus. The material was sent to the lab for culture…No relief. X Rays of both mastoids were negative…

So there we were. The Arthritis specialist blamed it all on a rare disease which may give a Rheumatoid picture—Disseminated Lupus Erythematosis; The Ear specialist blamed it all on the ears; a good Cardiologist would probably call it Subacute Bacterial Endocarditis…But the fever kept on spiking 104 degrees; 105 degrees; 104 degrees…Sulfadiazine didn't do anything. Two transfusions given her could have been sent to the Army for all the good it did her…

Two days ago she developed pneumonia; the right upper lobe is solid; her sputum yielded Pneumococcus type XIX…

Today I found Bile in her urine & could feel the liver somewhat enlarged. Pretty severe liver damage…

We still don't know. But the machine is starting to break down…

All my love darling
Aaron

Saturday 2/24 1 pm

Sweetheart:

You've got to cut that out darling, about wanting to nestle in my arms on a rainy afternoon and listen to good music or read poetry; or about being kissed until exhausted; or romping around the country…Have a heart! As I've been telling you during the past couple of weeks, I'm in the state of perpetual starvation and it isn't that the hospital isn't feeding me either. I haven't your reply to my question of my giving up work yet, so I'm going to decide about what I tell them for next week. That nurses aid that I met is no longer here I believe; or at any rate I haven't seen her around the hospital since. It has saved a lot of embarrassment; probably both ways. Let me know what you think anyway as I'll probably be using your money if I have to stop working. Altho I can probably get a job for a couple of weeks in April which would take care of it…

This morning we went over to the Peter Bent Brigham for the usual Saturday rounds. It is held in a beautiful amphitheatre with the Staff of the hospital all sitting in the front row; the patients wheeled in and demonstrated by the interne or clerk on the service; the complete history reviewed briefly; and then discussed by the staff with an authority discussing the disease if it is a rare or interesting one. Pushing a button lowers all the blinds by electricity so that the room is instantly prepared for showing slides— and slides are used about as frequently as the blackboard would be elsewhere for diagrams, pictures, tables…But that isn't what I was going to write about. Nor is it the cases presented, tho they were interesting enough. Rather the attitude of the guest speaker, Dr. Means, of the Mass. General Hospital (the blue blood hospital of New England; the Heart of the Mass. Medical Society). He treated the patients demonstrated just like experimental animals. They were to him a little better than monkeys to work on in so far as the reactions are closer to the ones to be found in his human patients; but not quite as good in so far as they couldn't be manipulated quite so easily. High grade monkeys…There was no consideration at all that these monkeys might have feelings as he talks about "How all these hypopituitary cases look very much alike"…like all cretins look somewhat alike! With the patient sitting there and the doctor obviously looking at him as tho at a new Baboon they just brought over from Australia…To the question of what to do with another patient he was interested solely in a biopsy of the liver to see what was going on there, although the operation could do the patient no good and probably would do a lot of harm…It is very difficult to get across by letter the total attitude, the insufferable smugness, the pompousness, the complete disregard of anyone who was not another medical man—and above all not even wealthy so that he could be one of his supporters…

Nor was he so very important that like Wagner one can say that he must be forgiven. Not at all!..There wasn't a bright young interne in the audience who couldn't do as well in the diagnosis and treatment of disease given the facilities of the MGH. It is just that he is entrenched, completely solid in his position, and can carry over his basic snobbishness, arrogance, hatred of the common people, with impunity. It's a rotten set up. The caste system that is breeding a breed of doctors that is completely detached from the laity—particularly the masses, the poor laity—is bound to get worse as it becomes more and more an hereditary affair. It's rotten enough now, God knows, and ought to be changed somehow…

Gosh I waxed vehement there, didn't I? Just that the attitude of "medicine being for the wealthy" which is practiced by these saviors of mankind, tireless fighters in the night, self sacrificing workers, of the noblest profession on earth…gets me. It's carried over to all aspects of the set up. Once the attitude is there on the top, as in any organization, it very soon becomes the dominant trend all the way down.

You know about the treatment of staff patients at the Chelsea Memorial; the skimping of laboratory work even tho I saw it kill one patient; the cheating and fakery that goes on there; the internes taking babies and tonsils while the doctor collects; the staff patient as a burden to be gotten out as quickly as possible, anyplace…

At the dinner table this afternoon, the head of the laboratory was telling us about her new worker who is very poor—she is being used on the West side patients…

Oh well,,,It is this kind of thing , only on more important items such as food for little children that make the revolutionaries…

I hope I can come in soon, dear. I miss you terribly.

Love
Aaron

Tuesday 2/27/45 11 pm

Darling:

I felt very good after talking to you last night; somehow, when I feel very small and discouraged, with all the wind out of my sails, feeling that not only is there nothing for the future but that even the past was just one long failure with mistake after mistake…then, talking to you for a little while makes me feel whole again and more at peace with my soul. It is very difficult to describe – You'll just have to understand…It is important for us not to succumb to each other's moods which are so very changeable; seeing clearly, or at least more hopefully, one can drag the other up from depression right along.

One of the boys told us that he enquired at the Bronx Hospital in person a few weeks ago about starting his internship early, and was told that they don't need us until the date of our official internship. That will be too bad, if true. I'll probably go over to see Mr. Superintendent if he hasn't written me by the time I'm in NY. Don't go off into the land of castles darling, in regards to the future Doctor Kelman. Actually there is nothing on the horizon right now, except the Army on May 2. That is the status quo. For anything else to happen some change will have to arise in the situation. We need positive results now, not negative. And time certainly is short.

We're still going down to the Peter Bent, Darling, and imbibing the wonderful stuff they hand out. I really can't imagine medicine being handled any better than is done there. There, the limitation on what is done for the patient is in the progress of medicine. But the best medicine of today, with all its complexities is being carried out in the school down the hill from us.

There is an interesting new approach to therapy which is coming out now, and I don't think I've written you about it yet. Dr. Thorne, the physician in chief of the Peter Bent, is pushing this therapy and doing a lot of work in its research and clinical evaluation. Briefly, the basic theory is that in diseases a lot of the constants of the internal environment are deranged, thereby doing a great deal of harm to the body and creating a lot of the symptoms of the disease.

Now what do I mean? I told you, probably too many times, of the wonderful physiological concept of an "internal environment" which the warm blooded animal carries around with him. Evolving from the ocean where the environment is pretty nearly constant, the animal living on land had a terrific problem of keeping his brain, eg, surrounded by a constant environment which was optimal for it. The blood, circulating in a closed system, was of course the answer. Yet the number of constants which had to be maintained, so as not to irreparably damage the delicate nerve cells, is quite large: the temperature, the acidity, the levels of Sodium, Chlorine, Calcium, Phosphorus, Sugar, Serum proteins, oxygen, carbon dioxide,-- and a host of others. To keep each of these substances bathing the brain at its constant level, an elaborate mechanism is present. Just as an example, in order to keep the temperature of the blood constant there is a very fine balance between heat forming –procedures such as burning of sugar in the liver and muscles (with if necessary shivering and getting goose pimples), and the heat dissipating procedures such as sweating, evaporation, the degree of dilatation of the skin capillaries…Controlling the whole works, as to which is going to go on more rapidly, the heat production or heat loss, is a very important center in the brain, the "thermostat." Now that is just one of the constants which must be maintained. More elaborate ones exist for many of the others. But the sum total of all these involved mechanisms, is a constant environment, a "milieu interne" which is at all times bathing the brain. The slightest departure will give rise to great many symptoms, and if prolonged will lead to irreversible damage. Of course, the rest of the body is also surrounded by this constant environment, and will only function well in it.

In disease, some of these constants are off. The acidity of the blood may go up, the serum proteins go down, the salts get way out of line, the sugar go haywire. The deviations may be present because of all sorts of pathologic changes in the body, in all sorts of disease. Yet no matter what the disease, acidosis or low blood sugar is very bad. With the modern laboratory at his command, Thorne is able to get analysis of the blood very frequently. He also has available the purified preparations which the blood is supposed to contain. He is thereby able to put in what is lacking by constant intravenous drip if necessary, taking constant samples of blood and having it analyzed so that he always knows just where he is. By this method he is able to give the body its optimum internal environment, thereby ameliorating a lot of the symptoms and actual damage of the disease, and assist the defense mechanisms of the body to work their hardest to overcome the disease itself.

Of course, where there is specific therapy such as Penicillin for an infection, that is given too. But even here, the body is kept in maximum fighting trim and in the least way susceptible to damage by the microorganisms, during the course of the illness.

The degree to which this sort of approach can be used depends upon the facilities. In the home all the doctor can do is to tell you to drink a lot of water in order to make up for the dehydration which attends most illnesses due to infection—thereby trying to correct the water constant of the blood and tissues. In the hospital, the small one even, we measure the amount of water needed by red counts, and give it intravenously, very often. In Harvard, Thorne can take care of the acidity, the vitamin levels, the electrolyte (salt) levels, and is now even putting in serum albumin to make up for its deficiency…

Gosh I'm sleepy now. One of the patients showed me the book by Clendening "The Human Body." It looks pretty good. With the smattering I've sent you, you really ought to enjoy it. If you read it, you can teach me some medicine.

Good night sweetheart
Aaron

Saturday 3/4/45 5 pm

Darling:

I'm just a little sleepy as I write this to you, having gone to sleep this afternoon after coming home from the conference at the Peter Bent. What a life, eh? I'll tell you what I weigh in my next letter after I find out. With this lazy life, no matter what my input of food is, the output of energy is still going to be far too short…

Sleepy or not, or better still, particularly when I'm sleepy, I get awful yearnings…I don't approve of celibacy. Sometimes, not often fortunately, I let my fancy fly as I lie down to nap, and imagine some very vivid situations with you taking a rather prominent part…But I don't think you understand, do you dear?

Last night Leo and Elliot were over; we wasted a lot of time talking and then did a few case histories. One of the former residents who is now a staff member came in to sleep in the resident's room so we gabbed away with him for about two hours getting to bed by 2. That is late—even for me. Medical student or no medical student, I need sleep—lots of it.

You know I'm very pleased with your promotion. Not only that you are worth marrying now that you are making so much money, but that I can feel your satisfaction in being given something to do which involves some responsibility and a little of the executive element. We all need that feeling. Despite all the protestations that you are a homebody, If given the opportunity I would have you, at least for a while, active in some activity apart from the home where you can feel that you are someone important . Even if only a little bit important. It gives nourishment to the ego, and makes for greater maturity I think. There is nothing worse than the timid, frightened little housewife who is a child to be protected—not a companion to be loved and respected. Two people make a team only if there are really two people. You can quote any of these trite sayings without giving me any credit at any time. Also, see lots more like them in Poor Richards Almanac…

I really can't keep on writing anything at all which makes sense. Being a little groggy, and with that awful feeling, all I can do in this mood is to wonder whether I oughtn't to come in to New York sooner. Like tomorrow. Why wait for the middle of March anyhow? But on second thought, I think that the weather is much too rotten to go anyplace now. Maybe it will only be raining two weeks from now, not cold and raining as it is now…

Your lectures on Sex and the Good Life sound very very good. Of course, I don't understand much about the subjects you write, (tho your letters are very well written and remarkably lucid,) but that the material presented does have a direct relationship to the mechanisms of behavior in the people all around us, there is little doubt. The types described, are to some extent extremes, particularly useful to describe the symptoms (like the typical medical cases given in Cecil's Medicine)—so that being aware of the manifestations of the various personalities we can better understand the people we're with—realizing that they are probably mild manifestations and combinations.

I'll try to get this letter out to you tonight, but I really don't know whether the mails will be collected in any of the boxes around here. But let it not be said that a little rain stopped me from mailing a letter to my girl!

I'll call you Monday at 9:30 darling.

Love
Aaron

Sunday 3/4/45 10:30 pm

Hello darling:

I didn't plan on writing again tonight; but why stick to plans anyway? It has been lovely up here this afternoon; full of the promise of spring—or something. It brought with it a gush of feeling for the out of doors. Gosh. I'd have liked to put on a heavy shirt and lumber jacket, sling a light lunch over my shoulder and go off into the woods with you—looking at the trees and birds, and just enjoying the air and the feel of the larger muscles of the body in motion…

Joe went out with the resident tonight. Did I ever tell you about Dr. Ostroger, "our Resident". Ostroger is one type of success story, too. He went thru Middlesex and graduated about three years ago. He took his internship in a small hospital in New York, and then obtained this residency at the Brigham which he has held for two years.

Ostroger is the fattest man I have ever seen. His terrific girth must have played a terrific part in his personality development. He is stupendous. Not a brain, he never-the-less is very competent in using his hands—or at least I think he is. He does IV and lumbar punctures very well; is a good first assistant in an operation; and can probably do a fairly good job at taking out a pair of tonsils and an appendix himself. His knowledge of the intricacies of medical theory is as deficient as any semblance of culture, art, music, letters…

Soon after coming to the Brigham, Ostroger began to look around for an office, and found one which was vacated by an established doctor going into the service. From that point on his residency was secondary. He arrived at the hospital nearly every morning, but left in time to do an evening practice, take night calls for the town of Medford, and do any anaesthesias in any other hospital he could get. His routine soon became that of coming up to this place at about 8 am; take care of whatever he could by lunch time; eat; sleep in the afternoon, and then leave for his office by 4:30. He'd muss up his bed before he left, so that on the record he was here all night. Nothing ever happened of course, some stupid therapy is going on, but I don't know if he could have improved the situation much if he were here…

Right now, Ostroger is making a fortune. His 150 dollars from the hospital, which is handed to him every month is just side money. Every anaesthesia is 10 or 15 dollars, and he can do 5-6 a week very easily. He has associated himself with a surgeon who kicks back 50%! The surgeon charges the patient $200 and gives Ostroger $100. He also collects for preoperative visits, visits in the hospital, and post operative visits at home. Usually he also either gives the anaesthesia or assists at the operation, so that he collects that fee too. As you can see, he is making considerably more on the operation than the surgeon—and since the kickback is illegal, it doesn't go down on the record for income tax purposes…As Ostroger said "Didn't I find the operation"—and very tempting it is too, to "find Operations".

Similarly for all consultant work. The urologist, the gynecologist, the ENT man, all kick back, and the one that kick backs the most gets his trade…Speaking to him about his X ray set up, he told us that if he really is out to get information, he sends the patient to an X ray man he knows who is good—but doesn't kick back; but usually, it is only to either impress the patient, confirm what he already knows, or simply an easy five dollars, by sending the patient to another X ray man who doesn't know anything—but who splits half of what he gets…

Ostroger gets literature from all the drug houses by the ton; all doctors do automatically. The ads are very elaborate, pseudo scientific; but essentially no different from the typical high pressure salesmanship used in selling useless stuff to the great american public. Only with the doctor it is more vicious. Selling him a useless preparation means that droves of his patients are going to be stuck with it; it doesn't cost the doctor anything…So we're warned continually in school not to take the patent preparations advertised at face value; rather to see the ingredients and realize very quickly that the same prescription can be written out by the Doctor in a far more efficient form at a fraction of the cost. Ostroger uses them all. He's constantly trying the patent medicines which just got in by the last mail on his patients. It saves him all the trouble of trying to figure out what could be used rationally, and a good prescription embodying those ingredients…

Ostroger is lonely. His family is in NY, and he has neither the time nor the personality for making close friends. He needs a wife badly; for his sexual life, for companionship of a sort, for the social needs of a doctor, to cook his meals for him, and to answer the telephone. (Right now he has a high school girl come in to answer the telephone every afternoon for about 6 hours and all day Saturday—for which he pays her $8 per week). Some of the good Jewish families of the town have tried to "show him a nice girl"—but they were usually no go. Tonight was another one of those "meeting a girl" so he asked one of us to go along—I refused…

As we see "our resident" only for a few minutes a day, we get along beautifully. Very little friction, there.

Tonight was quite nice up here; maybe it's that I'm alone that makes me want to talk to you. And this is the only way I can do that. Looking at the time I ought to be pretty dry by this point.

Also I'm sleepy

All my love dear
Aaron

Wednesday 3/7/45 11 pm

Gloria darling:

It's swell that you are fond of my letters and can secure some emotional satisfaction from them; I get quite a kick out of writing to you. In fact, writing these letters is to a large extent my only outlet. One must talk to someone about what goes on inside, of the thoughts that are being thunk, the things that one sees, the ideas revolving around inside the cranium…Without expression, I think the ideas, emotions…would hardly exist. Isn't there some psychological theory about there being no thought of motion without some motor component? There probably are no really clear ideas without expression. But that isn't the real reason for my writing—you know. I don't spend my evenings writing to any of my friends at all. I think that as I write and can almost visualize myself talking to you it gives some of the feeling of a visit…But then, you know just what I mean, you must be feeling the same thing. In fact, your letters have improved enormously in quality and quantity since those days three years ago when you started that letter writing marathon. I think that your letters are splendid now. For the next few months I think you ought to write at least two letters a day. If getting one a day is so much fun, imagine how I will enjoy getting them morning and afternoon (all right, I know that you are busy)

But to get away from these vain musings…Things are drawing to a head up here. I'm afraid that it's getting very, very tight. I don't know what to expect darling, but the story will partially be told in a few months. Joe was just put into 1A by his Board and is to get a pre induction physical by the end of the month. The story is that the Boards are getting us ready for being drafted on May 1. All the students of the lower three classes will certainly be drafted by then if the legislature doesn't pass a law giving us status before then. As for our class the situation is not clear. Smith told us to be sure we're in hospitals as soon as we graduate; and then to try to get the hospital to get our deferment as essential and not replaceable. I don't know just where I'll be able to go in May as my internship, you know, starts in July, with the other hospitals all pretty well filled up…At any rate I will have to get something, and then to see whether the "fait accompli" will get me deferred. So goes the everlasting tale…

I'll probably come in by bus sometimes next week, but that depends upon what you can take off, of course. I'll let you know exactly when I talk to you this Monday night. Hopefully, the weather won't be too bad. If it's at all nice I want to get some fresh air in. Up here as you know I've been living an almost plant like existence. If I'm not careful I'll develop radial symmetry…

Do you know dear, I've been terribly restless these past few weeks. Whether it is due to the lack of exercise, the rotten situation which is drawing near, the lack of variety in what I'm doing, or the love starvation I'm undergoing is difficult to determine. Probably the lack of exercise and love starvation. As you know there is a great increase in the Libido when the fellow sits around all day and doesn't get a chance to sublimate it in fruitful activity. So the answer may be a general restlessness. Or it may of course have nothing to do with it…A good game of handball would really be a godsend…If I weren't so lazy or had someone to play with, I'd probably stop writing to you of my "restlessness"—as tho you could do something about it. Joe isn't sex starved and he's just as restless. It's probably the food, then…

As usual, I'm getting sleepy darling. This letter is obviously not one of my learned treatises. In fact it is hardly a letter. Just a bunch of ramblings. It's a good thing that you can know pretty well what I feel or think no matter what I write, so that I can just sit at the typewriter and let the words come out. Sometimes I am surprised at the sentences that do write themselves down. Very interesting. Something like the stream of consciousness idea used by the psychiatrists so much…Only my fingers get mixed up and the words get spelled all wrong. This stream of consciousness is much easier having a psychiatrist around to take it all down…At any rate, you know that I'm in love with you—if by no other token than my sitting up in the middle of the night typing words so that I can make believe that I'm very close to you…

Good night darling,

Love

Aaron

(In March 1945, upon graduation from Middlesex, my Dad was accepted at Bronx Hospital as an interne. He gleefully packed up his few belongings and hastily moved back to New York. Shortly thereafter he married my mother. Here is where their story told by his letters ends, and my story was about to begin.)

POST-MORTEM AND PONDERINGS

Wow; what a journey! Little did I know at first that I'd be taking a trip back through time to an era before my birth but one that led to my conception, and reliving history, streaming live, through the words and lens of someone who was there.

When I first embarked on this project I had no idea what to expect. I knew my parents were apart for several years but didn't fully grasp the extent of a "long-distance relationship" in 1942. Today Brooklyn-Boston is practically a daily commute, and indeed many businessmen do this by train or air shuttle on a regular basis. Back in the day it was nearly an epic journey and the Greyhound Bus from Boston to Capital Station in Manhattan demanded time, planning, and finances, and was barely available once in a blue moon to the protagonists of this story. Telephone calls, even of the bare minimum three-minute variety, were a rare luxury and prohibitively expensive, and, needless to say, cell phones, texts, Skype, Facetime, etc. were not even a dream let alone on the horizon. So all that existed to connect was ink on paper and the USPS. It's remarkable that any relationships survived this challenge, let alone grew and flourished under the circumstances. Today, letter writing is pretty much a lost art. We're reduced to hurried emails, texts, tweets, which may convey data and information effectively but lack the personal touch and emotional resonance that a love letter enables. What a joy for me to enter the mind and heart of my Dad as he expressed his innermost thoughts and feelings in his letters to his beloved (the woman who would later become my Mom).

The View from Ground Level

Drilling down to my Dad's own experiences and impressions as he navigated the trials and tribulations of coming of age struck home in a way I never appreciated until now. The world I knew in the '60s was quite a different place than his of the 40's; but the more things change, the more they remain the same. While a college student I faced the terrifying prospect of being drafted and sent to the Vietnam War, as my Dad feared deployment to the European theatre. When I entered and matriculated through medical school, despite a generation of more scientific knowledge and breakthroughs, the approach, the subjects, the issues and challenges of entering this noble profession were no different. And when I met the love of my life (now *my* wife), I felt the same passion and yearning that he did for my Mom.

What impressed me most, and my primary takeaways, on this level are as follows:

1) The true measure of a man is not how he handles prosperity, but how he handles adversity; and Dad certainly measured up. He was a child of the Depression, grew up with his parents and two brothers in a tiny apartment, slept in a fold-out cot in the kitchen, and literally didn't have two nickels to rub together. He went to City College and worked wherever and doing whatever he could to support himself. One of his most enduring childhood memories was that the neighborhood doctor bought a new car every year. Dad had a vision, and he made it work despite the obstacles. He was a self-made man in every sense of the word.
2) It's hard to imagine working like a dog and chasing a dream with no assurance that any of it will pay off; but that's the situation my Dad found himself in, and had to face. But he soldiered on, day after day, despite the constant negativity bathing him and his classmates. Like the doughboys on Omaha Beach, facing seemingly insurmountable odds, he stuck to his guns and never wavered in his mission. He was a man with a plan. "Push on" was his mantra, and so he did. Now *that's* discipline, strength, persistence, optimism, hope, courage, and, above all, faith. My Dad was a man of faith and a believer. Lesser men would have given up, but not my Dad.

He knew what he wanted, stayed the course and he reached the finish line, despite the cards stacked against him. How many of us can say the same about ourselves? Not many…Not me, likely. I'm not half the man my Dad was.

3) The Zeitgeist of anti-Semitism was a heavy burden for Dad and his community. His parents left Eastern Europe to avoid persecution; but even the New World carried some Old World attitudes. Despite academic excellence, Dad struggled to gain acceptance to medical school, and the only available opportunity for him and his comrades in arms was a school that never gained recognition by the AMA. The enduring motif throughout his four year correspondence was the dreaded specter of the school closing prior to his graduation, and the ominous uncertainty of that event. It wasn't a matter of *if*, but *when*; and the future of the students was always in doubt: whether they would graduate at all, and, even if they did, whether they could work as doctors without state licensure. My Dad felt like a second-class citizen, relegated to inferior status, denied the fellowships, honors, accoutrements that a more prestigious degree would have afforded. Being in Boston, surrounded by academic centers of the highest caliber, attending guest lectures at Harvard, only highlighted the stark contrast between what was and what might have been. What a joy it was for him to see his son (my older brother) graduate from Harvard Medical School and train at "the other Brigham". He realized his dream through his children. I'm sure no father was ever prouder.
4) World War is undoubtedly a time of great anxiety, fear, and uncertainty about both the near and distant future. These emotions were the backdrop for so many of my Dad's letters. Even his near-obsessive use of the *ellipse* as a writing tool implies vagueness, wonder, uncertainty, insecurity, the predominant demons he dealt with on a daily basis. He was a worrier, no doubt, and remained one for the rest of his life. Genetic? Environmental? Both? Who knows…

5) Dad didn't suffer fools gladly, nor could he abide self-centered doctors who practiced medicine carelessly and selfishly, for their own benefit and to the detriment of their patients. Above all he felt that doctors were humanists, not technicians, and connecting with the patient on a personal level (not via the laboratory and diagnostic tests alone) was the best medicine. This is the story of a healer being born. He was thoughtful, and believed that his ears were his most valuable diagnostic tool. His experience in training uncovered a medical profession that leaned more heavily on technology than personal interaction. No lab test could trump talking to, listening to, and examining the patient, understanding the process, and making an astute educated diagnosis before blindly treating with a knee-jerk routine approach. He appreciated the intellectual aspects of medicine, the detective approach (much like the keenly observant and deductive approach of Sherlock Holmes whom Conan Doyle, a physician himself, modeled on an esteemed medical professor he admired). While others were content to memorize the facts and apply them blindly, for better or for worse, Dad searched beyond the "what" and "how" of disease and treatment to the "Why", and was frustrated at the lack of understanding that to this day plagues the scientist. He never stopped striving to master the mysteries of life itself. Were he not a physician, he likely would have made a good cleric or philosopher, who also deal with many of these very same questions.
6) Despite his obvious dissatisfaction and disrespect for many of his teachers, Dad never gave up and always kept his eye on the prize. If the lectures were unsatisfying, Dad sat in at better schools and read the texts over and over to compensate. If the hospitals were sub-par, Dad volunteered at other superior hospitals to learn what he was missing. He never settled for anything less than the best he could get and the best he could be.
7) Despite it all, Dad loved Medicine and loved being a doctor. In his eyes, if one *could* be a doctor, one *became* a doctor, no

ifs, ands, or buts. There was nothing better, and he fulfilled his destiny. Because of his background he faced a longer road and a steeper climb, but his vision would not be clouded or denied. Generations of his patients are forever-grateful.

8) Born shortly after the Bolshevik Revolution, it's not too surprising that Dad favored many Communist/Socialist beliefs. On a purely economic basis, from the perspective of a medical student viewing first-hand the inadequacies and inequities of medical care, Dad believed that a better health-care system was sorely needed, one in which everyone would have access to medical treatment regardless of ability to pay and no one would be left behind. Lenin would have been proud! Treatment very much depended on class distinction, and Dad objected mightily. At the time there was little he could do. Years later he charged his patients on a sliding scale, based on what they could afford, his little way of "sticking it to the man", providing the best medical care and treating every patient with dignity and respect. He clearly would have preferred a nationalized health system; his observations in medical school reflect that progressive attitude.
9) One of Dad's pet-peeves involved hospital administrators and managers who were not physicians. Nurses were the supervisors and he struggled mightily with this concept throughout his professional career, including his eventual position as founder of a private hospital in Queens, NY. It made no sense to him (nor to me for that matter) how anyone less than a properly trained and experienced doctor, with a full-time staff of similar assistants, could make the decisions necessary to deliver sophisticated up-to-date medical care. He likely realized that such an institutional organization was only possible in a system of socialized medicine where the priority was top-of-the line service for all, not the bottom line. Dad often reiterated this theme and perspective throughout his letters, finding fault with the system then in place that enabled and entitled the privileged few at the expense of the

masses. That issue and that debate continues to dominate the current conversation, with no true solution yet in sight.

10) Although I've always fancied myself a romantic, I see very little of that in my Dad (as expressed in these "love letters"). Considering that these words on paper were the mainstay of their developing romance, it seems strange that so little passion is expressed. I didn't expect, nor would I want to read, graphic and lurid details of his desires and their physical intimacy; yet I am still surprised at the dearth of "sexting" there be. It was a different time, I get it; and my Dad was somewhat of a reserved (dare I say prudish?) man. He was likely more open in person and in the bedroom than on paper. But I'm still somewhat surprised.
11) The Aaron Kelman I knew was an intellectual with diverse interests. Though a scientist by trade, he was deeply committed to, and passionate about, the arts, and these interests are evident in his letters. His oft-repeated references to classical music, the opera, philosophy, wide-ranging literature presage a life-long study of the social sciences. Never pompous, but always pedantic, his desire to teach at every opportunity, as evidenced in his writings to my Mom, often with the Socratic method, afforded me the best and broadest education I could have hoped for. He was truly a Renaissance man.

The View from 30,000 Feet

Beyond the emotional and visceral satisfaction and personal discoveries that arose from this adventure, historical and social insights into a fascinating period of American history were evident as well. My most fundamental takeaways from this altitude are as follows:

1) The 1940s, a mere 75 years ago, were a time of major gender discrimination and inequality. My grandparents

were traditionalists insofar as the men worked and provided financially, the women stayed at home, had babies, and took care of the household. Neither of my grandmothers was gainfully employed, nor did they expect their daughters to be so. Likewise my mother was groomed to assume a conventional role: marry a satisfactory mate, provide a suitable home, and beget appropriate children. No more, no less. Despite his oft-repeated expressions of love and commitment, my Dad's communications smack of condescension, superiority, even patriarchy. Oftentimes he approached "his girl" like she's a child, needed to grow up and become her own independent person, by no means his equal; and I suspect this attitude was not unusual "back in the day". He often judges, advises, and criticizes my Mom's attitudes and behaviors, both personal and professional. Whether she did the same is impossible to know without her letters to review. But it seems unlikely given the complete absence of any defense of his positions (implying a lack of challenge) or rebuttal of any contrary arguments. Comments regarding mutual acquaintances support this interpretation of gender attitudes of the day. Women grew up nurtured and protected in their parents' home until able to move into their husband's home, still supervised and managed, but by a different care-giver. Neither professional nor financial achievements were expected or necessary in a wife. Independence ("Women's Liberation" of the generation to come) was unheard of. "You've come a long way, baby" is an amazing understatement.

2) The "sexual revolution" of the 60's is most striking in contrast to the lives my parents lived a short generation before. No unsupervised (conjugal) visits away from home, chaperones de rigueur, no sleepovers, even between fiancés separated by circumstances beyond their control. The sexual tension is thick, oppressively evident,

and accelerating in direct proportion to time and distance. Contraception, unwanted pregnancy, abortion— taboo topics with potentially disastrous implications in the 1940s. Roe-v-Wade was still thirty years away. It's hard to imagine today.

3) My parents were first generation Americans, born of Russian émigré parents part of the wave of Eastern Europeans flooding the United States at the turn of the last century. WWII was in full bloom, and my parents' grandparents were being rounded up and stuffed in box cars on their way to execution as these letters were written. I find it strange that little to no mention is made of current events, public affairs, or the war effort. While medical school and my Dad's situation were difficult, it certainly pales in comparison to the plight of Eastern European Jews being hunted down by the Nazis. This is the one area of the story that confounds me. There is no mention of Pearl Harbor or D-Day, undeniably critical moments in our history. I can only assume that Americans were largely kept in the dark and misled as to the gravity, atrocities, and potential threat to the US occurring across the pond. It seems that avoiding the draft was the only concern of my Dad and his classmates, with nary a thought about those "over there" or "what if?" Clearly the world is a much smaller place now, with the 24-hour news cycle on multiple media outlets and embedded reporters on the front lines live streaming each invasion and sortie. The "Fireside Chats" were a whitewashed and unrealistic propaganda tool, qualifying as "fake news" in today's vernacular.
4) The Red Army was our ally in WW II, and their successes were our successes. The paradoxical but practical belief that "the enemy of my enemy is my friend" is very much at play here. Geopolitical conflicts make strange bedfellows, and, as counter-intuitive as it is today, the Soviets were our confreres during that terrible time. Who

knew that a few short years later we would be embroiled in a terrible cold war with nuclear implications that sobered us all? Apparently political expediency trumps all; likely always has and always will.

Coincidence or Karma?

Looking back on my Dad's experiences, and comparing them to my own at a similar time and place in our lives, reveals many parallels and uncanny overlaps. I'm especially interested in these great circles of life that somehow close over time, without any purposeful planning on our parts. Mark Twain famously said that history doesn't repeat itself, but often rhymes. A few of the more remarkable are as follows:

1) My Dad frequently describes his professors at Middlesex, predominantly refugees who fled Europe before the war, many Viennese with thick accents. When I entered medical school my teachers were by and large Americans, with one exception—an Anatomy teacher named Louie Bergmann, the very same Dr. Bergmann my father trained under 30 years earlier! How random is that! We uncovered this bizarre factoid one evening over dinner when I off-handedly mentioned that one of my professors would draw on the chalkboard using both hands at the same time—quite an unusual display of ambidexterity. A light went on in my father's eyes and he knew immediately who this man was. We arranged a luncheon date, and I sat quietly and listened attentively as these two men, professor and student, reunited after so many years, affectionately reminisced about a time long ago when they were both starting out, Dr. Bergmann in this country, my Dad in medical school, and the lives they led ever since. Dr. Bergmann had changed little (according to Dad), and he remains one of my most memorable and gifted mentors.

2) My parents grew up in Brooklyn but moved to Queens before I was born. I never visited my mother's (or father's) childhood homes, but when I discovered the letters, with my Mom's address, I decided to check it out. I didn't have very far to travel because my professional office in Brooklyn was literally down the block! Little did I know that ¾ of a century later, having lived in Queens, Connecticut, Manhattan, California, and Florida, I ended up in the same place where my mother grew up. Hmmm…
3) One of my Dad's most poignant and troubling experiences in medical school was caring for a relatively young patient with pancreatic cancer. At that time this diagnosis was a death sentence, and even my Dad, at his young stage, knew it. Forty years later my Dad was diagnosed with pancreatic cancer at age 68, still a relatively young man, practicing medicine full-time, in the prime of his life and looking forward to many golden years to come. But it was still a death sentence, and he still knew it. He passed away 3 months later. Enough said.
4) One of my Dad's frustrations voiced often in his letters was the limitations of clinical testing during his formative years. Blood and urine samples were collected and analyzed but only limited diagnostic data was available, and he frequently lamented that fact. Interestingly enough, a generation later saw a major breakthrough in laboratory diagnoses thanks to the research of my maternal uncle, Solly, my Dad's best friend. His work revolutionized the practice of medicine, overcame the deficiencies that frustrated my Dad back in the day, and earned a Nobel Prize in Medicine.
5) During their courtship, and their rare rendezvous, my mother and father would meet and spend the day together in New London, Connecticut, halfway between Brooklyn and Boston. During *my* courtship with the woman who would later become *my* wife, we too would meet and "rendezvous" in New London, where she attended Connecticut College. How curious that of all the cities in all the world we just so happened to meet and connect in the very same place, our

lives together intersected, and our futures evolved from this very same small New England town.

"All the world's a stage,
And all the men and women merely players;
They have their exits and their entrances,
And one man in his time plays many parts…"

So there it is, Aaron Kelman and Gloria Berson, two people caught in the happenstance of circumstance, trying to beat the odds and make it work. Life is a hell of a thing to happen to a person, and my parents overcame the obstacles and figured it out. Thank God! Otherwise I wouldn't be here today to tell their story. We all must play the hand that is dealt us, good or bad, and some do so more successfully than others. I daresay that my parents did a pretty good job, and their struggles are a model of persistence in the face of adversity, an example that love conquers all, and that we are bigger and better together than the sum of our parts… I couldn't be prouder…

CPSIA information can be obtained
at www.ICGtesting.com
Printed in the USA
BVHW08*1134011018
528933BV00008B/318/P

9 781632 637000